Patent Law Essentials

A Concise Guide

SECOND EDITION

Alan L. Durham

PRAEGER

Westport, Connecticut
London

Library of Congress Cataloging-in-Publication Data

Durham, Alan L., 1963–
    Patent law essentials: a concise guide / Alan L. Durham.—2nd ed.
     p. cm.
    Includes bibliographical references and index.
    ISBN 0–275–98205–X (alk. paper)
    1. Patent laws and legislation—United States. I. Title.
  KF3114.3.D87   2004
  346.7304'86—dc22   2004053103

British Library Cataloguing in Publication Data is available.

Library of Congress Catalog Card Number: 2004053103
ISBN: 0–275–98205–X

First published in 2004

Praeger Publishers, 88 Post Road West, Westport, CT 06881
An imprint of Greenwood Publishing Group, Inc.
www.praeger.com

Printed in the United States of America

The paper used in this book complies with the
Permanent Paper Standard issued by the National
Information Standards Organization (Z39.48–1984).

10 9 8 7 6 5 4 3 2 1

3/25/05

Contents

Preface

Since the first edition of this book appeared in 1999, the importance of intellectual property rights in today's society has become even more apparent. Millions of Americans share copyrighted works via the Internet, to the consternation of the music and film industries who, increasingly, turn to legal action to defend their interests. As these disputes run their course, copyright law will play a central role in shaping future technologies, business models, cultural developments and forms of personal expression. Patents too have become difficult to ignore. The mainstream press reports on the critical influence of patents in such fields as pharmaceuticals, biotechnology, software, and electronic commerce, frequently with the suggestion that overbroad patents, or their overzealous enforcement, may impede the very forces of innovation that patents are intended to promote. Patent owners, of course, vehemently disagree. In April 2004, a small company called Inter-Trust Technologies settled patent litigation against software giant Microsoft, which, if successful, could have stopped Microsoft from selling most of its product line. *Fortune* magazine called it "the biggest patent case ever." If the case was extraordinary in scale, it was, in other respects, typical. In an information economy, the control of ideas can make or break any business, large or small.

Several comprehensive treatises, including Professor Donald Chisum's remarkable 14-volume work, discuss patent law in exhaustive detail. They include much history, countless recitations of authority, and sophisticated analysis of every nuance. For readers needing these things, they are indispensable. The goals of this book are far more modest. As with the first edition, my intention is to present the essentials of patent law in the clearest terms possible, without oversimplifying or misrepresenting those areas where the law is genuinely complex. Whenever possible, I have used simple hypotheticals or examples from actual cases to illustrate a point. My hope is that I have produced a book that laymen can understand, but that is still sufficiently complete and up-to-date to be useful to professionals. I have taken particular care to include citations to recent authority in the footnotes, and many of the changes in the new edition will be found there. These footnotes can be ignored by readers who desire only the basics, but attorneys should find them a helpful reference.

More, perhaps, than attorneys who specialize in other fields, attorneys who specialize in patent law seem fascinated by the twists and turns, paradoxes and fine distinctions of the law itself, regardless of what it may mean for their clients. As others have observed, there is a kind of metaphysics in patent law's union of abstract ideas with the disposition of tangible property. Although the focus of this book is resolutely practical, I hope that some flavor remains of what makes patent law an intriguing intellectual exercise for those who devote their lives to its practice and study.

I would like to express my deepest appreciation to my friends and colleagues at the University of Alabama School of Law for their inspiration and encouragement. I am particularly grateful to Dean Kenneth Randall and the Law School Foundation for their support of my research. Once again I thank my former colleagues at Morrison & Foerster and Brown & Bain, who made the first edition of this book possible. Finally, many thanks to readers of the first edition who, directly or through online reviews, shared their thoughts and suggestions. Your kind words kindled my enthusiasm for a new edition.

CHAPTER 1

Overview

1.1 ORIGINS

The historical antecedents of the United States patent system are often traced to seventeenth-century England. Until then, a *patent* might refer to nothing more than a legally sanctioned monopoly, granted to reward a loyal subject or sold to raise funds for the exchequer. A merchant guild, for example, might purchase a patent for the exclusive right to sell playing cards. Freedom from competition allowed the patent owner to sell in larger volumes and at a higher price. Although this system was undoubtedly popular with the government and with the patent owners, these "odious monopolies" were a source of resentment to consumers and potential competitors. In 1624 the crown relented and the Statute of Monopolies, abolishing the general power of the monarch to grant exclusive rights, became law. Importantly, however, the statute ending the general practice of monopolies specifically exempted patents that allowed inventors the exclusive right to their inventions.

The tradition of granting patents to inventors continued in colonial America and, in spite of some skepticism by influential thinkers such as Thomas Jefferson, it was incorporated into the laws of the United States. The framers of the Constitution provided to Congress, in Article I, Section 8, the power to "promote the Progress of Science and [the] useful Arts, by securing for limited Times to Authors and inventors the exclusive Right to their respective Writings and Discoveries." This brief language is the source of both patent law and copyright law in the United States.[1] The specifics were left to Congress, whose

---

[1] When the Constitution was drafted, the term *science* was used in a broader sense than it is today, and was generally synonymous with *knowledge*. *Arts* also held a different meaning, and the term *useful arts* probably referred to what we would now call *technology*. Although somewhat counterintuitive, the prevailing view of legal historians is that patent law exists to advance the "arts," whereas copyright law exists to advance "science."

last wholesale revision of the Patent Act occurred in 1952, and to the Patent and Trademark Office (also known as the Patent Office or PTO), a division of the Department of Commerce created in 1836. The federal courts too have played a significant role in interpreting, supplementing, and perhaps, on some occasions, rewriting the rules set down by Congress.

Although patent law has evolved in some ways with the passage of time, the theories behind it are much the same today as they were in the beginning. One theory that still has an eighteenth-century flavor is that inventors possess a natural right to their inventions that must be recognized by law. The creation is naturally the property of the person who labored to create it. The more common theory, and the one most clearly reflected in the Constitution, is that patents provide the encouragement necessary for industrial advancement. If a budding Edison feared that the rewards of his inventive efforts would be reaped by copyists—copyists who did not even bear the costs of original research—he might abandon the laboratory for other pursuits. Society would then be denied the benefit of useful inventions. If, on the other hand, an inventor can obtain a patent ensuring that only he will profit from his invention, he is more likely to invest the time, effort, skill, and resources necessary to discover new technologies.

Patents also benefit society by making available precise descriptions of new inventions. A patent is a public document published by the United States government. One requirement of a patent is that it describe the invention, in both words and drawings, in such detail that other persons in the field can understand the invention and practice it themselves. During the term of the patent, this information may be of limited interest because only the patent owner and licensees have the legal right to practice the invention. Yet patents remain in force only for a limited time, and when the patent expires the invention enters the public domain. In theory at least, the millions of patents that have already expired are a resource that may be freely exploited by anyone, and even an unexpired patent can provide the inspiration for new and different approaches to technological problems.

The view that a patent is a kind of *bargain* between the inventor and the public, by which the inventor receives a limited monopoly in exchange for disclosing the invention to the public, is of more than theoretical interest. Together with the overall constitutional goal of promoting the "useful arts," the bargain model of patents helps to shape the specific rules that determine whether a patent is valid or invalid. In particular, this model will resurface as we examine the concepts of enablement and best mode in Sections 8.6–8.7.

1.2 SUMMARY AND ROADMAP

A book about patent law is difficult to organize because an understanding of one principle is so often dependent on an understanding of other principles, ad infinitum. As a *New Yorker* article once observed, patent law is "apt to plunge all but the stoutest minds into dizzying swirls of logic."[2] What follows is a sort of roadmap to this book that may keep the reader better oriented as we wind our way through the maze.

Chapter 1 (this chapter) introduces the reader to some of the history and theory underpinning patent law and concludes with a brief discussion of the laws, judicial opinions, and other authorities that are cited throughout this book.

Chapter 2 distinguishes patents from other forms of intellectual property rights with which patents are often confused. Specifically, Chapter 2 briefly discusses copyrights, which protect works of authorship such as writings, musical compositions, and illustrations; trademarks, which protect corporate names and logos; and trade secrets law, which protects confidential business information.

Chapter 3 leads the reader through a close examination of an actual United States patent, found in Appendix A. This includes the patent drawings, the *specification* (a detailed prose description of the inventor's work), and the *claims*. The claims are the last portion of a patent; they describe in careful terms exactly what the patented invention is.

Chapter 4 discusses the kinds of discoveries that can or cannot be patented, with sections devoted to abstract ideas, principles of nature, living organisms, artistic and literary creations, printed matter, and methods of doing business. Patent protection for computer software is a particularly thorny subject, and it is reserved for discussion with other specialized topics in Chapter 12.

Chapter 5 explains the process one goes through to obtain a patent from the United States Patent Office—a process known as *patent prosecution.* Some of the complexities discussed include patent applications that spawn offspring, known as *continuations, continuations-in-part,* or *divisional* applications; *interferences,* which are a procedure for determining which of two inventors who have competing patents or patent applications actually invented first; and *reissue* and *reexamination,* both procedures allowing the Patent Office a second look at applications that have already issued as patents.

Chapter 6 examines the issue of inventorship—that is, who should or should not be credited as an inventor—and how an inventor can convey rights to a patented invention, either by assignment or by license. Chapter 6 also discusses how rights to a patented invention can be conveyed, intentionally or unintentionally, by an *implied license.*

Chapter 7 deals with the issue of interpreting patent claims. This is a difficult but extremely important issue, because deciding what a patent claim *means* is the starting point for determining whether the patent is valid or infringed. Chapter 7 reviews some of the tools used to interpret patent claims, including *plain meaning,* the patent *specification,* and the *prosecution*

---

[2] John Seabrook, *The Flash of Genius,* The New Yorker, January 11, 1993, at 40.

history, which is a record of the applicant's dealings with the Patent Office. Chapter 7 also discusses special problems associated with claim *preambles* and certain specialized claim formats sometimes preferred by applicants. Among these are *product-by-process* claims, which describe the invention in terms of the way it is made, and *means-plus-function* claims, in which particular claim elements are described in terms of the function they perform.

Chapter 8 is one of the longer chapters in the book because it deals with the various conditions of patentability. If a patent application fails to meet any one of the conditions set out in this chapter, it should be rejected by the Patent Office. If the application nevertheless slips through the Patent Office, the patent can be held invalid by a court. In fact, in most cases where a charge of infringement results in a lawsuit, the accused infringer argues that the patent is invalid.

Chapter 8 begins with a general discussion of the conditions of patentability, including the presumption that any patent is valid until proven otherwise. The specific topics covered in the chapter include the *utility* requirement, which means that the patented invention must perform some useful function; the *definiteness* requirement, which means that the claims must be reasonably precise in identifying the patented invention; the *enablement* requirement, which means that the patent must include enough information so that others can practice the claimed invention without undue experimentation; the *best mode* requirement, which means that the inventor must have disclosed the best way he or she knew of practicing the invention at the time the application was filed; and the *written description* requirement, which means that the patent specification, as filed, must describe the invention ultimately claimed.

The *novelty* requirement, discussed next in Chapter 8, is in many respects the key to patentability. The novelty requirement means that the claimed invention must be *new* and *nonobvious*, in comparison to the prior art. Chapter 8 discusses the various kinds of prior art that may be relevant, including prior inventions, prior patents, and prior publications. Chapter 8 also discusses how the date of invention is determined, which can be a critical issue when deciding whether another invention, or a patent or publication, is actually *prior* art.

Chapter 8 discusses both *anticipation*, which means that the claimed invention can be found in the prior art, and *obviousness*, which means that even though nothing identical to the claimed invention is found in the prior art, the invention still would have been obvious to a person of ordinary skill. If an invention is obvious, perhaps as an elaboration or a combination of prior inventions, it is not considered an advance worthy of a patent. Obviousness is a difficult and subjective inquiry, invariably conducted in hindsight. Chapter 8 examines some of the "secondary considerations," such as commercial success, that are intended as more objective measures of whether an invention was obvious.

The chapter continues with a discussion of the *statutory bar* provisions, which can invalidate a patent if the applicant was too slow in filing an application after the occurrence of a critical event—such as an offer to sell a product embodying the invention. Chapter 8 concludes with an examination of double patenting. *Double patenting* is a ground for invalidating a patent if the same inventor had already patented the same invention. This prevents an inventor from obtaining multiple patents on the same thing, thereby extending the period of the patent monopoly beyond the intended span.

Chapter 9 examines two potential defenses to a charge of infringement, which, if successful, will result in a holding that a patent is unenforceable. If a patent is unenforceable, a court will not use its powers to prevent that patent from being infringed. The first such defense discussed in Chapter 9 is *inequitable conduct.* Because, generally speaking, patent prosecution happens in secret and only the applicant and the Patent Office participate, it is important to hold patent applicants to a high standard of candor and fair dealing during that process. Inequitable conduct occurs if an applicant intentionally deceives the Patent Office, or withholds critical information, during prosecution. The other unenforceability defense discussed in Chapter 9 is misuse. *Misuse* refers to attempts to leverage the patent monopoly beyond its intended scope—for example, by requiring that anyone practicing the patented invention purchase an *unpatented* product from the patent owner. This kind of "tying" and other forms of misuse may violate the federal antitrust laws, in addition to rendering a patent unenforceable.

Chapter 10 is another lengthy chapter because it deals with the subject of infringement. After a preliminary discussion covering the temporal and geographical limitations of a patent, Chapter 10 discusses direct and indirect infringement. *Direct* infringement includes making, using, selling, offering to sell, or importing into the United States something that falls within the scope of a patent claim. *Indirect* infringement means inducing or contributing to infringement by someone else—for example, by supplying a part that can only be used in a patented combination. An indirect infringer is liable in the same way that a direct infringer is liable.

Chapter 10 then discusses *literal* infringement, which occurs if the infringing product or process includes each and every element required by a patent claim, exactly as described. Next is a discussion of the "doctrine of equivalents," a doctrine holding that a product or process can still infringe a claim even though it is *different* from what the claim literally requires, as long as the differences are insubstantial. This is a difficult concept, even for experts and judges, so it is covered in some detail. Chapter 10 discusses how the doctrine of equivalents has evolved, and it examines some of the tests used to determine if a product or process is or is not equivalent to a claimed invention. The chapter also discusses limitations on the scope of equivalency imposed by the prosecution history, the patent disclosure, and the prior art. Chapter 10 further considers equivalency in the related context

of *means-plus-function* claims, as well as the "reverse doctrine of equivalents," which holds that a product does not infringe, even though it is literally described by the patent claims, if it is sufficiently "changed in
principle" from what the applicant actually invented. Finally, Chapter 10
discusses a little-used experimental-use exception to infringement.

Chapter 11 introduces the subject of patent litigation. Specific topics
discussed include jurisdiction and venue, which determine in what court a
suit for infringement can be filed; actions for declaratory judgment, which
permit an accused infringer to sue a patent owner instead of waiting to be
sued; burdens of proof, which determine who must prove what and how
compelling the evidence must be; and the roles of judge and jury in deciding the various issues presented in a typical case. Chapter 11 also examines the kinds of relief that can be won in a suit for patent infringement.
These include preliminary injunctions, which bar the continuance of the
allegedly infringing activity during the pendency of the lawsuit; permanent injunctions, which permanently bar infringing activity if the patent
owner prevails; and money damages, which compensate the patent owner
for past infringement. The last-named can be in the form of lost profits or
a reasonable royalty, and they can be increased as much as threefold if the
infringement is found to have been "willful." Chapter 11 also discusses
defenses that can limit the recovery of damages, including the 6-year statute of limitations, the patent owner's failure to properly mark products
that it has sold, laches, and equitable estoppel. *Laches* refers to unreasonable delay in filing suit that somehow prejudices the accused infringer.
Equitable estoppel refers to conduct by the patent owner that leads the
accused infringer to believe that the patent owner will not pursue a claim.

Chapter 11 ends with a brief discussion of the International Trade Commission, which is an alternative forum for raising a claim of patent infringement if
the accused products are imported into the United States from abroad.

Chapter 12 concludes the work with a discussion of several specialized
topics, including design patents, plant patents, foreign patents, and patents
claiming computer programs.

Appendices A and B provide, respectively, samples of actual utility and
design patents issued by the United States Patent Office.

1.3 SOURCES OF LAW

Several important sources of patent law will be referenced throughout
this book. One is the Patent Act, found at Title 35 of the United States Code
(U.S.C.). The Patent Act contains most of the legislation enacted by Congress that relates to patents. References to particular sections of the Act will
generally be in the format "35 U.S.C. § ____." Other important authorities
are the Code of Federal Regulations (37 C.F.R.) and the Manual of Patent

Examining Procedure (MPEP), which set forth detailed rules and regulations for obtaining a patent.

In addition to the statutes, rules, and regulations, one can find countless reported court decisions interpreting the patent laws. As in any other field of federal law, the controlling precedents are those of the United States Supreme Court. However, the Supreme Court only rarely accepts appeals in patent cases, leaving most of the decision making to the lower courts. The most significant of these lower courts, at present, is the Federal Circuit Court of Appeals. Established in 1982, the Federal Circuit, based in Washington, D.C., hears all appeals of patent-related cases, regardless of the place where the suit was initially filed. Except on those occasions when the Supreme Court intervenes, the Federal Circuit is the ultimate authority on what patent laws mean, and all inferior courts, as well as the Patent Office, are bound by its interpretations.

Cases referred to in this book are accompanied by citations, generally in the footnotes. The standard citation format includes the name of the case, followed by the volume of the official reporter in which it appears, the abbreviated name of the official reporter, the relevant page numbers, and in parentheses an identification of the court and the date of the decision. For example, *Vitronics Corp. v. Conceptronic, Inc.*, 90 F.3d 1576, 1582–83 (Fed. Cir. 1996), refers to a case of that name reported in Volume 90 of the *Federal Reporter* (Third Series) beginning at page 1576. The pages of particular interest are pages 1582–83, and the decision was rendered by the Federal Circuit Court of Appeals in 1996. These citations are provided in case the reader needs additional information or authority to support a particular proposition.

CHAPTER 2

Patents Distinguished from Other Rights

People sometimes confuse patents with copyrights or trademarks, saying, for example, that George Lucas has a *patent* on the name *Star Wars*. Patents, copyrights, trademarks, and trade secrets are all legal means of protecting *intellectual property*—a term referring to the intangible creations of the human mind in which the law recognizes some form of ownership. However, patents, copyrights, trademarks, and trade secrets are each governed by a unique body of rules and requirements, and, in spite of some overlap, they are generally designed to protect different sorts of intellectual creations. Therefore, a good starting point for explaining what a patent *is* may be to emphasize what it is *not*.

2.1 COPYRIGHTS

Copyrights protect "works of authorship," which is broadly defined by statute to include writings in the conventional sense and, among other things, dramatic works, musical compositions, choreography, paintings, sculptures, photographs, motion pictures, audio recordings, and architecture. To some degree, any work of authorship has an aspect of creative expression. Copyright protects this expression, not the underlying ideas. Although idea and expression are not always easy to sort out, one could, for example, borrow the information published in this book without violating its copyright. The copyright would be violated only by duplicating the book's language or organization. Language is a matter of expression and a product of the author's creative faculties. The information itself is on the side of ideas, and, no matter what labor was expended to compile it, it can be freely used without violation of copyright.[1]

Copyrights do not apply to technological innovations or to the useful features of products. For example, a new and more efficient spark plug design could not be copyrighted. Some useful products do have an aesthetic aspect that can protected by copyright, but the artistic component of the design must be distinguishable from the utilitarian component, which can only be patented. For example, a belt buckle might be copyrighted as a sculpture,[2] but the copyright cannot prevent the copying of some mechanical aspect of the design, such as an improved latching mechanism. In this respect a copyright is the antithesis of a patent, which is specifically intended to protect such technological advancements. If one had both a copyright and a patent on the same belt buckle, the copyright would protect only the aesthetic appearance of the belt buckle, and the patent would protect only the mechanism by which it worked.[3]

As we will see in Section 8.9, an invention is patentable only if it is sufficiently new and different when compared to prior inventions that persons skilled in the field would not have considered it obvious. In contrast, copyright law has no requirement of novelty per se. As long as the work of authorship is an original product of the author's imagination, a copyright cannot be denied simply because the work is similar to others that have gone before. This may be the case because of the difficulty of judging novelty or obviousness in relation to the kinds of creative works that are traditionally protected by copyright. Who can say whether the latest mystery novel is an obvious variation of the thousands that have gone before? By the same token, independent creation is a complete defense to infringement of copyright, regardless of the similarity of two works. If two songs are nearly identical to one another, but it can be shown that the second composer worked entirely on his own, without knowledge of the first composition, the second composer cannot be held to have infringed the copyright of the first.[4] Patent law is very different. One who innocently infringes a patent, perhaps not even knowing that the patent exists, can still be held accountable in the courts.

One area in which patent and copyright converge is in the protection of computer software. Software blurs the boundaries between a work of

---

[1] *See* Feist Publications, Inc. v. Rural Telephone Service Co., 499 U.S. 340, 347 (1991). (Facts are not copyrightable because they "do not owe their origin to an act of authorship.")

[2] *See* Kieselstein-Cord v. Accessories By Pearl, Inc., 632 F.2d 989 (2d Cir. 1980).

[3] Unless the patent were a *design* patent, a special category of patent discussed in Section 12.1.

[4] Although the similarity of the two works could be considered evidence that the second composer did not, in fact, work independently.

authorship and a machine. From the perspective of a programmer, a computer program is a kind of writing. It is expressed in a language, which resembles in some respects ordinary human languages, and the process of authorship involves some of the aesthetic choices and personal style associated with other forms of writing. Copyright, rather than patent, would seem the proper vehicle for protecting this expression. On the other hand, a program is akin to a machine part as soon as it is executed by a computer. The program controls the operation of the computer much as cogs and wheels may have controlled a machine of an earlier era. From this perspective, a computer program seems outside of the subject matter protected by copyright and more suitable for protection by patent.

Courts and scholars have struggled for decades to determine the proper application of copyright and patent law to computer software. At present, both forms of protection appear to be available, though each has its limitations. A computer program can be copyrighted, but this may not prevent someone else from extracting the functional aspects of the program to incorporate in a new program. The functional aspects of computer software can be patented as long as they meet the various requirements of patentability (such as novelty and nonobviousness) and as long as the patent steers clear of monopolizing an abstract idea, mathematical algorithm, or principle of nature. These special concerns are discussed in some detail in Section 12.4.

2.2 TRADEMARKS

Trademarks are governed by federal statutes, by state laws, and by common law. A trademark is a device, such as a word, phrase, or symbol, that is used to represent the origin of a product. A consumer who finds the word *Nike* on a shoe box, or the familiar Nike "swoosh" symbol, is entitled to presume that the shoe sold in the box is the genuine article. The overriding purpose of trademark law is the protection of consumers, and disputes in this area are usually resolved by determining whether consumers would be confused by the use of a mark that is similar to the mark of another business. If another shoe manufacturer adopted the name Nikke for its line of products, one could be sure that the original Nike would challenge such use as unfair and confusing. Patents are granted only on inventions—not on labels, logos, or brand names. Trademarks, on the other hand, do not secure exclusive rights to the functional aspects of a product.[5]

---

[5] Traffix Devices, Inc. v. Marketing Displays, Inc., 532 U.S. 23, 29 (2001).

2.3 TRADE SECRETS

Patents are not the only way that inventors can prevent others from taking advantage of their labors. Another option is to keep the invention a secret. An inventor cannot do both. As soon as a patent issues, the invention becomes public. This is a part of the bargain that the inventor strikes with the government in order to obtain the patent monopoly. However, the patent application process is, for the most part, confidential. If an inventor applies for a patent, but the application is rejected, the inventor can abandon the attempt and still retain some protection by keeping the invention a secret.

Whether an inventor is better advised to patent an invention or simply keep it a secret may depend on the nature of the invention. If it is something that will be revealed as soon as a product incorporating the invention is placed on the market, the notion of keeping the invention secret may be self-defeating. On the other hand, certain inventions can be exploited without making them public. For example, an ordinary product, indistinguishable from any other, might be manufactured less expensively because of an innovative process. Such a process might be better protected through secrecy than it would be by patent, because a patent would only last for a limited term. Similarly, the legendary secret formula of Coca-Cola has never been patented, apparently because the formula cannot be accurately determined by analyzing the finished product. Under these circumstances, secrecy provides Coca-Cola with better and longer-lasting protection.

If secret information is of the kind that gives one an advantage in business, it may be protectable under trade secret law. Trade secrets are largely governed by state laws, rather than federal law, so there is some geographic variation. However, about 40 states have adopted, in some form, a model statute known as the Uniform Trade Secrets Act. The definition of *trade secret* under the Uniform Act extends to various forms of information, including "a formula, pattern, compilation, program, device, method, technique, or process."[6] Although such things as formulas, devices, and processes are also within the area of potentially patentable inventions,[7] trade secret law imposes a different set of requirements. In order to qualify as a protectable trade secret under the Uniform Act, the information must "derive independent economic value, actual or potential, from not being generally known to, and not being readily ascertainable by proper means by, other persons who can obtain economic value from its disclosure or use."[8] In other words, not only must the informa-

---

[6] Uniform Trade Secrets Act § 1(4).

[7] Trade secret law can also be used to protect certain kinds of business information that would not be patentable—for example, customer lists and marketing plans. As long as information is secret and valuable to a business, it can be protected as a trade secret, even though it is not an invention in the usual sense.

[8] Uniform Trade Secrets Act § 1(4)(i).

tion be secret, it must also be *valuable*. In addition, the information must be "the subject of efforts that are reasonable under the circumstances to maintain its secrecy."[9] A company that is lax about security may be unable to resort to trade secret law to protect its information from use or disclosure. Patent law, in contrast, requires neither that an invention be economically valuable nor (under most circumstances) that it have been kept secret.[10]

Whereas patent law speaks of *infringement*, trade secret law forbids *misappropriation*. Misappropriation includes unauthorized disclosure or use of trade secret information by someone who has a duty to keep the information secret or limit its use.[11] Employees, for example, are generally duty-bound to refrain from using or disclosing the trade secret information of their employers. So is anyone who has signed a contract or confidentiality agreement promising to protect the information. An employee of a soda company who published his employer's secret formula on the Internet, or who used the formula to devise a rival soda, would likely be held guilty of trade secret misappropriation.

Misappropriation also includes the use of information known to be derived from someone under a duty to keep it confidential and acquisition of the secret information by "improper means."[12] A person who bribed a soda company employee in order to obtain its secret formula would likely be guilty of misappropriation. Finally, misappropriation can occur, under the Uniform Act, if trade secret information is used by persons who know that the information has come into their possession only because of a mistake. If a soda manufacturer received a fax from a competitor setting out a secret formula, and it was evident that the fax had actually been intended for someone else, the rival would probably not be permitted to keep the fax and use the formula.

Trade secret law differs from patent law in requiring either some connection with a duty (contractual or otherwise) to protect the confidential information, the use of "improper means" to acquire the information, or an evident mistake. If the information was acquired under other circumstances, it can be freely used. For example, the Uniform Act allows the acquisition of information by reverse engineering. *Reverse engineering* means beginning with the finished product and analyzing it to determine the process by which it was developed or the principle of its operation. As long as the finished product was acquired legitimately—by purchasing it on the open market, for example—it is not a violation of trade secret law to reverse engineer the product and use the resulting information in a competing product.

---

[9] Uniform Trade Secrets Act § 1(4)(ii).

[10] An exception arises if the invention was disclosed more than one year before a patent application was filed. See Section 8.10.

[11] Uniform Trade Secrets Act § 1(2)(ii).

[12] Uniform Trade Secrets Act § 1(2)(ii).

Hence, if a rival soda manufacturer could analyze a beverage and determine the formula by which it was manufactured, trade secret law (applying the Uniform Act) would not prevent the rival from discovering and using that information. Patent law, in contrast, does not distinguish between information acquired legitimately or illegitimately. A product can still infringe a patent, even though it was the result of reverse engineering or even independent development.

Trade secret law might seem at odds with patent law, which requires the public disclosure of information in exchange for exclusive rights. The Supreme Court, however, has ruled that the two bodies of law are not incompatible, and federal patent law does not preempt state trade secret laws.[13] One complements the other, and inventors are provided with a choice of means to protect their inventions, the most appropriate of which will be determined by the circumstances.

2.4 PATENTS

Patents cover practical inventions in the "useful arts." Any technological advance from a new microchip to an improved formula for bubble gum can be the subject of a patent. A special form of patent known as a *design patent* can protect some forms of artistic expression (see Section 12.1), but the usual kind of patent–the *utility patent*–applies only to technological inventions. As a result, a patent cannot be granted for a painting, a novel, a song, a product name, or a company logo.

In order to obtain a patent, an inventor must file an application with the United States Patent and Trademark Office, and the application must describe the invention in such a way that persons skilled in the field could practice the invention. The application must conclude with numbered *claims* that describe in precise terms exactly what the patent is intended to cover. A patent can be granted, or if granted can be held valid in the courts, only if the claims describe an invention that is both *new* and *nonobvious.* Patent law thus includes a requirement of novelty that is absent from copyright and trademark law.

Once an application issues as a patent, the patent remains in force until 20 years after the date the application was filed. During that time, no one without the permission of the patent owner can (within the geographical limits of the United States) make, use, sell, offer to sell, or import the invention described by the patent claims. To do so is an infringement of the patent, regardless of whether the infringer copied the inventor's ideas or discovered them independently. In contrast to trademark law, which requires that the protected mark be *used* in business, a patent owner can choose to practice the claimed invention, license it to others, or prevent its practice altogether.

---

[13] Kewanee Oil Co. v. Bicron Corp., 416 U.S. 470 (1974).

CHAPTER 3

Reading a Patent

Anyone interested in patent law should take the time to study an actual patent. Copies of three United States utility patents can be found in Appendix A of this book. The examples have been chosen for the sake of simplicity and brevity, and to show that inventors are still searching for a "better mousetrap."

The first patent claims a device for trapping a mouse with the help of a ping-pong ball. The mouse enters a tube, the tube tips forward as the mouse heads for the "smelly bait," and a ping-pong ball rolls down to block the mouse's escape. In the second patent, bait is used to lure the mouse onto a bridge. Although the bridge appears to be secure, the weight of the mouse causes the bridge to spin sideways, sending the mouse plunging headlong into a bucket. The trap claimed in the third patent is made from a soda can.

Although none of these inventions is complex, each patent includes the basic components found in patents awarded to the most sophisticated advancements. The first patent will be used as an example for most of the following discussion, but the reader should examine all three, in order to get a feel for the way patents are organized.

3.1 GENERAL INFORMATION

Patents are officially known by their serial numbers, printed at the top right-hand corner of the patent. For the sake of convenience, patents are often referred to by the last name of the first listed inventor or by the last three digits of the patent's serial number. The first patent in

Appendix A would be referred to as the Oviatt patent, or as the '918 patent. The date on which the patent issued appears directly below the serial number.[1]

The title of the patent appears at the top of the left-hand column: for example, "Mousetrap for Catching Mice Live." The title of a patent has little official significance and can sometimes be misleading.[2] The description of the "Mousetrap for Catching Mice Live" suggests that the trap can be immersed in water and the rodent drowned. The name of the inventor, or inventors, appears directly below the title, together with the inventor's address or home town. Beneath the inventor's name is the name of any person or company to whom the inventor assigned rights in the patent, prior to the date of issue.[3] Because the Oviatt patent shows no assignee, ownership of the patent evidently was retained by the inventor. Patent rights can be assigned after the patent issues. When this is the case, the transfer of ownership will not be evident from the patent itself, but it may be recorded in the Patent Office's prosecution history file.

Moving down the left-hand column, the next item to appear is the number of the application on which the patent was based. Each patent application submitted to the Patent Office is assigned a serial number. It is not the same serial number ultimately assigned to the patent itself. Although this can result in some confusion, it allows reference to applications that never issued as patents. The Oviatt patent is the result of a single application, numbered 347,890. Often the situation is more complicated. The applicant may have filed one application, which was rejected and abandoned in favor of a *continuation* or a *continuation-in-part* application. Sometimes this happens several times, resulting in a chain of applications preceding a particular patent. These complications are discussed in Sections 5.2–5.3. For now, it is enough to note that the "family history" of the patent, if any, can be found in the upper left-hand column of the patent, next to the bracketed number [63].

All patented inventions are assigned by the Patent Office to subject matter categories, which are sometimes narrowed to very particular fields. This is done so that the Patent Office (or anyone else for that matter) can conveniently search a given area and determine what has been patented so far.

---

[1] The bracketed number "[11]" to the left of the patent serial number, like the other bracketed numbers found at various places on the patent, is a matter of Patent Office formatting. All patents of a certain era have the number [11] next to the serial number, [45] next to the date of issue, [54] next to the title, [75] next to the names of the inventors and so forth. The numbers have no significance, other than in identifying the location of certain information.

[2] *See* Pitney Bowes, Inc. v. Hewlett-Packard Co., 182 F.3d 1298, 1312 (Fed. Cir. 1999) ("[T]he purpose of the title is not to demarcate the precise boundaries of the claimed invention but rather to provide a useful reference tool for future classification purposes. . . . [W]e certainly will not read limitations into the claims from the patent title.").

[3] *See* Section 6.2.

This classification information appears beneath the application family history, next to the bracketed numbers [51] and [52], the first number relating to international classification and the second to U.S. classification. In the case of the Oviatt patent, the mousetrap invention has been assigned to U.S. subject matter Class 43: "Fishing, Trapping and Vermin Destroying." It can be found specifically under subclasses 60 ("Traps:Imprisoning"), 61 ("Traps:Imprisoning:Swinging or Sliding Closure"), and 66 ("Traps:Self and Ever Set:Nonreturn Entrance:Victim Opened").

As discussed in Section 5.1, part of the Patent Office's duty on receiving an application is to search its collection of prior patents to determine whether the application claims something new. The Field of Search area shows the categories that were reviewed by the Patent Office in its search for earlier patents. In the case of the Oviatt patent, the Patent Office searched the same subclasses noted above, with the addition of subclasses 58 ("Traps"), 67 ("Traps:Self and Ever Set:Nonreturn Entrance:Victim Opened"), and 75 ("Traps:Self-Reset:Smiting"). The search categories established by the Patent Office provide a brief catalog of modern technology. Class 43, for example, is a testament to man's continuing war with the mouse, including subcategories for "impaling," "explosive," "choking or squeezing," and "electrocuting" traps, in addition to those that "smite."

Moving downward, the next section of the patent is a list of prior art references cited by the Patent Office during prosecution of the application. Prior art, discussed in Section 8.9.1, includes earlier patents and publications disclosing inventions similar to the one claimed by the patent applicant. The cited references are those that the Patent Office considered closest to the patented invention, though not so close as to prevent the patent from issuing. Looking once again to the Oviatt patent, the Patent Office cited three patents as prior art, two of them more than 75 years old: the Turnbo patent, issued in 1909; the Cushing patent, issued in 1917; and the Sackett patent, issued in 1988. All disclose some form of rat or mouse trap with a tilting mechanism to prevent the victim's escape.

Next to appear are the name of the patent examiner, or examiners, who reviewed the application for the Patent Office, and the name of the counsel or patent agent who represented the inventor during this process.

The paragraph entitled "Abstract" provides a summary of the invention.[4] This is the place to look for the gist of the invention, before tackling the detailed description that follows the drawings. The abstract typically includes a brief explanation of how the invention works and why it is useful.

---

[4] I use the term *invention* here to refer loosely to the technological advancement described in the patent disclosure. In a specific sense, the invention is defined by the patent claims. *See* Section 3.4.

3.2 DRAWINGS

After the abstract appear the patent drawings. These are often far more helpful in understanding the invention than a written description alone would be. Although drawings are not required for every patent, nearly all include some form of illustration. The Oviatt patent, like most patents, shows the invention from a variety of views so that all details are readily visible. Figures 3 and 8 show the invention before the mouse has sprung the trap. Figure 9 shows the movement of the ping-pong ball and the appearance of the trap after it has tipped forward on its pivot. Figure 2 is described as a "mouse eye view." Patents sometimes include exploded views, cross sections, or views of individual components when those views are helpful to understand the invention. Some patents include graphs or flow charts.

Patent drawings are generally surrounded by numbers and arrows, as are the drawings in the Oviatt patent. These are reference numbers corresponding to the written description of the invention found in the body of the patent. For example, the Oviatt patent identifies sphere 9 as the ping-pong ball, lump 10 as the bait, and rodent M as the mouse. Reading a patent sometimes requires a great deal of flipping back and forth to identify the components numbered in the drawings.[5]

Patent drawings sometimes depict different embodiments of the invention. Figure 1 of the Oviatt patent shows the trap set up on a stand made of wire, whereas Figure 5 shows the trap resting on the edge of a plastic ring. The inclusion of alternative embodiments shows that the inventor's ideas were not limited to a particular implementation of the invention.

3.3 SPECIFICATION

After the drawings comes the section of the patent referred to as the *specification*. The specification describes the invention, or technology related to the invention, in words rather than pictures. Often the specification begins with a "Background of the Invention" section discussing the technology as it existed before the patented invention was made. This allows the inventor to point out the shortcomings of what has gone before and highlight the advantages of the patented invention. The Oviatt patent begins in typical fashion by describing the health menace posed by mice and the disadvantages of typical traps that kill the mouse, where it is left to decompose, smell, and endanger children and pets. Oviatt then explains that his own invention avoids these problems by trapping the mouse alive.

Many specifications include a "Summary of the Invention" section, which is used to list the objectives of the patented invention. Oviatt states that the

---

[5] Note that the numbers used in labeling a patent drawing need not be consecutive. The Oviatt patent uses numbers 90 and 100, but there is no 89 or 99.

"main object" of his invention is to "trap a mouse alive." Other, subsidiary objectives are to provide an inexpensive trap, a trap that can be immersed in water to drown the mouse, and a trap that is reusable.

The next section of the Oviatt patent is, again in typical fashion, a "Brief Description of the Drawings." This portion of the patent explains in the most general way what is depicted in the drawings—for example, Figure 1 is a top view, Figure 3 is a cross section, and Figure 5 is an alternative embodiment.

The next section of the Oviatt patent is entitled "Description of the Preferred Embodiment." Almost any patent has a similar section where the inventor describes the "preferred embodiment" in great detail, identifying in the process all of the components visible in the drawings. The *preferred embodiment* means the inventor's favored implementation of the invention. Inventions are usually general concepts that, at a detailed level, could be implemented in any number of ways. In the Oviatt patent, the tilting tube and the rolling ball are general concepts that characterize the invention. Oviatt might be entitled to claim any mousetrap that shares those features. But in the specification, we learn of the inventor's preference for a ping-pong ball, and we are given two possible designs for the fulcrum on which the trap teeters—one a stand preferably made of wire, and the other a plastic ring with one flat edge.

Disclosure at this level of detail satisfies two requirements of the patent laws: that inventors provide in the specification sufficient information to allow persons skilled in the field to practice the invention, and that inventors disclose the *best* way they know of to practice the invention. These requirements, known respectively as the enablement and best mode requirements, are discussed in Sections 8.6 and 8.7. The details discussed in the specification *do not*, under most circumstances, limit what the patent covers. Even though the specification describes a ping-pong ball, the patent might still cover a similar mousetrap that used a rubber ball.

In fact, the Oviatt specification includes warnings to that effect. Just before the numbered claims, we find the following caveat:

Although the present invention has been described with reference to preferred embodiments, numerous modifications and variations can be made and still the result will come within the scope of the invention. No limitation with respect to the specific embodiments disclosed herein is intended or should be inferred.

Such warnings are common, though they are probably unnecessary.

3.4 CLAIMS

The last, and most important, section of a patent consists of the numbered claims. The *claims*, not the drawings or the specification, define what the patent "covers" and what will infringe. In the Oviatt patent we find eight claims.

Claims come in two forms–independent claims and dependent claims. An *independent* claim stands by itself, whereas a *dependent* claim explicitly refers to another claim and incorporates its terms by reference. Claim 1 of the Oviatt patent is an independent claim. Claim 2 is a dependent claim because it refers to "The mousetrap of claim 1 wherein. . . . " As a result, Claim 2 is read as though it incorporates all of the language of Claim 1, plus the additional language of Claim 2. Claim 3 is another dependent claim, which this time refers to Claim 2 ("The mousetrap of claim 2 wherein . . . "). Because Claim 2 depends from Claim 1, the effect of Claim 3 is to incorporate *all* of the language of Claims 1, 2, and 3.

Claims generally begin with a preamble that establishes the context of the invention. As discussed in Section 7.6, the preamble is sometimes treated as a limitation on the scope of the claim and sometimes as a mere introduction to the claim, in which case the preamble has no legal effect. This can have important consequences. For example, Claim 1 of the Oviatt patent begins with the preamble "A mousetrap comprising. . . . " If this were the last reference in the claim to a mouse, one could question whether the claim covered, for example, a squirrel trap that was otherwise identical to the device described in the claim.

The preamble usually ends with the term *consisting of* or *comprising*.[6] The indented paragraphs following the preamble are the claim "elements" or claim "limitations." The vast majority of patent claims are designed to cover a *combination* of elements or limitations. Looking at Claim 1 of the Oviatt patent, we find the following combination set forth:

1. A mousetrap comprising:

   a main tube having a central fulcrum means, a bait end, and a ball end;

   a base stand having a means to support the main tube at the fulcrum;

   said bait end further comprising mouse bait and a main tube closure;

   said ball end further comprising a ball and a main tube closure;

   an entrance tube depending down from the main tube at the central fulcrum means, and angled toward the ball end;

   said entrance tube having a mouse entrance adjacent a supporting surface for the base stand; and

   said main tube having a horizontal load position where said ball rests at the ball end, wherein a mouse enters the mouse entrance, walks toward the base up the entrance tube, and passes the fulcrum means, thereby causing the main tube to teeter down at the bait end, and cause the ball to roll down the main tube and then down the entrance tube, functioning to block an egress of the mouse out the mouse entrance.

---

[6] *See* Section 7.6.

Claim 1 of the Oviatt patent would cover any mousetrap that included each of the elements described. If a mousetrap did not incorporate one or more of the described elements, it would fall outside the scope of what was claimed. If a mousetrap did not tip like the Oviatt mousetrap, but instead relied on a spring-loaded mechanism to shoot a ping-pong ball down the tube to trap the mouse, that trap would lack the "fulcrum means" required by Claim 1, and it would fall outside the literal scope of the claim.[7]

The language used in patent claims is generally more formal and technical, and sometimes more obscure, than everyday language. Claim 1 of the Oviatt patent is not a particularly bad example, but it does include terms such as "fulcrum means," "supporting surface," "horizontal load position," and "egress," which might seem more grandiose than the invention requires. Claim drafters, whether inventors or attorneys, resort to such technical or pseudotechnical language because of the importance of the words to the legal effect of the patent. Insofar as possible, the claim language is required to describe exactly what the patent covers. Claim drafters therefore must be precise in their description of the invention but must not limit themselves by the choice of language to something narrower than the inventor intends to claim.

The Oviatt patent has three independent claims—Claims 1, 6, and 8—and five dependent claims. A patent generally can have as many claims as the inventor desires, although more claims can mean paying the Patent Office a higher fee. Each claim can be treated in some respects as if it were a separate patent. Although people often speak of a patent being infringed, it is really a claim, or a series of claims, that is infringed. A device may infringe one claim of a patent but not another, perhaps because of a minor variation in language. An inventor who describes the invention through more than one claim decreases the chance that a potentially infringing product will escape because of some small difference. Using more than one claim is also a hedge against the possibility that a claim will be held invalid by the courts. One claim may be held invalid, whereas another, with slightly different language, survives.[8]

Note how the Oviatt patent describes the same concept, in slightly different terms, in Claims 1, 6, and 8. Claim 1 speaks of a pair of tubes—a "main tube" and an "entrance tube." Claim 8, on the other hand, speaks of a "'Y' shaped tube." The Oviatt patent also illustrates how dependent claims are often used to include details described in the specification but omitted from the broader claims. For example, Claim 4 specifically limits the "ball" of Claim 1 to a "ping-pong ball." If it proved to be the case that a mousetrap had been invented prior to Oviatt's that used a rubber ball, the broader claim might be held invalid, whereas the narrow claim might not.

---

[7] *See* Section 10.5. As discussed in Section 10.6, a product that differs from what the claim literally requires may still infringe, under the doctrine of equivalents, if the differences are insubstantial.

[8] *See* 35 U.S.C. § 282 ("Each claim of a patent . . . shall be presumed valid independently of the validity of other claims . . . .").

CHAPTER 4

Patentable Subject Matter

The Supreme Court has suggested that the realm of patents embraces "anything under the sun that is made by man,"[1] but this is not literally true. First, the Constitution limits the power of Congress to the promotion of the "useful arts." These are generally understood to include technological endeavors rather than, for example, artistic or social endeavors. The language of the Patent Act further limits the types of creations that can be patented. Section 101 of the Patent Act (35 U.S.C. § 101) provides as follows:

Whoever invents or discovers any new and useful process, machine, manufacture, or composition of matter, or any new and useful improvement thereof, may obtain a patent therefor, subject to the conditions and requirements of this title.[2]

In order to be patented, an invention must fall within one of the statutory categories of "process, machine, manufacture, or composition of matter." Because these terms are deliberately broad, this is seldom an obstacle. Yet certain categories of invention or discovery have been held to exceed the statutory boundaries of patentable subject matter, or are sufficiently close to those boundaries as to generate controversy. The most important of these fall under the rubric of abstract ideas, principles of nature, living organisms, literary or artistic creations, printed matter, methods of doing business, and computer programs.

---

[1] Diamond v. Chakrabarty, 447 U.S. 303, 309 (1980).
[2] "Manufacture" is an abbreviated term for a product produced by a manufacturing process. "Composition of matter" is a broad term that is most often applied to chemical compounds and the like, but that could literally refer to any agglomeration of physical substances.

4.1 ABSTRACT IDEAS

The most general category of unpatentable subject matter, and perhaps the hardest to define, is the category of *abstract ideas*. Obviously, one can patent an idea if it is in the form of a new process, machine, manufacture, or composition of matter. One cannot, however, patent an idea that is without a material form or a practical application. For example, one probably could not patent the idea of renewable energy resources. The idea is a useful one, but to be patentable it should take the form of a particular kind of renewable energy resource. Patents are intended to reward and encourage those who make tangible contributions to the useful arts. If patents were awarded to abstract ideas rather than to practical applications of those ideas, the effect might be to discourage, rather than promote, advancements in those arts.

4.2 PRINCIPLES OF NATURE

Although the Patent Act defines *invention* as meaning "invention *or discovery*,"[3] the courts have long held that the truths of nature cannot be patented, even by the people who discover those truths. The clearest examples can be found in the formulas of mathematics or the physical sciences. Pythagoras may have been the first to appreciate that the sums of the squares of the two sides of a right triangle are equal to the square of the hypotenuse, but such insights do not qualify as patentable inventions. Similarly, Einstein could not have patented the relationship of mass to energy in the form of the equation $E = mc^2$. On the other hand, one could patent a novel apparatus, method, or composition of matter that puts a principle of nature to practical application: for example, a new surveying instrument that makes use of the Pythagorean theorem, or a nuclear reactor based on Einstein's discovery. Because the formulas of science and mathematics are generalized descriptions of the universe, any invention, at some level, can be described by those formulas. As long as the invention is not the formula itself but a useful application or embodiment of the formula, it is potentially patentable.

The rule against patenting a principle of nature has been applied to materials discovered in nature, as well as to abstract relationships and physical laws. The discovery of a new mineral in the earth would not entitle the discoverer to patent it.[4] On the other hand, one who discovers a specific *use* for a natural material, such as the treatment of a disease, can patent that method of use, so long as it is new and nonobvious.[5] If others discover further uses

---

[3] 35 U.S.C. § 100.

[4] Diamond v. Chakrabarty, 447 U.S. 303, 309 (1980).

[5] Similarly, a new use for an existing artificial compound can be patented, though the discoverer of the new use is not entitled to a patent on the compound itself. *See In re* Schoenwald, 964 F.2d 1122, 1124 (Fed. Cir. 1992).

for the material, those also are potentially patentable. Some problems can be avoided through careful claim drafting. One inventor was denied a patent on a shrimp that was beheaded and cleaned, but still protected by its shell.[6] Although the shrimp was no longer whole, that which remained was still a "product of nature" and in its original state. Had the inventor instead claimed a *method* of preparing a shrimp, that method would more likely be held patentable subject matter.

It might be argued that investigation into the principles of nature is a pursuit just as valuable as the development of technology, and that awarding patents to significant discoveries would encourage such investigation. Why then are patents unobtainable on newly discovered natural laws? At least two theories have been advanced. One holds that a patent on a principle of nature would simply be too broad. A principle may lead to a vast spectrum of practical applications, many of which could not have been foreseen by the discoverer of the principle. This may well be true. However, as we will see in Section 10.6.5, even inventions of the ordinary kind (such as machines, processes, and compositions of matter) may be applied after their invention in ways that the inventor could not have predicted. This is particularly true of "pioneering" inventions. These inventions, which establish entirely new fields of industry, are often regarded as those *most* worthy of a patent. Another, perhaps sounder, argument is that patent law should not take from the public that which it has formerly possessed. New inventions take nothing from the public because, by definition, the inventions did not exist before. On the other hand, principles of nature exist even before they are discovered, and the public may, in some sense, have used these principles before they were appreciated. The nuclear reactions that cause the sun to shine are described, in part, by Einstein's formula, but no one would suggest that the discovery of that formula should have entitled Einstein to a monopoly on sunshine.

4.3 LIVING ORGANISMS

Advances in technology sometimes compel a reassessment of the scope of protection available through the patent laws. Until recently, the idea of patenting a living animal might have seemed absurd. Even when an explorer discovered a species that was previously unknown, the explorer could not claim to have invented the species; the explorer merely discovered what was already there.[7] The situation has changed with the development of techniques allowing scientists to rearrange the genetic codes of

---

[6] Ex Parte Grayson, 51 U.S.P.Q. 413 (Pat. Off. Bd. App. 1941).

[7] A breeder might stake a stronger claim to invention, but the idea of patenting an improved cow or chicken seems never to have been seriously entertained before the era of genetic engineering.

existing species. Now biologists can truly claim to have invented a form of life that did not exist before. Still, the notion that a person or a company can claim a property interest in a life form is one that is unsettling to many people.

The Supreme Court, in *Diamond v. Chakrabarty*,[8] addressed the question of whether a genetically engineered bacteria, so devised that it could break down crude oil, could be patented. The bacteria was undeniably useful because it could be used to treat oil spills. It was also new. No naturally occurring bacteria possessed the same ability to break down all of the components found in crude oil. The Patent Office rejected Chakrabarty's patent application on the grounds that a living organism cannot be patented. The majority of the Supreme Court disagreed, holding that Congress had established a broad scope of patentability, and that if Congress wished to exclude genetically engineered life forms it would have to do so explicitly. The court also observed that the most important inventions may be those least foreseeable to the legislature. Literally speaking, new bacteria are "manufactures" and "compositions of matter," and are patentable as such.

The principles of *Chakrabarty*[9] have since been extended to multicellular organisms. In 1988, Harvard University obtained a celebrated patent on a genetically engineered mouse. The mouse is useful in laboratory studies because it is particularly susceptible to cancer. The PTO Board of Appeals and Interferences[10] has also held patentable a genetically altered oyster that can be enjoyed year-round, in contrast to naturally occurring oysters, which must be avoided during the summer months.[11] The Patent Office has announced that it will not permit a patent on a human being, though certain activists, so far unsuccessfully, have pressed claims to "human-animal chimeras" genetically combining the attributes of humans and other species. Their goal, apparently, is to foster debate.

Although a special kind of patent, discussed in Section 12.2, is available for plant life, the Supreme Court recently held that plant life is also appropriate subject matter for a utility patent.[12] This is a natural extension of *Chakrabarty*, although if Congress saw fit to create a specific set of rules governing plants, one might infer that plants were outside the scope of the preexisting statute.

---

[8] 447 U.S. 303 (1980).

[9] Cases are typically referred to by the name of the *first* litigant–for example, *Smith v. Jones* would be referred to as the *Smith* case. *Diamond v. Chakrabarty*, however, is generally referred to as the *Chakrabarty* case rather than the *Diamond* case. Diamond was the name of the acting Commissioner of Patents at the time the suit was filed. Since a number of cases can include the name of the Patent Commissioner (e.g., *Diamond v. Chakrabarty* and *Diamond v. Diehr*), using the name of the patent applicant, Chakrabarty, reduces ambiguity.

[10] *See* Section 5.1.

[11] Ex Parte Allen, 2 U.S.P.Q.2d 1425 (PTO Bd. App. & Int. 1987).

[12] J.E.M. AG Supply, Inc. v. Pioneer Hi-Bred Int'l, Inc., 534 U.S. 124 (2001).

4.4 ARTISTIC AND LITERARY CREATIONS

Generally speaking, the proper vehicle for protecting artistic and literary creations is copyright.[13] Utility patents are intended to protect, as the name implies, *useful* inventions. In this context, *useful* is meant in the narrow sense of a practical advancement in a technological art. Design patents are available for ornamental designs as applied to utilitarian objects, but they are a different kind of patent subject to a different set of rules.[14] If an inventor applies for a utility patent on what is essentially an ornamental feature, that application may be held outside of the subject matter permitted under 35 U.S.C. § 101. For example, a court in New York addressed the matter of whether garments that had been treated to produce a characteristic stonewashed jeans pattern could be patented.[15] The court determined that because the patterns did not affect the usefulness of the garments, the garments could only be protected by a design patent, not a utility patent.

4.5 PRINTED MATTER

Another exception to patentability concerns *printed matter*. Generally speaking, a manufactured article or composition of matter is not patentable if the only thing that distinguishes it from prior inventions is the presence of pictures or writing. One could not, for example, obtain a utility patent for a baseball cap merely because it bears a new team logo, even though the cap is new and useful, and caps, as such, are articles of manufacture.

On the other hand, an invention that involves printed matter may be patentable as long as the invention as a whole calls for a new structure, or the printed matter bears a novel functional relationship to the "substrate"—that is, the physical object on which the matter is printed. In one instance, an inventor applied for a patent on a scheme for deliberately mislabeling a measuring cup to solve the problem of measuring when making less than a full recipe. A cook who wishes to prepare, for example, one-third of the amount specified in a recipe may be left with the difficult task of measuring quantities such as 1/3 of 2/3 of a cup. The inventor conceived of a measuring cup for fractional portions. The cook who wishes to make a 1/3 recipe simply selects the 1/3 recipe cup, and when he fills the cup to the 2/3 cup mark, he actually has the desired 2/9 cup. Although the markings were the only difference between the inventor's measuring cups and other measuring cups, the useful relationship between the markings and the cups was enough to place the invention within the scope of patentable subject matter.[16]

---

[13] *See* Section 2.1.
[14] *See* Section 12.1.
[15] Levi Strauss & Co. v. Golden Trade S.r.L., 1995 U.S. Dist. LEXIS 4899 (S.D.N.Y. 1995).
[16] Application of Miller, 418 F.2d 1392 (C.C.P.A. 1969).

A similar issue can arise in the case of computer storage media, which function to store information, though not in printed form. Is a computer disk patentable merely because it contains new information? The answer may depend on the nature of the information. Under its current guidelines, the Patent Office will presume that a computer-readable storage medium that can be used to direct a computer to operate in a particular manner is an "article of manufacture" and falls within the scope of patentable subject matter. A CD-ROM, for example, that contains a new computer program will presumptively qualify as patentable subject matter. However, a known storage medium encoding data representing "creative or artistic expression," such as a work of art, literature, or music, will be considered nonstatutory.[17]

4.6 METHODS OF DOING BUSINESS

Perhaps because the constitutional phrase "useful arts" is generally regarded as equivalent to "technological arts," methods of doing business have traditionally been held beyond the purview of the patent laws. For example, an accounting method allowing users to enter, categorize, and total expenditures, and display the results in an expense analysis report, has been held unpatentable subject matter.[18] Arguably, such techniques are simply too remote from the disciplines of science and engineering to be thought suitable for the patent system. However, an *apparatus* used in business—like a cash register—would usually be considered patentable as a technological means to an end.

In recent years, computers have emerged as the universal tool for the conduct of a broad range of human activities, including the conduct of business. Any method of doing business in use today probably involves a computer in some way. A clever draftsman, instead of claiming the method per se, can claim the programmed computer as a system or apparatus, thereby

---

[17] MPEP § 2106. The Federal Circuit has opined that the printed matter cases have no relevance where the "matter" is to be processed not by a human mind, but by a computer. *In re Lowry*, 32 F.3d 1579, 1583 (Fed. Cir. 1994). However, if the distinguishing feature of the invention is in the form of stored information rather than revised structure, whether in the form of printing or information stored on a computer disk, the same concerns can be raised about the suitability of the invention for patent protection. The information, for example, might represent an advance in a literary or an artistic field rather than an advance in technology. Although it could be argued that a computer disk storing new data differs *structurally* from other disks, at a microscopic level, the same could be said of the printed page. The Patent Office has embarked on a reasonable course by attempting to distinguish between a computer program that causes a computer to function in a particular way, and stored data that merely represents a musical, literary, or artistic creation. Still, future court decisions will likely be necessary to sort out just when a computer disk with stored data is patentable and when it is not.

[18] *Ex Parte Murray*, 9 U.S.P.Q.2d 1819 (PTO Bd. Pat. App. & Int. 1988).

giving the invention a flavor of the technological arts. Should a method of doing business that would once have been considered unpatentable be patentable today, merely because the instrumentality has changed from pen and paper to computer?

This question still has not been answered definitively. One federal district court has concluded that a computer can make an otherwise unpatentable business method an invention suitable for patenting.[19] In this case, Merrill Lynch had the idea of combining in one financial service a brokerage account, a money market account, and a checking/credit card account. The combination of the three kinds of accounts supposedly produced "synergistic" benefits for the customer. The claims described a computerized "system," including means for entering, storing, manipulating, and communicating the information necessary to manage such a combined account. Although the court recognized that the account scheme itself would be "unpatentable if done by hand," the court held that drafting the claims in terms of a computerized system brought the invention within the realm of the "technological arts."[20]

In the similar case of *State Street Bank & Trust Co. v. Signature Financial Gp.*,[21] the Federal Circuit went so far as to reject the method-of-doing-business exception to patentability altogether. The patented invention in *State Street* involved a system for organizing a group of mutual funds under the common ownership of a partnership, an arrangement that produced economies of scale and tax advantages. The claims described a system and method for performing the necessary accounting, though in such broad terms that anyone creating such a fund and using a computer would necessarily infringe. The court found that the claims did not describe an unpatentably abstract algorithm[22] because the manipulation of data representing money is a "useful, concrete and tangible result." Examining the authority for a business methods exception to patentable subject matter, the court found such authority so unpersuasive that it took the opportunity to "lay this ill-conceived exception to rest."[23] The court did not, however, address the question of whether the patented invention in *State Street* represented any advancement in the useful or technological arts.

As methods of doing business become increasingly dependent on computers, questions regarding the patentability of business methods will often be subsumed within the larger question of when computer programs can be patented. This complex question is discussed in Section 12.4.

---

[19] Paine, Webber, Jackson & Curtis, Inc. v. Merrill Lynch, Pierce, Fenner & Smith, Inc., 564 F. Supp. 1358 (D. Del. 1983).

[20] *Paine, Webber,* 564 F. Supp. at 1369.

[21] 149 F.3d 1368 (Fed. Cir. 1998).

[22] *See* Section 12.4.

[23] *State Street,* 149 F.3d at 1375.

CHAPTER 5

Patent Prosecution

5.1 EXAMINATION

The process of applying for a patent, also known as *patent prosecution*, begins when the inventor, on his own or through his agent or attorney, files an application with the Patent Office for "examination." The application includes essentially the same things that a patent would include—a specification describing the invention in detail, drawings, and claims.[1] The Patent Office assigns the application to a patent examiner who has expert knowledge in the field of the invention. Because the Patent Office requires a filing fee, an issue fee, and various other fees, obtaining a patent can easily cost several thousand dollars, exclusive of any fees paid to a patent attorney or agent.[2]

The patent examiner searches for prior-art patents already granted on similar inventions to determine whether the invention claimed in the application is new and nonobvious.[3] The examiner also reviews the application to determine whether it meets the other requirements of a valid patent, such as having claims that are sufficiently definite.[4] After reviewing the application and searching for prior art, the examiner prepares a written Office Action to tell the applicant which claims are "allowed" or rejected and to explain any problems with the application. In many cases the examiner will

---

[1] As discussed below, a provisional application may omit the claims.
[2] Reduced fees are available to individuals and "small entities" (*see* MPEP § 509.02), but the costs are still considerable. A current fee schedule can be obtained by calling the General Information Services Division at (800) 786-9199 or by visiting the PTO Web site at http://www.uspto.gov.
[3] *See* Section 8.9.
[4] *See* Section 8.5.

reject the claims as originally filed on grounds that the invention is already disclosed in, or obvious in light of, prior patents.

Following such a rejection, the applicant is permitted to file a written response. Sometimes the response is to argue the point with the examiner and attempt to explain, on legal or technical grounds, why the claims should be allowed after all. Often, however, the response is to amend the claims in an effort to distinguish the invention from what has gone before. It is also possible to cancel claims or add new claims. When claims are amended, or new claims added, the applicant should explain why the changes overcome the problems found by the examiner.[5]

After a response from the applicant, the examiner prepares another Office Action, which may allow the claims or reject them once again. This process continues until the claims are allowed or until the examiner announces that the rejection is "final," which may occur at any time after the second rejection.[6] A final rejection can be appealed to the Patent Office Board of Appeals and Interferences, and from there to the Federal Circuit Court of Appeals.[7] If the situation appears hopeless, the application can be abandoned.

Although patent prosecution resembles a court proceeding in some respects—applicants are typically represented by attorneys who present legal arguments to the examiner "judge"—the situation differs in a very significant respect. In a typical court proceeding, the judge hears argument and evidence presented by adversaries having opposing points of view. Patent prosecution, on the other hand, is *ex parte*, meaning that there is no adversary present. A company that might infringe the patent has no opportunity to argue to the examiner that the patent should not issue. In fact, a potential infringer usually has no way even of knowing that the application is under consideration. It is the job of the examiner to represent the interests of the public and to ensure that a patent is not issued unless it meets all of the legal requirements. Yet the opportunity to present unrebutted arguments provides applicants with a great advantage, and that advantage is magnified in litigation by the presumption that all issued patents are valid.[8]

Because patent prosecution is ex parte, the individuals involved are held to a higher standard of candor and fair dealing than is typical of court proceedings. If, for example, the applicant is aware of information that might

---

[5] Although the claims can be amended, the specification cannot be changed to add "new matter." 37 C.F.R. § 1.118. New matter can be added only by filing a continuation-in-part. *See* Section 5.2.

[6] Recent legislation permits applicants to extend examination of disputed claims on payment of a fee, without the need to resort to the filing of a continuation of the kind discussed in Section 5.2. 35 U.S.C. § 132(b). A request under the new legislation is known as a Request for Continued Examination, or RCE.

[7] *See* 35 U.S.C. § 141. Alternatively, an applicant disappointed with the decision of the PTO Board may file a civil action in the United States District Court for the District of Columbia, from which any further appeal would be, again, to the Federal Circuit. *See* 35 U.S.C. § 145.

[8] *See* Section 8.2.

call into question whether the patent should issue—such as a close prior art reference—the applicant is required to bring that to the attention of the examiner. If the applicant, or the applicant's attorney, fails in that duty of candor, the patent may later be held unenforceable by a court.[9]

In some other countries, patent applications are made public or "laid open" after an initial examination by the patent office to allow the interested public to oppose the application. This lessens the likelihood that a patent will be granted simply because the patent office failed to discover the most pertinent prior art. The United States, which traditionally has conducted examinations in secret, recently enacted legislation requiring the publication of patent applications,[10] under some circumstances, 18 months after they are filed, or sooner at the request of the applicant.[11] Publication may be desired by the applicant because of the opportunity to obtain certain *provisional rights* before the patent issues.[12] Alternatively, an applicant can avoid publication by certifying that the invention has not and will not be the subject of an application in another country that *already* requires publication 18 months after filing.[13] Moreover, the law forbids, without the consent of the applicant, any form of third-party opposition or protest following the publication of the pending application.[14] Although the new rules may advantage patent applicants under some circumstances, they offer marginal benefits to potential challengers and prosecution remains, as before, ex parte.

Another recent change in the Patent Act is the addition of *provisional applications.*[15] A provisional application includes a specification and drawings, but it need not include any claim.[16] Within 12 months, the applicant must file an ordinary application or the provisional application will be deemed abandoned.[17] The advantage of a provisional application is that it allows an inventor to file an application and obtain a priority date[18] before the applicant is ready to formulate a claim.[19] In addition, although the applicant enjoys the benefits of an early filing date, the resulting patent does not expire until 20 years after the filing date of the ordinary application.[20] Nevertheless, applicants should approach this with caution. The benefit of the earlier filing date can be obtained only if the disclosures of the provisional

---

[9] *See* Section 9.1.

[10] This applies to utility patents, not design patents. *See* 35 U.S.C. § 122(b)(2)(A)(iv). Design patents are discussed in Section 12.1.

[11] 35 U.S.C. § 122(b).

[12] *See* Section 10.1.

[13] 35 U.S.C. § 122(b)(2)(B)(i).

[14] 35 U.S.C. § 122(c).

[15] *See* 35 U.S.C. § 111(b).

[16] 35 U.S.C. § 111(b)(2).

[17] 35 U.S.C. § 111(b)(5).

[18] *See* Section 8.9.3.

[19] *See* 35 U.S.C. § 119(e)(1).

[20] *See* Section 10.1.

application satisfy the requirements of Section 112, Paragraph 1, of the Patent Act, including the enablement,[21] best mode,[22] and written description[23] requirements. Because satisfaction of those requirements ultimately depends on what is *claimed*, preparing one's disclosure before one is ready to formulate a claim may be a hazardous affair.[24]

Prosecution is a slow process and may take years.[25] All of the documents filed by the applicant or by the examiner become part of the prosecution history of the patent. The prosecution history (also known as the *file history* or *file wrapper*) is made available to the public if the patent issues, and it is an important resource for interpreting what the claims mean. If in response to a rejection the applicant argues in favor of a narrow claim interpretation, that same interpretation is likely to be adopted by a court in any subsequent litigation.[26]

5.2 CONTINUATIONS AND CONTINUATIONS-IN-PART

In some instances, an applicant may choose to start over, in a sense, by filing a *continuation*. A continuation is an application that has the same disclosure as the prior application (i.e., the same specification) but new claims.[27] As long as the continuation is filed before the original application is abandoned, and as long as the continuation includes an explicit reference to the original application, the continuation, and any patent claims that issue from it, will be treated as though filed on the date that the original application was filed.[28] As in the case of reliance on a provisional application,[29] the earlier filing date may be important in determining the priority of the inven-

---

[21] *See* Section 8.6.

[22] *See* Section 8.7.

[23] *See* Section 8.8.

[24] *See* New Railhead Mfg, L.L.C. v. Vermeer Mfg. Co., 298 F.3d 1290 (Fed. Cir. 2002) (The disclosure of a provisional application did not adequately describe the later-claimed invention; consequently, the patentee could not obtain the early filing date necessary to avoid invalidation of the patent based on a public use bar (see Section 8.10.2).).

[25] An applicant who deliberately delays prosecution, perhaps to allow a market to expand before the patent is sprung on unsuspecting infringers, may be vulnerable to a defense of prosecution laches. See Section 11.8.3.3.

[26] *See* Section 7.3.

[27] *See* Transco Prods. Inc. v. Performance Contracting, Inc., 38 F.3d 551, 555 (Fed. Cir. 1994); M.P.E.P. § 201.07. There can be any number of reasons for filing a continuation. One is to permit the amendment of claims that have already been subject to a "final" rejection. *See Transco*, 38 F.3d at 559. The new availability of extended examination (35 U.S.C. § 132(b)) may reduce the need for continuations.

[28] *See* Mendenhall v. Cedarapids, Inc., 5 F.3d 1557, 1565 (Fed. Cir. 1993); 35 U.S.C. § 120; M.P.E.P. § 201.11. If the original application names more than one joint inventor, the continuation must name the same inventors, or a subset of them. 35 U.S.C. § 120; *In re Chu*, 66 F.3d 292, 297 (Fed. Cir. 1995).

[29] *See* Section 5.1.

tion as compared to other inventions or references.[30] The original application may be abandoned after the continuation is filed, or prosecution of the two applications may continue in parallel.

The second application may lead to another, and a chain of applications can be created in this way. The application that comes last on the chain will receive the benefit of the first application's filing date, as long as each link in the chain meets the requirements of continuity—that is, each application included the same disclosure as the one preceding it, and it was filed before the preceding application was abandoned. Related applications are often referred to using a family tree analogy, in which an earlier application may be referred to as the *parent* or *grandparent* of a later application.

On other occasions, an applicant may choose to file a *continuation-in-part* (or C-I-P). A continuation-in-part is like a continuation, but it includes additional disclosure in the specification.[31] A continuation-in-part might be filed if the applicant discovers an improvement on the basic invention disclosed in the original application and desires a patent claim to match. The important difference between a continuation and a continuation-in-part is that the latter is entitled to the filing date of the original application *only* as to claims supported by the disclosure of the original application.[32] Any claim supported by newly added material (referred to as *new matter*) is entitled only to the filing date of the continuation-in-part application.[33]

Suppose, for example, that an inventor files an application for a basic mousetrap on January 1, 2001. The application discloses and claims the combination of a spring, a latch, and a trigger to release the spring when disturbed by the mouse. Later that month, the inventor discovers a new kind of trigger that is less likely to release the spring prematurely. Because the original application is still in prosecution, the inventor files a continuation-in-part that discloses both the basic mousetrap design of the first application and the improved trigger. That application is filed on February 1, 2001. If the second application includes a claim having nothing to do with the new trigger, and the claim is fully supported by the disclosure of the original application, that claim will receive the benefit of the January 1 filing date. However, a claim that did refer to the new trigger would be entitled only to the February 1 filing date. If another inventor happened to have filed an application on a mousetrap trigger on January 15, the difference could be significant in determining priority.[34]

---

[30] *See* Section 8.9.2.

[31] *See Transco,* 38 F.3d at 555; M.P.E.P. § 201.08.

[32] The support must be adequate to satisfy the written description requirement of 35 U.S.C. § 112. See Section 8.8.

[33] *See* Augustine Medical, Inc. v. Gaymar Indus., Inc., 181 F.3d 1291, 1302 (Fed. Cir. 1999); Waldemar Link GmbH v. Osteonics Corp., 32 F.3d 556, 558 (Fed. Cir. 1994).

[34] *See* Section 8.9.2.

An exception to the rules just described arises if the matter newly added to the continuation-in-part application is *inherent* in the original application, even though not explicitly disclosed. Suppose that the inventor of the mousetrap realized that the design disclosed in the original application was more compact than most, so that the trap could be slipped into a smaller space. The inventor might decide to file a second application, styled as a continuation-in-part, explicitly pointing out this newly discovered advantage, and a claim might be drafted that referred explicitly to the trap's dimensions. As long as this characteristic had been inherent in the design originally disclosed, though not discussed, the claim would be entitled to the filing date of the original application.[35]

5.3 DIVISIONAL APPLICATIONS

Another complication in a patent family tree arises when, in the view of the examiner, the application claims more than one distinct invention. For example, the same application might claim both a new mousetrap design and a new artificial cheese to be used as bait, either of which could be used without the other. The examiner might determine that each was a separate invention, which should be claimed in its own application subject to its own fees and prior art search. When this occurs, the examiner issues a *restriction requirement* compelling the applicant to choose which of the two inventions to pursue. The other invention can be made the subject of a *divisional* application. The divisional application includes the pertinent part of the original disclosure, and it is entitled to the same filing date.[36]

5.4 INTERFERENCES

One responsibility of a patent examiner is to search for other patent applications that claim the same invention as the application under consideration. Because it is not uncommon for an invention to occur to two inventors at nearly the same time, it is also not uncommon for two patent applications to claim essentially the same thing. If such an application is discovered, the Patent Office will conduct an *interference proceeding* to determine which of the applications deserves priority.[37] Interference proceedings are conducted by the Board of Patent Appeals and Interferences, and examination

---

[35] *See* Therma-Tru Corp. v. Peachtree Doors Inc., 44 F.3d 988, 992–93 (Fed. Cir. 1995); Kennecott Corp. v. Kyocera Int'l, Inc., 835 F.2d 1419, 1421–23 (Fed. Cir. 1987).

[36] *See* 35 U.S.C. § 121; M.P.E.P. § 201.06; Transco Prods. Inc. v. Performance Contracting, Inc., 38 F.3d 551, 555 (Fed. Cir. 1994).

[37] *See* 35 U.S.C. § 135; Case v. CPC Int'l, Inc., 730 F.2d 745, 748 (Fed. Cir. 1984). Two applications claim the "same invention" if the invention of one is the same as, or obvious in light of, the invention of the other. 37 C.F.R. § 1.601 (i), (n).

of the interfering applications is generally halted until the interference is decided. In contrast to the usual course of patent prosecution, an interference is a trial-like adversarial proceeding in which each applicant has an opportunity to present evidence and argument in favor of its position.[38] An interference is time-consuming and can delay issue of a patent for years.

Although interferences are generally a contest between two or more pending applications, occasionally an interference occurs between an application and a patent that has already issued. In this case, the interference may occur at the instigation of the applicant, but the applicant must claim entitlement to an interference no more than 1 year after the patent has issued.[39]

Even if two applicants describe essentially the same invention, they are likely to use different language in their claims. In order to clarify what the disputed invention is, the Patent Office devises its own claims, known as *counts*, to describe the subject matter of the interference. A count may be identical to a claim submitted by one of the applicants, or it may be a new description of the invention. The purpose of the interference is to decide if both applications support a claim to the invention described by the count, and, if so, which applicant invented first. Although an applicant may be able to avoid an interference by denying any intention to claim the subject matter described by the count, the denial will prevent the applicant from afterwards obtaining a patent on that invention.[40]

In an interference, the applicant who was first to file is known as the "senior party" and other applicants are known as "junior parties." The senior party is presumed to have invented first, but that presumption can be overcome by evidence presented by a junior party.[41] Ultimately, the issue of which applicant was first to invent turns on questions of conception, reduction to practice, and diligence, all of which are discussed in Section 8.9.2. The victor in an interference can proceed with patent prosecution. The loser, barring an appeal,[42] must abandon his application or pursue claims to a different invention.

5.5 REISSUE

Apart from an interference, there are two instances in which an already issued patent may return to the Patent Office to undergo further proceed-

---

[38] Note that similar contests over priority can arise in the course of infringement litigation. *See* Section 8.9.1.3.

[39] 35 U.S.C. § 135(b). An interference can occur between *two* issued patents, but in this case the Patent Office has no jurisdiction. An interference between two issued patents must be conducted by a federal court. *See* 35 U.S.C. § 291.

[40] *See* 37 C.F.R. § 1.605(a).

[41] *See* Brown v. Barbacid, 276 F.3d 1327, 1332–33 (Fed. Cir. 2002).

[42] An appeal can be taken either to the Federal Circuit Court of Appeals or to a federal district court. *See* 35 U.S.C. § 146.

ings. They are known as *reissue* and *reexamination*. Reissue is a means for applicants to correct errors in a patent. The error may be a defect in the specification or drawings, or the applicant's claims may have been too broad or too narrow in comparison to what the applicant could rightfully claim.[43] If the claims are too narrow, they may fail to protect the full measure of the invention; if too broad, they may run afoul of the prior art.[44]

The reissue application cannot add new matter to the original application,[45] and any claims sought through reissue that would broaden the scope of the original claims must be applied for within 2 years of issue.[46] If a reissued patent is allowed, the original patent is "surrendered" in favor of the revised version.[47] The latter is enforceable from its own date of issue, and it expires when the original patent would have expired.[48] If any claims from the original patent are carried forward in substantially identical form in the reissued patent, those claims are enforceable as though they had been in effect from the issue date of the original patent. In other words, damages can be assessed for infringement after and *before* the reissue, even though the original claims were surrendered.[49] Patents that are the result of reissue proceedings can be identified by their serial numbers, which begin with the letters "Re."[50]

When applying for a reissue, the applicant must file a declaration identifying an error requiring correction and affirming that any errors occurred without deceptive intent.[51] What constitutes *error* can be a difficult issue. An applicant's deliberate choice to cancel a broad claim in favor of a narrow

---

[43] *See* 35 U.S.C. § 251. Minor errors of a clerical or typographical nature can be rectified without further examination by a certificate of correction. *See* 35 U.S.C. §§ 254–255.

[44] *See* Section 8.9.

[45] *See* Section 5.2. Furthermore, the reissue patent must claim the same invention *disclosed*, if not adequately claimed, in the original patent. *See* Hester Indus., Inc. v. Stein, Inc., 142 F.3d 1472, 1484 (Fed. Cir. 1998). This is similar to the written description requirement, discussed in Section 8.8.

[46] 35 U.S.C. § 251. This rule is strictly interpreted. If there is any conceivable device or method that would infringe the new claims but would not have infringed the original claims, the new claims are broader and cannot be obtained more than 2 years after the patent issued. *See* Tillotson, Ltd. v. Walbro Corp., 831 F.2d 1033, 1037 n.2 (Fed. Cir. 1987). On the other hand, an original claim and a reissue claim may be identical in scope, even if they do not use precisely the same words (e.g., one could refer to "12 inches" where the other refers to "one foot"). *See* Anderson v. International Eng'g & Mfg., Inc., 160 F.3d 1345, 1349 (Fed. Cir. 1998).

[47] 35 U.S.C. §§ 251–52.

[48] 35 U.S.C. § 251.

[49] *See* 35 U.S.C. § 252; Laitram Corp. v. NEC Corp., 952 F.2d 1357, 1360–61 (Fed. Cir. 1991).

[50] Note that *all* claims of a patent are examined during a reissue proceeding, including those that are unchanged from the original patent. A patentee who initiates a reissue proceeding, therefore, runs some risk that a claim already issued will be held invalid when looked at again. *See* Hewlett-Packard Co. v. Bausch & Lomb Inc., 882 F.2d 1556, 1563 (Fed. Cir. 1989).

[51] *See* 37 C.F.R. § 1.175. An earlier version of the rule also required the patentee to explain in detail the reason for the errors. *See* Shockley v. Arcan, Inc., 248 F.3d 1349, 1358 (Fed. Cir. 2001).

one in order to avoid prior art is not an error that can be corrected by reissue, even if the applicant has second thoughts.[52] On the other hand, a patent attorney's "failure to appreciate the full scope of the invention" generally is recognized as an error justifying reissue with broadened claims.[53]

Although patent claims can be broadened by reissue, the legislature foresaw the potential unfairness to anyone who steered clear of the original narrow claims, but not the new broader ones. To protect such persons, the law recognizes "intervening rights."[54] If, prior to the reissue, a person or corporation had made, used, purchased, imported, or offered to sell a product that did not infringe the original narrow claims, that person or corporation may continue to use that product, or may sell it to someone else or offer it for sale, even if doing so would infringe the broadened claims.[55] If, for example, a business had in its inventory items manufactured before the reissue that would infringe only the modified claims, that business would have the absolute right to sell those products after the reissue without incurring liability. Moreover, a court may allow additional items of the same nature to be made, used, or sold after the date of the reissue if "substantial preparation" to do so occurred before the reissue, and the court deems such measures equitable in light of the investments made and businesses commenced before the reissue.[56] A business that had invested in a factory to manufacture the newly infringing item would likely be allowed to continue producing and selling the item even after the reissue. Naturally, these rights do not extend to anyone who made no investments in an infringing activity until after the date of reissue.

5.6 REEXAMINATION

Reexamination allows the Patent Office to reconsider the validity of already issued claims in light of newly discovered prior art patents or printed publications. The purpose of reexamination is to provide a quicker and less expensive alternative to litigation when, for one reason or another,

---

[52] *See* Pannu v. Storz Instruments, Inc., 258 F.3d 1336, 1370-71 (Fed. Cir. 2001) (discussing the "recapture rule"). "Error under the reissue statute does not include a deliberate decision to surrender specific subject matter in order to overcome prior art, a decision which in light of subsequent developments in the marketplace might be regretted. It is precisely because the patentee amended his claims to overcome prior art that a member of the public is entitled to occupy the space abandoned by the patent applicant." Mentor Corp. v. Coloplast, Inc., 998 F.2d 992, 996 (Fed. Cir. 1993); *see also Hewlett-Packard*, 882 F.2d at 1565 (*error* must involve "inadvertence, accident, or mistake"). The rationale for the recapture rule is also relevant to prosecution history estoppel, discussed in Section 10.6.8.

[53] *See Hester*, 142 F.3d at 1479–80.

[54] *See* 35 U.S.C. § 252.

[55] *See* 35 U.S.C. § 252; *Shockley*, 248 F.3d at 1360. These absolute rights apply only to items that existed before the reissue, not to additional items of the same type. *Id.*

[56] *See* 35 U.S.C. § 252; *Shockley*, 248 F.3d at 1360–61.

the Patent Office failed to consider important prior art during the initial prosecution, and as a result the validity of the patent is in doubt. Reexamination differs from most Patent Office proceedings in one important respect. Whereas the public is generally denied any participation in patent prosecution, reexamination can be requested by anyone, including a licensee, an accused infringer, or a government agency.[57] All that is necessary to begin (besides the money to pay the reexamination fee) is knowledge of a prior patent or printed publication that casts doubt on the validity of some or all of the patent claims.[58]

The party requesting the reexamination must submit to the Patent Office a list of prior art and a statement explaining why it is pertinent.[59] A copy of the request is sent to the patent owner. Within 3 months, the Patent Office must decide whether the request raises "a substantial new question of patentability."[60] If the answer is no, the decision is final and unappealable. If the answer is yes, the Patent Office orders a reexamination. At that point the patent owner may file a statement, including any proposed changes to the claims, and the party requesting the reexamination may file a reply.[61]

If the traditional procedures are followed, from that point onward reexamination proceeds by the rules devised for ordinary patent prosecution, and the party requesting reexamination has no further involvement.[62] Recently, Congress created an alternative *inter partes* procedure allowing the requesting party much greater participation, including the opportunity to comment upon and rebut arguments made by the patent owner throughout the reexamination.[63] However, the party requesting inter partes reexamination cannot raise any invalidity arguments in subsequent litigation that were or *could have been* raised during the reexamination[64]—a drawback that may lead some to choose the traditional procedure.

If necessary, claims can be *narrowed* during reexamination so that they avoid the newly discovered prior art.[65] The patentee is not allowed to

---

[57] *See* 35 U.S.C. § 302; *In re Freeman*, 30 F.3d 1459, 1468 (Fed. Cir. 1994); Syntex (U.S.A.) Inc. v. U.S. PTO, 882 F.2d 1570, 1573 (Fed. Cir. 1989).

[58] Reexamination can be based only on prior patents or printed publications, not, for example, a claim of invalidity based on sales of the patented product prior to the application's "critical date." See Section 8.10.1. This limitation helps to keep reexamination proceedings comparatively simple and expedient.

[59] *See* 35 U.S.C. § 302.

[60] 35 U.S.C. § 303. According to recent legislation, the "new question" may be based on prior art already considered by the Patent Office. 35 U.S.C. § 303(a).

[61] 35 U.S.C. § 304. If the request for reexamination is made by someone other than the patentee, the patentee has no opportunity to make its views known until *after* the Patent Office has decided whether there is a "substantial new question of patentability." *See* 37 C.F.R. § 1.530(a); Platlex Corp. v. Mossinghoff, 771 F.2d 480, 483–84 (Fed. Cir. 1985).

[62] *See In re* Opprecht, 868 F.2d 1264, 1265 (Fed. Cir. 1989).

[63] *See* 35 U.S.C. §§ 311–318.

[64] 35 U.S.C. § 315(c).

enlarge the scope of the claims.[66] When the reexamination is concluded, the examiner issues a certificate canceling any claims held invalid, confirming any claims held patentable, and incorporating into the patent any new or revised claims.[67]

Although one would expect reexamination to be requested by someone wishing to attack the patent, sometimes it is requested by the patentee, as a way of *strengthening* a patent that might be held invalid in litigation. If the Patent Office finds that the claims are valid in spite of the additional prior art, a court is unlikely to hold otherwise. On the other hand, if the prior art is so close that the claims must be modified, reexamination provides an opportunity to do so. Thus, while a request for reexamination may signal doubts as to the validity of the patent, if the patent survives the process it is likely to be stronger than ever.

---

[65] However, "[u]nless a claim granted or conferred upon reexamination is identical to an original claim, the patent can not [*sic*] be enforced against infringing activity that occurred before issuance of the reexamination certificate. 'Identical' does not mean verbatim, but means at most without substantive change." Bloom Eng'g Co. v. North American Mfg. Co., 129 F.3d 1247, 1250 (Fed. Cir. 1997).

[66] 35 U.S.C. § 305.

[67] 35 U.S.C. § 307.

CHAPTER 6

Ownership and Other Rights

6.1 INVENTORSHIP

The right to obtain a patent initially belongs to the inventor.[1] When a patent application is filed it is important to designate the proper inventor of the subject matter claimed. A patent can name a single inventor, or it can name two or more joint inventors.[2] It is typically in the latter case that questions arise regarding who should or should not receive credit.

An inventor is anyone who participated in the mental act of *conceiving* the invention.[3] If two people work together on a project and both contribute to a patentable idea, both can be named on the application as joint inventors. This is true whether the specific contribution of each is difficult to identify, as may be the case when an idea arises from collaborative brainstorming,[4] or whether the contribution of each inventor is a discrete component of the whole.

---

[1] *See* 35 U.S.C. §§ 111, 115–16; Beech Aircraft Corp. v. EDO Corp., 990 F.2d 1237, 1248 (Fed. Cir. 1993).

[2] Where there is more than one inventor, each inventor, absent an agreement to the contrary, owns "a pro rata undivided interest in the entire patent, no matter what their respective contributions." Ethicon, Inc. v United States Surgical Corp., 135 F.3d 1456, 1465 (Fed. Cir. 1998). This is true even if an inventor contributed to the subject matter of only one claim in a patent having many claims. *Id.* at 1466.

[3] *See* Burroughs Wellcome Co. v. Barr Labs., Inc., 40 F.3d 1223, 1227–28 (Fed. Cir. 1994) ("Conception is the touchstone of inventorship, the completion of the mental part of invention."); Sewell v. Walters, 21 F.3d 411, 415 (Fed. Cir. 1994).

[4] *See* Canon Computer Sys., Inc. v. Nu-Kote Int'l, Inc., 134 F.3d 1085, 1088 (Fed. Cir. 1998) ("As any member of a large discussion group well knows, it is often difficult to remember who first said what.").

Not all contributions rise to the level of invention. Someone who had supervisory responsibility for a project but added nothing to the conception of the invention would not properly be considered an inventor. Similarly, someone who built or tested the completed invention, but did not contribute to its conception, could not be considered an inventor, no matter how important that person's contribution to the project as a whole.[5] Even someone who identifies a problem is not considered a co-inventor of the solution, in spite of the fact that identifying the problem is often a significant step. As one court observed, "[i]t is one thing to suggest that a better mousetrap ought to be built; it is another thing to build it."[6]

Deciding who should be credited as an inventor can be a difficult task, as illustrated by the case of *Hess v. Advanced Cardiovascular Sys., Inc.*[7] The invention was a balloon angioplasty catheter—a device that can be threaded through a narrowed artery and then inflated in order to reduce the blockage. The doctors responsible for the invention had tried various materials without success when they were referred to Mr. Hess, an engineer with Raychem who was familiar with their line of heat-shrinkable plastics. Hess identified specific materials and fabrication techniques that would provide the doctors with what they needed. The materials worked, the doctors obtained a patent, and the invention was a commercial success.

Eventually, Hess claimed that he should have been named on the patent as a co-inventor, because the invention would not have worked without his contribution. The Federal Circuit disagreed, noting that the inventors named on an issued patent are presumed to be the correct ones.[8] Hess's contribution was compared to that of a scientific treatise or a product catalog; he merely provided information regarding existing technology. "The principles [Hess] explained to [the doctors] were well known and found in textbooks. Mr. Hess did no more than a skilled salesman would do in explaining how his employer's product could be used to meet a customer's requirements."[9] Nevertheless, one can understand why Hess felt that identifying the right materials for the new application added

---

[5] *See Ethicon*, 135 F.3d at 1460 ("[O]ne does not qualify as a joint inventor by merely assisting the actual inventor after conception of the claimed invention. . . . Moreover, . . . one of ordinary skill in the art who simply reduced the inventor's idea to practice is not necessarily a joint inventor, even if the specification discloses that embodiment to satisfy the best mode requirement."); *Sewell*, 21 F.3d at 416–17. Although attorneys often assist inventors in preparing a patent application, they generally should not be considered joint inventors. *See* Solomon v. Kimberly-Clark Corp., 216 F.3d 1372, 1382 (Fed. Cir. 2000) ("An attorney performing that role should not be a competitor of the client, asserting inventorship as a result of representing his client.").

[6] *See* Buildex Inc. v. Kason Indus. Inc., 4 U.S.P.Q.2d 1803, 1805–6 (E.D.N.Y. 1987).

[7] 106 F.3d 976 (Fed. Cir. 1997).

[8] *Hess*, 106 F.3d at 980. The presumption can only be overcome by clear and convincing evidence. *Id.*

[9] *Hess*, 106 F.2d at 981.

more to the inventive idea than the passive contributions of a textbook author.

For two or more persons to be named as joint inventors, they must have *collaborated* in some way.[10] Two inventors who were unaware of each other's work could not be considered joint inventors, even if their efforts overlapped and even if the two inventors were employed by the same company.[11] Similarly, if inventor B simply builds on the published work of inventor A, the result is the sole invention of inventor B, not the joint invention of A and B.

On the other hand, joint inventors need not have physically worked together at the same time, nor is it necessary that the contribution of each be equivalent in type or amount.[12] If inventor A partially completed an invention, then passed it along to inventor B with the intention that inventor B complete it, A and B could be considered joint inventors of the finished invention. There are no distinctions drawn between co-inventors based on the significance, ingenuity, or timing of their contributions.[13]

Each joint inventor named on an application need not have contributed to every claim.[14] For example, if an application names A, B, and C as joint inventors, some claims may represent the work of A and B alone, or B and C alone, or A alone, or B alone, and so forth. Under one possible interpretation of the statute,[15] at least one claim of the joint application must embody the collective work of all the named inventors. However, the Patent Office has adopted the more liberal view that the application is proper as long as each inventor, jointly or *individually*, has contributed to at least one claim.[16] Although this could lead to joint applications including claims to unrelated inventions, the Patent Office has the power to issue a restriction requirement when that is the case.[17]

If an application names the wrong inventors (as can easily happen given the ambiguities in defining the role of inventor), the application, or issued

---

[10] *Burroughs*, 40 F.3d at 1227 ("A joint invention is the product of a collaboration between two or more persons working together to solve the problem addressed."); Credle v. Bond, 25 F.3d 1566, 1574 (Fed. Cir. 1994).

[11] Kimberly-Clark Corp. v. Procter & Gamble Dist. Co., 973 F.2d 911, 916 (Fed. Cir. 1992).

[12] 35 U.S.C. § 116; *Burroughs*, 40 F.3d at 1227.

[13] The contribution of an inventor cannot, however, be so minor as to be "insignificant." *See* Acromed Corp. v. Sofamor Danek Gp., Inc., 253 F.3d 1371, 1379 (Fed. Cir. 2001) ("a purported inventor must show that he made 'a contribution to the claimed invention that is not insignificant in quality, when that contribution is measured against the dimension of the full invention, and [did] more than merely explain to the real inventors well-known concepts and/or the current state of the art").

[14] 35 U.S.C. § 116; *Ethicon*, 135 F.3d at 1460 ("A contribution to one claim is enough.").

[15] 35 U.S.C. § 116.

[16] *See* 37 C.F.R. § 1.45 ("each named inventor must have made a contribution, individually or jointly, to the subject matter of at least one claim of the application").

[17] *See* Section 5.3.

patent, can be corrected to name the proper inventors without affecting the validity of the patent.[18] The incorrect naming of the inventors must, however, have occurred through error and without deceptive intent.[19] It cannot, for example, have been the product of a deliberate scheme to obtain an earlier priority date.

6.2 ASSIGNMENTS

Although the right to apply for a patent belongs to the inventor, and an application must at least be filed on the inventor's behalf,[20] a patent is commonly *owned* by someone other than the inventor. The transfer of ownership rights from the inventor to someone else is known as *assignment.* A common element of an employment contract, particularly in the case of engineers and scientists, is that any patentable inventions made by the employee in the course of employment must be assigned to the employer. Even if such a provision is not explicit in the employment contract, it is very likely to be implied if invention falls within the natural scope of the employee's duties.[21] Thus, although patents bear the name of individual inventors (hence the "Smith patent" or the "Jones patent"), actual rights to the patent often belong to a corporate assignee from the day the application is filed. In fact, a corporate assignee can prosecute a patent in the name of the inventor and ultimately obtain rights to the invention, even if the inventor refuses to cooperate.[22]

Patent rights are freely assignable like other forms of property.[23] A patent can be assigned not only from an employee to a corporation, but also from one corporation (or individual) to another. In a typical assign-

---

[18] *See* 35 U.S.C. §§ 116 (correction of inventorship for a pending application), 256 (correction of inventorship for an issued patent). If the inventors are incorrectly named, and the patent is not saved by correction, the patent can be considered invalid under § 102(f), discussed in Section 8.9.7. *See Solomon,* 216 F.3d at 1381; Pannu v. Iolab Corp., 155 F.3d 1344, 1349–50 (Fed. Cir. 1998). If the problem *is* corrected, the validity of the patent is restored, even for the period before the correction. Vikase Corp. v. American National Can Co., 261 F.3d 1316, 1329 (Fed. Cir. 2001). This is a rare example of a kind of "conditional invalidity."

[19] 35 U.S.C. §§ 116, 256.

[20] *See* 35 U.S.C. §§ 115–16.

[21] *See* Teets v. Chromalloy Gas Turbine Corp., 83 F.3d 403, 407 (Fed. Cir. 1996). Even if no agreement to assign is express or implied, if the invention was made by the employee on company time and using company materials, or if the employee introduced the practice of the invention into the employer's business, a court is likely to recognize a *shop right* benefiting the employer. A shop right is a nonexclusive, nontransferable right allowing the employer to practice the invention, royalty-free, even if the employee is allowed to patent the invention as an individual. *See* McElmurry v. Arkansas Power & Light Co., 995 F.2d 1576, 1580–82 (Fed. Cir. 1993).

[22] *See* 37 C.F.R. § 1.47.

[23] *See* 35 U.S.C. § 261.

ment, all rights, including the right to sue for infringement, pass to the new owner.[24]

6.3 LICENSES

A patent license is a more limited transfer of rights than an assignment. A licensor retains ownership of the patent but grants the licensee the right to practice the claimed invention, usually in exchange for some sort of royalty. A license can be exclusive or nonexclusive. If it is exclusive, there is only one licensee, and only that licensee has the right to practice the claimed invention. An exclusive licensee has the right to file suit against an infringer in order to preserve that exclusivity, though it may be necessary to sue in the patent owner's name or to join the patent owner as a co-plaintiff.[25] A nonexclusive licensee must rely on the patent owner to file suit.[26] Sometimes, but not always, a licensee obtains the right to sublicense others.

Some patent owners license their patents in order to obtain the royalty income. However, there is no requirement that a patent owner license anyone.[27] In some cases, the patent owner prefers the monopolistic, but perfectly legal, advantages of being the only producer of the patented product.[28] On occasion patent owners cross-license their patents, each patent owner granting to the other the right to practice some or all of the inventions in its patent portfolio. Where two or more companies hold basic patents in the same field of technology, this can be an expedient way to ensure that mutually destructive litigation does not take the place of competition in the marketplace.

6.3.1 Implied Licenses

Sometimes patent licenses are not express but implied.[29] An implied license is a reflection of the shared expectations of parties who have had dealings with one another, even if those expectations were not made

---

[24] *See* Rite-Hite Corp. v. Kelley Co., 56 F.3d 1538, 1551 (Fed. Cir. 1995); Ortho Pharmaceuticals Corp. v. General Institute, Inc., 52 F.3d 1026, 1030 (Fed. Cir. 1995). More limited assignments are also possible—for example, assignment of the rights to a patent as they pertain to a particular geographical area of the United States. *See* 35 U.S.C. § 261.

[25] *See* Rite-Hite Corp. v. Kelley Co., 56 F.3d 1538, 1552 (Fed. Cir. 1995); Ortho Pharmaceuticals Corp. v. General Institute, Inc., 52 F.3d 1026, 1030–31 (Fed. Cir. 1995); Abbott Labs. v. Diamedix Corp., 47 F.3d 1128, 1131 (Fed. Cir. 1995).

[26] *See Rite-Hite*, 56 F.3d at 1552; *Ortho*, 52 F.3d at 1031; *Abbott*, 47 F.3d at 1131.

[27] *See* 35 U.S.C. § 271(d)(4).

[28] Whether such exclusivity conferred any real market power would depend on whether there were other products that could substitute for the patented invention.

[29] Carborundum Co. v. Molten Metal Equipment Innovations, Inc., 72 F.3d 872, 878 (Fed. Cir. 1995).

explicit.[30] An implied license, like an express license, is a defense to a claim of infringement.[31]

6.3.1.1 First Sale

Because a patent owner has, among other rights, the exclusive right to "use" the patented invention, a patent owner might sell a patented article, only to forbid its use by the purchaser. Needless to say, most purchasers expect to use the things they buy. In order to fulfill this expectation and similar ones, whenever a patented article is purchased from the patent owner, without any express restriction or reservation of rights, the law recognizes an implied license allowing the purchaser to use the article, repair it,[32] or sell it to someone else. As stated in one Federal Circuit opinion, "an authorized sale of a patented product places that product beyond the reach of the patent. . . . The patent owner's rights with respect to the product end with its sale."[33] A patent owner who intends otherwise must make those intentions explicit.[34]

The *first sale* of a patented article, without restrictions, is said to "exhaust" the rights of the patent owner.[35] In other words, whatever compensation the patent owner receives from the first sale is all the patent owner can expect, even if the article is sold and resold, used and reused, many times.[36] The same result fol-

[30] *See Carborundum,* 72 F.3d at 878; McCoy v. Mitsuboshi Cutlery, Inc., 67 F.3d 917, 920 (Fed. Cir. 1995) (implied license arises from "entire course of conduct" between the parties).

[31] *Carborundum,* 72 F.3d at 878.

[32] Unless the repairs are so extensive that they are really a "reconstruction" of the patented invention. See Section 10.4.

[33] Intel Corp. v. ULSI Sys. Technology, Inc., 995 F.2d 1566, 1568 (Fed. Cir. 1993); *see also* Hewlett-Packard Co. v. Repeat-O-Type Stencil Mfg. Corp., 123 F.3d 1445, 1451 (Fed. Cir. 1997) ("Generally, when a seller sells a product without restriction, it in effect promises the purchaser that in exchange for the price paid, it will not interfere with the purchaser's full enjoyment of the product purchased. The buyer has an implied license under any patents of the seller that dominate the product or any uses of the product to which the parties might reasonably contemplate the product will be put.").

[34] Explicit restrictions *are* possible. For example, a patentee could sell an item with the requirement that it be used only once. Reuse of that item by the purchaser might then be considered an infringement. *See* Mallinckrodt, Inc. v. Medipart, Inc., 976 F.2d 700 (Fed. Cir. 1992). Some restrictions, however, may constitute misuse or an antitrust violation. See Section 9.2.

[35] *See United States v. Univis Lens Co.,* 316 U.S. 241, 250 (1942); Anton/Bauer Inc. v. PAG Ltd., 329 F.3d 1343, 1349 (Fed. Cir. 2003); Jazz Photo Corp. v. International Trade Comm'n, 264 F.3d 1094, 1105 (Fed. Cir. 2001); Bandag, Inc. v. Al Bolser's Tire Stores, Inc., 750 F.2d 903, 924 (Fed. Cir. 1984).

[36] The first sale must be an authorized sale by the patent owner or a licensee of the patent owner. If the product originated with an infringer, downstream purchasers can be held to infringe by using or reselling the product. *See Intel,* 995 F.2d at 1572–73 (Plager, J., dissenting). However, if the infringer was sued and compelled to pay money damages to the patentee, that payment amounts to a first sale and the infringing goods are subsequently beyond the reach of the patent. *See* King Instrument Corp. v. Otari Corp., 814 F.2d 1560, 1564 (Fed. Cir. 1987).

lows a first sale by a licensee of the patent owner; the licensee may owe royalties to the patent owner, but the article sold is afterwards "free of the patent."[37]

A similar rule applies where a patent claims a *method* and the patent owner sells an *apparatus* used in that method. For example, a patent might claim a "method of catching mice," and the apparatus sold might be a kind of mousetrap. Anyone who purchases a mousetrap expects to use it for catching mice, and if the only method of using the mousetrap is the same one claimed in the patent, the purchaser reasonably expects to use that method. Such expectations lead to the following rule: An unrestricted sale of an apparatus by the patent owner confers an implied license to practice a patented method if (1) the apparatus sold has no noninfringing uses, and (2) the circumstances of the sale otherwise plainly indicate that a license should be inferred.[38] On the other hand, if the apparatus has other uses, one cannot imply a license to the patented method.[39]

6.3.1.2 Legal Estoppel

Another situation in which a patent license can be implied falls under the heading of *legal estoppel.* Simply put, legal estoppel is a doctrine that prevents a patent owner from licensing one patent, only to make that license worthless by enforcing another.[40] Suppose that an inventor obtained two patents—one a broad patent covering a new mousetrap design, and the other a narrow patent covering a particular variation of that design. A mousetrap within the scope of the narrower patent would necessarily fall within the scope of the broader patent as well. Anyone who received an express license to the second patent would likely receive an implied license to the first under the principle of legal estoppel. Otherwise the patent owner could prevent the licensee from taking any benefit from the license it obtained.

6.3.1.3 Industry Standards

The preceding examples are merely specific instances in which a patent license is commonly implied. Any conduct by a patentee that could lead one

---

[37] *See* Unidisco, Inc. v. Schattner, 824 F.2d 965, 968 (Fed Cir. 1987).

[38] Met-Coil Sys. Corp. v. Korners Unlimited, Inc., 803 F.2d 684, 686 (Fed. Cir. 1986). The scope of the implied license may still depend on "what the parties reasonably intended . . . based on the circumstances of the sale." *See* Carborundum Co. v. Molten Metal Equipment Innovations, Inc., 72 F.3d 872, 878 (Fed. Cir. 1995). In *Carborundum,* for example, the parties disputed whether the implied license to practice a patented method lasted for the life of the patent, or expired when the purchased apparatus wore out. The court found that the parties could not have intended the license to outlast the apparatus. *Id.* at 878–79.

[39] *See Bandag,* 750 F.2d at 924. The alternative use need not be optimal, but it should be "reasonable." *See* Glass Equipment Development, Inc. v. Besten, Inc., 174 F.3d 1337, 1343 (Fed. Cir. 1999).

[40] *See* Spindelfabrik Suessen-Schurr Stahlecker & Grill GmbH v. Schubert & Salzer Maschinenfabrik Atiengesellschaft, 829 F.2d 1075, 1080 (Fed. Cir. 1987). "The rationale . . . is to estop the grantor from taking back that for which he received consideration." *Id.*

to infer a waiver or an abandonment of the patentee's rights may result in an implied license.[41] An increasingly common example involves the adoption of a patented technology as an industry standard. Many industries, such as the computer and telecommunications industries, depend on such standards to ensure that equipment from different manufacturers can work together. Once such a standard is adopted, companies in the industry are virtually compelled to conform. If the industry standard is covered by a patent, should all companies in the industry be forced to pay a royalty? In some cases the answer is yes, but if the patent owner promoted the adoption of the technology as a standard and gave the impression that the standard could be practiced free of obligations, the circumstances could establish an implied license.[42] Otherwise an industry could be lured into adopting a standard, only later to be faced with claims of infringement.

---

[41] *See* Wang Labs., Inc. v. Mitsubishi Electronics America, Inc., 103 F.3d 1571, 1580 (Fed. Cir. 1997).
[42] *See Wang,* 103 F.2d at 1575, 1581–82.

Interpreting Patent Claims

The claims are the most important part of any patent. They define what the patented invention is.[1] Hence, the first step in determining whether a patent is valid or infringed is to analyze the claims and determine precisely what they mean. This analysis is known as *claim construction* or *claim interpretation*.

Claims are written in the English language, but they often employ a technical vocabulary, the meaning of which is not immediately apparent. The following is an example of patent claim language, chosen more or less at random:

1. An aqueous cosmetic emulsion comprising:
    i) an isoparaffin;
    ii) a C8-C22 alkyl phosphate salt;
    wherein the isoparaffin and alkyl phosphate salt are present in a respective weight ratio of from about 40:1 to about 1:1, and said emulsion having a viscosity ranging from about 35 to about 90 Brookfield units as measured with a Brookfield Viscometer Model LTV using a #4 spindle rotating at 60 rpm at 25°C.[2]

The claim is for a hand lotion.

The obscurity of claim language can be traced to two sources. First, because patents are awarded to technological advancements, a technical vocabulary is often best suited to describe what the invention is. The language of the preceding example is probably meaningful to the chemist who invented the lotion and to other chemists who are likely to be reading the patent.

[1] Alloc, Inc. v. International Trade Comm'n, 342 F.3d 1361, 1368 (Fed. Cir. 2003).
[2] Conopco, Inc. v. May Dept. Stores Co., 46 F.3d 1556, 1560 (Fed. Cir. 1994).

Second, because of its legal significance, claim language must describe the invention precisely. If a narrow term is used instead of a more accurate broader term, the claims may fail to cover a product that was legitimately within the scope of the applicant's invention. If the preceding example had used the term "hand lotion" instead of "cosmetic emulsion," the claim might have been too narrow to cover a face cream that consisted of the same combination of materials. On the other hand, if a claim term is too broad, the patent may be anticipated by a prior art reference and made invalid.[3] The specific measure of viscosity in the preceding example may have been all that distinguished the invention from other lotions. Thus, everyday language that would serve as a casual description of an invention will not do for a patent claim. Finding the right words to describe an invention, from both a technical and legal viewpoint, is one of the most important tasks faced by a patent attorney.

Patent claims should be interpreted from the perspective of their intended audience—persons skilled in the field of the invention[4] at the time the patent application was filed.[5] When deciding what a patent claim means, guidance can be found in the following sources:

- The "ordinary meaning" or "plain meaning" of a word
- The specification
- The prosecution history
- Other claims

Although patentees sometimes testify as to what they *intended* a claim to mean, such subjective, post-hoc testimony carries little weight.[6]

7.1 PLAIN MEANING

The starting point for interpreting any term used in a patent claim is its *ordinary meaning* or *plain meaning* in the field of the invention.[7] That ordinary

---

[3] *See* Section 8.9.5.
[4] *See* Dayco Products, Inc. v. Total Containment, Inc., 258 F.3d 1317, 1324 (Fed. Cir. 2001) ("[W]e must always be conscious that our objective is to interpret the claims from the perspective of one of ordinary skill in the art. . . . If an argument offered in support of a particular claim construction is so convoluted and artificial that is would not be apparent to a skilled artisan reading the patent and the prosecution history, the argument is simply unhelpful to the performance of our task.").
[5] Kopykake Enterprises, Inc. v. Lucks Co., 264 F.3d 1377, 1383 (Fed. Cir. 2001).
[6] *See* Solomon v. Kimberly-Clark Corp., 216 F.3d 1372, 1379 (Fed. Cir. 2000); Senmed, Inc. v. Richard-Allan Medical Indus., Inc., 888 F.2d 815, 819 (Fed. Cir. 1989).
[7] CCS Fitness, Inc. v. Brunswick Corp., 288 F.3d 1359, 1366 (Fed. Cir. 2002) ("Generally speaking, we indulge a 'heavy presumption' that a claim term carries its ordinary and customary meaning."); *see also* Liebel-Flarsheim Co. v. Medrad Inc., 358 F.3d 898, 913 (Fed. Cir. 2004); Alloc, Inc. v. International Trade Comm'n, 342 F.3d 1361, 1368 (Fed. Cir. 2003).

meaning may not be immediately apparent, particularly if the term is a technical one.[8] Understandably, courts sometimes need assistance to understand terms that, to an expert, may be perfectly clear. At one time, the Federal Circuit sharply criticized resort to any extrinsic evidence, such as reference works or expert testimony, to assist in claim interpretation, except under the most extraordinary circumstances.[9] If one cannot rely on the intrinsic evidence—the patent itself and the prosecution history—then, the court reasoned, the claims are not properly serving their notice function.[10] Such evidence should be considered only as a last resort, when claim terminology, after study of the intrinsic evidence, remains stubbornly ambiguous.[11] Recently, however, the court has appeared more open to the use of certain kinds of extrinsic evidence, including dictionaries,[12] to assist a court in understanding the plain meaning of technical terms.[13] Even expert testimony may be admitted "to clarify the patented technology and to explain its meaning through the eyes of experience."[14] At the same time, courts are well aware that the opinions of experts are often colored by hindsight and

---

[8] *See* Teleflex, Inc. v. Ficosa North America Corp., 299 F.3d 1313, 1325 (Fed. Cir. 2002) ("the ordinary meaning must be determined from the standpoint of a person of ordinary skill in the relevant art").

[9] *See* Vitronics Corp. v. Conceptronic, Inc., 90 F.3d 1576, 1582–83 (Fed. Cir. 1996).

[10] *Vitronics,* 90 F.3d at 1583 ("The claims, specification, and file history, rather than extrinsic evidence, constitute the public record of the patentee's claim, a record on which the public is entitled to rely.").

[11] *Vitronics,* 90 F.3d at 1583.

[12] *See* Texas Digital Systems, Inc. v. Telegenix, Inc., 308 F.3d 1193, 1202–03 (Fed. Cir. 2002) ("Dictionaries are always available to the court to aid in the task of determining meanings that would have been attributed by those of skill in the relevant art to any disputed terms used by the inventor in the claims. . . . Dictionaries, encyclopedias and treatises, publicly available at the time the patent is issued, . . . are unbiased reflections of common understanding."); Interactive Gift Express, Inc. v. Compuserve Inc., 231 F.3d 859, 866 (Fed. Cir. 2000) ("Dictionaries, which are a form of extrinsic evidence, hold a special place. . . ."). Sometimes a general dictionary of the Webster's variety is used as an aid to deciphering a patent claim. *See, e.g.,* Greenberg v. Ethicon Endo-Surgery, Inc., 91 F.3d 1580, 1583 (Fed. Cir. 1996); Athletic Alternatives, Inc. v. Prince Mfg. Co., 73 F.3d 1573, 1579 (Fed. Cir. 1996). However, the best guide to the "plain meaning" of a technical term is often the technical literature, including specialized dictionaries, textbooks, research papers, and even other patents. *See* Toro Co. v. White Consolidated Indus., Inc., 199 F.3d 1295, 1299 (Fed. Cir. 1999) ("[T]he court must achieve the same understanding of the patent . . . as would a person experienced in the technology of the invention. Such a person would not rely solely on a dictionary of general linguistic usage. . . ."); Hoechst Celanese Corp. v. BP Chemicals Ltd., 78 F.3d 1575, 1580 (Fed. Cir. 1996).

[13] *See* Pitney Bowes, Inc. v. Hewlett-Packard Co., 182 F.3d 1298, 1308-09 (Fed. Cir. 1999) ("[I]t is entirely appropriate, even preferable, for a court to consult trustworthy extrinsic evidence to ensure that the claim construction it is tending to from the patent file is not inconsistent with clearly expressed, plainly apposite, and widely held understandings in the pertinent technical field."). Dictionary definitions may be consulted even before the patent specification or prosecution history. *See* Intellectual Property Development v. UA-Columbia Cablevision of Westchester Inc., 336 F.3d 1308, 1315 (Fed. Cir. 2003).

[14] Aqua-Aerobic Sys., Inc v. Aerators Inc., 211 F.3d 1241, 1245 (Fed. Cir. 2000).

the interests of the litigants who employ them. Consequently, expert
testimony is treated with appropriate skepticism, and it may not "correct
errors or erase limitations or otherwise diverge from the description of the
invention as contained in the patent documents."[15]

7.2 THE SPECIFICATION

If a word has an ordinary or plain meaning, one might suppose that its
interpretation would be uncontroversial, yet words as simple as "on" and
"a" have been the subject of intense debate in the context of infringement
litigation.[16] One reason for this is that a patent applicant can be "his own
lexicographer"–which is to say, an applicant can devise his own vocabulary
to describe the invention.[17] Words can be used in ways that differ from their
ordinary sense, or new words can be invented. Nevertheless, if the applicant
uses words in a specialized or unusual sense, that sense must be made clear
in the patent specification.[18] Words used in a patent claim cannot have a
secret meaning.[19]

The patent specification is a place for the applicant to elaborate on the
invention, and it serves as a "dictionary" to define, expressly or by implication, any specialized meaning to be given to terms used in the claims.[20]
Accordingly, the specification is "the single best guide to the meaning of a
disputed term."[21] In all cases it is relevant, and in many it is dispositive.[22] If
the specification clearly shows that the applicant did not use a term in its
ordinary sense, the specification takes precedence.[23]

Although the specification is an indispensable tool for claim interpretation,
there is always a danger that it will be used not to *define* a term used in a claim,

15 *Aqua-Aerobic,* 211 F.3d at 1245.
16 Senmed, Inc. v. Richard-Allan Medical Indus., Inc., 888 F.2d 815, 819 (Fed. Cir. 1989);
   North American Vaccine, Inc. v. American Cyanamid Co., 7 F.3d 1571, 1575–76 (Fed. Cir.
   1993).
17 Alloc, Inc. v. International Trade Comm'n, 342 F.3d 1361, 1368 (Fed. Cir. 2003) ("A patent
   applicant may consistently and clearly use a term in a manner either more or less expansive
   than its general usage in the relevant art, thereby expanding or limiting the scope of the
   term in the context of the patent claims."); Abbott Labs. v. Novopharm Ltd., 323 F.3d 1324,
   1330 (Fed. Cir. 2003); Bell Atlantic Network Services, Inc. v. Covad Communications Gp.,
   Inc., 262 F.2d 1258, 1268 (Fed. Cir. 2001); Vitronics Corp. v. Conceptronic, Inc., 90 F.3d
   1576, 1582 (Fed. Cir. 1996).
18 *See Bell Atlantic,* 262 F.3d at 1268; *Vitronics,* 90 F.3d at 1582. The specification "must clearly
   redefine a claim term 'so as to put a reasonable competitor or one reasonably skilled in the
   art on notice that the patentee intended to so redefine that claim term.'" Elekta Instrument
   S.A. v. O.U.R. Scientific Int'l. Inc., 214 F.3d 1302, 1307 (Fed. Cir. 2000).
19 Intellicall, Inc. v. Phonometrics, Inc., 952 F.2d 1384, 1387–88 (Fed. Cir. 1992).
20 *See Bell Atlantic,* 262 F.3d at 1268; *Vitronics,* 90 F.3d at 1582.
21 *Vitronics,* 90 F.3d at 1582.
22 *Vitronics,* 90 F.3d at 1582.
23 *See Bell Atlantic,* 262 F.3d at 1268.

but to *add limitations* that do not appear in the claim at all. A specification is required to describe specific examples, or *preferred embodiments*, that fall within the scope of the patent claims, but are not coextensive with them.[24] The details of these preferred embodiments do not limit the scope of the claims, unless the claims say so.[25]

Consider, for example, the claims in *In re Paulsen*,[26] which described a "portable computer" with a hinged case allowing the display screen to be latched in an upright position during use. The patentee argued that the term "portable computer" did not include a calculator. If the claims did cover a calculator, they would be found invalid because of a prior Japanese patent. The patentee pointed out that the specific portable computer disclosed in the specification incorporated a sophisticated display, advanced data processing capability, communications ports, and other attributes that are characteristic of a laptop personal computer rather than a calculator. Nevertheless, the court found that none of these things were required by the claims. Since the claims merely said "portable computer," and the court found that a calculator was a kind of portable computer as that term is generally understood, the claims were broad enough to include a calculator.[27]

Sometimes, as in *Paulsen*, the patentee is motivated to read into the claims limitations found in the specification, in order to narrow the claims sufficiently to avoid the prior art. In other cases, it is the accused infringer who

---

[24] *See* Section 3.3. It is seldom correct to interpret claim language to exclude the patentee's own preferred embodiments. *See Vitronics*, 90 F.3d at 1583 ("[s]uch an interpretation is rarely, if ever, correct and would require highly persuasive evidentiary support"). On occasion, however, no other reading of the claim language is possible. *See Elekta*, 214 F.3d at 1308 ("in light of the prosecution history and the unambiguous language of the amended claim, we conclude that this is the rare case in which such an interpretation is compelled").

[25] Prima Tek II, L.L.C. v. Polypap, S.A.R.L., 318 F.3d 1143, 1148–49 (Fed. Cir. 2003) ("Notwithstanding the fact that the claim language must be examined in light of the written description [in the specification], limitations may not be read into the claims from the written description. . . . Similarly, the mere fact that the patent drawings depict a particular embodiment of the patent does not operate to limit the claims to that specific configuration."); Teleflex, Inc. v. Ficosa North America Corp., 299 F.3d 1313, 1326 (Fed. Cir. 2002) ("the claims must be read in view of the specification . . . but limitations from the specification are not to be read into the claims"). "Even when the specification describes only a single embodiment, the claims of the patent will not be read restrictively unless the patentee has demonstrated a clear intention to limit the claim scope using 'words or expressions of manifest exclusion or restriction.'" Liebel-Flarsheim Co. v. Medrad Inc., 358 F.3d 898, 906 (Fed. Cir. 2004). Resolving the tension between interpreting claim language in light of the specification and reading into the claim limitations found only in the specification depends upon "how the specification characterizes the claimed invention." *Alloc*, 342 F.3d at 1370. The specification may "refer[] to a limitation only as a part of less than all possible embodiments," or it may "suggest[] that the very character of the invention requires [that] the limitation be a part of every embodiment." *Id.* If "the specification makes clear at various points that the claimed invention is narrower than the claim language might imply, it is entirely permissible and proper to limit the claims." *Id.*

[26] 30 F.3d 1475 (Fed. Cir. 1994).

[27] *Paulsen*, 30 F.3d at 1479–80.

seeks to read in those limitations in order to narrow the claim and avoid infringement. In neither case is the practice allowed. Note that there is sometimes a fine line between reading in a limitation absent from the claims and using the specification to *interpret* the claims in a particular fashion.[28] The patentee in *Paulsen*, for example, might have argued that *computer* is a term with various meanings and that reading the claim language *in light of* the specification would suggest the narrower meaning.[29]

There is one important exception to the rule that limitations found only in the specification cannot be read into the claims. This exception applies to claims drafted in the means-plus-function format provided for in Paragraph 6 of 35 U.S.C. § 112. Claims of this type are discussed in Section 7.7.4.

7.3 THE PROSECUTION HISTORY

Another resource for interpreting claim language is the prosecution history.[30] This is (ideally) a complete record of the proceedings before the Patent Office, and it includes any remarks or representations that may have been made by the applicant concerning the proper interpretation of the claims.[31] Claims must be interpreted in the same way in litigation as they were in the Patent Office.[32] Otherwise applicants could treat their claims as the proverbial "nose of wax" to be twisted one direction in prosecution (perhaps to avoid a close prior art reference), then another direction in litigation (perhaps to encompass an accused product similar to that

---

[28] *See Liebel-Flarsheim*, 358 F.3d at 904; Interactive Gift Express, Inc. v. Compuserve Inc., 231 F.3d at 859, 865–66 (Fed. Cir. 2000).

[29] *See, e.g.*, Ethicon Endo-Surgery, Inc. v. U.S. Surgical Corp., 93 F.3d 1572, 1578 (Fed. Cir. 1996).

[30] *See* Section 5.1. Note that, during prosecution, claims are given their "*broadest* reasonable interpretation" in order to ensure that there is no encroachment on the prior art. Springs Window Fashions LP v. Novo Indus., L.P., 323 F.3d 989, 995 (Fed. Cir. 2003). This bias does not apply in subsequent infringement litigation.

[31] *See* Johnson v. Stanley Works, 903 F.2d 8182, 817 (Fed. Cir. 1990). Sometimes, however, matters are decided in a telephone conference, of which there is often an inadequate record.

[32] *See* Rheox, Inc. v. Entact, Inc., 276 F.3d 1319, 1325 (Fed. Cir. 2002) ("Arguments and amendments made during prosecution of a patent application must be examined to determine the meaning of terms in the claims. . . . 'The prosecution history limits the interpretation of the claim terms so as to exclude any interpretation that was disclaimed during prosecution.'"); Vitronics Corp. v. Conceptronic, Inc., 90 F.3d 1576, 1583 (Fed. Cir. 1996); Southwall Technologies, Inc. v. Cardinal IG Co., 54 F.3d 1570, 1576 (Fed. Cir. 1995). Arguing during prosecution that a term has a narrow meaning, an applicant may "disclaim" a broader meaning. *See* Golight Inc. v. Wal-Mart Stores Inc., 355 F.3d 1327, 1333 (Fed. Cir. 2004); Omega Eng'g, Inc. v. Raytek Corp., 334 F.3d 1314, 1324 (Fed. Cir. 2003) ("[W]here the patentee has unequivocally disavowed a certain meaning to obtain his patent, the doctrine of prosecution disclaimer attaches and narrows the ordinary meaning of the claim congruent with the scope of the surrender.")

reference).[33] Such inconsistency in interpretation would pervert the process of examination, and it would hinder potential competitors who should be entitled to rely on the public record in judging the scope of the patentee's claims.[34]

Occasionally, a court will overlook what was obviously a *mistaken* characterization of the invention by the applicant during prosecution.[35] This is appropriate, however, only when the error is so apparent that a reasonable person reading the prosecution history would not be misled.[36]

7.4 OTHER CLAIMS

Sometimes the meaning of language in one claim is clarified by comparison to the language of another claim. This particularly arises in the context of the *doctrine of claim differentiation*, which holds that each claim should be presumed to differ in scope from every other claim. The assumption is that an applicant would not intentionally draft two claims that covered, in different words, precisely the same subject matter.[37] The doctrine of claim differentiation is not absolute, however. Sometimes the only reasonable interpretation of a claim is one that makes it redundant.[38]

[33] *See Vitronics,* 90 F.3d at 1583; *Southwall,* 54 F.3d at 1578.

[34] *See Springs Window Fashions,* 323 F.3d at 995 ("The public notice function of a patent and its prosecution history requires that a patentee be held to what he declares during the prosecution of his patent. A patentee may not state during prosecution that the claims do not cover a particular device and then change position and later sue a party who makes that same device for infringement."). On the other hand, it should not be necessary for competitors to look beyond the patent itself to understand what the claims mean. The specification ought to provide all of the information required. If the claim interpretation suggested by the patent itself is one that favors a competitor, it could be argued that the patentee should not be entitled to rely on the prosecution history for a different interpretation.

[35] *See, e.g.,* Intervet America, Inc. v. Kee-Vet Labs., Inc., 887 F.2d 1050, 1053-1054 (Fed. Cir. 1989).

[36] *See* Biotec Biologische Naturverpackungen GmbH v. Biocorp, Inc. 249 F.3d 1341, 1348 (Fed. Cir. 2001) ("An error in the prosecution record must be viewed as errors are in documents in general; that is, would it have been apparent to the interested reader that an error was made, such that it would be unfair to enforce the error."); Hockerson-Halberstadt, Inc. v. Avia Gp. Int'l, Inc., 222 F.3d 951, 957 (Fed. Cir. 2000) (distinguishing *Intervet* and denying the patentee the requested "mulligan that would erase from the prosecution history the inventor's disavowal of a particular aspect of a claim term's meaning").

[37] *See* Kraft Foods, Inc. v. International Trading Co., 203 F.3d 1362, 1366 (Fed. Cir. 2000) ("two claims of a patent are presumptively of different scope"); Beachcombers, Int'l, Inc. v. Wildwood Creative Prods., Inc., 31 F.3d 1154, 1162 (Fed. Cir. 1994) (interpretation that would render a claim superfluous is "presumptively unreasonable"); Tandon Corp. v. U.S. Int'l Trade Comm'n, 831 F.2d 1017, 1023 (Fed. Cir. 1987). If a dependent claim adds a limitation to an independent claim (see Section 3.4), it is presumed that that new limitation is not present, implicitly, in the independent claim. Liebel-Flarsheim Co. v. Medrad Inc., 358 F.3d 898, 910 (Fed. Cir. 2004).

7.5 VALIDITY

Another basic principle of claim interpretation is that claims should, if possible, be read in a manner that preserves their validity.[39] The source of this rule is obscure, but probably the underlying assumption is that a claim approved by the Patent Office should be presumed valid,[40] and the interpretation that supports validity must be the one that the Patent Office had in mind. Like the doctrine of claim differentiation, this principle does not justify a claim interpretation that is unreasonable or simply contrary to the evidence.[41]

One rule of claim interpretation that *is* absolute is that a claim must be interpreted in the same way when the issue is infringement as it is when the issue is validity.[42] If, for example, a claim is interpreted in a narrow fashion to avoid a potentially invalidating prior art reference, that same narrow interpretation must be applied when comparing the claim to the accused product. The meaning of a claim cannot change to suit the convenience of the patent owner.[43]

---

[38] *See Kraft Foods*, 203 F.3d at 1368 (claim differentiation "is 'not a hard and fast rule'"); *Tandon*, 831 F.2d at 1023–24.

[39] Liebel-Flarsheim Co. v. Medrad Inc., 358 F.3d 898, 911 (Fed. Cir. 2004); Tate Access Floors, Inc. v. Interface Architectural Resources, Inc., 279 F.3d 1357, 1367 (Fed. Cir. 2002); Karsten Mfg. Corp. v. Cleveland Golf Co., 242 F.3d 1376, 1384 (Fed. Cir. 2001); Apple Computer, Inc. v. Articulate Sys., Inc., 234 F.3d 14, 24 (Fed. Cir. 2000) ("'claims should be read in a way that avoids ensnaring the prior art if it is possible to do so'"). The axiom applies, however, only if the meaning of the claim remains ambiguous in spite of the normal procedures of claim interpretation. *Liebel-Flarsheim*, 358 F.3d at 911.

[40] *See* Section 8.2.

[41] *Apple Computer*, 324 F.3d at 24; Rhine v. Casio, Inc., 183 F.3d 1342, 1245 (Fed. Cir. 1999) ("We . . . have consistently employed the caveat, 'if possible,' to our instruction that claims should be construed to sustain their validity."); Quantum Corp. v. Rodime, PLC, 65 F.3d 1577, 1584 (Fed. Cir. 1995) ("Although [courts] construe claims, if possible, so as to sustain their validity . . . it is well settled that no matter how great the temptations of fairness or policy making, courts do not redraft claims."). There is, accordingly, no "practicing the prior art" defense to infringement. If the defendant's product is identical to the prior art and the claim reads on both, the claim is simply invalid. *See Tate Access Floors*, 279 F.3d at 1367. The rule against rewriting claims also applies when a literal reading effectively spoils the invention. In *Chef American Inc. v. Lamb-Weston Inc.*, 358 F.3d 1371 (Fed. Cir. 2004), the claims called for dough to be heated *to* 400 degrees, rather than *at* 400 degrees. Dough heated to 400 degrees would be burned to a crisp, but the court maintained that the claims meant what they said. *See Id.* at 1374 ("we construe the claim as written, not as the patentees wish they had written it").

[42] Amgen, Inc. v. Hoechst Marion Roussel, Inc., 314 F.3d 1313, 1330 (Fed. Cir. 2003); Amazon.com, Inc. v. Barnesandnoble.com, Inc., 239 F.3d 1343, 1351 (Fed. Cir. 2001); C.R. Bard, Inc. v. M3 Sys., Inc., 157 F.3d 1340, 1363 (Fed. Cir. 1998); Atlantic Thermoplastics Co. v. Faytex Corp., 970 F.2d 834, 846 (Fed. Cir. 1992); Smithkline Diagnostics, Inc. v. Helena Labs. Corp., 859 F.2d 878, 882 (Fed. Cir. 1988).

7.6 PREAMBLES

One peculiar rule of claim interpretation involves the *preamble*–the first paragraph of a patent claim that typically ends with the word *comprising*. In the claim set out at the beginning of this chapter, the preamble language is "An aqueous cosmetic emulsion comprising. . . ." The preamble often characterizes the category of invention or its intended use–for example, a mousetrap or a "cosmetic emulsion"–but it does not in itself recite the checklist of claim elements that defines the patented invention. In such cases, the preamble is not considered a claim limitation, and this can have important consequences. Imagine, for example, a product identical to the cosmetic emulsion described in the example but used as an industrial lubricant. If the preamble were disregarded, the lubricant would infringe the claim.

A preamble is treated as a claim limitation only "if it recites essential structure or steps, or if it is 'necessary to give life, meaning, and vitality' to the claim."[44] This is a nebulous distinction. On occasion the preamble is clearly a substantive part of the claim because the "body" of the claim that follows includes references to the preamble. For instance, the body of the claim used as an example refers to "said emulsion." It is therefore likely that a court would consider the "aqueous cosmetic emulsion" language to be a claim limitation.[45] On other occasions, preamble language is treated as essential because the applicant relied upon it to distinguish the invention from the prior art.[46] On the other hand, if the preamble states an intended use or environment for the invention, but the remainder of the claim is sufficient by itself to describe what the invention *is*, then the preamble will not be considered a part of the claim.[47]

If the claim read without the preamble would leave one guessing as to what the invention really was, the preamble would probably be considered

[43] A disadvantage borne by patent owners in litigation is that they must find a single claim interpretation that supports a finding of *both* validity and infringement. An accused infringer, on the other hand, can be satisfied with an interpretation that renders the claim invalid *or* a different interpretation that renders the claim not infringed. Which interpretation the court chooses may be a matter of indifference to the accused infringer.

[44] *In re* Cruciferous Sprout Litigation, 301 F.3d 1343, 1347 (Fed. Cir. 2002); Catalina Mktg. Int'l, Inc. v. Coolsavings.com, Inc., 289 F.3d 801, 808 (Fed. Cir. 2002). Yet there is no litmus test for deciding whether a preamble should be considered a claim limitation. *See* Corning Glass Works v. Sumitomo Electric U.S.A., Inc., 868 F.2d 1251, 1257 (Fed. Cir. 1989). "To say that a preamble is a limitation if it gives 'meaning to the claim' may merely state the problem rather than lead one to the answer." *Id.* The decision must be made in the context of the entire patent, which may establish "'what the inventors actually invented and intended to encompass by the claim.'" *Catalina,* 289 F.3d at 808. In particular, structure or steps recited in the preamble and "underscored as important by the specification" are more likely to be considered claim limitations. *Id.*

[45] *See Catalina,* 289 F.3d at 808 ("dependence on a particular disputed preamble phrase for antecedent basis may limit claim scope because it indicates a reliance on both the preamble and claim body to define the claimed invention").

[46] *See Cruciferous Sprout,* 301 F.3d at 1347; *Catalina,* 289 F.3d at 808.

a claim limitation. In *Diversitech Corp. v. Century Steps, Inc.*,[48] for example, the claim referred to an equipment-supporting base comprising a foam core and a cementitious coating. Without the preamble, the claim would have referred to the core and the coating, but one would have no idea what the invention really was. In *Diversitech* the court found that the preamble was necessary to define the invention. In contrast, in *STX LLC v. Brine, Inc.*,[49] the preamble boasted that the patented lacrosse stick would provide "improved handling and playing characteristics." Because the remainder of the claim stood alone as a structurally complete description of the stick, the court did not find that the preamble language limited the claim.[50]

On the subject of preambles, it is important to note the difference between *comprising* and *consisting of,* the two phrases that typically conclude a claim preamble. *Comprising* is a term of art, understood to mean that the invention consists of the following combination of claim elements, by themselves or in combination with additional elements.[51] *Consisting of,* on the other hand, is understood to mean "the following elements *and no others.*" *Comprising* is the broader and generally more useful term. If the preamble ends with *consisting essentially of,* the claim allows additional unrecited ingredients, but only if they do not change the basic characteristics of the combination.[52]

7.7 SPECIAL CLAIM FORMATS

Several specialized claim formats are available to inventors who wish to use them.

7.7.1 Jepson Claims

One specialized claim format is known as a *Jepson claim.*[53] A Jepson claim is a claim to an improvement on a product that already exists. The Jepson format includes a recitation of the preexisting components in the preamble and the improvement in the body of the claim.[54] For example:

---

[47] "[A] preamble is not limiting 'where a patentee defines a structurally complete invention in the claim body and uses the preamble only to state a purpose or intended use for the invention.'" *Catalina,* 289 F.3d at 808; *see also* Pitney Bowes, Inc. v. Hewlett-Packard Co., 182 F.3d 1298, 1305 (Fed. Cir. 1999). "[P]reamble language merely extolling benefits or features of the claimed invention does not limit the claim scope without clear reliance on those benefits or features as patentably significant." *Catalina,* 289 F.3d at 809.

[48] 850 F.2d 675, 677–78 (Fed. Cir. 1988).

[49] 211 F.3d 588 (Fed. Cir. 2000).

[50] *STX,* 211 F.3d at 591.

[51] *See* Carl Zeiss Stiftung v. Renishaw PLC, 945 F.2d 1173, 1178 (Fed. Cir. 1991); Water Technologies Corp. v. Calco, Ltd., 850 F.2d 660, 666 (Fed. Cir. 1988).

[52] *See Water Technologies,* 850 F.2d at 666.

[53] Named after *Ex parte Jepson,* 243 O.G. 525 (Ass't Comm'r Pat. 1917), the case that first approved the format.

[54] *See* Ethicon Endo-Surgery, Inc. v. U.S. Surgical Corp., 93 F.3d 1572, 1577 (Fed. Cir. 1996).

In an instrument marker pen body including an ink reservoir and means for receiving a writing tip, *the improvement comprising* a pen arm holding means consisting of an integrally molded hinged member adapted to fold against a surface of the pen body and to be locked against said surface by engageable locking means and to receive and secure in place against said surface a pen arm when said hinged member is in its folded and locked position.[55]

The words "In a [preexisting device], the improvement comprising" are typical of a Jepson claim. The significance of a Jepson claim is that the elements recited in the preamble are claim limitations, and the patent applicant, by implication, admits that those elements exist in the prior art.[56]

7.7.2 Markush Claims

Another specialized claim format is the *Markush claim*, generally used to describe chemical and biological inventions. A Markush claim includes a claim element selected from a group of possibilities—for example, "a sugar selected from the group consisting of sucrose, fructose, and lactose."[57] Markush groups are used when there is no generic term that conveniently describes the desired claim element.[58]

7.7.3 Product-by-Process Claims

Whereas most patent claims can be characterized as process, apparatus, or composition of matter claims, a so-called *product-by-process* claim straddles the usual categories. A product-by-process claim, as the name suggests, describes a product made by a specific process. Traditionally, product-by-process claims have been used when the invention is best described in terms of how it is made rather than what it is.[59] Consider how an omelet could be described to someone who had never seen one. One might attempt to describe an omelet in physical or chemical terms, but a better approach would be to provide the recipe. At one time product-by-process claims were allowed only when the invention could not be described except through the "recipe"—for example, when the precise physical characteristics of the product could not be determined. Now they are allowed even if they are not strictly necessary.

There has been much debate about the role to be given the process in interpreting a product-by-process claim. In *Scripps Clinic & Research Foun-*

---

[55] Pentec, Inc. v. Graphic Controls Corp., 776 F.2d 309, 312 (Fed. Cir. 1985) (emphasis added).

[56] *Pentec,* 776 F.2d at 315.

[57] For an example of a Markush claim, see *North American Vaccine, Inc. v. American Cyanamid Co.,* 7 F.3d 1571, 1573 (Fed. Cir. 1993).

[58] *See* Application of Weber, 580 F.2d 455, 457 n.4 (C.C.P.A. 1978).

[59] *See In re* Thorpe, 777 F.2d 695, 697 (Fed. Cir. 1985).

dation v. Genentech, Inc.,[60] the Federal Circuit held that the process
described in a product-by-process claim could be ignored when determining the scope of the claim. In other words, if the claim recited the product
of process X, an *identical product* made by a *different process* would still
infringe.[61] According to this way of thinking, the process recited in a product-by-process claim is provided only as a way to define the product. The
subject matter of the claim is still the omelet, not the recipe. This interpretation of the law follows the practice of the Patent Office in determining if a
product-by-process claim should issue. The Patent Office will not issue a
product-by-process claim unless it finds that the product, not just the process, is something new.[62]

However, in *Atlantic Thermoplastics Co. v. Faytex Corp.,*[63] a different panel
of Federal Circuit judges rejected the earlier interpretation and held that the
process set forth in a product-by-process claim does limit the claim, at least
in litigation, so an identical product made by a different process does not
infringe.[64] According to this court, the *Scripps Clinic* rule was contrary to
Supreme Court authority and the hornbook principle of patent law that all
elements of a claim are essential in determining infringement. Although it
acknowledged that different standards are applied in patent prosecution, the
court noted that this discrepancy is not unique. For example, the Patent
Office will give claims their "broadest reasonable interpretation," whereas
no such rule applies in litigation.[65]

Conflict in the Federal Circuit can be resolved through a procedure
allowing an expanded, or en banc, panel of all the judges on the Federal Circuit to review the case and decide collectively how the conflict will be settled. Unfortunately, the procedure was not followed in this instance, and the
conflict between *Scripps Clinic* and *Atlantic Thermoplastics* remains. As a rule,
if two decisions of the Federal Circuit conflict, the earlier one (i.e., *Scripps
Clinic*) takes precedence.[66] Yet if *Scripps Clinic* really was contrary to
Supreme Court precedent (a matter on which the Federal Circuit judges dis-

[60] 927 F.2d 1565 (Fed. Cir. 1991).
[61] "[T]he correct reading of product-by-process claims is that they are not limited to product
prepared by the process set forth in the claims." *Scripps Clinic,* 927 F.2d at 1583 (Fed. Cir.
1991).
[62] *See Thorpe,* 777 F.2d at 697.
[63] 970 F.2d 834 (Fed. Cir. 1992).
[64] *Atlantic Thermoplastics,* 970 F.2d at 847.
[65] *Atlantic Thermoplastics,* 970 F.2d at 846. The court suggested, but did not clearly state, that a
product-by-process claim involving a new process but an old product would be held valid in
litigation, even though it would be (or should be) rejected by the Patent Office. If this were
not true, it would violate the principle that claims must be given the same interpretation for
infringement as for validity. *See Id.*
[66] Newell Co. v. Kenney Mfg. Co., 846 F.2d 787, 765 (Fed. Cir. 1988). Relying on this principle, a lower court in Illinois rejected the reasoning of *Atlantic Thermoplastics* in favor of *Scripps
Clinic. See* DeKalb Genetics Corp. v. Northrup King Co., 1997 U.S. Dist. LEXIS 14275 (N.D.
Ill. 1997).

agree), then the Supreme Court authority would control. More than a decade later, it is still impossible for anyone to say precisely what the law is.

7.7.4 Means-Plus-Function Claims

One form of specialized claim format that has become extremely common is the means-plus-function format authorized by 35 U.S.C. § 112, ¶ 6. At one time, courts held that a claim to an apparatus must describe the features of the apparatus in precise physical terms rather than in terms of the functions they perform. So, for example, a claim to a mousetrap could properly refer to a "steel spring" but could not refer simply to a "means for snapping the trap shut." The latter claim would literally cover a mousetrap with a steel spring, a plastic spring, a rubber band, or any other mechanism that might close the trap. Such a claim would not adequately define the invention, since it could cover many things that the patentee had not invented or disclosed.

Permitting a patentee to describe a feature of the invention in terms of its function does have certain advantages, however. In the prior example, the inventor might have in mind the steel spring, the plastic spring, the rubber band, and dozens of other means for snapping the trap shut, and the choice of which to use might have little to do with the essence of the invention. A person skilled in designing mousetraps who read the patent might also realize that various forms of springs and elastic bands could be used. In this situation, it would seem pointless to require the inventor to provide a long list of every variety of spring, rubber band, or similar device that the inventor could imagine. Moreover, it might be too easy for a competitor to avoid the patent simply by coming up with a closing mechanism that the patentee had neglected to list.

The result of this tension between convenience and the need for specificity in claim drafting was legislative compromise, embodied in § 112, ¶ 6:

> An element in a claim for a combination may be expressed as a means or step for performing a specified function without the recital of structure, material or acts in support thereof, and such claim shall be construed to cover the corresponding structure, material or acts described in the specification and equivalents thereof.

Thus, an inventor can choose to describe an element of the invention as a physical structure (i.e., "steel spring") or as a means for performing a specified function (i.e., "means for snapping the trap shut"), leaving it to the specification to describe the physical structure that performs the function. If the inventor chooses the latter option, the claim will cover the specific structure disclosed in the specification and equivalents of that structure (i.e., a mousetrap with a steel spring or the equivalent of a steel spring).[67] Deciding just what is equivalent is a matter discussed in Section 10.7.

Although any claim element including the word means is presumed to be a means-plus-function element construed in accordance with § 112, ¶ 6,[68] that presumption can be rebutted if the claim element, contrary to the language of § 112, ¶ 6, does recite structure.[69] For example, in *Envirco Corp. v. Clestra Cleanroom, Inc.*,[70] the Federal Circuit held that a claim element calling for a "second baffle means" was not a means-plus-function element, because the claim recited structural information concerning the location and formation of the baffle.[71] The difference is significant; when a claim element is construed as a means-plus-function element, the patent owner is put to the additional burden of demonstrating that the structures of the accused product are identical or equivalent to the structures disclosed in the patent specification. Some patent applicants seem to overuse the means format, perhaps not appreciating the risks.[72]

Note that § 112, ¶ 6 applies only to a "claim for a combination." A single means claim is still considered invalid.[73] One could not claim, for example, just "a means for catching a mouse" and leave it at that. The means-plus-function format can be used only when the claim breaks down the invention into specific components.

7.7.5 Step-Plus-Function Claims

The language of § 112, ¶ 6 also provides for a *step-plus-function* claim—in other words, a process claim in which a step of the process is described

---

[67] "When multiple embodiments in the specification correspond to the claimed function, proper application of [§ 112, ¶ 6] generally reads the claim element to embrace each of those embodiments." Micro Chemical, Inc. v. Great Plains Chemical Co., 194 F.3d 1250, 1258 (Fed. Cir. 1999); *see also* Creo Prods., Inc. v. Presser, Inc., 305 F.3d 1337, 1346 (Fed. Cir. 2002). If *no* embodiment described in the specification provides structure to support the means-plus-function element, then the claim is invalid on grounds of indefiniteness. Intellectual Property Development Inc. v. UA-Columbia Cablevision of Westchester Inc., 336 F.3d 1308, 1319 (Fed. Cir. 2003).

[68] Allen Eng'g Corp. v. Bartell Indus., Inc., 299 F.3d 1336, 1347 (Fed. Cir. 2002); *Micro Chemical*, 194 F.3d at 1257.

[69] *See Micro Chemical*, 194 F.3d at 1257 ("[The] presumption collapses . . . if the claim itself recites sufficient structure, material, or acts to perform the claimed function."). The presumption also fails if the claim element recites no function for the means to perform. *See Allen Eng'g*, 299 F.3d at 1347. An element that does *not* use the word *means* is presumed *not* to be a means-plus-function element. However, that presumption will be rebutted and § 112, ¶ 6 applied if, even in the absence of the "means" language, the element "nonetheless relies on functional terms rather than structure or material to describe performance of the claimed function." *Micro Chemical*, 194 F.3d at 1257.

[70] 209 F.3d 1360 (Fed. Cir. 2000).

[71] *Envirco*, 209 F.3d at 1365.

[72] *See Allen Eng'g*, 299 F.3d at 1348 (patent applicant was "clearly enamored of the word 'means,'" using it repeatedly where, due to the recitation of structure, such use did not trigger § 112, ¶ 6).

[73] *See In re Hyatt*, 708 F.2d 712, 714 (Fed. Cir. 1983).

solely in terms of the "function" performed by that step, without the recital of a specific "act." Such a claim would cover the act described in the specification and its equivalents.[74] Although it is comparatively easy to distinguish between a *function* and a *structure*, it is much more difficult to distinguish between a *function* and an *act.* Returning to the mousetrap example, a claim element that referred to a "means for snapping the trap shut" would clearly be a means-plus-function claim element, because other than the generic term *means*, the physical structure is described solely in terms of the function it performs. Imagine, however, a mouse-trapping process claim, one element of which is "closing the trap to imprison the mouse." Is "closing the trap" (or for that matter "imprisoning the mouse") a function or an act? Does it describe the step itself or only the result of the step?

According to the Federal Circuit, a *function* refers to "*what* a claim element ultimately accomplishes."[75] An *act* corresponds to "*how* the function is accomplished."[76] This would suggest that "imprisoning the mouse" is a function, and "closing the trap" is an act. However, it is difficult to maintain the supposed distinction. In *Masco Corp v. U.S.*, the court held that "transmitting a force" was an act because "transmitting" described *how* the force was conveyed through mechanical parts.[77] Yet "transmitting a force" could be understood as a necessary result, accomplished by the action of any number of mechanical contrivances—more of a *what* than a *how.*

The Federal Circuit seems reluctant to construe any claim as a step-plus-function claim, which is understandable given the difficulties. It has observed that "[i]f we were to construe every process claim containing steps described by an 'ing' verb, such as passing, heating, reacting, transferring, etc. into a step-plus-function limitation, we would be limiting process claims in a manner never intended by Congress."[78] Unless patentees find the step-plus-function option indispensable, which is unlikely considering how seldom courts hold it to apply, perhaps the best solution would be legislation removing the problematic language from § 112, ¶ 6.

---

[74] The term *step for* suggests an intention to invoke § 112, ¶ 6, though the term *steps of* does not. Masco Corp. v. U.S., 303 F.3d 1316, 1327 (Fed. Cir. 2002).

[75] *Masco*, 303 F.3d at 1327 (emphasis in original).

[76] *Masco*, 303 F.3d at 1327 (emphasis in original); *see also* Seal-Flex, Inc. v. Athletic Track and Court Construction, 172 F.3d 836, 849–50 (Fed. Cir. 1999) (Rader, J., concurring).

[77] *Masco*, 303 F.3d at 1328; *see also* O.I. Corp. v. Tekmar Co., 115 F.3d 1576, 1583–84 (Fed. Cir. 1997) ("the step[] of . . . passing the [material] through a passage" construed as an "act" rather than a function).

[78] *O.I. Corp.*, 115 F.3d at 1583.

CHAPTER 8

Conditions of Patentability

8.1 EXAMINATION VERSUS LITIGATION

Before a patent is issued, the application must go through a process of *examination* by the Patent Office.[1] The purpose of the examination is to ensure that the application meets the various requirements of *patentability*. These requirements, which are explained in some detail later in this chapter, include the following:

- The invention must have *utility*.
- The claims must be *definite*.
- The specification must *enable* the practice of the invention and must disclose the inventor's *best mode* of practicing the invention.
- The claimed invention must be *novel*—that is, it must be new and *nonobvious* in comparison to the prior art.

In spite of the examination process, patents are sometimes issued that fail to meet these fundamental requirements. This is not always the fault of the Patent Office. For example, the Patent Office cannot judge whether a claim is novel in comparison to an earlier product if, as not infrequently occurs, the Patent Office is not even aware of the earlier product. Moreover, patent examination is not a practical forum for inquiring into certain questions, such as whether the information disclosed in a specification really reflects the applicant's "best mode." Questions like these can be explored effectively only in an adversarial proceeding. For all of these reasons, courts have the

---

[1] *See* Section 5.1.

power to find an issued patent invalid,[2] and a finding of invalidity is a complete defense to any charge of infringement.[3]

The patentability requirements discussed in this chapter are relevant in the examination process, where they can be grounds for rejecting an application, and in the litigation context, where they can be grounds for holding an already issued patent invalid. There are some procedural differences in the way these requirements are enforced in the Patent Office as compared to a court. For example, when judging whether a claim is novel, the Patent Office will give the claim its "broadest reasonable construction."[4] A court will not.[5] Nevertheless, the rules and precedent that apply in one context generally apply in the other context as well.

8.2 THE PRESUMPTION OF VALIDITY

Although courts have the power to hold an issued patent invalid, they do not discount the work of the Patent Office entirely. All patents are presumed to be valid, and the burden of overcoming that presumption rests with the accused infringer.[6] The presumption can only be overcome by "clear and convincing evidence" of invalidity.[7] This standard of proof is something less than the "beyond a reasonable doubt" standard of criminal law,[8] but it requires more than just a preponderance of the evidence. Consequently, a challenge to the validity of a patent is always an uphill battle. Note that the presumption of validity applies only after a patent has issued; there is no presumption in the Patent Office that an application meets the requirements of patentability.[9]

---

[2] *See* Quad Environmental Technologies Corp. v. Union Sanitary Dist., 946 F.2d 870, 876 (Fed. Cir. 1991) ("The courts are the final arbiter of patent validity and, although courts may take cognizance of, and benefit from, the proceedings before the patent examiner, the question is ultimately for the courts to decide, without deference to the rulings of the patent examiner.").

[3] Lough v. Brunswick Corp., 86 F.3d 1113, 1123 (Fed. Cir. 1996).

[4] *See In re* Morris, 127 F.3d 1048, 1054 (Fed. Cir. 1997) ("the PTO applies to the verbiage of the proposed claims the broadest reasonable meaning of the words in their ordinary usage as they would be understood by one of ordinary skill in the art, taking into account whatever enlightenment by way of definitions or otherwise that may be afforded by the written description contained in the applicant's specification").

[5] *See* Atlantic Thermoplastics Co. v. Faytex Corp., 970 F.2d 834, 846 (Fed. Cir. 1992).

[6] 35 U.S.C. § 282; Apotex USA, Inc. v. Merck & Co., 254 F.3d 1031, 1036 (Fed. Cir. 2001); Budde v. Harley-Davidson, Inc., 250 F.3d 1369, 1376 (Fed. Cir. 2001); Therma-Tru Corp. v. Peachtree Doors Inc., 44 F.3d 988, 992 (Fed. Cir. 1995). The presumption is "related to the presumption that the PTO does its job properly." Superior Fireplace Co. v. Majestic Prods. Co., 270 F.3d 1358, 1367 n.1 (Fed. Cir. 2001).

[7] Intellectual Property Development Inc. v. UA-Columbia Cablevision of Westchester Inc., 336 F.3d 1308, 1319 (Fed. Cir. 2003); *Apotex*, 254 F.3d at 1036; *Budde*, 250 F.3d at 1376; *Therma-Tru*, 44 F.3d at 992.

[8] Trans-World Mfg. Corp. v. Al Nyman & Sons, Inc., 750 F.2d 1552, 1559 (Fed. Cir. 1984).

[9] *In re* Morris, 127 F.3d 1048, 1054 (Fed. Cir. 1997).

Some older cases suggest that the presumption of validity is weakened or nullified when validity is challenged on grounds that were not considered by the Patent Office, such as a prior art reference of which the Patent Office was unaware. The Federal Circuit has adamantly maintained that the presumption of validity is ever-present and unchanging, no matter what grounds of invalidity may be asserted,[10] but it has admitted that the presumption is easier to overcome when the grounds are new.[11] Perhaps the difference is only one of semantics. In any event, deference to the Patent Office is more understandable when the Patent Office has already considered the issue than when it has not.

The presumption of validity applies separately to each claim of a patent.[12] Even if Claim 1 has been proven invalid by clear and convincing evidence, Claim 2 is unaffected until a challenger proves that it, too, is invalid. Generally, a patentee's goal in litigation is to prove infringement of at least one valid claim.

8.3 ASSIGNOR ESTOPPEL

Consider the following scenario. An inventor obtains a patent on a new apparatus and then assigns all rights to his employer.[13] The inventor receives valuable consideration for the assignment—perhaps a bonus. Afterward the inventor leaves his employer to form his own company and produces a product that is covered by the patent. If the former employer accuses the inventor of infringing the patent, can the inventor claim that the patent is invalid?

The answer is no. Anyone who assigns patent rights to another in exchange for valuable consideration[14] implicitly acknowledges the validity of the patent and gives up the right to challenge that validity at a later time.

[10] Hybritech Inc. v. Monoclonal Antibodies, Inc., 802 F.2d 1367, 1375 (Fed. Cir. 1986) ("the presumption remains intact and on the challenger throughout the litigation, and the clear and convincing evidence standard does not change").

[11] Ultra-Tex Surfaces, Inc. v. Hill Bros. Chemical Co., 204 F.3d 1360, 1367 (Fed. Cir. 2000) (describing the "additional burden" faced by the challenger who relies on "the very same references that were before the examiner"); *Hybritech,* 802 F.2d at 1375 ("the introduction of prior art not before the examiner may facilitate the challenger's meeting [its] burden of proof").

[12] 35 U.S.C. § 282 ("Each claim of a patent . . . shall be presumed valid independently of the validity of other claims; dependent or multiple dependent claims shall be presumed valid even though dependent upon an invalid claim."). There is one very specialized exception involving obviousness challenges to claims describing substances produced by biotechnological processes. See 35 U.S.C. §§ 282, 103(b)(1).

[13] See Section 6.2.

[14] The "valuable consideration" need not be a separate payment or bonus. Where the inventor/assignor is an employee of a corporation, that employee's regular salary is likely to be considered adequate consideration, at least if the invention was within the scope of the inventor/assignor's employment. See Diamond Scientific Co. v. Ambico, Inc., 848 F.2d 1220, 1225 (Fed. Cir. 1988).

This principle, known as *assignor estoppel,* is a matter of fairness: "[a]n assignor should not be permitted to sell something and later assert that what was sold is worthless, all to the detriment of the assignee."[15] The rule applies to the individual who assigned the patent, and it may apply to others with whom that individual is involved. For example, if the company accused of infringing the patent is not owned by the inventor/assignor, but it employs him in a position of responsibility, that company may still be barred from contesting the validity of the patent.[16]

8.4 UTILITY

Section 101 of the Patent Act states that a patent may be granted to the discoverer of a "new and useful" invention. Article 1, Section 8 of the Constitution also speaks of promoting the "useful arts." From these sources, the courts have derived the rule that an invention must be useful before it can be patented.[17] This is known as the utility requirement.[18]

A broad range of inventions are considered useful in terms of patentability, even if they serve a relatively trivial purpose. In addition to patents on such clearly useful inventions as microchips and pharmaceuticals, one can find many patents claiming toys, novelties, and the like. If they serve their purpose, they are sufficiently useful to receive a patent.[19] The only kinds of invention categorically excluded from patentability on grounds of nonutility are those whose purpose is deemed illegal or immoral. Until 1977, gambling machines were held to lack utility.[20] The exclusion still applies to any inven-

---

[15] *Diamond Scientific,* 848 F.2d at 1224; *see also* Mentor Graphics Corp. v. Quickturn Design Sys., Inc., 150 F.3d 1374, 1378 (Fed. Cir. 1998) ("Without exceptional circumstances (such as an express reservation by the assignor of the right to challenge the validity of the patent or an express waiver of the assignee of the right to assert assignor estoppel), one who assigns a patent surrenders with that assignment the right to later challenge the validity of the assigned patent.").

[16] *See* Shamrock Technologies, Inc. v. Medical Sterilization, Inc., 903 F.2d 789, 793 (Fed. Cir. 1990).

[17] *See* Stiftung v. Renishaw PLC, 945 F.2d 1173, 1180 (Fed. Cir. 1991).

[18] The concept of utility does not apply to design patents, discussed in Section 12.1.

[19] "The threshold of utility is not high: An invention is 'useful' under section 101 if it is capable of providing some identifiable benefit." Juicy Whip, Inc. v. Orange Bang, Inc., 185 F.3d 1364, 1366 (Fed. Cir. 1999). One patent demonstrating the potential breadth of the concept of utility is U.S. patent No. 5,457,821, entitled "Hat Simulating a Fried Egg." According to the specification, "[t]he hat finds utility, for example, as an attention-getting item in connection with promotional activities at trade shows, conventions, and the like. Further the hat is useful in connection with egg sale promotions in the egg industry." Perhaps a design patent would have been more appropriate. See Section 12.1.

[20] *See* Tol-O-Matic, Inc. v. Proma Produkt-Und Marketing Gesellschaft M.b.H, 945 F.2d 1546, 1552 (Fed. Cir. 1991).

tion useful only in committing a crime or fraud–for example, a method of counterfeiting currency.[21]

One of the more curious utility cases of recent years is *Juicy Whip, Inc. v. Orange Bang, Inc.*,[22] where the invention was a beverage dispenser, like one might see at the concession stand of a movie theater, which *appeared* to dispense the beverage from a supply in a glass bowl. In fact, the beverage was mixed elsewhere just as it was dispensed. The latter is more practical, but somehow less tempting to purchasers.[23] Even though the purpose of the invention was to mislead consumers, the court found that the invention had utility. As the court observed, "[i]t is not at all unusual for a product to be designed to appear to viewers to be something it is not." Examples include imitation diamonds and simulated leather.[24] Even if the practice is deceptive, it is the task of other government agencies, not the Patent Office, to protect consumers from such deception.[25] In any event, the case illustrates how inclusive the concept of utility has become.

Although it might be argued that an invention is useful only if it is an improvement over the prior art, this is not required. An invention can still be patented even if it is inferior to, or no better than, existing devices or methods.[26] As the Federal Circuit has observed, "[a]n invention need not be the best or the only way to accomplish a certain result, and it need only be useful to some extent and in certain applications."[27]

It would be difficult, and perhaps pointless, for the Patent Office to attempt to assess in every case whether the claimed invention is really an improvement. Although an invention is inferior to its predecessors in some respects, it may be superior in others. In many cases, the advantages of a particular invention cannot be fully appreciated until long after it is patented. In the end, the Patent Office is simply not in the business of judging

[21] "'All that the law requires is that the invention should not be frivolous, or injurious to the well-being, good policy, or good morals of society. The word *useful* therefore is incorporated into the act in contradistinction to mischievous or immoral.'" *Tol-O-Matic*, 945 F.2d at 1553 (emphasis in original). Even the exception for inventions with immoral or illegal purposes "has not been applied broadly in recent years." *Juicy Whip*, 185 F.3d at 1366–67.

[22] 185 F.3d 1364 (Fed. Cir. 1999).

[23] "The display bowl is said to stimulate impulse buying by providing the consumer with a visual beverage display. A premix display bowl, however, has a limited capacity and is subject to contamination by bacteria." *Juicy Whip*, 185 F.3d at 1365.

[24] *Juicy Whip*, 185 F.3d at 1367. The comparison may be a bit unfair. Imitation goods may *substitute* for the real thing without, necessarily, *fooling* anyone. The purpose of the beverage dispenser seems to have been only to mislead.

[25] *Juicy Whip*, 185 F.3d at 1368.

[26] Demaco Corp. v. F. Von Langsdorff Licensing Ltd., 851 F.2d 1387, 1390 (Fed. Cir. 1988) ("The patent statute does not require that a patentable invention be superior to all prior devices.").

[27] *Stiftung*, 945 F.2d at 1180; *see also* Envirotech Corp. v. Al George, Inc., 730 F.2d 753, 762 (Fed. Cir. 1984) ("the fact that an invention has only limited utility and is only operable in certain applications is not grounds for finding lack of utility").

whether one invention is better than another. This is one reason why the popular conception of a patent as an award for technological achievement is misguided. In spite of the frequent attempts of advertising to imply that a product is "so good it's patented," patents are a reflection of novelty, not of merit.

Inventions are required to achieve a minimum level of operability, since an invention that fails to work at all cannot be said to have utility.[28] In most cases, the Patent Office accepts the applicant's representation that the invention is operable; the Patent Office is not equipped to perform experiments to test whether an invention works as advertised. Occasionally, however, the nature of the invention raises suspicions. Applications for perpetual motion machines, which are impossible according to the most fundamental principles of physics, are sometimes submitted. When the Patent Office receives an application for an invention that so defies conventional wisdom, the applicant may be required to come forward with experimental evidence demonstrating that the invention actually does work.[29] In one case where the claimed device purported to produce more energy than it consumed, the Patent Office arranged for tests to be conducted by the Bureau of Standards. Unfortunately, the tests were not a success.[30]

New pharmaceuticals present a special problem because years of testing may be required to demonstrate that they are safe and effective. In *In re Brana*,[31] the Federal Circuit held that animal studies could provide sufficient evidence of utility, even though FDA approval would require further testing.[32] The court explained that if full FDA approval were required before a patent could be granted, the costs would discourage some companies from patenting, and perhaps from developing, potentially important discoveries.

[28] Process Control Corp. v. Hydreclaim Corp., 190 F.3d 1350, 1358 (Fed. Cir. 1999); *Tol-O-Matic*, 945 F.2d at 1553 (referring to the "total incapacity" that could lead to a finding of non-utility). On the other hand, if a claimed invention achieves some of its objectives, but not others, it will still be deemed to have utility. *Stiftung*, 945 F.2d at 1180 ("'When a properly claimed invention meets at least one stated objective, utility under § 101 is clearly shown.'"). Note that if a claimed invention is an impossibility, the patent fails on grounds of enablement (see Section 8.6) as well as utility. *Process Control*, 190 F.3d at 1358.

[29] One example of an invention met with skepticism is discussed in *Fregau v. Mossinghoff*, 776 F.2d 1034 (Fed. Cir. 1985). The claimed method was supposed to enhance the density and flavor of beverages by passing them through a magnetic field. The Patent Office did not consider the experimental evidence offered by the applicant convincing. Curiously, the Patent Office also found several examples of close, and equally unbelievable, prior art.

[30] *See* Newman v. Quigg, 877 F.2d 1575 (Fed. Cir. 1989). Inventions based on cold fusion are currently treated with great skepticism, but baldness cures have entered the realm of the believable. *See In re* Swartz, 232 F.3d 862 (Fed. Cir. 2000) (cold fusion); *In re* Cortright, 165 F.3d 1353 (Fed. Cir. 1999) (baldness cures).

[31] 51 F.3d 1560 (Fed. Cir. 1995).

[32] "Usefulness in patent law, and in particular in the context of pharmaceutical inventions, necessarily includes the expectation of further research and development. The stage at which an invention in this field becomes useful is well before it is ready to be administered to humans." *Brana*, 51 F.3d at 1568.

A patent specification must disclose the utility of the claimed invention, so difficulties can arise if it is unclear from the specification what the invention is supposed to do. This is rarely, if ever, the case with apparatus claims, but it can occur when the invention is a chemical compound and the application fails to specify how the compound should be used. To state, for example, that a compound can be used to form a "film" may be an inadequate statement of utility, if the usefulness of such a film is not clear.[33] These problems are most likely to arise when the applicant attempts to rely on a foreign patent application in order to establish priority.[34] This is because other countries have different requirements regarding the disclosure of utility in a patent application.[35]

Although the Patent Office has limited means to challenge claims on grounds of inoperability or impossibility, this is not necessarily the case in litigation. A party charged with patent infringement may offer evidence demonstrating that whatever is required by the claim is either physically impossible or useless.[36] On the other hand, if a claim actually has been infringed, a court will be reluctant to find that the invention lacks utility. As one court observed, "People rarely, if ever, appropriate useless inventions."[37]

8.5 DEFINITENESS

The function of patent claims is to identify what is covered by the patent. If patent infringement can be compared to trespassing, the claims serve as the boundary markers that define what is, or is not, an encroachment on the inventor's exclusive territory.[38] The law therefore requires that the claims have a definite meaning understandable to those skilled in the art. This requirement is embodied in the second paragraph of 35 U.S.C. § 112, which provides that the "specification shall conclude with one or more claims particularly pointing out and distinctly claiming the subject matter which the applicant regards as his invention."

---

[33] *See In re* Ziegler, 992 F.2d 1197, 1201–1203 (Fed. Cir. 1993).
[34] See Section 12.3.
[35] *See* Cross v. Iizuka, 753 F.2d 1040 (Fed. Cir. 1985).
[36] *See* Raytheon Co. v. Roper Corp., 724 F.2d 951, 956–57 (Fed. Cir. 1983).
[37] *Raytheon*, 724 F.2d at 959.
[38] *See* S3 Inc. v. Nvidia Corp., 259 F.3d 1364, 1369 (Fed. Cir. 2001) ("The purpose of claims is not to explain the technology or how it works, but to state the legal boundaries of the patent grant.").

The test for compliance is whether a person experienced in the field of the invention, reading the claims and the patent specification, would understand the scope of the subject matter covered by the claims.[39] If the claims are so vague or unclear that those in the industry cannot reasonably determine what does or does not infringe the patent,[40] the claims may be held unpatentable or invalid.[41] Yet because language is inherently imprecise, the law requires only such precision in claim drafting as the subject matter permits.[42] In *Orthokinetics, Inc. v. Safety Travel Chairs, Inc.*,[43] for example, the patent claimed a wheel chair with a part "so dimensioned" that it could be inserted in the space between the seats and doorframe of an automobile. The claim did not state exactly what those dimensions should be, nor could it have stated them precisely since they would vary depending on the model of the automobile (although the dimensions for any particular automobile could be obtained easily). The court held that the claim language was not indefinite, because it was as precise as the subject matter permitted: "The patent law does not require that all possible lengths corresponding to the spaces in hundreds of different automobiles be listed in the patent, let alone that they be listed in the claims."[44]

The test for indefiniteness is whether the claim language is understandable when read in light of the specification. One function of the specification

[39] *See* Intellectual Property Development Inc. v. UA-Columbia Cablevision of Westchester Inc., 336 F.3d 1308, 1319 (Fed. Cir. 2003); LNP Eng'g Plastics, Inc. v. Miller Waste Mills, Inc., 275 F.3d 1374, 1359 (Fed. Cir. 2001); *S3*, 259 F.3d at 1367; Morton Int'l, Inc. v. Cardinal Chemical Co., 5 F.3d 1464, 1470 (Fed. Cir. 1993); Shatterproof Glass Corp. v. Libbey-Owens Ford Co., 758 F.2d 613, 624 (Fed. Cir. 1985) ("'[i]f the claims, read in light of the specification, reasonably apprise those skilled in the art both of the utilization and scope of the invention, and if the language is as precise as the subject matter permits, the courts can demand no more.'"). Like enablement, discussed in Section 8.6, definiteness is determined from the perspective of one skilled in the art at the time the patent application was filed. W.L. Gore & Assoc, Inc. v. Garlock, Inc., 721 F.2d 1540, 1557 (Fed. Cir. 1983).
[40] *See* All Dental Prodx, LLC v. Advantage Dental Prods., Inc., 309 F.3d 774, 779–80 (Fed. Cir. 2002) ("'The primary purpose of the definiteness requirement is to ensure that the claims are written in such a way that they give notice to the public of the extent of the legal protection afforded by the patent, so that interested members of the public, *e.g.*, competitors of the patent owner, can determine whether or not they infringe.'"); *see also* Oakley, Inc. v. Sunglass Hut Int'l, 316 F.3d 1331, 1340 (Fed. Cir. 2003).
[41] Recently, the Federal Circuit has described the indefiniteness threshold as "somewhat high"–requiring a claim that is "insolubly ambiguous" and impossible to narrow. *See* Amgen, Inc. v. Hoechst Marion Roussel, Inc., 314 F.3d 1313, 1342 (Fed. Cir. 2003). A claim is not indefinite merely because its terms are difficult to understand or because reasonable persons might reach different conclusions. Bancorp Services L.L.C. v. Hartford Life Insurance Co., 359 F.3d 1367, 1372 (Fed. Cir. 2004).
[42] Hybritech Inc. v. Monoclonal Antibodies, Inc., 802 F.2d 1367, 1385 (Fed. Cir. 1986); *see also* *S3*, 259 F.3d at 1367. It has been observed that a patent claim is "'one of the most difficult legal instruments to draw with accuracy.'" Slimfold Mfg. Co. v. Kinkead Indus., Inc., 810 F.2d 1113, 1117 (Fed. Cir. 1987).
[43] 806 F.2d 1565 (Fed. Cir. 1986).
[44] *Orthokinetics*, 806 F.2d at 1576.

is to serve as a dictionary or glossary for any claim terms that might have a specialized meaning.[45] The specification may provide a specific definition for otherwise vague claim language, or it may provide a test for measuring whether a product falls within the intended meaning of the claim.[46] Even if some experimentation is required to determine the boundaries of the claim, the claim will not be held indefinite if the language is as precise as the subject matter permits.[47] The prosecution history also may provide information to clarify the meaning of a disputed term.[48]

In spite of the requirement that claims use definite language, words of degree such as *generally, approximately,* and *substantially equal to* are commonly used.[49] Although these terms are inherently inexact, they are often tolerated because they are "as precise as the subject matter permits." For example, in *Rosemount, Inc. v. Beckman Instruments, Inc.*,[50] the patent claims described a device for measuring pH, having one component "in close proximity" to another. The court found that "close proximity" was a term used and understood in the industry. Had the inventor been forced to specify a precise dimension (e.g., "within .5 centimeters"), the claim would likely have been narrower than the true scope of the invention. Moreover, requiring a precise definition of *close proximity* in the patent specification would "turn the construction of a patent into a mere semantic quibble that serves no useful purpose."[51]

On the other hand, a court will treat words of degree with suspicion if, in litigation, the patentee argues that the term is broad enough to encompass the accused product but narrow enough to avoid the prior art, with no suggestion as to where the line in-between should be drawn. In *Amgen, Inc. v. Chugai Pharmaceuticals Co.*,[52] the patentee claimed a protein

---

[45] *See* Beachcombers, Int'l, Inc. v. Wildwood Creative Products, Inc., 31 F.3d 1154, 1158 (Fed. Cir. 1994) ("As we have repeatedly said, a patentee can be his own lexicographer provided the patentee's definition, to the extent it differs from the conventional definition, is clearly set forth in the specification.").

[46] *See* Seattle Box Co. v. Industrial Crating & Packing, Inc., 731 F.2d 818, 826 (Fed. Cir. 1984); *Shatterproof Glass,* 758 F.2d at 624; *W.L. Gore,* 721 F.2d at 1557–58.

[47] "[T]he fact that some experimentation may be necessary to determine the scope of the claims does not render the claims indefinite." Exxon Research & Eng'g Co. v. U.S., 265 F.3d 1371, 1379 (Fed. Cir. 2001).

[48] *See All Dental Prodx,* 309 F.3d at 780 ("The prosecution history can . . . be relied upon to clarify claim meaning and hence provide definiteness."); Texas Instruments Inc. v. U.S. Int'l Trade Comm'n, 871 F.2d 1054, 1063 (Fed. Cir. 1989) ("The public is entitled to know the scope of the claims but must look to both the patent specification and the prosecution history, especially where there is doubt concerning the scope of the claims.").

[49] *See* Andrew Corp. v. Gabriel Elec., Inc., 847 F.2d 819, 821 (Fed. Cir. 1988).

[50] 727 F.2d 1540 (Fed. Cir. 1984).

[51] *Rosemount,* 727 F.2d at 1547. The Patent Office guidelines also require only a "reasonable degree of particularity and distinctness." M.P.E.P. § 2173.02. "Some latitude in the manner of expression and the aptness of terms should be permitted even though the claim language is not as precise as the examiner might desire." *Id. See also Oakley,* 316 F.3d at 1341 ("a patentee need not define his invention with mathematical precision").

[52] 927 F.2d 1200 (Fed. Cir. 1991).

having a "specific activity" of "at least about 160,000 IU/AU." A prior art product exhibited a specific activity of 128,620 IU/AU. Because nothing in the claims, the specification, the prosecution history, or the prior art provided any hint as to whether, for example, a protein having a specific activity of 145,000 IU/AU would come within the scope of the claims, the court held that the term "about" was insufficiently definite in the context of that particular patent.

When a claim is drafted in reasonably definite terms, it provides competitors of the patent owner with fair warning of what will or will not infringe the patent. If claim language is vague, competitors must proceed at their peril, and the uncertainty provides the patent owner with what is, in effect, a broader claim. However, the laudable effects of the definiteness requirement are undermined to some extent by the *doctrine of equivalents*.[53] According to that doctrine, even a product that is not literally described by the claim language may infringe, if the differences are "insubstantial." The effect is to add an extra dimension of uncertainty to every patent claim. The tension between the definiteness requirement and the doctrine of equivalents is one of the reasons that the latter doctrine, though long established, is often criticized.[54]

8.6 ENABLEMENT

As discussed in Section 1.1, a patent can be regarded as a bargain between the inventor and the public. In exchange for a monopoly on the invention for a period of years, the inventor must disclose the invention in such clear terms that, when the patent has expired, the public at large can take advantage of the invention. This concept is behind the *enablement* and *best mode* requirements.[55] The enablement requirement is derived from the following language of 35 U.S.C. § 112:

> The specification shall contain a written description of the invention, and of the manner and process of making and using it, in such full, clear, concise, and exact terms as to *enable* any person skilled in the art to which it pertains, or with which it is most nearly connected, to make and use the same.

To satisfy the enablement requirement, the patent must describe the invention in such clear and exact terms that persons "skilled in the art"[56] can make and use the invention without "undue experimentation."[57] Because

---

[53] *See* Section 10.6.

[54] *See* Section 10.6.3.

[55] The enablement requirement also helps to fix the date of invention for purposes of determining priority. See Section 8.9.2. The inclusion of an enabling disclosure in a patent application demonstrates that the applicant had a completed invention no later than the filing date.

[56] *See* Section 8.9.6.

[57] Amgen, Inc. v. Hoechst Marion Roussel, Inc., 314 F.3d 1313, 1334 (Fed. Cir. 2003); Process Control Corp. v. Hydreclaim Corp., 190 F.3d 1350, 1358 (Fed. Cir. 1999); Enzo Biochem, Inc. v. Calgene, Inc., 188 F.3d 1362, 1371 (Fed. Cir. 1999).

patents are intended to be read and used by those skilled in the art, the specification need not include information that such persons would already know.[58] A patent on an improved radio antenna, for example, need not disclose the entire theory and practice of how to build a radio, beginning with Marconi. Persons skilled in the radio art would know the basics already and would only have to be informed of the inventor's improvement in order to take advantage of the invention.[59]

It is also not required that a patent disclosure be so detailed that the invention can be practiced without experimentation. The only requirement is that such experimentation not be "undue."[60] The definition of *undue* varies depending on the nature of the invention and expectations in the industry.[61] Experimentation that takes a great deal of time may not be considered undue if the experiments are routine, and the specification provides clear guidance as to what must be done. In the biotechnology industry, for example, isolating cells that will produce a desired antibody may require testing many cells and discarding all but a few. If such screening is routine and the patent specification tells the experimenter how to proceed, the patent will still be considered enabling.[62] The test is whether, under the circumstances, the amount of experimentation required would be unreasonable.

Sometimes patentees risk violating the enablement requirement when they attempt to reserve as a trade secret some piece of information necessary to practice the claimed invention.[63] In one case, a patentee obtained claims to a machine tool control system but did not disclose the proprietary software that made the system work.[64] Without better evidence that commercially available software could be substituted, the court found the patent nonenabling. To have constructed the necessary software from scratch would have required 1 1/2 to 2 years of "undue" experimentation. On the other hand, another patent that failed to disclose software necessary to prac-

---

[58] "[A] patent need not teach, and preferably omits, what is well known in the art." Hybritech Inc. v. Monoclonal Antibodies, Inc., 802 F.2d 1367, 1384 (Fed. Cir. 1986).

[59] *See* S3 Inc. v. Nvidia Corp., 259 F.3d 1364, 1371 (Fed. Cir. 2001) ("The law is clear that patent documents need not include subject matter that is known in the field of the invention and is in the prior art, for patents are written for persons experienced in the field of the invention. . . . To hold otherwise would require every patent document to include a technical treatise for the unskilled reader. Although an accommodation to the 'common experience' of lay persons may be feasible, it is an unnecessary burden for inventors and has long been rejected as a requirement of patent disclosures."); Ajinomoto Co. v. Archer-Daniels-Midland Co., 228 F.3d 1338, 1346–47 (Fed. Cir. 2000) (offering similar observations in the context of the best mode requirement).

[60] *See Enzo*, 188 F.3d at 1371 ("'The key word is "undue," not "experimentation."'").

[61] Factors to consider may include the amount of experimentation required, the presence or absence of guidance in the patent disclosure, the skill of those practicing in the field, and the extent to which the art is "predictable." *See Enzo*, 188 F.3d at 1371.

[62] *See In re* Wands, 858 F.2d 731 (Fed. Cir. 1988).

[63] *See* Section 2.3.

[64] White Consolidated Indus. v. Vega Servo-Control, Inc., 713 F.2d 788 (Fed. Cir. 1983).

tice the invention was held to be valid because writing the necessary software would have been a comparatively quick and straightforward task for an experienced programmer.[65]

In the case of inventions that depend on the use of living materials, such as microorganisms or cultured cells, words alone may be insufficient to enable one skilled in the art to make and use the invention. A sample of the biological materials may be necessary to begin. In such cases, inventors can satisfy the enablement requirement by depositing samples of the material in a certified depository where they are available to researchers in the field.[66] In other cases, it may be sufficient to direct researchers to commercial sources of supply or provide them with the directions necessary to produce the materials for themselves.

As far as the enablement requirement is concerned, the specification need disclose only some manner in which the invention can be practiced. It need not disclose every manner of practicing the invention, or even the best manner.[67] It is also not required that the inventor understand or disclose the principles that make the invention work, as long as it does work. If the specification provides the information needed to make and use the invention, the patentee's theory as to why it works can be completely wrong.[68]

Whether a specification is enabling is measured retrospectively based on the resources available when the patent application was filed. Later developments in the art are irrelevant.[69] If the invention requires a skill that was developed only after the filing date of the patent application, the patent cannot be considered enabling. By the same token, if a patent was enabling as of its filing date, no later developments in the art can undo that fact. A patent on a bulletproof vest could be enabling as of its filing date and remain a valid patent, even though later advancements in weaponry rendered the disclosed embodiments ineffective.

---

[65] Northern Telecom, Inc. v. Datapoint Corp., 908 F.2d 931 (Fed. Cir. 1990). The absence of a specific disclosure of software is also a potential best mode violation. See Section 8.7. However, "it is generally sufficient if the functions of the software are disclosed, it usually being the case that creation of the specific source code is within the skill of the art." Robotic Vision Sys., Inc. v. View Eng'g Inc., 112 F.3d 1163, 1166 (Fed. Cir. 1997).

[66] *See* 37 C.F.R. § 1.802; M.P.E.P. § 2401 *et seq; Ajinomoto*, 228 F.3d at 1345–46.

[67] Engel Indus., Inc. v. Lockformer Co., 946 F.2d 1528, 1533 (Fed. Cir. 1991). Failure to disclose the best manner known to the inventor may violate the best mode requirement. See Section 8.7.

[68] *See Process Control*, 190 F.3d at 1359 ("an otherwise valid patent covering a meritorious invention should not be struck down simply because of the patentee's misconceptions about scientific principles concerning the invention"); *In re* Cortright, 165 F.3d 1353, 1359 (Fed. Cir. 1999) ("'[I]t is not a requirement of patentability that an inventor correctly set forth, or even know, how or why the invention works.'"); Newman v. Quigg, 877 F.2d 1575, 1581 (Fed. Cir. 1989).

[69] *See* Plant Genetic Sys., N.V. v. DeKalb Genetics Corp., 315 F.3d 1335, 1339 (Fed. Cir. 2003); *Enzo*, 188 F.3d at 1371; *In re* Wright, 999 F.2d at 1557, 1562–63 (Fed. Cir. 1993).

8.6.1 Scope of Enablement

Some of the most troubling enablement questions arise when the patent claims are substantially broader than the specific embodiments disclosed in the specification. Patent claims can be, and often are, generic. For example, a claim might (hypothetically) cover *every* mousetrap that included the combination of (1) a spring, (2) a latch, and (3) a trigger to unhook the latch and release the spring when disturbed by a mouse. The specification might disclose in detail only *one* example of such a trap—with a particular kind of spring, latch, and trigger. If the claim covers other versions of the trap that are not discussed at all, is the specification adequate to enable one skilled in the art to practice the claimed invention?

It is often said that the enabling disclosure in the specification must be "commensurate in scope" with the breadth of the claims.[70] However, the rules to be applied generally depend on the kind of invention that is claimed. If the invention is a mechanical one or an electrical circuit, the art is regarded as *predictable*, meaning that if one embodiment of the invention is disclosed, persons skilled in the art will understand how to make and use other variations.[71] If, for example, the specification discloses a plastic spring for the mousetrap, persons skilled in the art will know how to substitute a steel spring.

Other arts, such as chemistry and biotechnology, are considered relatively *unpredictable*. Even a tiny change in the structure of a molecule may have large and unanticipated effects. Here, the patentee may be forced to

---

[70] *See, e.g.,* Chiron Corp. v. Genetech Inc., 363 F.3d 1247, 1253 (Fed. Cir. 2004); Amgen, Inc. v. Chugai Pharmaceutical Co., 927 F.2d 1200, 1213 (Fed. Cir. 1991); *see also* National Recovery Technologies, Inc. v. Magnetic Separation Sys., Inc., 166 F.3d 1190, 1195–96 (Fed. Cir. 1999) ("The enablement requirement ensures that the public knowledge is enriched by the patent specification to a degree at least commensurate with the scope of the claims. The scope of the claims must be less than or equal to the scope of the enablement."). Some cases state that the patent specification must enable "the full scope of the claimed invention." *See, e.g., Chiron,* 363 F.3d at 1253; Plant Genetic Sys., N.V. v. DeKalb Genetics Corp., 315 F.3d 1335, 1339 (Fed. Cir. 2003); Durel Corp. v. Osram Sylvania, Inc., 256 F.3d 1298, 1306 (Fed. Cir. 2001). However, the expertise of those skilled in the art, and the possibility of routine experimentation, may serve to "'fill gaps, interpolate between embodiments, and perhaps even extrapolate beyond the disclosed embodiments, depending upon the predictability of the art.'" *Chiron,* 363 F.3d at 1253. "Pioneer" inventions, which establish an entirely new field of inquiry (see Section 10.6.7), may support broad claims, but they are subject to the same requirement that the claims "bear a reasonable correlation to the scope of enablement." *See Plant Genetic Sys.,* 315 F.3d at 1339–40. "Nacent technologies" demand a "specific and useful teaching." *Chiron,* 363 F.3d at 1254. On the other hand, "[t]he law does not expect an applicant to disclose knowledge invented or developed after the filing date. Such disclosure would be impossible." *Id.* These various pronouncements clearly leave counsel much room for argument.

[71] "If an invention pertains to an art where the results are predictable, e.g., the mechanical as opposed to the chemical arts, a broad claim can be enabled by disclosure of a single embodiment. . . ." Spectra-Physics, Inc. v. Coherent, Inc., 827 F.2d 1524, 1533 (Fed. Cir. 1987).

draft claims that are more limited in scope and closer to the specific embodiments disclosed in the specification. One patentee claimed all possible sequences of DNA that would produce the protein EPO, which stimulates the production of red blood cells, or any analog of EPO that would have a similar effect.[72] The specification disclosed the information needed to prepare EPO and just a few of its analogs. The court found that the number of possible DNA sequences within the scope of the claim vastly outstripped the enabling disclosure: "There may be many other genetic sequences that code for EPO-type products. [The patentee] has told us how to make and use only a few of them and is therefore not entitled to claim all of them."[73]

This distinction between the predictable and unpredictable arts strikes some as unsatisfactory. If a claim in the mechanical arts can be considered enabled even though it encompasses embodiments that are "inadequately disclosed" in the specification,[74] of what use is the predictability of the art? Is it true that mechanical contrivances are invariably more predictable than chemistry? Where do newer arts, such as that of computer programming, fall? But for now, at least, it is clear that broad claims will be more readily tolerated in the mechanical and electrical arts than in the arts of chemistry and biotechnology.

8.7 BEST MODE

The *best mode* requirement, like the enablement requirement, arises from the language of 35 U.S.C. § 112, which provides that a specification "shall set forth the best mode contemplated by the inventor for carrying out his invention." The best mode means the best manner of practicing the invention, or the best operative example, known to the inventor. If the inventor of a hypothetical mousetrap envisioned two variants of the claimed invention, one using an inferior plastic spring and the other a superior steel spring, the best mode requirement would demand that the better embodiment be disclosed in the patent, even though both came within the scope of the generic claim.

Like the enablement requirement, the best mode requirement reflects the bargain model of patent law. If a patentee is to be awarded a monopoly on an invention for a period of years, the public is entitled to disclosure of the best that the patentee has to offer. If there were no best mode requirement, patentees might be tempted to disclose the least effective or most impractical embodiments of their inventions, perhaps reserving the better embodi-

[72] *Amgen*, 927 F.2d at 1212–14.
[73] *Amgen*, 927 F.2d at 1213–14.
[74] *Spectra-Physics*, 827 F.2d at 1533.

ments as trade secrets. The result would do little to advance the "useful arts."[75]

Where the enablement requirement can be satisfied by the disclosure of *any* operable mode of practicing the invention, the best mode requirement compels disclosure of the one mode believed by the inventor to be the best.[76] The relevant time period is the time at which the patent application was filed, and the relevant perspective is that of the inventor.[77] If the inventor believed the disclosed mode to be the best, the best mode requirement is satisfied even if the inventor was mistaken at the time, or even if other modes were later discovered that even the inventor would acknowledge as better than the one disclosed in the patent specification. The patent does not have to be updated to disclose later-discovered improvements.[78]

Because satisfaction of the best mode requirement is dependent on the subjective beliefs of the inventor, violation of the requirement may be difficult to prove. Sometimes in litigation the inventor's contemporaneous documents are used to show that a better mode was recognized but not disclosed.[79] One can also consider the means adopted by the patentee for commercializing the invention. For example, in *Northern Telecom, Inc. v. Datapoint Corp.*,[80] the patent described a system for capturing data on standard audiocassettes. Employees of the patent owner testified that cassettes with special characteristics, different from those of ordinary audiocassettes, had been ordered by the patent owner for its own use. This evidence helped to establish a violation of the best mode requirement.[81]

The best mode requirement also has an objective component: Was the best mode known to the inventor at the time the patent application was filed *dis-*

---

[75] "[T]he best mode requirement . . . ensure[s] that a patent applicant plays 'fair and square' with the patent system. It is a requirement that the *quid pro quo* of the patent grant be satisfied. One must not receive the right to exclude others unless at the time of filing he has provided an adequate disclosure of the best mode known to him of carrying out the invention." Amgen, Inc. v. Chugai Pharmaceutical Co., 927 F.2d 1200, 1209–10 (Fed. Cir. 1991). In some cases, a better mode may have been devised by someone other than the inventor, after the date of invention but before the filing of the patent application. If the inventor is aware of this better mode before the application is filed, it must be disclosed in the specification, even though it does not represent the inventor's own work, and he could not claim it in the patent. *See* Graco, Inc. v. Binks Mfg. Co., 60 F.3d 785, 789 (Fed. Cir. 1995).

[76] *See* Teleflex, Inc. v. Ficosa North America Corp., 299 F.3d 1313, 1330 (Fed. Cir. 2002) (distinguishing between best mode and enablement requirements).

[77] *See* Bayer A.G. v. Schein Pharmaceuticals, Inc., 301 F.3d 1306, 1314 (Fed. Cir. 2002) ("Unlike enablement, the existence of a best mode is a purely subjective matter depending upon what the inventor actually believed at the time the application was filed.").

[78] *See* Transco Prods. Inc. v. Performance Contracting, Inc., 38 F.3d 551 (Fed. Cir. 1994). Constant changes in patent disclosures, to account for progressive improvements in technology, might cause more administrative difficulties than the benefits would warrant. The addition of new disclosure might also cause difficulty in applying the "new matter" rules. See Section 5.2.

[79] *See, e.g.,* Dana Corp. v. IPC Ltd. Partnership, 860 F.2d 415, 418–420 (Fed. Cir. 1988).

[80] 908 F.2d 931 (Fed. Cir. 1990).

[81] *Northern Telecom,* 908 F.2d at 940.

closed in the application in such clear terms that persons skilled in the art, reviewing the patent specification, would recognize it as the best mode and have sufficient information to practice it themselves?[82] Even if the specification includes a general reference to the best mode, the reference may be so lacking in detail that, as a practical matter, the best mode is concealed.[83] Alternatively, the best mode may be disclosed together with so many inferior modes that the best mode is inadequately differentiated.[84] The determination of whether the best mode was adequately disclosed must take into account the level of skill in the art and the extent to which particular information would be understood by those of ordinary skill, even if it were not made explicit.[85]

Although a patent specification must reveal the inventor's best mode of practicing the invention, the level of detail that must be included is not unlimited. The focus is on the invention *as claimed*.[86] The specification need not be equivalent to a "product specification" or a blueprint for mass production. It need not, for example, disclose all of the dimensions, tolerances, drawings, and other information that a factory foreman would need to gear up for production.[87] Such detailed information would be impractical to include in every patent, and it would be an unnecessary gift to the patentee's competitors. Still, the line between best mode and product specification can be a difficult one to draw.

In *Christianson v. Colt Industries*,[88] the court held that patents to various parts of the M-16 rifle were not invalid, even though they failed to disclose the dimensions and tolerances that would have been necessary for others to manufacture interchangeable parts. Because interchangeability was not required by the claims, the production details were deemed separable from

---

[82] *See Bayer*, 301 F.3d at 1320; Eli Lilly & Co. v. Barr Labs., Inc., 222 F.3d 973, 981 (Fed. Cir. 2000); Fonar Corp. v. General Electric Co., 107 F.3d 1543, 1548 (Fed. Cir. 1997).

[83] *See* U.S. Gypsum Co. v. National Gypsum Co., 74 F.3d 1209, 1215 (Fed. Cir. 1996); Spectra-Physics, Inc. v. Coherent, Inc., 827 F.2d 1524, 1536 (Fed. Cir. 1987).

[84] *See* Randomex, Inc. v. Scopus Corp., 849 F.2d 585, 592 (Fed. Cir. 1988) (Mayer, J., dissenting).

[85] *See* Chemcast Corp. v. Arco Indus. Corp., 913 F.2d 923, 927 (Fed. Cir. 1990). On the other hand, the best mode requirement cannot be satisfied *solely* by reference to information already known in the art. *Bayer*, 301 F.3d at 1314. The applicant still must *disclose* the best mode. *See* Robotic Vision Sys., Inc. v. View Eng'g, Inc., 112 F.3d 1163, 1165 (Fed. Cir. 1997) ("While a disclosure . . . is to be understood from the standpoint of one skilled in the relevant art, a certain basic disclosure is needed of the best mode."). It would not be sufficient, for example, that one skilled in the art could discover the best mode by reviewing technical literature in the field. *See Bayer*, 301 F.3d at 1314 ("Because of the subjective nature of the best mode inquiry, the best mode disclosure requirement—unlike enablement—cannot be met by mute reference to the knowledge of one of skill in the art. The reason is pragmatic. It is unreasonable if not impossible to require the ordinary artisan to peer into the inventor's mind to discover his or her idiosyncratic preferences as of the filing date. Rather, because the existence of a best mode of carrying out the invention is by definition known only to the inventor, section 112 demands actual disclosure regardless of whether, as an abstract matter, practicing that mode would be within the knowledge of one of ordinary skill in the art."). As is so often the case in patent law, there is only a fine distinction between evaluating the patent disclosure in light of knowledge available to those skilled in the art (which is permitted) and resorting to other sources to supply deficiencies in the patent disclosure (which is not permitted).

the best mode of the invention, even though, as a practical matter, the absence of those details would prevent others from competing in the market for rifle parts. The patents were still adequate to allow one to manufacture *a* rifle, even if it was not a rifle that the army, which required interchangeability with M-16 parts, would care to purchase.

Similarly, a patent applicant is not always required to disclose the details of components that may be used *with* the claimed invention but that are not part of the claimed invention itself. To borrow an analogy used by the court in *Randomex, Inc. v. Scopus Corp.*,[89] the inventor of a new engine might have to disclose the kind of fuel that was best for its operation, but the inventor of the engine would not have to disclose the best formula for making that fuel. It would be sufficient to disclose the fuel by brand name, as long as that brand, or its equivalent, was readily available. Engines and fuels are different arts, and a patent claiming only the engine need not disclose how to manufacture the fuel.

One case that put this principle to practice is *DeGeorge v. Bernier*,[90] where the claimed invention was electrical circuitry that would automatically indent paragraphs composed on a word processor. Even though the applicant did not disclose any details of the word processor, the court found no violation of the best mode requirement or the enablement requirement. The applicant did not claim to have invented a word processor, and one could practice the best mode of the *invention* even in conjunction with an inferior word processor.

---

[86] *See Bayer*, 301 F.3d at 1315; *Teleflex*, 299 F.3d at 1329–30 (best mode analysis "must begin and remain focused on the language of the claim," as opposed, for example, to "unclaimed subject matter relating to production details dictated by customer requirements"). Recent statements by the Federal Circuit suggest that an inventor need not disclose preferred methods of *making or using* the claimed invention, unless the claims show that such methods are a part of "carrying out the invention" or "materially affect[] the properties of the claimed invention." *See Bayer*, 301 F.3d at 1315. If the claim described the mechanical aspects of a novel mousetrap, the *enablement* requirement would demand an adequate description of how to make and use the trap without "undue experimentation." See Section 8.6. However, the inventor might not be required to disclose the *best* method of making or using the trap, so long as the claims were about the mechanical aspects of the trap, as opposed to its manufacture or use. The result would be different only if the inferior method of manufacture (or use) resulted in a mechanically inferior mousetrap. If a method of manufacture was disfavored because it was more expensive, but it produced an identical mousetrap, it would have nothing to do with "carrying out the invention" and need not be disclosed. In any event, the analysis in *Bayer* suggests a strong focus on the *claimed* invention, which may assist in resolving some difficult best mode issues.

[87] *See Bayer*, 301 F.3d at 1314–1315 (inventor's "every preference" need not be disclosed); *Teleflex*, 299 F.3d at 1331 ("[t]he best mode requirement does not extend to 'production details'").

[88] 822 F.2d 1544, 1562–63 (Fed. Cir. 1987).

[89] 849 F.2d 585, 590 (Fed. Cir. 1988).

[90] 768 F.2d 1318, 1324–25 (Fed. Cir. 1985).

Whether an inventor is required to disclose such information as the names of companies supplying parts or the trade names of ingredients used in the inventor's composition depends on the particular facts of the case.[91] If, for example, only one company sells an ingredient pure enough to produce an effective version of the patented compound, the inventor would probably be required to disclose the name of that company—at least if that information was not already generally known.[92] In other cases, the name of a supplier might be a convenience, but its absence would not prevent others from practicing the inventor's best mode.

Companies that have manufactured a product prior to the filing date of their patent are particularly vulnerable to claims of a best mode violation. Something can always be found in the patentee's product or in its manufacturing methods that was not disclosed in the patent. Whatever that thing is, it will be singled out by those challenging the validity of the patent, who will argue that the patentee must have considered that thing the best choice or the patentee would have chosen something else.[93] In the end, the court will have to decide whether that choice is sufficiently related to the claimed invention that it should have been disclosed as the best mode, or whether it is a choice that has little to do with the invention itself.

Some cases have suggested that the best mode requirement is violated only if the best mode was deliberately concealed.[94] Other cases, although still speaking of concealment, suggest the concealment can be unintentional.[95] The latter view seems to have prevailed.[96] However, whether or not the concealment was intentional can still have important consequences. Under some circumstances, intentional concealment of the best mode can be considered inequitable conduct[97] that will render all claims of the patent, and possibly those of related patents, unenforceable.[98]

---

[91] *See Transco,* 38 F.3d at 560.

[92] *See U.S. Gypsum,* 74 F.3d at 1214 (because the inventor did not know the composition of or method of manufacturing a critical ingredient, "he was required, at a minimum, to provide supplier/trade name information").

[93] *See* Wahl Instruments, Inc. v. Acvious, Inc., 950 F.2d 1575, 1581 (Fed. Cir. 1991). Here the knowledge of persons skilled in the art may be relevant: "[R]outine details" need not be disclosed where "one skilled in the art is aware of alternative means . . . that would still produce the best mode of the claimed invention." *Teleflex,* 299 F.3d at 1332; *see also Eli Lilly,* 222 F.3d at 981, 984. Disclosure of the best mode may be satisfactory even if "some experimentation is necessary." *Eli Lilly,* 222 F.3d at 984.

[94] "Invalidity for violation of the best mode requires intentional concealment of a better mode than was disclosed." Brooktree Corp. v. Advanced Micro Devices, Inc., 977 F.2d 1555, 1575 (Fed. Cir. 1992).

[95] "[O]nly evidence of 'concealment,' whether *accidental* or intentional, is considered." Spectra-Physics, Inc. v. Coherent, Inc., 827 F.2d 1524, 1535 (Fed. Cir. 1987) (emphasis added).

[96] *See U.S. Gypsum,* 74 F.3d at 1215–16.

[97] See Section 9.1.

[98] *See* Consolidated Aluminum Corp. v. Foseco Int'l, Ltd., 910 F.2d 804 (Fed. Cir. 1990) (application's disclosure was of a "fictitious" and "inoperable" mode).

A best mode violation occurs only if the best mode contemplated *by the inventor* is inadequately disclosed in the patent specification. Knowledge of better modes will not be imputed to the inventor through legal fictions. For example, if other engineers working for the same corporation knew of an improvement to the basic invention, but that improvement was not communicated to the inventor before the filing date of the patent, failure to disclose that improvement in the patent specification would not violate the best mode requirement.[99] This result might encourage a "head in the sand" mentality among corporations, who could isolate researchers just to avoid the disclosure of more information than necessary. On the other hand, § 112 literally refers only to the knowledge of the inventor, not the inventor's colleagues or employer, and it could be difficult to determine whether the inventor had been deliberately shielded from knowledge of improvements to his invention.

8.8 THE WRITTEN DESCRIPTION REQUIREMENT

Another requirement of a valid patent is the so-called *written description requirement*, taken from the following language of 35 U.S.C. § 112, ¶ 1:

> The specification shall contain a *written description* of the invention, and of the manner and process of making and using it, in such full, clear, concise, and exact terms as to enable any person skilled in the art to which it pertains, or with which it is most nearly connected, to make and use the same.

The written description requirement is one of the more nebulous concepts in patent law, in part because it is so easily confused with the definiteness and enablement requirements, and in part because its function seems largely redundant of those other tests. It is, after all, the function of the *claims* to describe the invention in precise terms.[100] Why should the *specification* be required to describe the invention? On the other hand, if the description simply means an *enabling disclosure*, as the remainder of the sentence seems to imply, why infer a description requirement as something distinct from the enablement requirement?

The Federal Circuit made some attempt to sort out the confusion in *Vas-Cath Inc. v. Mahurkar.*[101] As the court explained, the written description requirement can be characterized in part as an historical accident, traceable to the late eighteenth century when patents were not required to have claims. In those days, it was the function of the specification not only to enable the practice of the invention, but also to describe it so as to warn potential infringers. Today, the written description requirement most often comes into play where the claims have *changed* during prosecution of the patent application.

As discussed in Section 5.1, claim language is regularly changed or amended as a normal part of the process of patent prosecution. The patent examiner may object to the language of the claims as filed for any number of reasons, including the applicant's failure to distinguish the invention from the prior art. A common response to such an objection is to modify the language of the claims. An applicant may decide to modify the claims as filed, or add more claims, even without an objection from the examiner, if the applicant thinks of new and better ways to describe the invention. Such changes are allowed as long as the new claims are adequately supported by the specification *as filed*. In most cases, the specification does not change during prosecution.

The filing date of the patent application is often critical to establishing the priority of the invention—in other words, whether the applicant is entitled to a patent because he was the first to invent, or whether the applicant is not entitled to a patent because someone else invented first.[102] If an application was filed on a particular date, fully describing and enabling the practice of the invention, then the applicant's date of invention is, at the very latest, his filing date. Suppose, however, that the claims are amended during prosecution, so that they describe a new and different invention than what is disclosed in the original specification. In such a case, the date on which the patent application was filed would have no bearing on the actual date of invention. The written description requirement prevents this result by requiring a match between the invention as claimed and the invention as "described" in the specification. In some cases, the test is characterized as whether the claims are "adequately supported" by the specification,[103] or whether the specification was sufficient to demonstrate, to persons skilled in the art, that the applicant "possessed" the invention.[104] The description

---

[102] A foreign patent application can be of similar importance if the applicant relies on that application for his "filing date." See Section 12.3.

[103] *Vas-Cath*, 935 F.2d at 1560.

[104] *See* Moba, B.V. v. Diamond Automation, Inc., 325 F.3d 1306, 1320 (Fed. Cir. 2003) (the description requirement "has always required sufficient information in the original disclosure to show that the inventor possessed the invention at the time of the original filing"); Purdue Pharma L.P. v. Faulding Inc., 230 F.3d 1320, 1323 (Fed. Cir. 2000) ("Put another way, one skilled in the art, reading the original disclosure, must immediately discern the limitation at issue in the claims."); Lampi Corp. v. American Power Prods., Inc., 228 F.3d 1365, 1378 (Fed. Cir. 2000). Note that possession itself is not the issue, but the adequacy of the disclosure to *demonstrate* possession. Hence, the description requirement as a rule cannot be satisfied by other evidence, such as sworn testimony, that the applicant did possess (though he did not adequately describe) the claimed invention. *See* Enzo Biochem, Inc. v. Gen-Probe Inc., 296 F.3d 1316, 1330 (Fed. Cir. 2002). One can, however, satisfy the description requirement by the deposit of sample biological materials in certain cases where a verbal or pictorial description would be impossible. *See id.*

requirement "'guards against the inventor's overreaching by insisting that he recount his invention in such detail that his future claims can be determined to be encompassed within his original creation.'"[105]

It may appear that the enablement requirement, discussed in Section 8.6, would prevent an applicant from claiming more than the original application can support. If a modified claim really reflected a new and different invention, it would seem unlikely that the specification as filed would be adequate to enable one to practice that invention. However, according to the Federal Circuit and its predecessor court, "'it is possible for a specification to *enable* the practice of invention as broadly as it is claimed, and still not *describe* that invention.'"[106]

An example of this distinction can be found in *Martin v. Mayer*,[107] where the invention concerned an electrical cable constructed of various layers, including a conductor, a dielectric, and a "high frequency absorption medium." One of the claims at issue concerned a "harness" composed of more than one such cable. The specification as filed disclosed only a single cable. A person skilled in the art might have been *enabled* by the description of the solitary cable to construct a harness of several cables (particularly if the later-filed claim suggested it), but the specification included no written description of the harness to demonstrate that the applicant actually had conceived of that invention when the application was filed.[108]

The same issue can arise if the specification, as originally filed, discloses a single species of a later-claimed genus. For example, the specification might disclose one example of a chemical compound within the broader group eventually claimed. The specification could enable persons skilled

---

[105] *Vas-Cath*, 935 F.2d at 1561; *see also In re Wright*, 866 F.2d 422, 424 (Fed. Cir. 1989) ("When the scope of a claim has been changed by amendment in such a way as to justify an assertion that it is directed to a *different invention* than was the original claim, it is proper to inquire whether the newly claimed subject matter was *described* in the patent application when filed as the invention of the applicant. That is the essence of the so-called 'description requirement.'" (emphasis in original)). If the patentee is attempting to rely on the filing date of a parent or grandparent application (see Section 5.2), and that application does not adequately describe the subsequent claim, the result may not be that the claim is invalid but only that it cannot rely on the earlier filing date. *See* Reiffin v. Microsoft Corp., 214 F.3d 1342, 1346 (Fed. Cir. 2000).

[106] *Vas-Cath*, 935 F.2d at 1561 (emphasis in original).

[107] 823 F.2d 500 (Fed. Cir. 1987).

[108] *See also* Lockwood v. American Airlines, Inc., 107 F.3d 1565, 1572 (Fed. Cir. 1997) (the specification must describe the invention itself, not only so much as necessary to make the invention *obvious*). *Martin* actually arose from an interference. See Section 5.4. Interferences are procedures conducted by the Patent Office to determine which one of two or more applicants claiming the same subject matter is the first and true inventor. The claims (or "counts") addressed in the interference often differ from the claims as originally filed by one or more of the parties to the interference, and one of the issues that may be debated is whether a specification, as filed, shows that the applicant had invented the subject matter of the count.

in the art to produce the other compounds in the genus–the single example in the specification, together with the claim's indication of a broader
genus, might be enough guidance to allow production of each compound
without undue experimentation.[109] However, the disclosure of the single
species in the specification may be inadequate to show that the applicant
had conceived of the broader genus at the time the patent application was
filed.[110]

If a claim is broadened by omitting some detail of the preferred embodiment disclosed in the specification, a court may examine whether the omitted detail is "critical." In *In re Peters*,[111] for example, the specification
disclosed an improved flat-panel television display, one element of which
was tapered. Although the claims originally called for a tapered element,
this limitation was later removed as unnecessary. The Patent Office held that
the modified claim violated the written description requirement, because the
specification as filed did not demonstrate that the applicant was in possession of the broader invention (i.e., tapered *and* untapered elements). The
Federal Circuit reversed the decision.

> The broadened claims merely omit an unnecessary limitation that had restricted
> one element of the invention to the exact and non-critical shape disclosed in the orig-
> inal patent. In sum, nothing in the original disclosure indicates or suggests that the
> tapered shape of the tips was essential or critical to either the operation or patentabil-
> ity of the invention.[112]

Since the original specification showed that the tapering was not important,
the *invention* described by the applicant was not limited to that embodiment.[113]

Thus, a patent satisfies the written description requirement if the specification "conveys with reasonable clarity to those skilled in the art that, as of

---

[109] *See* Section 8.6.

[110] *See* Regents of the University of California v. Eli Lilly & Co., 119 F.3d 1559, 1567–68 (Fed. Cir.
1997); Vas-Cath, 935 F.2d at 1561–62. The reverse can happen as well. The early disclosure
of a large genus may lack any "blaze marks" leading persons skilled in the art to (and showing
possession of) a particular species later singled out in a claim. *See Purdue Pharma*, 230 F.3d at
1326. "[O]ne cannot disclose a forest in the original application, and then later pick a tree out
of the forest and say here is my invention." *Id.*

[111] 723 F.2d 891 (Fed. Cir. 1983).

[112] *Peters*, 723 F.2d at 893–94.

[113] The *Martin* opinion does not discuss whether the difference between a single cable and a bun-
dle of cables is critical. However, the court referred to uncontradicted evidence that "such
bundling was not conventional as applied to cables with a conductive outer layer." 823 F.2d
at 505. Note that in *Cooper Cameron Corp. v. Kvaerner Oilfield Prods., Inc.*, 291 F.3d 1317, 1323
(Fed. Cir. 2002), the Federal Circuit distanced itself from the notion that there is an "essential
element" or "critical element" test, characterizing the use of such terms as an expression of
"the unremarkable proposition that a broad claim is invalid when the entirely of the specification clearly indicates that the invention is of a much narrower scope." *See also* Amgen, Inc.
v. Hoechst Marion Roussel, Inc., 314 F.3d 1313, 1333 (Fed. Cir. 2003).

the filing date [of the application], he or she was in possession *of the invention.* The invention is, for purposes of the 'written description' inquiry, *whatever is now claimed.*[114] This does not mean that the specification has to describe the later-claimed invention in the very same terms.[115] In *In re Wright*,[116] for example, the claim language "not permanently fixed," as applied to a micro-capsule powder used in an imaging process, did not appear in the specification. However, the specification included enough information, including a warning that the powder should not be disturbed, to show that the invention as originally contemplated and disclosed included powder that was "not permanently fixed."

It is important that the invention be described in terms adequate to show that the applicant has *invented* the claimed subject matter, not just that he has a plan for doing so. This problem has been known to arise where the patent claims a particular variety of DNA. "An adequate written description of DNA requires more than a mere statement that it is a part of the invention and reference to a potential method for isolating it; what is required is a description of the DNA itself."[117] In these cases it is difficult to disentangle the written description requirement from the enablement requirement. In *Fiers v. Revel*,[118] for example, the court seemed to fear that the applicants were claiming an invention much broader than what they had so far achieved: "Claiming all DNA's that achieve a result without defining the means that will do so is not in compliance with the description requirement; it is an attempt to preempt the future before it has arrived."[119] Unless the issue arises from a discrepancy between the originally filed specification and a *modified* claim, this concern should be one that can be adequately addressed by the enablement requirement.[120]

The description requirement certainly seems most useful, and most distinct from the other requirements of patentability, when claims have changed during prosecution. Some judges of the Federal Circuit believe that it should be invoked *only* as "a priority policeman."[121] On a few occasions, however, the description requirement has been enforced (particularly in the context of biotechnology inventions) as an absolute requirement of disclosure, even when

---

[114] *Vas-Cath*, 935 F.2d at 1563–64 (emphasis in original); *see also* Waldemar Link v. Osteonics Corp., 32 F.3d 556, 559 (Fed. Cir. 1994).
[115] *See Lampi*, 228 F.3d at 1378.
[116] 866 F.2d 422, 425 (Fed. Cir. 1989).
[117] Fiers v. Revel, 984 F.2d 1164, 1170 (Fed. Cir. 1993). Recently, the Federal Circuit has stated that functional descriptions of genetic material may sometimes be adequate. *See Enzo Biochem*, 296 F.3d at 1324.
[118] 984 F.2d 1164 (Fed. Cir. 1993).
[119] *Fiers*, 984 F.2d at 1171.
[120] *See* Section 8.6.
[121] Enzo Biochem, Inc. v. Gen-Probe Inc., 63 U.S.P.Q.2d 1618, 1624 (Fed. Cir. 2002) (nonprecedential opinion; Rader, J., dissenting).

claims have not been changed so as to make the *timing* of the disclosure the

issue.[122] One can still inquire whether the specification demonstrates *possession of the invention*, and perhaps, in that way, guard against overambitious claiming accompanied by an inadequate quid pro quo of disclosure. Again, however, the enablement requirement, which is an easier test to define and perhaps to satisfy, arguably covers that ground already.

8.9 NOVELTY

An invention can be patented only if it is new. Hence, an important part of patent prosecution and patent litigation is comparing the claimed invention to prior inventions to determine whether the claims are *novel*. Prior inventions, as well as patents, patent applications, and publications that disclose prior inventions, are known as *prior art references*. The various kinds of prior art references are listed in 35 U.S.C. § 102, a complex provision discussed in detail in the sections that follow. If a claimed invention is identical to one or more prior art references, the claim is said to be *anticipated*.[123] If the claimed invention differs from the prior art, but the differences are of the sort that would occur to a person of ordinary skill, the claim is said to be *obvious*.[124] Either is sufficient grounds for holding a claim unpatentable or invalid.

8.9.1 Categories of Prior Art

Section 102 is one of the most important provisions of the Patent Act, but because of its length and structure it is also one of the most difficult to grasp. The provision begins "[a] person shall be entitled to a patent unless . . ." and the following seven paragraphs (§ 102(a)–§ 102 (g)) list various circumstances under which a patent *cannot* be granted, most of them related to a lack of novelty. If a patent issued even though it violates one of these conditions, the patent can be held invalid by the courts.

8.9.1.1 Prior Knowledge, Use, Patents, and Publications (§ 102(a))

---

[122] *See Moba*, 325 F.3d at 1320. The first case to use the description requirement in this fashion seems to have been *Regents of the University of California v. Eli Lilly & Co.*, 119 F.3d 1559 (Fed. Cir. 1997). In *University of Rochester v. G.D. Searle & Co.*, 358 F.3d 916 (Fed. Cir. 2004), the Federal Circuit, addressing this issue more squarely than before, held that the description requirement applied "whether a question of priority has arisen or not." *Id.* at 924. Although early cases of this sort had dealt with "genetic materials," the principle "applies to all types of inventions." *Id.* at 925.

[123] *See* Section 8.9.5.

[124] *See* Section 8.9.6.

Section 102(a) of the Patent Act reads as follows:

A person shall be entitled to a patent unless–
(a) the invention was known or used by others in this country, or patented or described in a printed publication in this or a foreign country, before the invention thereof by the applicant for patent. . . .

This section identifies four kinds of prior art reference that might invalidate a patent if they occurred before the applicant's date of invention:[125]

- Prior knowledge of the invention by others in *this* country
- Prior use of the invention by others in *this* country
- A prior patent on the invention in *any* country
- A prior "printed publication" of the invention in *any* country[126]

Prior knowledge, prior use, patents, and printed publications, are four common categories of prior art. One feature they share is that, to some degree, they all place the invention in the possession of the public.[127] If an invention has already been the subject of a patent or printed publication, or if the invention is one that has already been known or used, granting a patent on the invention would not "promote the progress of . . . the useful arts."[128] On the contrary, it would take away an invention that the public had already enjoyed. In § 102, "[s]ociety, speaking through Congress and the courts, has said 'thou shalt not take it away.'"[129]

Although prior knowledge, prior use, patents, and publications are fairly straightforward concepts, they have been refined through judicial analysis, primarily to clarify the extent to which a reference must be publicly available. For example, while *known* or *used* could literally refer to secret knowledge or secret use, § 102(a) has been interpreted to require knowledge or use that is accessible to the public.[130] Similarly, the term *patented* means that the invention was *disclosed* in a patent, not merely that it was encompassed within the scope of a broad patent claim.[131] *Patented* can refer to the rights

[125] The *date of invention* is discussed in Section 8.9.2.
[126] Prior use or knowledge of the invention in a foreign country is excluded from § 102(a), perhaps because in an earlier era such knowledge or use would have been difficult to verify. The increasingly global nature of both commerce and scientific research has spurred some commentators to suggest that the national distinctions embodied in § 102(a) are out of date.
[127] *See* Carella v. Starlight Archery & Pro Line Co., 804 F.2d 135, 139 (Fed. Cir. 1986). A prior patent at least gives the public *knowledge* of the invention and the expectation of possessing it as soon as the patent has expired.
[128] See Section 1.1.
[129] Kimberly-Clark Corp. v. Johnson & Johnson, 745 F.2d 1437, 1453–54 (Fed. Cir. 1984).
[130] *See* Minnesota Mining & Mfg. Co. v. Chemque, Inc., 303 F.3d 1294, 1301 (Fed. Cir. 2002); Woodland Trust v. Flowertree Nursery, Inc., 148 F.3d 1368, 1370 (Fed. Cir. 1998) ("in order to invalidate a patent based on prior knowledge or use, that knowledge or use must have been available to the public").
[131] *See In re* Benno, 768 F.2d 1340, 1346 (Fed. Cir. 1985).

granted by foreign countries, even if they differ somewhat from U.S. patent rights,[132] but the foreign patent must be "available to the public."[133]

"[D]escribed in a printed publication" may be the language of § 102(a) that has received the most intense judicial scrutiny.[134] The courts have made clear that "printed" is not to be taken too literally. Information that is distributed through other media, such as photographs, CD-ROMs, or microfilm, can qualify as printed publications.[135] The two critical characteristics of a printed publication are (1) that it is "accessible" to the public and (2) that it includes an "enabling disclosure."

Accessible means "interested members of the public could obtain the information if they wanted to."[136] Most books, technical journals, and other materials normally thought of as publications are clearly accessible to the public, but inventions are sometimes disclosed in classified documents or documents distributed only on a confidential basis (e.g., documents for the internal use of a corporation). Those do not qualify as publications.[137] On the other hand, distribution of even a small number of copies without restriction can be considered sufficient.[138]

Some of the most difficult cases arise when a document has not been distributed, but it has been made available in a library or similar collection. In *In re Hall*,[139] for example, the potentially invalidating reference was a doctoral thesis. The thesis had not been published in the usual sense, but it had been deposited in a university library in Germany where it was, theoreti-

---

[132] *See In re* Carlson, 983 F.2d 1032 (Fed. Cir. 1992).
[133] *See Carlson*, 983 F.2d at 1037. The standard of "availability" is rather low. *See id.* at 1037–38 (a German Geschmacksmuster can qualify as a patent under § 102, even if one must travel to a courthouse in a remote German city in order to see the design to which it applies). Note that a patent document can also constitute a printed publication.
[134] The same term also appears in the statutory bar provision of 35 U.S.C. § 102(b). See Section 8.10.
[135] *See In re* Hall, 781 F.2d 897, 898 (Fed. Cir. 1986) ("The statutory phrase 'printed publication' has been interpreted to give effect to ongoing advances in the technologies of data storage, retrieval, and dissemination.").
[136] Constant v. Advanced Micro-Devices, Inc., 848 F.2d 1560, 1569 (Fed. Cir. 1988). If the publication is *accessible*, it is irrelevant whether anyone in particular *actually* reviewed it. *Id.*
[137] *See* Northern Telecom, Inc. v. Datapoint Corp., 908 F.2d 931, 936–37 (Fed. Cir. 1990); *but c.f.* Cooper Cameron Corp. v. Kvaerner Oilfield Prods., Inc., 291 F.3d 1317, 1323–24 (Fed. Cir. 2002) (in spite of a "confidential" label, a report may have been sufficiently available to the public to qualify as prior art). Restricted publications might serve as evidence of a prior invention under § 102(g). See Section 8.9.1.3
[138] *See* Massachusetts Institute of Technology v. A.B. Fortia, 774 F.2d 1104, 1109 (Fed. Cir. 1985) (paper that was discussed at a conference attended by 50 to 100 interested persons and that was distributed "on request" to at least six persons without restrictions, constituted a publication); *but cf.* Preemption Devices, Inc. v. Minnesota Mining & Mfg. Co., 732 F.2d 903, 906 (Fed. Cir. 1984) (six copies of an article sent to a "friend" were not a publication). Sometimes the "interested public" to whom the publication must be available is a relatively small group. *See Cooper Cameron*, 291 F.3d at 1324.
[139] 781 F.2d 897 (Fed. Cir. 1986).

cally, available for review. The court held that "a single catalogued thesis in one university" might "constitute sufficient accessibility to those interested in the art exercising reasonable diligence."[140] In *In re Cronyn*,[141] however, the court held that three undergraduate theses did not constitute printed publications. The court held that, in this case, the documents "were not accessible to the public because they had not been either cataloged or indexed in a meaningful way."[142] They could have been located only by sorting through a collection of index cards kept in a shoebox in the university's chemistry department. These cases obviously draw fine, and somewhat arbitrary, distinctions. Although the undergraduate theses in *Cronyn* would have been difficult to track down, as a practical matter the thesis in *Hall* might have been equally elusive. Still, the courts must draw the line somewhere, and they repeatedly emphasize the importance of the particular facts in each case.[143]

The other important requirement of a printed publication is that it include an *enabling disclosure* of the invention.[144] An enabling disclosure is a description of the invention that would allow a person skilled in the art to make and use the invention without undue experimentation.[145] If, for example, a marketing brochure boasts of the advantages of a process, but it does not include enough information to allow the process to be duplicated, the brochure lacks an enabling disclosure.[146] In deciding whether a disclosure is enabling, the knowledge that would be available to those of skill in the art can be taken into account. In other words, the publication does not have to include information that would already be known to persons of ordinary skill.[147]

8.9.1.2 *Prior Applications (§ 102(e))*[148]

Another category of prior art reference, not discussed in § 102(a), is a patent *application*. The circumstances under which a patent application can constitute prior art are set forth in § 102(e). Section 102(e) has evolved into a

---

[140] *Hall*, 781 F.2d at 900.

[141] 890 F.2d 1158 (Fed. Cir. 1989).

[142] *Cronyn*, 890 F.2d at 1161.

[143] *See, e.g., Cronyn*, 890 F.2d at 1161.

[144] Amgen, Inc. v. Hoechst Marion Roussel, Inc., 314 F.3d 1313, 1354 (Fed. Cir. 2003); Helefix Ltd. v. Blok-Lok, Ltd., 208 F.3d 1339, 1347 (Fed. Cir. 2000); *In re* Epstein, 32 F.3d 1559, 1568 (Fed. Cir. 1994); Constant v. Advanced Micro-Devices, Inc., 848 F.2d 1560, 1569 (Fed. Cir. 1988). A publication need not be enabling to serve as evidence of *obviousness*, discussed in Section 8.9.6. *See Amgen*, 314 F.3d at 1357.

[145] The enabling disclosure requirement also applies to patent specifications. See Section 8.6.

[146] *See Helefix*, 208 F.3d at 1346–48; Reading & Bates Construction Co. v. Baker Energy Resources Corp., 748 F.2d 645, 651–52 (Fed. Cir. 1984).

[147] *In re* Donohue, 766 F.2d 531, 533 (Fed. Cir. 1985).

[148] There is no apparent logic to the ordering of paragraphs in § 102. They will therefore be discussed in the order that seems easiest to understand, rather than in the order in which they appear in the statute.

complex paragraph freighted with cross-references to other portions of the Patent Act, but the gist of it is the addition of the following to the list of potential prior art references:

- A patent application, filed by *another* inventor in the United States,[149] before the applicant's date of invention, *if* that application eventually *issued* as a patent or was *published* under the rules[150] now permitting the publication of applications.

Thus, if inventor A had a patent application on file before inventor B had conceived of the same invention, then inventor A's application would be prior art to inventor B, even if inventor's A's application neither issued as a patent, nor was published as an application, until some later date. Note that § 102(e) applies only to patent applications that are eventually published or converted into issued patents.

8.9.1.3 Prior Inventions (§ 102(g))

A final category of prior art reference[151] is embodied in § 102(g)(2):

A person shall be entitled to a patent unless—(g)(2) before the applicant's invention thereof, the invention was made in this country by another inventor who had not abandoned, suppressed, or concealed it. . . .

Made, in this context, means "invented." Thus, § 102(g)(2) adds the following category of prior art reference to those set forth in §§ 102(a) and (e):

- An invention by another inventor, in this country, which had not been abandoned, suppressed, or concealed.

Two inventors, working independently, can conceive of the same invention. The telephone, for example, is said to have been invented independently, and almost simultaneously, by Alexander Graham Bell and Elisha Gray. In other countries, priority is awarded to the first inventor to file a patent application, but in the United States the patent goes to the first to *invent*. Section 102(g) denies a patent to an applicant who was not the first to invent.[152]

---

[149] Under certain circumstances, an international application may qualify. *See* 35 U.S.C. § 102(e)(1).

[150] *See* Section 5.1.

[151] Other than those that apply only to the statutory bar provisions discussed in Sections 8.10–8.11.

[152] Section 102(g)(2) may be invoked in litigation in order to invalidate an issued patent. *See* Dow Chemical Co. v. Astro-Valcour, Inc., 267 F.3d 1334, 1339 (Fed. Cir. 2001); Sandt Technology, Ltd. v. Resco Metal & Plastics Corp., 264 F.3d 1344, 1350 (Fed. Cir. 2001); Apotex USA, Inc. v. Merck & Co., 254 F.3d 1031, 1035 (Fed. Cir. 2001). If the contest for priority occurs in the course of prosecuting a patent application, the result can be an interference proceeding, discussed in Section 5.4. In that event, § 102(g)(1) controls. The rule is much the same, except that work in some foreign countries can suffice to establish priority, whereas § 102(g)(2) is restricted to prior invention in the United States.

There is, however, an important exception. The first invention does not count against a later inventor if the first invention was "abandoned, suppressed, or concealed."[153] An invention is "deemed abandoned, suppressed, or concealed if, within a reasonable time after completion, no steps are taken to make the invention publicly known."[154] Abandonment, suppression, and concealment can be inferred if, after a reasonable period of time, the first inventor has not filed a patent application, used the invention in public, embodied the invention in a product for sale, or described the invention in a publication.[155] This exception to the "first to invent" rule rewards those who make inventions available to the public, and penalizes those who hide or abandon inventions.[156]

If the delay in publicizing an invention, or applying for a patent, is more than a few years, abandonment may be presumed.[157] The presumption can be overcome by evidence that efforts to perfect the invention caused the delay.[158] On the other hand, efforts to *commercialize* the invention cannot excuse an applicant's failure to file promptly.[159] In *Lutzker v. Plet*,[160] where the invention was a device for making canapés, the first inventor (Lutzker) waited more than four years after completing the invention before disclosing it to the public at a trade show. By the time of the trade show, the second inventor (Plet) had invented the device independently and filed a patent application. Lutzker argued that the delay should be excused because it had been due to efforts to perfect the invention. The Patent Office, affirmed by the court, disagreed. The

---

[153] As with other invalidity defenses, the challenger of an issued patent must prove prior invention under § 102(g) by clear and convincing evidence. *Dow Chemical*, 267 F.3d at 1339. If the challenger is successful, the burden shifts to the patentee to produce evidence that the invention was abandoned, suppressed or concealed. *Id.* If that evidence is sufficient to create at least a genuine issue of fact (see Section 11.7), it up to the challenger, once again, to rebut the evidence of abandonment, suppression, or concealment by clear and convincing evidence to the contrary. *Id.*

[154] Correge v. Murphy, 705 F.2d 1326, 1330 (Fed. Cir. 1983). Concealment may be a choice actively pursued by the prior inventor, or the unplanned result of delay. *See Apotex*, 254 F.3d at 1038.

[155] *See Dow Chemical*, 267 F.3d at 1342; *Correge*, 705 F.2d at 1330.

[156] *See* Checkpoint Sys., Inc. v. U.S. Int'l Trade Comm'n, 54 F.3d 765, 761 (Fed. Cir. 1995).

[157] *See* Lutzker v. Plet, 843 F.2d 1364, 1367 (Fed. Cir. 1988) (discussing cases in which delays of 29 months to four years were held sufficient to show abandonment, suppression, or concealment). However, there is no period of time that is unreasonable *per se*. *See Dow Chemical*, 267 F.3d at 1342–43. "Rather a determination of abandonment, suppression or concealment has 'consistently been based on equitable principles and public policy as applied to the facts of each case.'" *Checkpoint*, 54 F.3d at 761.

[158] *See Lutzker*, 843 F.2d at 1367.

[159] If the prior inventor never intended to file a patent application but, instead, meant to introduce the invention to the public by a product, courts are far more tolerant of commercial activities as an excuse for delay. *See Dow Chemical*, 267 F.3d at 1343; *Checkpoint*, 54 F.3d at 762. This means, oddly enough, that the prior inventor who never filed a patent application himself may be better off, because he can more easily invalidate the subsequent patent to someone else.

[160] 843 F.2d 1364 (Fed. Cir. 1988).

delay was attributed to the development of a recipe book, packaging, and other things unrelated to the invention itself. Lutzker was therefore found to have abandoned, suppressed, or concealed the invention, and his activities did not prevent the issuance of a patent to Plet.[161]

Two points should be mentioned about the timing of an abandonment. First, the abandonment can be nullified if the first inventor renews his efforts to patent the invention, or to make it available to the public, before the second inventor "enters the field."[162] The first inventor would be credited with the date of renewed activity as his date of invention. Thus, if Lutzker had begun work on a patent application before Plet entered the field, his earlier inactivity could have been overlooked. Second, § 102(g) refers to prior inventions that "had" not been abandoned, suppressed, or concealed, implying that an invention abandoned, suppressed, or concealed *after* the entry into the field of the second inventor would still be effective as prior art.[163]

8.9.2 Date of Invention

To evaluate whether a patent, patent application, publication, or other reference is *prior* art under §§ 102(a) or (e), it is necessary to determine the patentee's (or applicant's) date of invention. In applying § 102(g), it is necessary to determine the date of invention of both the patentee (or applicant) and the alleged prior inventor. References *subsequent* to the patentee's (or applicant's) date of invention have no relevance under these statutory provisions.[164]

Invention, as defined in patent law, involves two steps: conception and reduction to practice.[165] *Conception* is the mental act of invention–the moment of insight when the inventor imagines the thing that ultimately will be claimed. As formally defined by the Federal Circuit, conception requires the formation in the inventor's mind of "a definite and permanent idea of the invention, including every feature of the subject matter sought to be patented."[166] If the inventor has done no more than recognize a problem, the conception of the invention is still incomplete.[167] Conception is complete

---

[161] The court was influenced by the fact that the recipe book and other items accounting for the delay were not related to the disclosure in Lutzker's eventual patent application. *Lutzker*, 843 F.2d at 1367–68.

[162] *See Lutzker*, 843 F.2d at 1368; Paulik v. Rizkalla, 760 F.2d 1270, 1275–76 (Fed. Cir. 1985).

[163] The language of the statute seems clear. However, the Federal Circuit has not ruled on this issue, and it could be argued that ignoring a later abandonment would hinder the policy of making inventions available to the public.

[164] They may, however, be relevant under the statutory bar provisions (see Section 8.10), and they may have a bearing on obviousness as instances of *near-simultaneous invention* (see Section 8.9.6.1).

[165] The Supreme Court has implied that conception is the more important of the two. *See* Pfaff v. Wells Electronics, Inc., 525 U.S. 55, 60 (1998) ("The primary meaning of the word 'invention' in the Patent Act unquestionably refers to the inventor's conception rather than to a physical embodiment of that idea."). However, as discussed below, reduction to practice still plays an important role in establishing priority.

only when the inventor finds the *solution* to a problem, and the solution is worked out in sufficient detail, in the inventor's mind, that persons of ordinary skill in the art could put the inventor's ideas to practice without extensive research or undue experimentation.[168]

Reduction to practice means reducing the idea to a physical embodiment and, in most cases, testing it to confirm that it will work.[169] In the case of an apparatus, reduction to practice means that the apparatus was assembled, at least in prototype. In the case of a method, reduction to practice means that the method was actually performed. A patent claim is not reduced to practice until there is a physical embodiment that includes all of the elements of the claim.[170]

The amount of testing of the physical embodiment necessary for reduction to practice varies considerably depending on the nature of the invention. The courts are instructed to employ a "common sense approach."[171] Some devices are considered so simple, and their effectiveness so obvious, that no testing at all is required.[172] Other inventions require careful evaluation under conditions that duplicate, or simulate, the intended working environment of the invention. The testing required is whatever is reasonably necessary to demonstrate that the invention will work.[173] Even where testing is required, it is not necessary to demonstrate that the invention is so refined that it is ready to market.[174] A prototype that is not yet of commercial quality may be sufficient to show that the principle of the invention is sound.[175] Moreover, "[t]esting

---

[166] Sewall v. Walters, 21 F.3d 411, 415 (Fed. Cir. 1994); *see also* Singh v. Brake, 317 F.3d 1334, 1340 (Fed. Cir. 2003) ("'Conception is the formation "in the mind of the inventor of a definite and permanent idea of the complete and operative invention, as it is thereafter to be applied in practice."'"); Slip Track Sys., Inc. v. Metal-Lite, Inc., 304 F.3d 1256, 1262–63 (Fed. Cir. 2002); Brown v. Barbacid, 276 F.3d 1327, 1335–36 (Fed. Cir. 2002). A mere research plan coupled with a vague hope of success does not amount to a conception. *See* Hitzeman v. Rutter, 243 F.3d 1345, 1356–57 (Fed. Cir. 2001); Burroughs Wellcome Co. v. Barr Labs., Inc., 40 F.3d 1223, 1228 (Fed. Cir. 1994) ("An idea is definite and permanent when the inventor has a specific, settled idea, a particular solution to the problem at hand, not just a general goal or research plan he hopes to pursue."). An inventor who has stumbled across a patentable invention must recognize it, though he need not appreciate that it is, in fact, patentable. *See* Rosco, Inc. v. Mirror Lite Co., 304 F.3d 1373, 1381 (Fed. Cir. 2002); *Hitzeman*, 243 F.3d at 1358–59.

[167] *See* Morgan v. Hirsch, 728 F.2d 1449 (Fed. Cir. 1994).

[168] *See Singh*, 317 F.3d at 1334; *Brown*, 276 F.3d at 1336.

[169] *See Slip Track*, 304 F.3d at 1265 ("In order to establish actual reduction to practice, the inventor must prove that he constructed an embodiment or performed a process that met all the limitations of the claim, and that he determined that the invention would work for its intended purpose. . . . [The latter] may require testing, depending on the character of the invention and the problem that it solves."); Scott v. Finney, 34 F.3d 1058 (Fed. Cir. 1994); Newkirk v. Lulejian, 825 F.2d 1581, 1582 (Fed. Cir. 1987).

[170] *See* Eaton v. Evans, 204 F.3d 1094, 1097 (Fed. Cir. 2000).

[171] *Scott*, 34 F.3d at 1061.

[172] *See Slip Track*, 304 F.3d at 1265 ("Some devices are so simple and their purpose and efficacy so obvious that their complete construction is sufficient to demonstrate their workability.").

need not show utility beyond a possibility of failure, but only utility beyond a probability of failure."[176]

In a few cases, courts have held the subject matter of an invention to be so unpredictable that the invention could not be fully *conceived* until experiments had been performed and the results evaluated. Conception and reduction to practice are, in these cases, simultaneous. This circumstance is most likely to occur in the fields of chemistry and biotechnology, where useful combinations can sometimes be discovered only by trial and error.[177] In *Smith v. Bousquet*,[178] for example, the court held that the effectiveness of a chemical as an insecticide, on particular species and under particular conditions, could not be predicted until realistic experiments were carried out. Until then, plans to use the chemical as an insecticide were mere hope or speculation, not an invention.[179]

The reduction to practice discussed so far is *actual* reduction to practice. The filing of a patent application is considered a *constructive* reduction to practice.[180] *Constructive* is a word often used in the law when an act is treated as though it were one thing, when it is actually something else.[181] Although filing a patent application is not a reduction to practice at all, it is treated as though it were for purposes of fixing the date of invention. Therefore, an inventor who never produces a physical embodiment of the invention, or who does so only later, will be considered to have reduced to practice on the date the patent application was filed.[182] In any case, the filing date of the application is the presumptive date of invention for any patent, pending proof of earlier conception and reduction to practice.[183]

---

[173] "[The] common sense approach prescribes more scrupulous testing under circumstances approaching actual use conditions when the problem includes many uncertainties. On the other hand, when the problem to be solved does not present myriad variables, common sense similarly permits little or no testing to show the soundness of the principles of operation of the invention." *Scott*, 34 F.3d at 1063; *see also* Taskett v. Dentlinger, 344 F.3d 1337, 1341 (Fed. Cir. 2003).

[174] "Reduction to practice does not require 'that the invention, when tested, be in a commercially satisfactory stage of development.'" *Scott*, 34 F.3d at 1061. *See also* Loral Fairchild Corp. v. Matsushita Elec. Indus. Co., 266 F.3d 1358, 1362–63 (Fed. Cir. 2001) ("Once the invention has been shown to work for its intended purpose, reduction to practice is complete. . . . Further efforts to commercialize the invention are simply not relevant. . . ."); DSL Dynamic Sciences Ltd. v. Union Switch & Signal, Inc., 928 F.2d 1122, 1126 (Fed. Cir. 1991).

[175] *See Scott*, 34 F.3d at 1062.

[176] *Scott*, 34 F.3d at 1062.

[177] *See* Mycogen Plant Science, Inc. v. Monsanto Co., 243 F.3d 1316, 1330 (Fed. Cir. 2001) ("The doctrine of simultaneous conception and reduction to practice is somewhat rare but certainly not unknown, especially in the unpredictable arts such as chemistry and biology."), *vacated on other grounds*, 535 U.S. 1109 (2002).

[178] 111 F.2d 157 (C.C.P.A. 1940).

[179] More recently, the concept of simultaneous conception and reduction to practice has been applied to inventions involving DNA. *See, e.g., Mycogen*, 243 F.3d at 1330–31; Amgen, Inc. v. Chugai Pharmaceutical Co., 927 F.2d 1200, 1206–07 (Fed. Cir. 1991).

[180] Cooper v. Goldfarb, 154 F.3d 1321, 1327 (Fed. Cir. 1998).

[181] See the discussion of constructive notice in Section 11.8.3.2.

If *date of invention* were always synonymous with *date of reduction to practice*, life would be simpler. In fact, the date of conception must also be taken into account because of the following complication introduced by § 102(g):

> In determining priority of invention under this subsection, there shall be considered not only the respective date of conception and reduction to practice of the invention, but also the reasonable diligence of one who was first to conceive and last to reduce to practice, from a time prior to conception by the other.

In other words, when two inventors contend for the title of "first to invent," either in the context of an interference proceeding or a prior art challenge to an issued patent, the inventor who was first to conceive but last to reduce to practice will prevail, if, but *only* if, he was diligent in reducing the invention to practice.[184]

The easiest cases to resolve are those in which the first inventor to conceive of the invention is also the first to reduce to practice. Suppose, for example, that inventor A, who has received a patent, sues an infringer. The infringer argues that the invention of inventor B is prior art to inventor A's patent under § 102(g). If inventor A's date of conception precedes inventor B's date of conception, *and* inventor A's date of reduction to practice precedes inventor B's date of reduction to practice, inventor B's work is not prior art. If the situation is reversed (i.e., inventor B's dates of conception and reduction to practice precede inventor A's respective dates), then inventor B's invention is prior art to inventor A. In neither case is anyone's diligence an issue. When, however, the first inventor to conceive was last to reduce to practice, diligence comes into play. To return to the example, if inventor A was the first to conceive of the invention, but before he could reduce the invention to practice inventor B both conceived and reduced to practice, the patent to inventor A would be valid only if inventor A had been diligent from a time *prior* to B's date of conception.[185]

---

[182] Treating the filing of a patent application as equivalent to producing a physical embodiment of the invention is not so far-fetched, since the application should include all of the information necessary to allow one skilled in the art to complete such an embodiment without undue experimentation. If it does not include that information, the patent will be invalid for lack of enablement. See Section 8.6.

[183] Bausch & Lomb, Inc. v. Barnes-Hind/Hydrocurve, Inc., 796 F.2d 443, 449 (Fed. Cir. 1986).

[184] *See Pfaff,* 525 U.S. at 61 ("[A]ssuming diligence on the part of the applicant, it is normally the first inventor to conceive, rather than the first to reduce to practice, who establishes the right to patent."); *Brown,* 276 F.3d at 1337. The Federal Circuit has applied the diligence principle in the context of § 102(a). *See In re* Mulder, 716 F.2d 1542, 1545 (Fed. Cir. 1983) (printed publication); Loral Fairchild Corp. v. Matsushita Elec. Indus. Co., 266 F.3d 1358, 1365–66 (Fed. Cir. 2001) (Newman, J., dissenting). However, the recent addition of the phrase "under this subsection" may suggest that it is only appropriate in the prior invention context of § 102(g).

[185] *See In re* Jolley, 308 F.3d 1317, 1326 (Fed. Cir. 2002). The time period that begins just before a rival's conception and ends with one's own reduction to practice is frequently called the *critical period* for diligence. *See, e.g.,* Scott v. Koyama, 281 F.3d 1243, 1247 (Fed. Cir. 2002); Bey v. Kollonitsch, 806 F.2d 1024, 1025–26 (Fed. Cir. 1986). Earlier lapses in diligence can be overlooked.

The rules can be more easily visualized with the aid of a time line. In the following examples, C stands for the date of conception and RTP for the date of reduction to practice. Time progresses from left to right. Assume that inventor A has received a patent. Inventor B developed the same invention independently, and his work is alleged to be prior art under § 102(g). In the first example, B's invention is not prior art because he was last to conceive and last to reduce to practice:

A: C - - - - - - - - - RTP
B: C - - - - - - - - - - - - RTP

In the second example, B's invention is prior art because he was first to conceive and first to reduce to practice:

A: C - - - - - - - - - - - - RTP
B: C - - - - - - - - - RTP

In the third example, A was first to conceive, but B was first to reduce to practice. B's invention is not prior art *if* A was diligent, though not as swift as B, in reducing his invention to practice:

A: C - - - - - - - - - - - - - - RTP (diligent?)
B: C - - - - - RTP

In the last example, B was first to conceive, but A was first to reduce to practice. B's invention is prior art *if* B was diligent in reducing his invention to practice:

A: C - - - - - RTP
B: C - - - - - - - - - - - - - - RTP (diligent?)

The purpose of this rather confusing set of rules is to reward inventors who are the first to conceive of an idea, while at the same time encouraging inventors to bring their ideas to a practical end, or a public disclosure, as soon as possible.

Diligence in this context means reasonable efforts to reduce the invention to practice or to file a patent application. Diligent effort must be relatively continuous. Some excuses have been recognized for lapses of effort—most notably the need to complete some other invention before the first can be reduced to practice.[186] The courts will also consider "the reasonable everyday problems and limitations encountered by an inventor," including illness, poverty, the need for an occasional vacation, or the need to make a living by other means.[187] Efforts to fund or commercialize the invention, or time devoted to an unrelated invention, are not considered adequate excuses for delay.[188]

---

[186] *See, e.g.,* Keizer v. Bradley, 270 F.2d 396 (C.C.P.A. 1959).

[187] *See* Griffith v. Kanamaru, 816 F.2d 624, 626–27 (Fed. Cir. 1987). If the reduction to practice had been a constructive reduction to practice, accomplished by filing a patent application, the patent attorney's need to work on other applications can be considered an adequate excuse for delay, if the applications were handled in the order received, or if there was a need to work on related applications as a group. *See Bey,* 806 F.2d at 1028–30.

Although diligence seems the inverse of abandonment or concealment, and the factual considerations are similar, remember that they are distinct issues under § 102(g). Abandonment can negate a prior art reference that was both conceived *and* reduced to practice before the patentee entered the scene. Diligence is an issue only in the rarer circumstance that the first inventor to conceive was the last to reduce to practice.

8.9.3 Burdens of Proof–Conception, Reduction to Practice, and Diligence

If a question of priority turns on the filing date of a patent application or the publication date of a technical journal, the proof is relatively straightforward. The filing date of a patent application is a matter of public record, and the publication date of a journal is usually easy to verify. If, however, priority depends on dates of conception and reduction to practice, the facts can be much harder to establish. A conception date, in particular, can be a difficult thing to prove because the essential activity occurs entirely in the mind of the inventor.

Whenever there is a successful invention, there are sure to be those who purport to have had the same idea first. By the same token, it is easy for any patentee faced with prior art to claim that his conception occurred even earlier. The courts have therefore established certain rules governing the proof required to establish conception and reduction to practice.

First, the date on which a patent application is filed is presumed to be the applicant's date of invention in the absence of other evidence.[189] During prosecution of a patent application, if the applicant needs to establish an earlier date of invention in order to predate a potential prior art reference, this can be accomplished under certain circumstances by means of a sworn affidavit from the inventor establishing prior conception and reduction to practice.[190] This is known as *swearing behind* a reference. In litigation, dates of conception and reduction to practice must be demonstrated by "clear and convincing evidence."[191] This is true whether it is the patentee who is trying to disqualify potential prior art, or whether it is the accused infringer who is attempting to establish prior conception and reduction to practice by another in order to make a case for invalidity under § 102(g).[192]

---

[188] *See Griffith*, 816 F.2d at 627–28. As in the case of abandonment or concealment, the line between work on the invention and unrelated commercial activity can be difficult to draw. "Precedent illustrates the continuum between, on the one hand, ongoing laboratory experimentation, and, on the other hand, pure money-raising activity that is entirely unrelated to practice of the process." *Scott*, 281 F.3d at 1248 (holding that construction of facilities for large-scale practice of the claimed process sufficed to show diligence).

[189] *See* Ecolochem, Inc. v. Southern California Edison Co., 227 F.3d 1361, 1371 (Fed. Cir. 2000) (date of invention presumed to be filing date of parent application); Bausch & Lomb, Inc. v. Barnes-Hind/Hydrocurve, Inc., 796 F.2d 443, 449 (Fed. Cir. 1986).

[190] *See* 37 C.F.R. § 1.131.

[191] *See* Section 8.2.

A date of conception cannot be established entirely by the inventor's own testimony. Such testimony is simply too untrustworthy. Instead, a claim to a conception date must be *corroborated*, usually by the testimony of a noninventor who was made aware of the inventor's work soon after the date in question.[193] For this reason, engineers involved in organized research programs often have their laboratory notebooks periodically reviewed, signed, and dated by a colleague.[194] Such a notebook can be the best evidence of what was conceived and when,[195] and it is a practice strongly recommended to anyone pursuing work that may eventually prove patentable. Dates of reduction to practice and allegations of diligence also must be corroborated by evidence independent of the inventor.[196] Although eyewitness testimony is often best, corroboration is subject to a rule of reason that allows the inventor's claims to be substantiated by any evidence sufficient to establish credibility.[197] For example, testimony regarding a reduction to practice might be corroborated by dated invoices for the parts that were used to build an embodiment of the invention.[198]

[192] The ultimate burden of proof on validity, however, always remains with the party challenging the patent. *See* Innovative Scuba Concepts, Inc. v. Feder Indus., Inc., 26 F.3d 1112, 1115 (Fed. Cir. 1994).

[193] *See* Rosco, Inc. v. Mirror Lite Co., 304 F.3d 1373, 1382 (Fed. Cir. 2002) ("It is well established that a party claiming his own prior inventorship must proffer evidence corroborating his testimony."); Sandt Technology, Ltd. v. Resco Metal and Plastics Corp., 264 F.3d 1344, 1350 (Fed. Cir. 2001) ("'This rule addresses the concern that a party claiming inventorship might be tempted to describe his actions in an unjustifiably self-serving manner in order to obtain a patent or to maintain an existing patent.'").

[194] The colleague, however, cannot be a co-inventor. See Section 6.1.

[195] *See Sandt Technology*, 264 F.3d at 1350–51 ("Documentary or physical evidence that is made contemporaneously with the inventive process provides the most reliable proof that the inventor's testimony has been corroborated."). In comparison, "post-invention oral testimony is more suspect, as there is more of a risk that the witness may have a litigation-inspired motive to corroborate the inventor's testimony, and that the testimony may be inaccurate." *Id.* at 1351.

[196] Cooper v. Goldfarb, 154 F.3d 1321, 1330 (Fed. Cir. 1998) (corroboration of reduction to practice); Hahn v. Wong, 892 F.2d 1028, 1032–33 (Fed. Cir. 1989). The Federal Circuit has described the standard for corroborating reduction to practice as "more stringent." Singh v. Brake, 222 F.3d 1362, 1370 (Fed. Cir. 2000). Perhaps that is because reduction to practice requires the inventor to take things farther than conception. *See id.* ("a notebook page may well show that the inventor *conceived* what he wrote on the page, whereas it may not show that the experiments were *actually performed*, as required for a reduction to practice" (emphasis in original)).

[197] *See Sandt Technology*, 264 F.3d at 1350; *Singh*, 222 F.3d at 1367; *Cooper*, 154 F.3d at 1330 ("In order to corroborate a reduction to practice, it is not necessary to produce an actual over-the-shoulder observer. Rather, sufficient circumstantial evidence of an independent nature can satisfy the corroboration requirement."). In *Woodland Trust v. Flowertree Nursery, Inc.*, 148 F.3d 1368, 1371 (Fed. Cir. 1998), the court listed a number of factors relevant to whether the testimony of a corroborating witness satisfies the rule of reason. These include the interest of the corroborating witness in the subject matter of the suit and the amount of time that has elapsed since the events in question.

[198] *See* Lacotte v. Thomas, 758 F.2d 611, 613 (Fed. Cir. 1985).

8.9.4 Prior Work by the Same Inventor

The kinds of prior art listed in §§ 102(a), (e), and (g) are limited, expressly or by implication, to prior inventions, patents, patent applications, printed publications, public knowledge, or public use attributable to persons *other than the inventor*.[199] This limitation can be difficult to apply in cases where a patent names two or more joint inventors.[200] For example, can a publication by A alone be considered prior art to the joint invention of A and B? In these cases, courts resort to the concept of the *inventive entity*, which is simply a way of referring to a specific group of inventors. A reference can be considered prior art to a patent or patent application if it is attributable to a different inventive entity. This is true whether the prior inventive entity is composed of entirely different individuals, or whether some individuals are common to both inventive entities. Thus, a publication by A, describing his work alone, could invalidate the subsequent patent of A and B together.[201] A publication describing the work of A and B together could invalidate a subsequent patent to A alone. But a publication describing the work of A and B together would not be prior art to the subsequent patent of A and B.[202] Note that the question is not who *wrote* the publication, but rather whose *invention* the publication describes. A publication by A and B describing the work of A alone would not be § 102(a) prior art to A's subsequent patent.[203]

Section 103(c) provides another twist. Even if a prior invention is attributable to a different inventive entity, if the invention is *only* a potential reference under § 102(e), (f), or (g), and if the prior invention and the subsequent application are owned by the *same person* (or both are subject to an obliga-

---

[199] *In re Katz,* 687 F.2d 450, 454 (C.C.P.A. 1982); *see also* Rapoport v. Dement, 254 F.3d 1053, 1056 (Fed. Cir. 2001) (report cannot be cited as prior art against its author). Section 102(a) refers to an invention "patented or described in a printed publication . . . before the invention thereof by the applicant." Although there is no explicit exception for the applicant's own work, clearly the applicant himself cannot patent or describe an invention in a printed publication before he has at least conceived it. It might be possible for the applicant to produce a patent or publication in comparison to which his later invention is *obvious* (*see* Section 8.9.6), but the courts have generally ruled out the use of an inventor's own work as the basis for an obviousness challenge. *See Katz,* 687 F.2d at 454. An important exception is created by the *statutory bar* provisions (see Sections 8.10–8.11). A statutory bar, based either on anticipation or obviousness, can be triggered by the inventor's own activities, if they occur more than one year before an application is filed. Also, a prior patent by the same inventor can raise issues of double patenting. *See* Section 8.12.

[200] *See* Section 6.1.

[201] This is one occasion on which A and B might reconsider whether B was properly named as a joint inventor. If B's contribution did not rise to the level of invention, and if B was named as an inventor only accidentally, it would be possible to correct the patent to name only A as the inventor, thereby removing the prior publication as a potential prior art reference. *See* Section 6.1.

[202] Unless, again, it could suffice for a statutory bar under § 102(b). *See* Section 8.10.

[203] *See Katz,* 687 F.2d at 455.

tion to assign to the same person[204]), the prior invention cannot render the subsequent patent invalid for obviousness.[205] This provision applies most often where several people are working on a project for the same corporation,[206] and it prevents the work of one person from invalidating the work of a colleague, recognizing that both are generally working under the same direction and toward the same goal.

8.9.5 Anticipation

Establishing that a patent, patent application, publication, or other potential reference falls within one of the categories of prior art set forth in § 102 is only a first step. Even if a reference falls within one of the prior art categories, and even if it can be shown to be *prior* art to the patent or application in question, it still must be determined whether or not the invention claimed is novel when compared to the reference. If the claimed invention is identical to subject matter disclosed or embodied in the prior art reference, the claim is *anticipated* and invalid for lack of novelty.

Determining whether a claim is anticipated by a prior art reference is a procedure very similar to determining if a product infringes a claim.[207] First, the claim must be *construed* to determine exactly what it means. The rules of claim construction are discussed in Chapter 7. Note that whatever construction is applied to a claim when the issue is infringement is the same construction that must be applied when the issue is validity. A claim can have only one meaning.[208] After the claim has been construed, it must be compared to the reference to determine whether the reference includes each and every element of the claim.[209] In other words, the claim is used as a checklist, and every element of the claim must find an exact match in the reference.[210]

---

[204] *See* Section 6.2.

[205] *See* Section 8.9.6.

[206] The law generally treats a corporation as a "person." People are "natural persons."

[207] *See* Chapter 10.

[208] *See* Section 7.5.

[209] *See* Teleflex, Inc. v. Ficosa North America Corp., 299 F.3d 1313, 1335 (Fed. Cir. 2000) (describing the "two-step procedure").

[210] *See Teleflex,* 299 F.3d at 1335; Crown Operations Int'l, Ltd. v. Solutia Inc., 289 F.3d 1367, 1375 (Fed. Cir. 2002); Glaverbel Societe Anonyme v. Northlake Marketing & Supply, Inc., 45 F.3d 1550, 1554 (Fed. Cir. 1995) ("Anticipation . . . requires identity of invention: the claimed invention, as described in appropriately construed claims, must be the same as that of the reference, in order to anticipate."). The tests of anticipation and literal infringement (see Section 10.5) are so similar, it is sometimes said that whatever would literally infringe a claim if it came later in time, anticipates if it came before. *See* Dow Chemical Co. v. Astro-Valcour, Inc., 267 F.3d 1334, 1339 (Fed. Cir. 2001). However, because anticipation can be based on references that would not infringe (e.g., the description of an invention in a publication), the infringement test of anticipation may be more confusing than helpful.

Anticipation requires that all of the elements of a claim be found in a *single* reference.[211] This is because combining the teachings of one reference with the teachings of another reference might be sufficiently inventive to warrant a patent.[212] The question, in such a case, is whether the combination was non-obvious. Obviousness is a separate ground of invalidity discussed in the next section. In any event, if the invention represents the combination of features found in more than one reference, it is not invalid on grounds of anticipation.

If the prior art reference is a patent or printed publication, it anticipates only if it discloses or *teaches* each and every element of the claimed invention, when read by a person skilled in the art.[213] A particular claim element can be mentioned *explicitly* in the reference,[214] or it can be *inherent*.[215] Suppose, for example, that a claim to a mousetrap required a "flexible" spring, and a prior publication disclosed a mousetrap with a steel spring of certain dimensions. Even if the publication did not refer to the flexibility of the spring, the spring described might be inherently flexible because of its materials and design. In this situation, the flexible spring element of the claim would be met by the reference, even though it was not explicit.[216]

Although anticipation requires that all of the elements of a claim be found in one reference, it may be proper to look to other references as an aid to *understanding* the anticipatory reference.[217] It is not proper to look to other references to fill in claim elements missing in the primary reference.[218]

---

[211] *Teleflex*, 299 F.3d at 1335; *Crown*, 289 F.3d at 1375; *In re* Bond, 910 F.2d 831, 832 (Fed. Cir. 1990).

[212] *See* Clearstream Wastewater Sys., Inc. v. Hydro-Action, Inc., 206 F.3d 1440, 1445 (Fed. Cir. 2000) (combination claims "can consist of new combinations of old elements;" individual elements of those combinations "may, and often do, read on the prior art").

[213] Like a patent disclosure, an anticipating reference must be "enabling." *See* Elan Pharmaceuticals, Inc. v. Mayo Foundation for Medical Education and Research, 346 F.3d 1054 (Fed. Cir. 2003) ("The disclosure in an assertedly anticipating reference must be adequate to enable possession of the desired subject matter. It is insufficient to name or describe the desired subject matter, if it cannot be produced without undue experimentation."); Amgen Inc. v. Hoechst Marion Roussel, Inc., 314 F.3d 1313, 1354 (Fed. Cir. 2003). On the other hand, a reference can be enabling, and anticipating, even if what it describes has not actually been attempted. *See Elan*, 346 F.3d at 1055.

[214] The reference, however, does not have to describe a claim element in precisely the same words used in the patent claim. *See Bond*, 910 F.2d at 832 (anticipation is not an *"ipsissimis verbis"* test).

[215] *See* Eli Lilly & Co. v. Barr Labs., Inc. 251 F.3d 955, 970 (Fed. Cir. 2001) ("A reference is anticipatory if it discloses every limitation of the claimed invention either explicitly or inherently. . . . A reference includes an inherent characteristic if that characteristic is the 'natural result' flowing from the reference's explicitly explicated limitations."); Telemac Cellular Corp. v. Topp Telecom, Inc., 247 F.3d 1316, 1327 (Fed. Cir. 2001) ("'Under the principles of inherency, if the prior art necessarily functions in accordance with, or includes, the claimed limitation, it anticipates.'"); Verdegaal Bros., Inc. v. Union Oil Co., 814 F.2d 628, 633 (Fed. Cir. 1987). Although anticipation requires that every claim element be found in a single reference, other references can be used to prove the fact of inherency. *Teleflex*, 299 F.3d at 1335; Continental Can Co. v. Monsanto Co., 948 F.2d 1264, 1268–69 (Fed. Cir. 1991).

This relatively clear distinction was blurred somewhat by the decision in *In re Graves*.[219] There the Federal Circuit held that a reference lacking a claim element could still be held to anticipate, if the missing element was "within the knowledge of a skilled artisan."[220] This sounds suspiciously close to an obviousness test, rather than the classic test of anticipation, and it is not clear how far in this direction the Federal Circuit is willing to go.[221]

If a patent claims a broad genus, a reference that includes a single species of the genus will anticipate the claim.[222] For example, a claim that specified a fuel composed of (among other things) "10 to 50 percent methane" would be anticipated by a prior fuel that met all of the other claim elements and that was composed of 25 percent methane. The claim is anticipated because it would otherwise prevent the practice of at least one fuel combination already in use. The converse, how-

---

[216] The Federal Circuit has issued conflicting statements on whether an inherent characteristic must have been *recognized* in order to count for anticipation. Some opinions state that the inherent characteristic must be "necessarily present" and "so recognized by persons of ordinary skill." Finnegan Corp. v. International Trade Comm'n., 180 F.3d 1354, 1365 (Fed. Cir. 1999); *see also Crown*, 289 F.3d at 1377. On other occasions, the court has observed that "[i]nherency is not necessarily coterminous with the knowledge of those of ordinary skill in the art," and "[a]rtisans of ordinary skill may not recognize the inherent characteristics of functioning of the prior art." *In re* Cruciferous Sprout Litigation, 301 F.3d 1343, 1349 (Fed. Cir. 2002); *see also* E.I. du Pont de Nemours & Co. v. Phillips Petroleum Co., 849 F.2d 1430, 1436 (Fed. Cir. 1988). The more recent decisions disavow the requirement of recognition. *See, e.g.,* Toro Co. v. Deere & Co., 355 F.3d 1313, 1320–21 (Fed. Cir. 2004); Schering Corp. v. Geneva Pharmaceuticals, Inc., 339 F.3d 1373, 1377 (Fed. Cir. 2003). Recognition may be superfluous if beneficial characteristics were present in the prior art, and the advantages were enjoyed whether anyone knew it or not. If certain vegetable sprouts always included cancer-preventing chemicals, the people who ate them reaped the benefits, even if unknowingly. *See Cruciferous Sprout*, 301 F.3d at 1350 (the inherent characteristics "have existed as long as the sprouts themselves. . . . It matters not that those of ordinary skill heretofore may not have recognized these inherent characteristics of the sprouts"). In some instances, however, failure to recognize an inherent characteristic may negate the benefits. For example, if a diet described in a publication could cure cancer but no one realized it, the diet would not be prescribed to those who could benefit from it. The Federal Circuit has not explained things in quite this fashion, but it seems a plausible way to resolve the conflict. *See* EMI Gp. North America, Inc. v. Cypress Semiconductor Corp., 268 F.3d 1342, 1350–51 (Fed. Cir. 2001) (attempting a comparatively opaque distinction between "theoretical mechanisms or rules of law," which need not be appreciated to be inherent, with other characteristics, where recognition helps establish inherency "for every combination of a claim's limitation").

[217] *See Teleflex*, 299 F.3d at 1335; Bristol-Meyers Squibb Co. v. Ben Venue Labs., Inc., 246 F.3d 1368, 1379 (Fed. Cir. 2001); *In re* Baxter Travenol Labs., 952 F.2d 388, 390 (Fed. Cir. 1991). When used in that limited fashion, the additional references need not be *prior* art. *See Bristol-Meyers*, 246 F.3d at 1379.

[218] *Teleflex*, 299 F.3d at 1335 ("Although we have permitted the use of additional references to confirm the contents of the allegedly anticipating reference . . . we have made clear that anticipation does not permit an additional reference to supply a missing claim limitation.").

[219] 69 F.3d 1147 (Fed. Cir. 1995).

[220] *Graves*, 69 F.3d at 1152.

[221] *See Teleflex*, 299 F.3d at 1334–35 (rejecting an argument based on *Graves* and reiterating that additional prior art references cannot fill gaps in the allegedly anticipating reference).

ever, is not true.[223] If a claim called for a fuel composed of exactly 25 percent methane, and a prior publication discussed such a fuel with a methane concentration of anywhere from 10 to 50 percent, the claim requiring exactly 25 percent would not be anticipated. It might or might not be invalid for obviousness.

8.9.6 Obviousness (35 U.S.C. § 103)

Obviousness is a concept drawn from the following language of 35 U.S.C. § 103(a):

A patent may not be obtained though the invention is not identically disclosed or described as set forth in section 102 of this title, if the differences between the subject matter sought to be patented and the prior art are such that the subject matter as a whole would have been obvious at the time the invention was made to a person having ordinary skill in the art to which said subject matter pertains.

Like anticipation, obviousness is a ground for rejecting a patent claim in the course of prosecution or invalidating a patent claim in the course of infringement litigation. Obviousness, however, does not require that the claimed invention be identical to the prior art. Instead, obviousness focuses on the differences between the claim and the prior art, and asks whether those differences are really inventive, or whether they are differences that might have occurred to anyone of ordinary skill. Like § 102, § 103 prevents a patent claim from taking from the public what, in a sense, it already possesses.[224]

Obviousness is judged from the perspective of the "person of ordinary skill in the art" at the time the invention was made.[225] The person of ordinary skill in the art is a mythical everyman whose perspective is often called upon in patent law, not only in context of obviousness but also, for example, in deciding whether a patent specification enables the practice of the claimed invention.[226] The person of ordinary skill is not an inventor or innovator but a person of ordinary competence who does the expected thing.[227]

---

[222] *See Eli Lilly,* 251 F.3d at 971 ("Our case law firmly establishes that a later genus claim limitation is anticipated by, and therefore not patentably distinct from, an earlier species claim."); Atlas Powder Co. v. Ireco, Inc., 190 F.3d 1342, 1346 (Fed. Cir. 1999) ("[I]f granting patent protection on the disputed claim would allow the patentee to exclude the public from practicing the prior art, then that claim is anticipated, regardless of whether it also covers subject matter not in the prior art."); Chester v. Miller, 906 F.2d 1574, 1577 (Fed. Cir. 1990).

[223] *See* Minnesota Mining & Mfg. Co. v. Johnson & Johnson Orthopaedics, Inc., 976 F.2d 1559, 1572 (Fed. Cir. 1992) (although patentee's claims were "subsumed" in a prior reference's "generalized disclosure," this did not constitute "literal identity" of invention). Disclosure of a sufficiently limited genus *might* anticipate a species of the genus, even if the prior art did not name that species specifically. *See Bristol-Meyers,* 246 F.3d at 1380. The detailed description of a small genus might be equivalent to an explicit description of each of its members.

[224] Obviousness looks to the differences between the claimed invention and the prior art, but the invention still must be viewed "as a whole." *See* Para-Ordnance Mfg., Inc. v. SGS Imports Int'l, Inc., 73 F.3d 1085, 1087 (Fed. Cir. 1995); Ryko Mfg. Co. v. Nu-Star, Inc., 950 F.2d 714, 717 (Fed. Cir. 1991).

The level of expertise and education required of the person of ordinary skill varies depending on the art. In a very sophisticated art, a person of ordinary skill might have a Ph.D. and years of hands-on experience. In a less sophisticated art, the person of ordinary skill might be a shade tree mechanic. If a court is called upon to decide whether or not a claimed invention is obvious, it first must decide what level of skill represents ordinary skill in the art at the time the invention was made.[228]

Nonobviousness should not be confused with complexity. Sometimes the simplest inventions are the most innovative.[229] Moreover, the invention need not have been the result of a *flash of genius*–the kind of sudden inspiration that led Archimedes to shout "Eureka!" An invention that is the product patient experimentation, or that is discovered entirely by accident, is just as patentable as one that arises from pure mental effort.[230] The only requirement is that the invention would not have occurred to a person of ordinary skill. This principle accounts for the first sentence of § 103(c), which provides, rather cryptically, that "[p]atentability shall not be negatived by the manner in which the invention was made."

[225] *See* Amgen Inc. v. Hoechst Marion Roussel, Inc., 314 F.3d 1313, 1352 (Fed. Cir. 2003); Arkie Lures, Inc. v. Gene Larew Tackle, Inc., 119 F.3d 953, 956 (Fed. Cir. 1997) (the decision regarding obviousness "is made not from the viewpoint of the inventor, but from the viewpoint of a person of ordinary skill in the field of the invention"); Custom Accessories, Inc. v. Jeffrey-Allan Indus., Inc., 807 F.2d 955, 962 (Fed. Cir. 1986) (The question is whether the invention would have been obvious to one of ordinary skill in the art of the invention–"not to the judge, or to a layman, or to those skilled in remote arts, or to geniuses in the art.").

[226] *See* Section 8.6.

[227] Standard Oil Co. v. American Cyanamid Co., 774 F.2d 448, 454 (Fed. Cir. 1985) ("A person of ordinary skill in the art is . . . presumed to be one who thinks along the lines of conventional wisdom in the art and is not one who undertakes to innovate, whether by patient, and often expensive, systematic research or by extraordinary insights, it makes no difference which.").

[228] *See* Ruiz v. A.B. Chance Co., 234 F.3d 654, 666 (Fed. Cir. 2000). Factors that may be considered include "1) the types of problems encountered in the art; 2) the prior art solutions to those problems; 3) the rapidity with which innovations are made; 4) the sophistication of the technology; and 5) the educational level of active workers in the field." *Id.* at 666–67. An invention may be obvious to a person of ordinary skill even if it would not be obvious to a layperson. On the other hand, an invention that would be obvious to a person of *extraordinary* skill can still be patentable. Inventors and patentees are often assumed to be persons of extraordinary skill. *See* Kloster Speedsteel AB v. Crucible Inc., 793 F.2d 1565, 1574 (Fed. Cir. 1986).

[229] *See* Gentry Gallery, Inc. v. Berkline Corp., 134 F.3d 1473, 1478 (Fed. Cir. 1998) ("simplicity alone is not determinative of obviousness"); *In re* Oetiker, 877 F.2d 1443, 1447 (Fed. Cir. 1992) ("Simplicity is not inimical to patentability."); Demaco Corp. v. F. Von Langsdorff Licensing Ltd., 851 F.2d 1387, 1390–91 (Fed. Cir. 1988) ("Nor does the patent statute require that an invention be complex in order to be nonobvious.").

[230] *See* Graham v. John Deere Co., 383 U.S. 1, 15 (1966); Life Technologies, Inc. v. Clontech Labs., Inc., 224 F.3d 1320, 1325 (Fed. Cir. 2000) ("the path that leads an inventor to the invention is . . . irrelevant to patentability"); *In re* Dow Chemical Co., 837 F.2d 469, 472 (Fed. Cir. 1988) ("[m]ost technological advance is the fruit of methodical, persistent investigation"); Vandenberg v. Dairy Equipment Co., 740 F.2d 1560, 1565 (Fed. Cir. 1984).

The standard of patentability is not whether the invention would have been "obvious to *try.*"[231] If, for example, there were a long list of compounds that might prove to be an effective treatment for a disease, any one of which would be obvious to try, the discovery that a particular compound on that list is an effective treatment might still be a nonobvious invention.[232] The deciding factor is whether a person skilled in the art, contemplating that particular compound, would have had a "reasonable expectation of success" before the discovery had been made.[233] Although it is a confusing approach to distinguish between *obvious to do* and *obvious to try,* it at least acknowledges that important and nonobvious inventions can arise from laborious trial and error. This particularly seems to be the case in the fields of chemistry and biotechnology.

Sometimes an invention would have been obvious from a *technological* point of view, but not from a *business* point of view. Suppose, for example, that a patent claimed a mousetrap of a prior design, but with certain parts made of solid gold. The patentee might argue that the mousetrap was nonobvious because no one would have believed a solid gold mousetrap to be a profitable item. Perhaps the inventor was a marketing genius, who realized that a solid gold mousetrap would be a successful novelty gift for the wealthy. Patents, however, are meant to encourage the *technological* arts. Therefore, even if the mousetrap was ingenious from a marketing standpoint, it would be unpatentable if obvious from a technological standpoint.[234]

Whereas anticipation requires that all the elements of the claimed invention be found in a single prior art reference, obviousness can be based on the *combination* of more than one reference. If, for example, some elements of the claimed invention were found in one technical journal, and the remaining elements were found in another journal, it could be argued that the combination of one with the other would have been obvious to a person of ordinary skill who was aware of both.

---

[231] Novo Nordisk A/S v. Becton Dickinson & Co., 304 F.3d 1216, 1220 (Fed. Cir. 2002); Ecolochem, Inc. v. Southern California Edison Co., 227 F.3d 1361, 1374 (Fed. Cir. 2000); *In re* Deuel, 51 F.3d 1552, 1559 (Fed. Cir. 1995).

[232] *See In re* Baird, 16 F.3d 380, 382 (Fed. Cir. 1994) ("A disclosure of millions of compounds does not render obvious a claim to three compounds, particularly when the disclosure indicates a preference leading away from the claimed compounds.").

[233] *See* Boehringer Ingelheim Vetmedica, Inc. v. Schering-Plough Corp., 320 F.3d 1339, 1352 (Fed. Cir. 2003) (prior reports of failure negated "reasonable expectation of success"); *In re* O'Farrell, 853 F.2d 894, 903–04 (Fed. Cir. 1988); *In re* Merck & Co., 800 F.2d 1091, 1097 (Fed. Cir. 1986). Another "obvious to try" situation might occur if a publication included "a general disclosure [to] pique the scientist's curiosity, such that further investigation might be done as a result of the disclosure, but the disclosure itself [did] not contain a sufficient teaching of how to obtain the desired result." *In re* Eli Lilly & Co., 902 F.2d 943, 945 (Fed. Cir. 1990).

[234] *See* Orthopedic Equipment Co. v. U.S., 702 F.2d 1005, 1013 (Fed. Cir. 1983) ("[T]he fact that the two disclosed apparatus would not be combined by businessmen for economic reasons is not the same as saying that it could not be done because skilled persons in the art felt that there was some technological incompatibility that prevented their combination. Only the latter fact is telling on the issue of nonobviousness.").

It is not necessary that any person skilled in the art actually considered such a combination before the claimed invention was made. Instead, courts often imagine the hypothetical "person of ordinary skill in the art" standing in a workshop, surrounded by all of the relevant patents, publications, and other prior art references.[235] The question then becomes, would such a person, confronting the problem solved by the invention and aware of all of these references, have found it obvious to make the claimed combination?

The references that may be considered include any of the kinds of prior art set forth in § 102, as long as they are in "the field of the inventor's endeavor" or an *analogous art.* An analogous art is one that is "reasonably pertinent to the particular problem with which the inventor is involved"—in other words, an art that an inventor would look to for solutions or ideas.[236] For example, in *In re Paulsen*,[237] the claimed invention concerned a case for a portable computer hinged in such a way that it could be closed tight for carrying or latched in an upright position for viewing the display screen. The court found it appropriate to consider references concerning hinges and latches, even if they were not in the portable computer field:

> The problems encountered by the inventors . . . were problems that were not unique to portable computers. They concerned how to connect and secure the computer's display housing to the computer while meeting certain size constraints and functional requirements. . . . We agree with the Board that given the nature of the problems confronted by the inventors, one of ordinary skill in the art "would have consulted the mechanical arts for housings, hinges, latches, springs, etc."[238]

In *In re Oetiker*,[239] on the other hand, the court found insufficient evidence that a person working on hose clamps would have been motivated to consider fasteners used in clothing.[240]

In judging whether a claimed invention would have been obvious, it is important to avoid the use of hindsight.[241] After an invention has been

---

[235] *See* Para-Ordnance Mfg. v. SGS Imports Int'l, Inc., 73 F.3d 1085, 1088 (Fed. Cir. 1995). However, the visual image of the art "tableau" has been criticized by the judge who first created it, perhaps because it suggests the use of hindsight in selecting the references to "hang in the workshop." *See* Standard Oil Co. v. American Cyanamid Co., 774 F.2d 448, 454 n.3 (Fed. Cir. 1985) (referring to the "unfortunate popularity" of the tableau imagery).

[236] *See* Wang Labs., Inc. v. Toshiba Corp., 993 F.2d 858, 864 (Fed. Cir. 1993); *In re* Clay, 966 F.2d 656, 659 (Fed. Cir. 1992). Note that the pertinent art should be defined in terms of the *problem* faced by the inventor, not the *solution* embodied in the patented invention. The latter would introduce inappropriate hindsight. *See* Monarch Knitting Machinery Corp. v. Sulzer Morat GmbH, 139 F.3d 877, 881 (Fed. Cir. 1998).

[237] 30 F.3d 1475 (Fed. Cir. 1994).

[238] *Paulsen*, 30 F.3d at 1481–82.

[239] 977 F.2d 1443 (Fed. Cir. 1992).

[240] *Oetiker*, 977 F.2d at 1447.

[241] *See* Crown Operations Int'l., Ltd. v. Solutia Inc., 289 F.3d 1367, 1376 (Fed. Cir. 2002); *In re* Kotzab, 217 F.3d 1365, 1369 (Fed. Cir. 2000); *Para-Ordnance*, 73 F.3d at 1087.

made, it may be all too easy to claim that it was obvious.[242] Obviousness must be judged from the perspective of one of ordinary skill in the art "at the time the invention was made." Accordingly, one cannot prove obviousness by simply canvassing the prior art, using the patent itself as a guide, until all the elements of the invention have been found.[243] Rather, one must show some preexisting *suggestion* or *motivation* to combine the references in the manner claimed.[244] This does not mean that one reference must include an explicit reference to the other, but it does mean there must be something, either in the references themselves or in the general knowledge available in the art, that would have led a person of ordinary skill to combine those particular references in the manner claimed, and with a reasonable expectation of success.[245]

Sometimes a prior reference *teaches away* from the claimed invention. To teach away means to suggest that the claimed combination should be avoided as undesirable or ineffective.[246] This is one factor to consider in deciding whether certain references render a claimed invention obvious. Nevertheless, sufficient disclosure can render an invention obvious and unpatentable, even if the reference suggests that the invention is an inferior approach.[247]

It seems easier to conclude that the claimed invention was an obvious one if there are a large number of similar ideas found in the prior art. How-

---

[242] "Good ideas may well appear 'obvious' after they have been disclosed, despite having been previously unrecognized." *Arkie Lures*, 119 F.3d at 956.

[243] *See Crown*, 289 F.3d at 1376 ("'Determination of obviousness cannot be based on the hindsight combination of components selectively culled from the prior art to fit the parameters of the patented invention.'"); *Life Technologies*, 224 F.3d at 1326 ("It is axiomatic that a claimed invention is not obvious solely because it is composed of elements that are all individually found in the prior art."); *In re* Gorman, 933 F.2d 982, 987 (Fed. Cir. 1991) ("It is impermissible . . . simply to engage in a hindsight reconstruction of the claimed invention, using the applicant's structure as a template and selecting elements from references to fill the gaps.").

[244] *See Boehringer*, 320 F.3d at 1354; Beckson Marine, Inc. v. NFM, Inc., 292 F.3d 718, 727 (Fed. Cir. 2002); *Crown*, 289 F.3d at 1376; *Kotzab*, 217 F.3d at 1370. Even when the invention is alleged to be an obvious variation of a single prior art reference, there must be a motivation to alter that reference as required to produce the claimed invention. *See* Sibia Neurosciences, Inc. v. Cadus Pharmaceutical Corp., 225 F.3d 1349, 1356 (Fed. Cir. 2000).

[245] *See* Ruiz v. A.B. Chance Co., 357 F.3d 1270, 1276–77 (Fed. Cir. 204) (the "suggestion" to combine need not be explicit, but may be found in "the nature of the problem to be solved"); *Crown*, 289 F.3d at 1376 ("There must be a teaching or suggestion within the prior art, within the nature of the problem to be solved, or within the general knowledge of a person of ordinary skill in the field of the invention, to look to particular sources, to select particular elements, and to combine them as combined by the inventor.").

[246] *See In re* Haruna, 249 F.3d 1327, 1335 (Fed. Cir. 2001); *In re* Gurley, 27 F.3d 551, 553 (Fed. Cir. 1994) ("A reference may be said to teach away when a person of ordinary skill, upon reading the reference, would be discouraged from following the path set out in the reference, or would be led in a direction divergent from the path that was taken by the applicant."). Note that "teaching away" is not relevant to anticipation. Celeritas Technologies, Ltd. v. Rockwell Int'l Corp., 150 F.3d 1354, 1361 (Fed. Cir. 1998) ("A reference is no less anticipatory if, after disclosing the invention, the reference then disparages it.").

ever, one can reach the opposite conclusion, reasoning that where so many inventors came so close to the claimed invention, but still managed to be different, there must be something about the claimed invention that everyone else missed.[248] A defendant in a patent case who is attempting to prove obviousness must decide whether it is more persuasive to weigh in with every reference available or to select only the few that are most similar to the claimed invention.

Although obviousness determinations are highly fact-specific,[249] a pair of examples will give the reader some flavor for how the decisions are made. In *In re Gorman*,[250] the claimed invention was a novelty lollipop in the shape of a thumb. The elements of the claimed invention included a thumb-shaped candy core; a protective covering, also thumb-shaped, which served first as a mold for the candy core and then as a "toy and novelty item for placement upon the thumb of the user;" a lollipop stick; a plug of chewing gum or similar edible material to seal the bottom of the candy; and a plastic or cardboard disk at the base of the "thumb."

The prior art located by the Patent Office included thirteen references. Some showed candy or ice cream formed in a rubbery mold, which served double-duty as a wrapper for the product. One ice cream product on a stick included a similar cardboard base. Other references (believe it or not) disclosed thumb-shaped candies and confections. Edible plugs also had been disclosed for sealing liquid inside of candy and ice cream products. Although Gorman's claim was very detailed, and none of the references included all of the things that Gorman claimed, the Patent Office found that the combination still would have been obvious to any person of ordinary skill. The Federal Circuit affirmed: "The various elements Gorman combined . . . are all shown in the cited references in various subcombinations, used in the same way, for the same purpose as in the claimed invention."[251]

In *Moleculon Research Corp. v. CBS, Inc.*,[252] however, the Federal Circuit upheld the determination of the trial court that the claimed invention was not obvious. There the invention was a cube-puzzle of the kind popularized by Rubik's Cube. In fact, Rubik's Cube was the product accused of infringement. The claims described a puzzle in the shape of a subdivided cube, the pieces of which could be scrambled and restored by rotating the facets of the cube. CBS, which owned the rights to Rubik's Cube, argued that the claims were obvious in light of a prior patent, to one Gustafson, disclosing a spheri-

---

[247] *See Gurley*, 27 F.3d at 553 ("A known and obvious composition does not become patentable simply because it has been described as somewhat inferior to some other product for the same use.").

[248] *See Gorman*, 933 F.2d at 986.

[249] Even though the ultimate determination of obviousness is a "question of law." See Section 11.4.

[250] 933 F.2d 892, 897 (Fed. Cir. 1991).

[251] *Gorman*, 933 F.2d at 987.

[252] 793 F.2d 1261 (Fed. Cir. 1986).

cal puzzle with a subdivided, rotatable shell. A person skilled in the art might have *considered* converting Gustafson's sphere puzzle into a cube with rotating faces, but nothing in the art suggested that such a change would have been desirable. On the contrary, the evidence showed that Gustafson, while considering other shapes, had dismissed a cube as inadequate.[253] Moreover, one expert described the cube as a "quantum leap" from the sphere.[254] On the basis of this evidence, the lower court properly concluded that even someone aware of Gustafson's sphere would not have found it obvious to make the cube.

Even these two examples are enough to prove the Federal Circuit's observation that "[t]he obviousness standard, while easy to expound, is sometimes difficult to apply."[255] An obviousness analysis requires a difficult act of the imagination. The decision maker, whether a patent examiner or judge, must view the situation from the perspective of another person (a person of ordinary skill in the art), at a different time (the time the invention was made), while ignoring information that has to be foremost in the decision maker's mind (the disclosure of the invention in the patent itself).[256] And even if the decision maker can manage this feat, obviousness can still seem a matter of opinion. It is not hard to imagine *Gorman* or *Moleculon* reaching an opposite conclusion.

8.9.6.1 *Secondary Considerations*

Because the obviousness determination is such a difficult and subjective one, courts have increasingly emphasized the importance of *secondary considerations*. Secondary considerations are factors that are believed to provide objective evidence of obviousness or nonobviousness. A leading case on secondary considerations is *Graham v. John Deere Co.*,[257] one of the Supreme Court's infrequent opinions in the area of patent law. The court suggested that in deciding the fundamental question of obviousness, it might be appropriate to consider "secondary considerations" such as "commercial success, long felt but unsolved needs, failure of others, etc."[258] Under subsequent Federal Circuit precedent, consideration of these factors has become mandatory.[259]

---

[253] *Moleculon*, 793 F.2d at 1268.

[254] *Moleculon*, 793 F.2d at 1268.

[255] Uniroyal, Inc. v. Rudkin-Wiley Corp., 837 F.2d 1044, 1050 (Fed. Cir. 1988).

[256] *See Uniroyal*, 837 F.2d at 1050–51.

[257] 383 U.S. 1 (1966).

[258] *Graham*, 383 U.S. at 17–18. The factors specifically mentioned in *Graham* may be given greater weight than others subsumed in the "etc." *See* Ecolochem, Inc. v. Southern California Edison Co., 227 F.3d 1361, 1380 (Fed. Cir. 2000).

[259] *See* Ruiz v. A.B. Chance Co., 234 F.3d 654, 667 (Fed. Cir. 2000) ("Our precedents clearly hold that secondary considerations, when present, must be considered in determining obviousness."); Hybritech, Inc. v. Monoclonal Antibodies, Inc., 802 F.2d 1367, 1380 (Fed. Cir. 1986) (secondary considerations are more than "icing on the cake"); Stratoflex, Inc. v. Aeroquip Corp., 713 F.2d 1530, 1539 (Fed. Cir. 1983).

Secondary considerations include the following:

• Commercial success
• Long-felt need
• Failure of others
• Industry recognition
• Expressions of skepticism or disbelief
• Unexpected results
• Copying
• Near-simultaneous invention

The secondary consideration most frequently encountered is commercial success. Commercial success means evidence that a product covered by a patent claim has earned substantial profits in the marketplace. In theory, an invention that has been successful in the marketplace could not have been an obvious one. Otherwise, someone else would have stepped ahead of the inventor in order to reap the available rewards.[260]

There are at least three possible objections to this theory. First, the theory works only if the success of the invention had been foreseeable. Second, *someone* has to be first to invent, even if the invention is an obvious one and the rewards are substantial. Finally, commercial success can be due to any number of factors other than the claimed invention, including marketing know-how, advertising, manufacturing techniques, quality control, price, or features of the product other than those covered by the claim. In order to meet this last objection, a *nexus* must exist between the success and the claimed invention.[261] Nexus means a logical, cause-and-effect relationship between the success of the product and the claimed invention. Such a connection might be shown in a number of ways, including consumer surveys, comparisons to similar products, or testimony concerning the relative advantages of the claimed invention.[262]

---

[260] *See* Dickey-John Corp. v. Int'l Tapetronics Corp., 710 F.2d 329, 346–47 (7th Cir. 1983) ("If individuals believe there is 'a fortune waiting in the wings' for the person who solves the problem, we infer that with such an incentive, many artisans were actually attempting to find the solution. The longer they failed to do so, the stronger the inference that it took extraordinary skill to solve the problem.").

[261] *See* Brown & Williamson Tobacco Corp. v. Philip Morris Inc., 229 F.3d 1120, 1130 (Fed. Cir. 2000); *Ecolochem,* 227 F.3d at 1377; Sibia Neurosciences, Inc. v. Cadus Pharmaceutical Corp., 225 F.3d 1349, 1358–59 (Fed. Cir. 2000); Demaco Corp. v. F. Von Langsdorff Licensing Ltd., 851 F.2d 1387, 1392 (Fed. Cir. 1988).

[262] *See Demaco,* 851 F.2d at 1392–93. "[I]f the marketed product embodies the claimed features, and is coextensive with them, then a nexus is presumed and the burden shifts to the party asserting obviousness to present evidence to rebut the presumed nexus." *Brown & Williamson,* 229 F.3d at 1130. One way to rebut the presumption might be to show that other products embodying the patented invention were commercial failures; hence, the successful product must owe its success to something other than the invention. *See id.*

Commercial success is useful as a secondary consideration to patentees or applicants who have marketed a product covered by the claim. Commercial success can also be premised on a product marketed by someone else—even an infringer—as long as there is a nexus between the success of the product and the invention claimed.[263] Success in licensing[264] may also be offered as evidence of commercial success.[265]

The other secondary considerations are relatively straightforward. If there had been a long-felt need for an invention, or if others had tried and failed to solve the problem addressed by the invention, it is reasonable to infer that the invention was not an obvious one. Otherwise the problem would have been solved before, and the need already satisfied.[266] Reactions to the invention by persons skilled in the art can also be important. If experts in the field praised the invention or, even better, if they expressed skepticism or disbelief that anyone had solved the problems overcome by the invention, this also serves as evidence of nonobviousness.[267] Unexpected results can be useful in showing that an invention was not an obvious one, particularly where the results are unexpectedly good.[268] Finally, because imitation is the sincerest form of flattery, copying of the invention can be taken as objective evidence that the invention was not obvious.[269]

All of the secondary considerations discussed so far are potential evidence of *nonobviousness*.[270] Near-simultaneous invention is one secondary consideration that is positive evidence of *obviousness*. If an invention is made independently by

---

[263] *See Brown & Williamson,* 229 F.3d at 1130.

[264] See Section 6.3.

[265] *See In re* GPAC Inc., 57 F.3d 1573, 1580 (Fed. Cir. 1995).

[266] *See* Advanced Display Sys., Inc. v. Kent State University, 212 F.3d 1272, 1285 (Fed. Cir. 2000) (failure of others); Gambro Lundia AB v. Baxter Healthcare Corp., 110 F.3d 1573, 1579–80 (Fed. Cir. 1997); *In re* Dow Chemical Co., 837 F.2d 469, 472 (Fed. Cir. 1988) ("Recognition of need, and difficulties encountered by those skilled in the field, are classical indicia of unobviousness.").

[267] *See Ecolochem,* 227 F.3d at 1380 (acclamation); Monarch Knitting Machinery Corp. v. Sulzer Morat GmbH, 139 F.3d 877, 885 (Fed. Cir. 1998) ("general skepticism" as evidence of nonobviousness); Gillette Co. v. S.C. Johnson & Son, Inc., 919 F.2d 720, 726 (Fed. Cir. 1990) (skepticism toward "new-fangled approach" evidenced nonobviousness); Environmental Designs, Ltd. v. Union Oil Co., 713 F.2d 693, 697–98 (Fed. Cir. 1983). "Teaching away" (see Section 8.9.6) can be one form of expressing skepticism. *See Monarch Knitting,* 139 F.3d at 885 ("[i]n effect, 'teaching away' is a more pointed and probative form of skepticism").

[268] *See* Richardson-Vicks Inc. v. Upjohn Co., 122 F.3d 1476, 1483 (Fed. Cir. 1997).

[269] *Advanced Display,* 212 F.3d at 1285–86; Diversitech Corp. v. Century Steps, Inc., 850 F.2d 675, 679 (Fed. Cir. 1988); Panduit Corp. v. Dennison Mfg. Co., 776 F.2d 1082, 1099 (Fed. Cir. 1985). But c.f. *Ecolochem,* 227 F.3d at 1380 (Copying "is only equivocal evidence of nonobviousness in the absence of more compelling objective indicia;" copying could have occurred only because of "'a general lack of concern for patent property.'").

[270] The absence of commercial success, long-felt need, and the other indicia of nonobviousness has generally been held a "neutral factor," rather than positive evidence of obviousness. *See* Gentry Gallery, Inc. v. Berkline Corp., 134 F.3d 1473, 1478 (Fed. Cir. 1998); *Medtronic,* 799 F.2d at 739 n.13.

another inventor, at nearly the same time as the applicant or patentee, this is evidence that the invention was not the result of uncommon effort or insight. Rather, the art may simply have progressed to the point where the claimed invention was the obvious next step.[271] Note that an independent, near-simultaneous invention can serve as objective evidence of obviousness, even if that invention occurred shortly after the invention by the patentee or applicant, thereby disqualifying it as potential prior art under § 102.

8.9.7 Derivation (§ 102(f))

One rule of patentability that almost goes without saying is that an applicant cannot claim someone else's invention. This rule is embodied in 35 U.S.C. § 102(f), which states that a patent cannot be obtained if the applicant "did not himself invent the subject matter sought to be patented." If the purported inventor took the idea from someone else, the claim is unpatentable or, if already issued, invalid. A defense based on § 102(f) is usually referred to as a *derivation* defense, because the claim is said to be derived from someone else's invention.[272]

A derivation defense requires proof, by clear and convincing evidence, (1) that the invention was fully conceived by another person before it had been conceived by the purported inventor, and (2) that the conception was communicated to the purported inventor.[273] The information communicated must have been an enabling disclosure of the invention,[274] not merely information that could have made the invention obvious.[275]

8.10 SECTION 102(b) STATUTORY BARS

The previous discussion of § 102 concerned the effect of events occurring before the applicant's *date of invention*. The portions of § 102 that deal with these events (paragraphs (a), (e), and (g)) ensure that on the date of the applicant's invention, the invention was new. Paragraph (b) of § 102 serves a different purpose. Section 102(b) ensures that the applicant did not delay too long in filing a patent application after the occurrence of certain key events.

---

[271] *See Ecolochem*, 227 F.3d at 1379; *In re* Merk & Co., 800 F.2d 1091, 1098 (Fed. Cir. 1986).

[272] *See* Eaton Corp. v. Rockwell Int'l Corp., 323 F.3d 1332, 1344 (Fed. Cir. 2003); Price v. Symsek, 988 F.2d 1187, 1190 (Fed. Cir. 1993).

[273] *Eaton*, 323 F.3d at 1344; Gambro Lundia AB v. Baxter Healthcare Corp., 110 F.3d 1573, 1576 (Fed. Cir. 1997). The claim of prior conception must be corroborated (see Section 8.9.3). Lacks Indus., Inc. v. McKechnie Vehicle Components USA, Inc., 322 F.3d 1335, 1349 (Fed. Cir. 2003).

[274] *Eaton*, 323 F.3d at 1344. Enabling disclosures are discussed in Section 8.6.

[275] *Gambro*, 110 F.3d at 1577–78. *Gambro* suggests that one could never base a finding of obviousness on the kind of disclosure contemplated in § 102(f). However, the Federal Circuit later decided that a § 102(f) disclosure, combined with other references, *can* lead to a finding of obviousness. Oddzon Prods., Inc. v. Just Toys, Inc., 122 F.3d 1396, 1403–04 (Fed. Cir. 1997).

Section 102(b) provides as follows:

A person shall be entitled to a patent unless—

(b) the invention was patented or described in a printed publication in this or a foreign country or in public use or on sale in this country, more than one year prior to the date of the application for patent in the United States. . . .

Section 102(b) is similar to 102(a) in that both refer to prior patents, printed publications and public use.[276] However, § 102(b) differs fundamentally from § 102(a) in three respects. First, § 102(b) adds the "on sale" language. Second, a § 102(b) reference often arises from the actions of the applicant himself, whereas a § 102(a) reference can only arise from the acts of a third party. Finally, the important date for § 102(b) is not the date of the invention, but a date exactly *one year before the patent application was filed.*[277] This date is known as the application's *critical date.*

Imagine the following scenario. On January 1, 2000, an inventor conceives of a better mousetrap, and on January 2, 2000, the inventor reduces the invention to practice by constructing a prototype in his workshop. January 2, 2000, is the date of the invention, and that date is corroborated by a witnessed laboratory notebook. On January 3, 2000, the inventor submits a complete description of the mousetrap to the *Inventor's Newsletter,* which publishes the description on February 1, 2000. On February 2, 2001, the inventor files a patent application. The critical date of the application, under § 102(b), is February 2, 2000. The publication in the *Inventor's Newsletter* on February 1, 2000, is not prior art under § 102(a) because it did not occur before the applicant's date of invention. However, the publication did occur before the critical date. Consequently, if the publication included a complete and enabling description of the invention, the patent application would be rejected under § 102(b).

In essence, § 102(b) provides a one-year grace period after the first patent, publication, public use, or offer to sell that relates to the claimed invention.[278] An inventor has that long to file a patent application, or the right to a patent is lost. Any problems that might arise from the inventor's own activities can be avoided simply by ensuring that a patent application is on file within one year of the date of invention. This practice should be adopted by all inventors, though frequently it is not.

The rationale for § 102(b) is threefold. First, and most generally, it encourages diligence by penalizing inventors who are lazy, or inclined to suppress

---

[276] The definition of *printed publication* under § 102(a) also applies under § 102(b). *See* Section 8.9.1.1.

[277] When prosecution results in a chain of related applications, a later application may be entitled to the effective filing date of a preceding application for purposes of § 102(b). *See* Section 5.2.

[278] *See* Woodland Trust v. Flowertree Nursery, Inc., 148 F.3d 1368, 1370 (Fed. Cir. 1998).

their inventions, or who for some other reason delay in filing a patent application.[279] Second, it prevents the public from being misled where the availability of the invention to the public, without evidence that the inventor intends to obtain a patent, might create the impression that the invention is up for grabs.[280] Finally, it prevents what could be an unwarranted extension of the inventor's monopoly powers beyond the 20 years contemplated by the patent system.[281] If there were no § 102(b), an inventor might delay seeking patent protection indefinitely, and the mere threat that he would do so eventually could prevent potential competitors from daring to compete. On the other hand, an inventor does need a certain amount of time to perfect the invention, judge whether it is worth pursuing, and prepare a patent application.[282] Section 102(b) establishes one year as the period that most effectively balances the needs of the inventor against the needs of the public.

The prohibitions of § 102(b) are commonly known as *statutory bars.* A statutory bar can prevent the issuance of a claim in a patent application, or it can be used to challenge the validity of an issued patent claim in subsequent infringement litigation. A reference that qualifies under § 102(b) can also be used as the basis for a finding of obviousness.[283] In some cases, a reference can qualify as prior art under either § 102(a) or § 102(b). If so, § 102(b) can provide the simpler analysis because it relies on the easily determined critical date of the patent application, rather than the often difficult to determine date of invention.

8.10.1 The On-Sale Bar

The most frequently encountered statutory bar is probably the *on-sale bar* created when the inventor, or a third party,[284] takes steps to commercialize the

---

[279] *See* Special Devices, Inc. v. OEA, Inc., 270 F.3d 1353, 1357 (Fed. Cir. 2001); La Bounty Mfg., Inc. v. U.S. Int'l Trade Comm'n, 958 F.2d 1066, 1071 (Fed. Cir. 1992) ("The general purpose behind [the] section 102(b) bars is to require inventors to assert with due diligence their right to a patent through the prompt filing of a patent application.").

[280] *See* Continental Plastic Containers v. Owens Brockway Plastic Prods., Inc., 141 F.3d 1073, 1079 (Fed. Cir. 1998) ("[t]he primary policy underlying the 'public use' case is that of detrimental public reliance"); Baxter Int'l, Inc. v. Cobe Labs., Inc., 88 F.3d 1054, 1058 (Fed. Cir. 1996).

[281] *See Continental Plastic,* 141 F.3d at 1079 ("the primary purpose underlying the 'on sale' case is that of prohibiting the commercial exploitation of the design beyond the statutorily prescribed time period"); *Baxter Int'l,* 88 F.3d at 1058; Ferag AG v. Quipp, Inc., 45 F.3d 1562, 1566 (Fed. Cir. 1995).

[282] *See Baxter Int'l,* 88 F.3d at 1058 (policies behind § 102(b) include "'allowing the inventor a reasonable amount of time following sales activity to determine the potential economic value of a patent'").

[283] *See* Elmer v. ICC Fabricating, Inc., 67 F.3d 1571, 1574 (Fed. Cir. 1995); Baker Oil Tools, Inc. v. Geo Vann, Inc., 828 F.2d 1558, 1563 (Fed. Cir. 1987).

[284] *See* Special Devices, Inc. v. OEA, Inc., 270 F.3d 1353, 1355 (Fed. Cir. 2001) ("By phrasing the statutory bar in the passive voice, Congress indicated that it does not matter who places the invention 'on sale'; it only matters that someone—inventor, supplier or other third party—placed it on sale.").

claimed invention more than one year before the filing date of the patent application. An on-sale bar arises if a product embodying the claimed invention, or rendering it obvious, was sold or offered for sale before the critical date.[285] A single sale, or a single offer to sell, is sufficient to invoke the statutory bar.[286]

Disputes frequently arise over whether certain activity did or did not constitute a sale or definite offer to sell. For example, an inventor may contend that a commercial relationship with a potential customer was not related to a bona fide sale of patented product, but rather to a joint development effort. In *Continental Can Co. v. Monsanto Co.*,[287] a plastics company entered into an agreement with the Coca-Cola Company to develop a plastic bottle. Under the agreement, the companies would work together to produce a suitable bottle, with the plastics company making the bottles and Coca-Cola testing them. If a satisfactory bottle were developed, Coca-Cola would purchase the bottles from the plastics company, under terms that were partially negotiated. The plastics company produced bottles in a variety of shapes, including one that allegedly embodied the patent claim in question, but the project was abandoned when tests proved unsuccessful.[288] Although the trial court found that the relationship had placed the patented bottle on sale before the critical date, the Federal Circuit disagreed and reversed:

> Although Admiral Plastic's hope was surely commercial sales, and the record shows that prices and quantities were discussed, this does not of itself place the subject matter "on sale" in the sense of § 102(b). The . . . bottle was a part of a terminated development project that never bore commercial fruit and was cloaked in confidentiality. While the line is not always bright between development and being on sale . . . in this case the line was not crossed.[289]

---

[285] *See* Keystone Retaining Wall Sys., Inc. v. Westrock, Inc., 997 F.2d 1444, 1451 (Fed. Cir. 1993).

[286] Intel Corp. v. U.S. Int'l Trade Comm'n, 946 F.2d 821, 830 (Fed. Cir. 1991). An offer to sell must be so definite and final that, applying traditional principles of contract law, acceptance of that offer would form a binding contract. *See* Linear Technology Corp. v. Micrel, Inc., 275 F.3d 1040, 1048–52 (Fed. Cir. 2001) (general dissemination of advertising, newsletters and data sheets did not constitute such an offer); Group One, Ltd. v. Hallmark Cards, Inc., 254 F.3d 1041, 1046 (Fed. Cir. 2001). The *offer* itself is sufficient even if it was declined. Scaltech, Inc. v. Retec/Tetra, L.L.C., 269 F.3d 1321, 1328 (Fed. Cir. 2001).

[287] 948 F.2d 1264 (Fed. Cir. 1991).

[288] *See Continental Can*, 948 F.2d at 1269.

[289] *Continental Can*, 948 F.2d at 1270. A sale or offer to sell must be to a separate entity. A transaction between related corporations that was completed purely for accounting purposes would not constitute a genuine "sale," at least if the "selling" entity "so controls the purchaser that the invention remains out of the public's hands." *See* Ferag AG v. Quipp, Inc., 45 F.3d 1562, 1567 (Fed. Cir. 1995). On the other hand, sales *to the patentee* by an independent supplier, not for purposes of experiment or development but in preparation for release to the general public, can invalidate a patent. *See Special Devices*, 270 F.3d at 1355-57. Note that *licensing* someone to practice the invention (see Section 6.3) is not a sale that triggers § 102(b). *In re* Kollar, 286 F.3d 1326, 1330–34 (Fed. Cir. 2002).

A transaction does not constitute a bar under § 102(b) if it is part of an *experimental use*—that is, if the primary object of the "sale" was not to profit from the invention, but to test it in the field.[290] Although a court will consider a variety of factors in deciding if a sale was for purposes of commerce or experiment, at a minimum the seller must inform the purchaser that the goods are experimental, and the seller must retain sufficient control over the goods to conduct the required monitoring or tests.[291] A court will also consider whether the seller kept the kind of records that would suggest experimentation, whether the seller required the purchaser to keep the activities confidential, whether payment was received, and whether the sale was accompanied by promotional efforts.[292] Keeping track of customer responses and complaints after sale of a new product is not sufficient to show that the sales were primarily experimental.[293] Moreover, the experiments have to relate to the *claimed invention.* If the experiments relate to some other aspect of a product, or if they are nothing more than marketing tests to gauge consumer demand, the sale is not within the experimental use exception.[294]

One issue that long divided opinion is the extent to which the invention must be complete before it can be offered for sale in a manner triggering § 102(b).[295] The Supreme Court eventually decreed, in *Pfaff v. Wells Electronics, Inc.*,[296] that the invention must be "ready for patenting" before the critical date in order for a sale or offer to sell to be invalidating.[297] Once the invention is ready for patenting, there is no excuse to delay (more than one year) filing a patent application. *One* way to demonstrate that the invention was ready for patenting is an actual reduction to

---

[290] *See* Pfaff v. Wells Electronics, Inc., 525 U.S. 55, 64 (1998) ("[A]n inventor who seeks to perfect his discovery may conduct extensive testing without losing his right to obtain a patent for his invention—even if such testing occurs in the public eye. The law has long recognized the distinction between inventions put to experimental use and products sold commercially."); EZ Dock, Inc. v. Schafer Sys., Inc., 276 F.3d 1347, 1352–53 (Fed. Cir. 2002) (sale may have been primarily to test dock in rougher waters). To qualify as experimental, the transaction must have been "primarily for purposes of experimentation," rather than profit. Allen Eng'g Corp. v. Bartell Indus., Inc., 299 F.3d 1336, 1352–53 (Fed. Cir. 2002).

[291] *See* Paragon Podiatry Lab., Inc. v. KLM Labs., Inc. 984 F.2d 1182, 1186–87 (Fed. Cir. 1993); La Bounty Mfg., Inc. v. U.S. Int'l Trade Comm'n, 958 F.2d 1066, 1071–72 (Fed. Cir. 1992).

[292] *See Allen Eng'g,* 299 F.3d at 1353-55; U.S. Environmental Prods. Inc. v. Westall, 911 F.2d 713, 717 (Fed. Cir. 1990).

[293] *See Paragon,* 984 F.2d at 1187–88.

[294] *See EZ Dock,* 276 F.3d at 1353; *In re* Smith, 714 F.2d 1127, 1135–36 (Fed. Cir. 1983).

[295] *See, e.g.,* UMC Electronics Co. v. U.S., 816 F.2d 647 (Fed. Cir. 1987) (where the majority held that an invention need not be reduced to practice to be offered for sale, and Judge Smith penned a sharp dissent).

[296] 525 U.S. 55 (1998).

[297] *Pfaff,* 525 U.S. at 67. The court speaks of the invention being "ready for patenting" *before the critical date,* rather than before the date of the offer to sell. *Id.* This suggests that the event triggering the commencement of the one-year grace period could be the event that makes the invention ready for patenting (such as a reduction to practice), if that event occurs subsequent to the offer.

practice.[298] An inventor who has reduced the invention to practice—building the claimed apparatus or performing the claimed method—should be ready to prepare the kind of enabling disclosure required in a patent application.[299] Alternatively, one can demonstrate that an invention was ready for patenting through "drawings or other descriptions of the invention that were sufficiently specific to enable a person skilled in the art to practice the invention."[300] If such descriptions were available to the inventor, they could have been incorporated in a patent application. Consequently, an offer to sell an invention that has yet to be built can bar or invalidate a subsequent patent. In *Pfaff*, for example, the inventor had such confidence in his ability to proceed directly from an engineering drawing to a finished product that he offered to sell the product in large quantities before any had been made.[301] That drawing showed that the invention was ready for patenting, so the offer, before the critical date, invalidated the patent.

8.10.2 The Public Use Bar

Public use of the claimed invention before the application's critical date can also operate as a bar under § 102(b), but it is subject to the same experimental use exception. Some inventions must be tested in a more-or-less public environment, and if it is clear that the use is experimental it will not invalidate a claim.[302] Because § 102(b) refers to "public" use, a use that is observed only by persons under an obligation of secrecy does not invoke the statutory bar.[303]

When the inventor demonstrates his invention to a few friends or associates, the determination of whether such use was *public* can be difficult. In

---

[298] *Pfaff*, 525 U.S. at 67.

[299] *See* Section 8.6.

[300] *Pfaff*, 525 U.S. at 67. An invention may be fully conceived but not yet "ready for patenting" if the development necessary for putting the invention to practice is incomplete. *See* Space Sys./Loral, Inc. v. Lockheed Martin Corp., 271 F.3d 1076, 1080–81 (Fed. Cir. 2001). On the other hand, the invention can be "ready for patenting" even if the inventor does not yet have perfect confidence that it will work. *See* Robotic Vision Sys., Inc. v. View Eng'g, Inc., 249 F.3d 1307, 1312 (Fed. Cir. 2001) ("It will be a rare case indeed in which an inventor has no uncertainty concerning the workability of his invention before he has reduced it to practice."). Whether an invention was "ready for patenting" or "not quite ready for patenting" is certain to be a matter of frequent dispute.

[301] *See Pfaff*, 525 U.S. at 58. As the inventor testified at his deposition: "Q. It was in a drawing. Is that correct? A. Strictly in a drawing. Went from the drawing to the hard tooling. That's the way I do my business. Q. Boom-boom? A. You got it. Q. You are satisfied, obviously, when you come up with some drawings that it is going to go—'it works'? A. I know what I am doing, yes, most of the time." *Id.*, 525 U.S. at 58 n.3.

[302] *See* Pfaff v. Wells Electronics, Inc., 525 U.S. 55, 64 (1998); Netscape Communications Corp. v. Konrad, 295 F.3d 1315, 1320 (Fed. Cir. 2002); Allied Colloids Inc. v. American Cyanamid Co., 64 F.2d 1570, 1574 (Fed. Cir. 1995).

Moleculon Research Corp. v. CBS, Inc.,[304] the inventor displayed a model of his cube puzzle to a few university colleagues. The "personal relationships and surrounding circumstances" were sufficient for the court to find that the inventor had retained control over the invention and the distribution of information concerning it, even though there was no express agreement of confidentiality.[305] In contrast, a jury in *Beachcombers v. Wildwood Creative Products, Inc.*[306] found that a demonstration of an improved kaleidoscope to 20–30 party guests was a public use, and the Federal Circuit affirmed. The purpose of the demonstration was "getting feedback on the device," and the host made no efforts toward secrecy.[307]

   Although it does not fit neatly in the categories of "public use" or "on sale," a commercial use of the invention by the applicant before the critical date, even if that use does not make the invention itself a matter of public knowledge, is considered sufficient to invoke the statutory bar.[308] Suppose, for example, that the applicant invented a more efficient method of manufacturing copper wire. If the finished product resembled any other copper wire, no one outside of the factory might know anything of the improved process. Nevertheless, if the applicant used that process, and profited from it, prior to the critical date of the patent application, the Federal Circuit has held that such use forfeits the right to obtain a patent.[309] Here there is a difference between the activities of the patent applicant and unrelated third parties. If a third party made commercial use of the method before the applicant's critical date, but such use did not disclose the invention to the public, § 102(b) does not apply.[310] Perhaps the distinction exists because an inventor's own secret but commercial use, or a third party's nonsecret com-

---

[303] *See* Minnesota Mining & Mfg. Co. v. Chemque, Inc., 303 F.3d 1294, 1301 (Fed. Cir. 2002) (public use "includes any use of the claimed invention by a person other than the inventor who is under no limitation, restriction or obligation or secrecy to the inventor"); *Netscape*, 295 F.3d at 1320–21.

[304] 793 F.2d 1261 (Fed. Cir. 1986).

[305] *Moleculon*, 793 F.2d at 1266.

[306] 31 F.3d 1154 (Fed. Cir. 1994).

[307] *Beachcombers*, 31 F.3d at 1160.

[308] *See* Special Devices, Inc. v. OEA, Inc., 270 F.3d 1353, 1357 (Fed. Cir. 2001); Woodland Trust v. Flowertree Nursery, Inc., 148 F.3d 1368, 1370-71 (Fed. Cir. 1998). Sometimes the bar is characterized as an on-sale bar, sometimes a public use bar. *See Special Devices*, 270 F.3d at 1357 (characterizing *Woodland Trust* as referring to the on-sale bar); *Woodland Trust*, 148 F.3d at 1998 (citing cases referring to "public use"). In the paradoxical words of *Kinzenbaw v. Deere & Co.*, 741 F.2d 383, 390 (Fed. Cir. 1984), "[a] commercial use is a public use even if it is kept secret."

[309] *See* D.L. Auld Co. v. Chroma Graphics Corp., 714 F.2d 1144, 1147–48 (Fed. Cir. 1983) (secret commercial use by "applicant for patent or his assignee" triggers § 102(b)). Sale of a product that *embodies* the patented invention, without, somehow, disclosing it, triggers § 102(b) regardless of who sold it. *In re* Epstein, 32 F.3d 1559, 1568 (Fed. Cir. 1994); J.A. LaPorte, Inc. v. Norfolk Dredging Co., 787 F.2d 1577, 1583 (Fed. Cir. 1986). Perhaps that is because the sale of the claimed invention itself does not straddle the public use and on-sale bars as problematically as the sale of a product made by a secret *process*.

mercial use, can put the inventor on notice of the need to file promptly.[311] A secret third party use, on the other hand, could catch the inventor off guard.

8.11 OTHER STATUTORY BARS (35 U.S.C. §§ 102(c), (d))

A similar type of statutory bar is created by 35 U.S.C. § 102(d), which provides as follows:

A person shall be entitled to a patent unless—

(d) the invention was first patented or caused to be patented, or was the subject of an inventor's certificate, by the applicant or his legal representatives or assigns in a foreign country prior to the date of the application for patent in this country on an application for patent or inventor's certificate filed more than twelve months before the filing of the application in the United States. . . .

Simply put, an inventor who applies for a patent in a foreign country, waits more than twelve months before filing in the United States, and receives the foreign patent before filing in the United States will be denied a United States patent.[312] As in the case of § 102(b), § 102(d) promotes diligence in filing and prevents the extension of the patent monopoly.[313] Anyone who applies for a patent in a foreign country and plans to obtain a United States patent is well advised to file in the United States no more than twelve months later, thereby avoiding the risk that the foreign patent will be granted sooner than expected.

Finally, one other rarely used form of statutory bar arises from § 102(c), which provides that an inventor is not entitled to a patent if "he has abandoned the invention."[314] *Abandoning the invention* means abandoning the right to *patent* the invention. Mere delay in filing a patent application does not show that the invention was abandoned,[315] although it can have important consequences in a priority contest under § 102(g),[316] and it can allow the imposition of an on-sale or similar bar under § 102(b). However, if an inventor were to announce to the public that he would not patent his invention, such an announcement might constitute an abandonment.[317]

---

[310] *Woodland Trust*, 148 F.3d at 1371 ("when an asserted prior use is not that of the applicant, § 102(b) is not a bar when that prior use or knowledge is not available to the public").

[311] *See Special Devices*, 270 F.3d at 1355.

[312] *See* Bayer AG v. Schein Pharmaceuticals, Inc., 301 F.3d 1306, 1312 (Fed. Cir. 2002).

[313] *See In re* Kathawala, 9 F.3d 942, 947 (Fed. Cir. 1993).

[314] *See* Oddzon Prods., Inc. v. Just Toys, Inc., 122 F.2d 1396, 1402 (Fed. Cir. 1997).

[315] *See* Paulik v. Rizkalla, 760 F.2d 1270, 1272 (Fed. Cir. 1985) ("'the mere lapse of time' will not prevent the inventor from receiving a patent").

[316] *See* Section 8.9.1.3.

[317] An *application* can be "abandoned" and then refiled, without abandoning the invention in terms of § 102(c). The abandonment could, however, sacrifice the early filing date of the application for purposes of § 102(b).

8.12 DOUBLE PATENTING

An inventor is entitled to one patent on one invention.[318] If more than one patent could be obtained on the same invention, an inventor could extend the period of exclusivity beyond what the law intends.[319] For example, an inventor could apply for one patent in 2005 and a second on the same invention in 2015, thereby obtaining the equivalent of a 30-year patent. To prevent this result, a claim can be held unpatentable or invalid if it duplicates the subject matter of a claim in an earlier patent to the same inventor. This is referred to as *double patenting*. Double patenting can also be found where the claims are attributable to different "inventive entities"[320] but are owned by a common assignee.[321]

Double patenting comes in two forms. The first is *same invention double patenting*, which means that the later claim is substantially identical in scope to the earlier claim.[322] The prohibition against same invention double patenting is said to have a statutory basis in 35 U.S.C. § 101, which states that "[w]hoever invents or discovers any new and useful process . . . may obtain *a* patent therefor."[323] The more common form of double patenting is *obviousness-type double patenting*, which means that the later claim, though not identical, is only an obvious variation of the earlier claim.[324] The reasoning behind this prohibition is that once a patent has expired, the public should be at liberty to use not only the precise invention claimed, but also variations that would be obvious to one of ordinary skill.[325]

Issues of obviousness-type double patenting often arise when an inventor seeks to patent both a broad genus and a narrow species of that genus. For example, an inventor might conceive of both a generic design for a new mousetrap and a specific variation of that design using a particularly sensitive trigger. If the inventor obtained a patent on the broad invention first and then sought a patent on the variation or improvement, the question would be whether the variation was obvious in light of the more general design. If not, the inventor would be entitled to both patents.[326] On the

---

[318] *In re* Leonardo, 119 F.3d 960, 965 (Fed. Cir. 1997).

[319] *See In re* Goodman, 11 F.3d 1046, 1053 (Fed. Cir. 1993); General Foods Corp. v. Studiengesellschaft Kohle MbH, 972 F.2d 1272, 1279–80 (Fed. Cir. 1992) ("The basic concept of double patenting is that the *same* invention cannot be patented more than once, which, if it happened, would result in a second patent which would expire some time after the original patent and extend the protection timewise." (emphasis in original)).

[320] *See* Section 8.9.4.

[321] *See In re* Longi, 759 F.2d 887, 893 (Fed. Cir. 1985).

[322] *See Leonardo,* 119 F.3d at 965; *Goodman,* 11 F.3d at 1052; *Longi,* 759 F.2d at 892.

[323] *See Leonardo,* 119 F.3d at 965; *Longi,* 759 F.2d at 892.

[324] *See* Eli Lilly & Co. v. Barr Labs., Inc., 251 F.3d 955, 967–68 (Fed. Cir. 2001); Georgia-Pacific Corp. v. U.S. Gypsum Co., 195 F.3d 1322, 1326 (Fed. Cir. 1999); *Goodman,* 11 F.3d at 1052; *Longi,* 759 F.2d at 892.

[325] *See Leonardo,* 119 F.3d at 965 (referring to obviousness-type double patenting as a "judicially created" doctrine); *Longi,* 759 F.2d at 892–93.

other hand, if the inventor obtained the narrower patent first and the broader patent second, the second patent would almost certainly be held obvious in light of the first. This result conforms with the rule derived in the context of § 102 that a claim to a genus is anticipated if a single species of that genus is found in the prior art.[327]

On rare occasions the inventor actually filed the application for the broader patent *first*, and it issued second only because of delays in prosecution over which the inventor had no control. Under these circumstances, the second patent is denied only if each claimed invention would be obvious in light of the other–a so-called two-way test of obviousness.[328] Although this can result in an extension of the patent monopoly beyond the contemplated period, where it was not the patentee's fault the extension is not considered "unjustified."[329] Note that the term of patents applied for after June 7, 1995, runs from their filing date rather than their issue date, as was previously the case, so this particular concern will eventually be eliminated.

Obviousness-type double patenting can be "cured," in a sense, by the filing of a *terminal disclaimer* with the Patent Office.[330] A terminal disclaimer is a binding statement that (1) a later patent will expire at the same time as a prior patent, and (2) the later patent will be enforceable only as long as it and the prior patent are commonly owned.[331] The voluntary curtailment of the term of the second patent removes any concern that the existence of two similar patents will improperly extend the duration of the patent monopoly. The requirement of common ownership eliminates the additional risk that the two similar patents might be assigned to different parties, each of whom could press duplicative and harassing claims against a potential infringer.[332]

---

[326] It is true that the combination of both patents, issued at different times, might prevent anyone from making the specific mousetrap for a period of more than 20 years. This is not considered improper. If one product embodies several distinct patentable inventions, each such invention can result in a patent. When a particular patent expires, that invention is available to the public *as long as* it is practiced in a way that does not violate some other patent. *See In re* Kaplan, 789 F.2d 1574, 1577–78 (Fed. Cir. 1986).

[327] *See* Section 8.9.5. Although this is classified as an instance of obviousness-type double patenting, *see Goodman*, 11 F.3d at 1052–53, one can conceive of cases in which the full scope of a genus is not obvious merely from the disclosure of a species of the genus. Perhaps this would be better classified as *anticipation-type* double patenting. *See Eli Lilly*, 251 F.3d at 968 (claim in second patent is not "patentably distinct . . . if the later claim is obvious over, or anticipated by, the earlier claim").

[328] A two-way approach for obviousness-type double patenting is also adopted whenever one of the patents at issue is a utility patent and the other is a design patent. *See In re* Dembiczak, 175 F.3d 994, 1002 (Fed. Cir. 1999).

[329] *In re* Braat, 937 F.2d 589, 595 (Fed. Cir. 1991). The two-way test is *not* appropriate if the applicant is at least partially responsible for the delay in issuing the first-filed application, *see Eli Lilly*, 251 F.3d at 968 n.7, or if the applicant could have filed all of the claims in one application, *In re* Berg, 140 F.3d 1428, 1434 (Fed. Cir. 1998).

[330] *See Goodman*, 11 F.3d at 1052; *Longi*, 759 F.2d at 894; 35 U.S.C. § 253.

[331] *See* 37 C.F.R. § 1.321(c); *In re* Van Ornum, 696 F.2d 937, 944–48 (C.C.P.A. 1982).

[332] *See Van Ornum*, 686 F.2d at 944–45.

The terminal disclaimer mechanism provides inventors with some incentive to further develop their patented ideas, even in ways that might be considered obvious, and to disclose those developments to the public through additional patents.[333] This procedure applies only to obviousness-type double patenting; same invention double patenting cannot be remedied by a terminal disclaimer. A terminal disclaimer is also no protection against grounds of invalidity other than double patenting.[334]

Sometimes related patents will issue as the result of a *restriction requirement*.[335] A restriction requirement results when the patent examiner, during prosecution, finds that an application claims two or more distinct inventions. The applicant must elect which invention to pursue in the pending application, and if the applicant wishes to pursue one of the other inventions, the applicant must file a *divisional* application. That application and the original application may each result in a patent. Because, in this case, the existence of two separate patents is attributable to the Patent Office's determination that each application represents a distinct invention, the patents are immune from a challenge of double patenting.[336] A different result would be unfair to the applicant. But if the claims of the separate applications evolve during the course of prosecution, as they sometimes do, the applicant must maintain "consonance"–that is, the claims cannot be changed in such a way that what was formerly patentably distinct is no longer so. If consonance is lost, so is the immunity from double patenting.[337]

---

[333] *See* Quad Environmental Technologies Corp. v. Union Sanitary Dist., 946 F.2d 870, 873 (Fed. Cir. 1991).

[334] *See Quad,* 946 F.2d at 874.

[335] *See* Section 5.3.

[336] *See* 35 U.S.C. § 121; Applied Materials, Inc. v. Advanced Semiconductor Materials America, Inc., 98 F.3d 1563, 1568 (Fed. Cir. 1996); Gerber Garment Technology, Inc. v. Lectra Sys., Inc., 916 F.2d 683, 687 (Fed. Cir. 1990).

[337] *See Gerber*, 916 F.2d at 688.

CHAPTER 9

Enforceability Defenses

Certain defenses to a claim of patent infringement produce, if successful, a holding that the patent is *unenforceable* rather than *invalid*. The most important of these are the inequitable conduct and misuse defenses.[1] If a patent is unenforceable, it cannot be the basis of an infringement claim.

9.1 INEQUITABLE CONDUCT

In a court proceeding, the presence of an adversary helps to keep the litigants honest. If one party shades the truth or withholds important evidence from the court, the other party will expose the error, if it can. As discussed in Section 5.1, patent prosecution is *ex parte*, meaning that persons who might oppose the issuance of a patent have no opportunity to participate. If the applicant misrepresents the facts, there is no one to contradict him. Moreover, the Patent Office often relies heavily on information provided by the applicant. The applicant's sales activities, for example, might be enough to raise a statutory bar under 35 U.S.C. § 102(b),[2] but the patent examiner generally knows about those activities only what the applicant chooses to tell. Nevertheless, every issued patent enjoys a presumption of validity.

Because an applicant could take unfair advantage of this situation, applicants are charged with a duty of candor more demanding than what

---

[1] Another unenforceability defense might be raised where ownership of a patent subject to a terminal disclaimer had been transferred, contrary to the requirement that patents linked by a terminal disclaimer remain commonly owned. *See* Section 8.12.

[2] *See* Section 8.10.1.

is normally expected of parties in an adversarial proceeding. Applicants are required to disclose to the patent examiner any information that is "material" to the issuance of the patent under consideration.[3] Applicants are not affirmatively required to *search* for such information. They are not, for example, required to search the prior art for potentially invalidating references.[4] But if the applicant is aware of such a reference, that information must be divulged. This duty extends to the applicant, to the applicant's attorneys, and to anyone else who has substantial involvement in the application process.[5] A failure to meet the required duty of candor is known as *inequitable conduct.*

Inequitable conduct may be raised as a defense in patent infringement litigation, and, if it is proven, the patent will be held unenforceable.[6] Although technically the patent may not be invalid, the effect is much the same, with one important exception. If a single claim of a patent is invalid (for example, because it is anticipated by a prior art reference), the remaining claims of the patent can survive if they do not suffer the same defect.[7] In contrast, if an applicant obtained a single patent claim through inequitable conduct, the *entire patent* is unenforceable.[8] This result often makes inequitable conduct a more attractive defense than, for example, anticipation, even though both defenses could be based on the same prior art reference.

An inequitable conduct defense can be based on a misrepresentation made to the Patent Office, or a withholding of information. In either case,

---

[3] 37 C.F.R. § 1.56.

[4] *See* Brasseler, U.S.A. I, L.P. v. Stryker Sales Corp., 267 F.3d 1370, 1382 (Fed. Cir. 2001) ("a duty to investigate does not arise where there is no notice of the existence of material information"); FMC Corp. v. Hennessy Indus., Inc., 836 F.2d 521, 526 n.6 (Fed. Cir. 1987). The "possibility that material information may exist" is not enough to trigger a duty to inquire; there must be some clue "suggest[ing] the existence of specific information the materiality of which may be ascertained with reasonable inquiry." *Brasseler,* 267 F.3d at 1382. On the other hand, an applicant cannot cultivate ignorance if there are sufficient warnings of invalidating prior art. *See id.* at 1380 ("where an applicant knows of information the materiality of which may be so readily determined, he or she cannot intentionally avoid learning of its materiality"); Hewlett-Packard Co. v. Bausch & Lomb Inc., 882 F.2d 1556, 1562 (Fed. Cir. 1989) (wrongful intent may be inferred from evidence of "studied ignorance"). Usually an attorney can rely on information provided by the applicant, unless there is a reason to doubt its accuracy or completeness. *See Brasseler,* 267 F.3d at 1382-83 ("[t]here is no need for an attorney to pursue a fishing expedition").

[5] 37 C.F.R. § 1.56(c); *Brasseler,* 267 F.3d at 1383 n.6. Note that "inventors represented by counsel are presumed to know the law." *Brasseler,* 267 F.3d at 1385.

[6] Bristol-Myers Squibb Co. v. Rhone-Poulenc Rorer, Inc., 326 F.3d 1226, 1233 (Fed. Cir. 2003).

[7] 35 U.S.C. § 288.

[8] Baxter Int'l, Inc. v. McGaw, Inc., 149 F.3d 1321, 1332 (Fed. Cir. 1998) ("It is . . . settled law that inequitable conduct with respect to one claim renders the entire patent unenforceable."); Kingsdown Medical Consultants, Ltd. v. Hollister, Inc., 863 F.2d 867, 874 (Fed. Cir. 1988). Unenforceability can even extend to another patent if the patents are found sufficiently related. This is sometimes referred to as *infectious unenforceability. See Baxter,* 149 F.3d at 1327.

two elements must be proven: *materiality* and *intent.*[9] Both standards have been subject to conflicting definitions over the years, suggesting that the courts have had difficulty in defining the conduct that should be considered inequitable.

Materiality means that the information withheld or misrepresented was of sufficient importance to warrant the penalties associated with inequitable conduct. One test of materiality is whether the patent would have issued if the examiner had known the correct information. This is sometimes called the "but for" test—in other words, *but for* the misrepresentation, would the patent have issued?[10] Another, less restrictive test is whether there is a *substantial likelihood* that a *reasonable patent examiner* would have considered the information *important* in deciding whether the application should issue as a patent.[11] Information can be material as defined by this test even if, ultimately, the examiner would have decided that the patent should issue.[12]

The latter test has been adopted by the Federal Circuit as the *threshold* test of materiality.[13] If the withheld or misrepresented information does not meet this threshold, the inequitable conduct defense necessarily fails. The source of the threshold standard was the Patent Office's own Rule 56, but that rule was amended in 1992 to adopt a new definition of materiality. According to the new definition, information is material if, by itself or in combination with other information, it is inconsistent with a position taken by the applicant, or it is sufficient to establish a *prima facie* case of unpatentability.[14] The latter means that the information initially compels a conclusion of unpatentability (under a preponderance-of-the-evidence burden of proof), before any evidence in favor of patentability is considered.[15] It remains to be seen how or if the new standard changes the Federal Circuit's threshold of materiality.[16]

---

[9] *Brasseler*, 267 F.3d at 1379–80; Perceptive Biosystems, Inc. v. Pharmacia Biotech, Inc., 225 F.3d 1315, 1318–19 (Fed. Cir. 2000).

[10] This test comes in two flavors—the "subjective but for" test, and the "objective but for" test. The subjective test is whether the particular examiner involved would have allowed the application to issue as a patent if not for the challenged conduct. *See* American Hoist & Derrick Co. v. Sowa & Sons, Inc., 725 F.2d 1350, 1362–63 (Fed. Cir. 1984). This can only be determined if the examiner testifies, a practice that the Patent Office does not endorse. The more practical "objective but for" test asks whether a reasonable examiner would have allowed the patent to issue. *See id.*

[11] *Brasseler*, 267 F.3d at 1380; Molins PLC v. Textron, Inc., 48 F.3d 1172, 1179 (Fed. Cir. 1995). In a close case, it is best to assume that the information is material. *See Brasseler*, 267 F.3d at 1386 ("we have repeatedly warned practitioners that in close cases, where the materiality of the information is uncertain, disclosure is required").

[12] *See* Li Second Family Ltd. Partnership v. Toshiba Corp., 231 F.3d 1373, 1380–81 (Fed. Cir. 2000) (the standard of materiality is "not whether the information would conclusively decide the issue of patentability"). "[A]ffirmative misrepresentations by the patentee, in contrast to misleading omissions, are more likely to be regarded as material." Hoffman-La Roche, Inc. v. Promega Corp., 323 F.3d 1354, 1367 (Fed. Cir. 2003).

[13] *Brasseler*, 267 F.3d at 1380.

[14] 37 C.F.R. § 1.56(b).

[15] 37 C.F.R. § 1.56(b).

Under any standard, information cannot be material if it is cumulative of other information available to the examiner. For example, if the information is a withheld prior art reference, it is not material if the examiner considered prior art that was just as pertinent, or more pertinent, than the reference in question.[17] Also, if the applicant withheld information but the examiner discovered it on his own, the applicant's action could not be considered inequitable conduct.[18]

The *intent* threshold of inequitable conduct is as important as the materiality threshold. If information was withheld or misrepresented by the applicant because of an innocent mistake, the applicant did not commit inequitable conduct, no matter how material the information may have been. At one time, some courts considered *gross negligence* to be sufficient intent to warrant a finding of inequitable conduct.[19] However, in *Kingsdown Medical Consultants v. Hollister Inc.,*[20] the Federal Circuit, resolving conflicting precedent, held that inequitable conduct can only occur if the applicant or attorney deliberately attempted to deceive the Patent Office.[21] Hence, a lapse that is the result of carelessness, even gross carelessness, does not amount to inequitable conduct.

Note that intent to deceive can be proven by indirect evidence. It is rare that inequitable conduct will be proven by an applicant's admission or a "smoking gun" document referring to a planned deception. Rather, the proof is likely to be found in circumstances where the information was so important, and the situation so devoid of any possibility of an excuse, that one must conclude that the deception was deliberate.[22]

If the information withheld or misrepresented meets the threshold test of materiality, and if there is also proof of intent to deceive, the ultimate deci-

---

[16] If the previous rule was in effect at the time the application was prosecuted, the Federal Circuit has applied the older standard. *See, e.g., Brasseler,* 267 F.3d at 1380. With respect to more recent applications, as recently as May 23, 2003, the Federal Circuit had yet to decide whether it would adopt a revised standard of materiality. *See* Dayco Prods., Inc. v. Total Containment, Inc., 329 F.3d 1358, 1364 (Fed. Cir. 2003) (observing that the outcome would have been the same under either standard).

[17] LNP Eng'g Plastics, Inc. v. Miller Waste Mills, Inc., 275 F.3d 1347, 1360 (Fed. Cir. 2001) ("an applicant need not disclose a material reference if it is cumulative to or less material than those already before the examiner"); GFI, Inc. v. Franklin Corp., 265 F.3d 1268, 1274 (Fed. Cir. 2001).

[18] *Molins,* 48 F.3d at 1185; Scripps Clinic Research Foundation v. Genentech, Inc., 927 F.2d 1565, 1582 (Fed. Cir. 1991) ("When a reference was before the examiner, whether through the examiner's search or the applicant's disclosure, it cannot be deemed to have been withheld from the examiner.").

[19] *See, e.g.,* Driscoll v. Cebalo, 731 F.2d 878, 885 (Fed. Cir. 1984).

[20] 863 F.2d 867 (Fed. Cir. 1988) (resolution of conflicting precedent decided *en banc*).

[21] *Kingsdown,* 863 F.2d at 876 ("We adopt the view that a finding that particular conduct amounts to 'gross negligence' does not of itself justify an inference of intent to deceive; the involved conduct, viewed in light of all of the evidence, including evidence indicative of good faith, must indicate sufficient culpability to require a finding of intent to deceive."); *see also Brasseler,* 267 F.3d at 1382 ("a finding or deceptive intent may not be based solely on gross negligence").

sion of whether there was inequitable conduct is left to the discretion of the judge,[23] who must balance the materiality of the information against the seriousness of the intent.[24] The more important the information, the less the required showing of intent before the patent will be held unenforceable.[25]

Charges of inequitable conduct have become so routine in patent litigation that the Federal Circuit has referred to them as "an absolute plague."[26] It is difficult to say whether this reflects a low standard of ethics among applicants and patent attorneys, or just the readiness of accused infringers to raise every conceivable defense.

9.2 MISUSE

The patent system strikes a delicate balance between, on the one hand, the desire to encourage innovation by rewarding inventors with exclusive rights to their inventions and, on the other hand, the desire to promote healthy competition in the marketplace. Although the essence of the patent system is the grant of a monopoly, it is still a monopoly of limited scope and duration. If a patent owner attempts to leverage the advantage of a patent into something beyond its intended boundaries, the patent owner may be held to have committed *misuse*.[27] Like the inequitable con-

---

[22] "'[S]moking gun' evidence is not required in order to establish an intent to deceive. . . . Rather, this element of inequitable conduct must generally be inferred from the facts and circumstances surrounding the applicant's overall conduct." Paragon Podiatry Lab., Inc. v. KLM Labs., Inc., 984 F.2d 1182, 1189–90 (Fed. Cir. 1993); s*ee also Hoffman-La Roche*, 323 F.3d at 1371 ("Intent . . . is typicaly proved inferentially . . . and a finding of intent does not require a confession from the stand by the inventor or the prosecuting attorney."); *Bristol-Myers*, 326 F.3d at 1239; *Li Second Family*, 231 F.3d at 1381. "A mere denial of intent to mislead (which would defeat every effort to establish inequitable conduct) will not suffice." *GFI*, 265 F.3d at 1275.

[23] *Perseptive Biosystems*, 225 F.3d at 1318 ("The defense of inequitable conduct is entirely equitable in nature, and thus not an issue for a jury to decide.").

[24] *See Perseptive Biosystems*, 225 F.3d at 1319 ("Once the threshold levels of materiality and intent have been established, the trial court is required to weigh materiality and intent. . . . In light of all of the circumstances, the court must then determine whether the applicant's conduct is so culpable that the patent should be held unenforceable."); *Molins*, 48 F.3d at 1178.

[25] *See Bristol-Myers*, 326 F.3d at 1234 ("when balanced against high materiality, the showing of intent can be proportionately less"); *Brasseler*, 267 F.3d at 1381; *Perseptive Biosystems*, 225 F.3d at 1319.

[26] Burlington Indus., Inc. v. Dayco Corp., 849 F.2d 1418, 1422 (Fed. Cir. 1988).

[27] *See* C.R. Bard, Inc. v. M3 Sys., Inc., 157 F.3d 1340, 1372 (Fed. Cir. 1998) ("Patent misuse relates primarily to a patentee's actions that affect competition in unpatented goods or that otherwise extend the economic effect beyond the scope of the patent grant."); Atari Games Corp. v. Nintendo of America, Inc., 897 F.2d 1572, 1576 (Fed. Cir. 1990) ("a patent owner may not take the property right granted by a patent and use it to extend his power in the marketplace improperly, i.e. beyond the limits of what Congress intended to give in the patent laws"); Windsurfing Int'l, Inc. v. AMF, Inc., 782 F.2d 995, 1001 (Fed. Cir. 1986) (a misuse defense "requires that the alleged infringer show that the patentee has impermissibly broadened 'the physical or temporal scope' of the patent grant with anticompetitive effect").

duct defense, the misuse defense leads, if successful, to a holding that the patent is unenforceable.

An early example of overreaching by a patent owner can be found in *Morton Salt Co. v. G.S. Suppiger.*[28] Suppiger obtained a patent on a machine used in the canning industry for adding salt tablets to the contents of the cans. Only the machine was patented; the salt tablets were not. Nevertheless, when Suppiger leased its machines to canneries, it licensed the canneries to use the machines only if they agreed to buy all of their salt tablets from a Suppiger subsidiary. The Supreme Court viewed this extension of the patent grant as improper and held that a patent owner guilty of such practices could not look to a court for relief.[29] Today such conduct might be characterized as misuse.

Although there is no exhaustive list of the kinds of behavior that constitute misuse, the following often raise questions:

- A patent license, such as that discussed in *Morton Salt*, which compels the licensee to purchase separate, unpatented goods from the patent owner. This is called a *tying arrangement.*[30]
- A patent license that forbids the licensee from dealing with the patent owner's competitors. This is sometimes called *tying-out* in contrast to the *tying-in* found in *Morton Salt*.
- A patent license granted only on the condition that *other* patents are also licensed, even though the other patents may be undesired or even invalid.[31]
- An attempt to extend the collection of royalty payments past the expiration of the patent term.[32]
- A patent license that attempts to fix downstream prices.

The misuse defense covers some of the same territory as the federal antitrust laws,[33] at least where the challenged activity takes the form of a threat to competition. Conduct may rise to the level of misuse without violating the antitrust laws,[34] but similar considerations of *market power*, anticompetitive effects, and business justifications appear in either context,[35] particularly after

[28] 314 U.S. 488 (1941).
[29] *Morton Salt*, 314 U.S. at 492–94.
[30] See Virginia Panel Corp. v. Mac Panel Co., 133 F.3d 860, 869 (Fed. Cir. 1997) (referring to tying of "staple good[s]" as an example of "per se patent misuse"); Senza-Gel Corp. v. Seiffhart, 803 F.2d 661 (Fed. Cir. 1986). Note that it is not misuse to demand that licensees purchase from the patent owner goods which, if purchased from someone else, could supply the basis of a claim of contributory infringement—for example, goods useful only in practicing the patented invention. *See* 35 U.S.C. § 271(d). Contributory infringement is discussed in Section 10.4.
[31] It is common for patent owners to license a group of related patents as a package—an arrangement that may be convenient for the licensee as well as for the patent owner. The potential of misuse exists only if the patent owner refuses to license individual patents on reasonable terms.
[32] *See* Brulotte v. Thys Co., 379 U.S. 29, 33 (1964); *Virginia Panel*, 133 F.3d at 869.

changes to 35 U.S.C. § 271. Section 271 now states that it is misuse to condition a patent license on the sale of a separate, unpatented product only if the patent owner has market power in the relevant market.[36] The same limitation applies to patent licenses offered only as a group.[37]

Market power is a concept developed in the setting of antitrust law, and perhaps only an economist could provide a thorough definition. In general terms, market power means the ability to alter the conditions of trade, and in particular to raise prices, beyond what could be accomplished in a competitive market. Whether a company has market power depends on the availability of acceptable substitutes for whatever goods or services that company controls. Thus, if *Morton Salt* had applied the current version of § 271, the court might have considered whether Suppiger's patented salt depositing machines were so superior that it could compel canneries to obtain a patent license, even at the cost of having to purchase unpatented salt tablets from Suppiger's subsidiary. If the canneries could easily have chosen another machine without such restrictions, Suppiger would not have had the power to restrain competition.

Even where a misuse defense is dependent on a demonstration of anticompetitive effects, it is not necessary that the party raising the defense have suffered those anticompetitive effects personally. Protection of the public from abusive practices, and denial of relief to those undeserving of the court's protection, are reasons enough to hold a patent unenforceable, no matter what effect the challenged conduct has had on the litigants in a particular case.[38]

Some conduct that might seem anticompetitive is not considered misuse. For example, it is not misuse to grant only a limited number of licenses to a patent, to grant no licenses to a patent, or to completely suppress an invention by neither practicing it nor licensing it.[39] It is up to the patentee to decide whether the invention will be exploited during the term of the

---

[33] The federal antitrust laws (e.g., the Sherman Antitrust Act, 15 U.S.C. §§ 1–7) are designed to protect competition in the marketplace. Because a patent is a *legal* form of monopoly, efforts to enforce a patent within its legitimate scope do not violate the antitrust laws. *See In re* Independent Service Organizations Antitrust Litigation, 203 F.3d 1322, 1326 (Fed. Cir. 2000) (generally a patent owner who brings suit to enforce right to exclude is exempt from antitrust laws). Antitrust concerns should arise only if the patent was obtained by fraud or known to be invalid, or if the suit was a "mere sham." *See id.; Atari,* 897 F.2d at 1576.

[34] *Morton Salt,* 314 U.S. at 494; C.R. Bard, Inc. v. M3 Sys., Inc., 157 F.3d 1340, 1372 (Fed. Cir. 1998).

[35] *See Virginia Panel,* 133 F.3d at 869 (discussing "rule of reason" applied to some practices alleged to be misuse); *Windsurfing,* 782 F.2d at 1002 (unless conduct has been deemed *per se* anticompetitive, there must be a showing that it "tends to restrain competition unlawfully in an appropriately defined market").

[36] 35 U.S.C. § 271(d). "A patent alone does not demonstrate market power." *Independent Service Organizations,* 203 F.3d at 1325.

[37] 35 U.S.C. § 271(d).

[38] *Morton Salt,* 314 U.S. at 493–94.

patent. In only a few cases have courts found this result so injurious to the public welfare that they have refused to enjoin infringement, a decision that is tantamount to granting a compulsory license.[40]

Unlike invalidity, or unenforceability resulting from inequitable conduct, unenforceability resulting from misuse is reversible. The patent can be enforced again as soon as the objectionable conduct has ceased and any lingering effects have "dissipated."[41]

---

[39] *See* 35 U.S.C. § 271(d) (stating that "refus[al] to license or use any rights to the patent" is not an act of misuse); *Independent Service Organizations*, 203 F.3d at 1326; Cygnus Therapeutics Sys. v. Alza Corp., 92 F.3d 1153, 1160 (Fed. Cir. 1996) ("a patentee may, if it wishes, do nothing with the subject matter of the patent"); King Instruments Corp. v. Perego, 65 F.3d 941, 950 (Fed. Cir. 1995) ("The market may well dictate that the best use of a patent is to exclude infringing products, rather than to market the invention."); Rite-Hite Corp. v. Kelley Co., 56 F.3d 1538, 1547 (Fed. Cir. 1995).

[40] *See Rite-Hite*, 56 F.3d at 1547–48.

[41] *Morton Salt* 314 U.S. at 493; *see also Senza-Gel*, 803 F.2d at 668 n.10.

CHAPTER 10

Infringement

The owner of a patent has the exclusive right to make, use, sell, offer to sell, or import into the United States the invention described by the claims.[1] Anyone else who engages in those activities, without the permission of the patent owner, is an *infringer.* An infringer can be sued for money damages[2] and can be compelled by a court to cease the infringing activities.

10.1 PATENT TERM

Generally speaking, the exclusive rights conferred by a patent begin on the date the patent issues and expire 20 years after the filing date of the application (or any earlier application cited for purposes of priority).[3] Consequently, the term of the patent will vary depending on how long it takes for the application to make its way through the Patent Office. A patent issued in 2005 on an application filed in 2000 would last only 15 years, expiring in 2020.[4]

Until recently, the term of a patent was seventeen years from the date of *issue.*[5] Consequently, long delays in prosecution, sometimes due to maneuvering by the applicant, occasionally resulted in patents issuing on inventions

---

[1] *See* 35 U.S.C. § 271(a).

[2] *See* Section 11.8.

[3] 35 U.S.C. § 154(2).

[4] The 20-year term applies to utility patents. Design patents, discussed in Section 12.1, have a term of 14 years from the date of issue. 35 U.S.C. § 173.

[5] Due to the change from a 17-year to a 20-year term, patents applied for prior to June 8, 1995, are entitled to the greater of the 20-year term provided by the current statute, or the term of 17 years from issue provided by the former statute. 35 U.S.C. § 154(c).

that had already been in public use for decades.[6] In 1990, for example, computer chip manufacturers learned that a patent had been issued to one Gilbert Hyatt claiming the basic concept of the microprocessor—already the subject of a long-established and lucrative industry. This patent appeared at such a late date because it took 21 years and the prosecution of a long chain of related applications before the patent issued. Because the application process was conducted in secret, none of the chip manufacturers knew of the patent until, from their perspective, it was too late to do anything about it. The current practice of measuring the effective term of a patent from its filing date reduces the incentive for applicants to delay prosecution and surprise an industry with a so-called "submarine patent."

Under the current rules, if the examination is unduly delayed and the PTO bears the blame, the term of the patent may be extended accordingly.[7] The term may also be extended if a successful appeal,[8] an interference proceeding,[9] or certain kinds of regulatory delay,[10] such as FDA review of the patented product, prevent the patentee from enjoying the full term of its commercial monopoly.

In the event a patent application is published before its date of issue,[11] the patentee enjoys *provisional rights*, meaning the right to demand a reasonable royalty from anyone who practiced the patented invention in the interval.[12] These rights apply only against parties with *actual notice* of the patent application,[13] and they can be collected only after the patent has issued. Such rights are one incentive for applicants to publish their applications, even when the law does require it.[14] Except for these provisional rights, an applicant with a "patent pending" has no exclusive rights until the patent issues. On the other hand, with few exceptions,[15] the patentee can demand that

---

[6] Calculated delay may allow an accused infringer to raise the defense of prosecution laches. *See* Section 11.8.3.3.

[7] *See* 35 U.S.C. § 154(b).

[8] *See* 35 U.S.C. § 154(b)(1)(C).

[9] *See* 35 U.S.C. § 154(b)(1)(C). Interference proceedings are discussed in Section 5.4.

[10] *See* 35 U.S.C. §§ 155–156.

[11] *See* Section 5.1.

[12] 35 U.S.C. § 154(d). The invention claimed in the issued patent must be "substantially identical" to the invention claimed in the published application. *Id.*

[13] 35 U.S.C. § 154(d)(1)(B).

[14] *See* Section 5.1.

[15] One exception involves a claim to a "method of doing or conducting business." *See* 35 U.S.C. § 173(a)(3). An accused infringer who can demonstrate that, acting in good faith, it (1) reduced to practice the claimed method at least one year before the filing date of the patent, and (2) used the method commercially before the filing date of the patent, may continue to use the method without the patentee's consent. *See* 35 U.S.C. § 273(b). This recently created defense to infringement protects parties who already invested in a method of doing business, but whose use of that method was not sufficiently public to trigger a statutory bar. *See* Section 8.10. It remains to be seen how broadly the term "method of doing or conducting business" will be interpreted. The other instance of intervening rights arises in the context of reissued patents. *See* Section 5.5.

infringing activity cease when the patent issues, even if it had already begun. Warnings of a "patent pending" advise potential infringers that they should not begin what they may not be permitted to continue. One should remember, however, that many pending applications result in relatively narrow patent claims, or are denied altogether.

10.2 GEOGRAPHIC LIMITATIONS

United States patent law does not apply to activities that take place entirely in another country.[16] The sale or use of a patented product in Japan, for example, is not an infringement of a United States patent, although it could be an infringement of a corresponding Japanese patent. The law also provides an explicit exception for inventions built into vehicles, such as aircraft, that may enter the United States temporarily. If a United States patent covered a design for landing gear, and a Japanese airliner with the claimed landing gear flew into the United States to deliver passengers, the use of the patented landing gear in the United States would not infringe the patent.[17]

In two respects, United States patent law does take notice of activities occurring in another country. First, delivering the *components* of a patented invention from the United States to a foreign country, where they will be assembled into the claimed combination, can be an infringement of a United States patent.[18] The legal analysis mirrors that of contributory infringement or inducement of infringement in the United States, topics discussed in Section 10.4. Second, it can be an infringement of a United States patent to import, use, sell, or offer to sell in the United States a product made in a foreign country by a *process* patented in the United States.[19] This prevents the evasion of United States patents by moving production overseas.[20]

---

[16] *See* Rotec Indus., Inc. v. Mitsubishi Corp., 215 F.3d 1246, 1251 (Fed. Cir. 2000) ("These extraterritorial activities . . . are irrelevant to the case before us, because '[t]he right conferred by a patent under our law is confined to the Unites States and its territories, and infringement of this right cannot be predicated of acts wholly done in a foreign country.'").

[17] *See* 35 U.S.C. § 272; National Steel Car. Ltd. v. Canadian Pacific Railway Ltd., 357 F.3d 1319, 1325–26 (Fed. Cir. 2004). The exception applies to countries offering reciprocal privileges.

[18] *See* 35 U.S.C. § 271(f); Waymark Corp. v. Porta Sys. Corp., 245 F.3d 1364, 1367 (Fed. Cir. 2001). In fact, it is sufficient that the components were exported with the *intention* that they be combined. Proof that they were *actually* combined is not required. *Waymark,* 245 F.3d at 1367–68. In that respect, § 271(f) differs from contributory infringement or inducement. *See id.*

[19] 35 U.S.C. § 271(g); Biotec Biologische Naturverpackungen GmbH v. Biocorp, Inc., 249 F.3d 1341, 1351–52 (Fed. Cir. 2001).

[20] *See* Eli Lilly & Co. v. American Cyanamid Co., 82 F.3d 1568, 1571–72 (Fed. Cir. 1996).

The latter provision does not apply if the product is "materially changed by subsequent processes," or if the product "becomes a trivial and nonessential component of another product."[21] So, for example, if the patent claimed a process for refining aluminum, it would probably not be an infringement to import an automobile having an aluminum ashtray, even if the material from which the ashtray was made could be traced back to the patented process. At some point, the imported product becomes too far removed from the claimed process to regard the importation of that product as an infringement.

10.3 STATE OF MIND

Generally speaking, the intentions of the infringer are irrelevant to infringement. A patent can be infringed even by someone who is unaware that the patent exists.[22] On the other hand, infringement that *is* intentional, referred to as *willful infringement*, can result in an award of increased damages, up to three times the amount of damages that could be recovered from an innocent infringer, together with attorneys' fees. These increased awards, intended as a penalty or deterrent, are discussed in Section 11.8.2.

Indirect infringement, discussed in Section 10.4, is an exception to the general rule. Inducement of infringement and contributory infringement, both forms of indirect infringement, do require an awareness of the patent and knowledge of the infringing acts.

10.4 DIRECT AND INDIRECT INFRINGEMENT

One who, without authority, makes, uses, sells, offers to sell, or imports into the United States a product covered by a patent is a *direct infringer.* One who is not a direct infringer may be held equally liable for encouraging or contributing to infringement by someone else. This is sometimes referred to as *indirect* or *dependent* infringement.[23]

---

[21] 35 U.S.C. § 271(g); *see also Biotec,* 249 F.3d at 1352; *Eli Lilly,* 82 F.3d at 1572; Bio-Technology General Corp. v. Genentech, Inc., 80 F.3d 1553, 1560 (Fed. Cir. 1996). Of course, whether the product of a patented process has been "materially changed" is a matter of degree and can be a difficult question. Because the statute is relatively new, there have been few opportunities so far for the courts to clarify how the rule will be applied.

[22] Hilton Davis Chemical Co. v. Warner-Jenkinson Co., 62 F.3d 1512, 1519 (Fed. Cir. 1995) (en banc) ("Intent is not an element of infringement. . . . A patent may exclude others from practicing the claimed invention, regardless of whether the infringers even know of the patent."), *rev'd on other grounds,* Warner-Jenkinson Co. v. Hilton-Davis Chemical Co., 520 U.S. 17 (1997); *see also* Florida Prepaid Postsecondary Education Expense Board v. College Savings Bank, 527 U.S. 627, 645 (1999) ("Actions predicated on direct patent infringement . . . do not require any showing of intent to infringe"); Jurgens v. CBK, Ltd., 80 F.3d 1566, 1570 n.2 (Fed. Cir. 1996) (infringement is "a strict liability offense").

Indirect infringement comes in two forms—*inducement* of infringement and *contributory* infringement. The concept of inducement is the simpler one. Anyone who actively induces the infringement of a patent by another may be held liable as an infringer.[24] Consider the case of *Moleculon Research Corp. v. CBS, Inc.*[25] CBS sold the popular toy known as Rubik's Cube, a product that Moleculon believed to infringe its patent on a rotating-cube puzzle. Some of the claims, rather than describing the puzzle as a physical object, instead claimed a method of solving the puzzle by rotating the facets of the cube. These method claims could be directly infringed only by someone performing the steps of the method—that is, by someone using the puzzle. It would have been impractical, however, to file suit against every consumer who purchased Rubik's Cube. Even though CBS did not directly infringe those method claims, the court found that it could be held liable for inducing infringement by purchasers, largely because it sold puzzles and instruction sheets that would lead purchasers to practice the method.[26]

Although a direct infringer can be completely innocent of the existence of the patent, one who induces infringement must know of the patent and must intend to cause the infringing acts.[27] Where such intent is found, it is even possible to hold officers or directors of a corporation liable for an infringement by their corporation, if they "actively assisted" in that infringement.[28] This is one instance in which the corporate form will not shield officers or directors from personal liability for the acts of their corporation. Because it is seldom possible to prove the necessary intent, such liability still is comparatively rare.[29]

A *contributory infringer* is one who imports, sells, or offers to sell a component of a patented combination, or a material or apparatus to be used in a patented process, if all of the following conditions are met:[30]

23 *See* RF Delaware, Inc. v. Pacific Keystone Technologies, Inc., 326 F.3d 1255, 1268 (Fed. Cir. 2003) ("dependent infringement"); Moba, B.V. v. Diamond Automation, Inc., 325 F.3d 1306, 1318 (Fed. Cir. 2003) ("indirect infringement"). In any case of indirect infringement, there must be evidence of a related *direct* infringement by someone else. *RF Delaware*, 326 F.3d at 1268; Husky Injection Molding Sys. Ltd. v. R & D Tool Eng'g Co., 291 F.3d 780, 784 (Fed. Cir. 2002); Arthur A. Collins, Inc. v. Northern Telecom Ltd., 216 F.3d 1042, 1048–49 (Fed. Cir. 2000). However, that direct infringement can be shown by circumstantial evidence. *See* Moleculon Research Corp. v. CBS, Inc., 793 F.2d 1261, 1272 (Fed. Cir. 1986).
24 35 U.S.C. § 271(b).
25 793 F.2d 1261 (Fed. Cir. 1986).
26 *Moleculon*, 794 F.2d at 1272.
27 *See Moba*, 325 F.3d at 1318 ("Although § 271(b) does not use the word 'knowingly,' this court has uniformly imposed a knowledge requirement."); Manville Sales Corp. v. Paramount Sys., Inc., 917 F.2d 544, 553 (Fed. Cir. 1990). Some courts may impose a "knew *or should have known*" standard of knowledge. *See Manville*, 917 F.2d at 553.
28 *See Manville*, 917 F.2d at 553; Orthokinetics, Inc. v. Safety Travel Chairs, Inc., 806 F.2d 1565, 1578–79 (Fed. Cir. 1986).
29 *See* Al-Site Corp. v. VSI Int'l, Inc., 174 F.3d 1308, 1331 (Fed. Cir. 1999).
30 35 U.S.C. § 271(c); *Husky*, 291 F.3d at 784.

- The item is a "*material part* of the patented invention."
- The item is imported, sold, or offered for sale with *knowledge* that the item was "*especially made or especially adapted*" for use in an infringing manner.[31]
- The item is *not* a "staple article or commodity of commerce suitable for substantial noninfringing use."

Many patented combinations include individual elements that themselves are common and unpatentable. The Oviatt mousetrap design (see Appendix A) includes an ordinary ping-pong ball. The Oviatt patent cannot prevent anyone from making, using, importing, selling, or offering to sell ping-pong balls, which have obvious uses unrelated to the mousetrap invention. The inventor's legitimate monopoly extends only to the claimed combination. Suppose, however, that someone sold the remaining components of the Oviatt mousetrap, without the ping-pong ball. Because all of the claims of the Oviatt patent require a ball, selling the remaining pieces would not directly infringe the patent.[32] However, it is likely that anyone who purchased the incomplete trap would eventually supply the missing ball, thereby forming an infringing combination. If the patent owner were forced to sue only those who formed that combination—consumers who purchased an incomplete trap and supplied their own ping-pong ball—enforcement of the Oviatt patent would be impractical.

Patent law treats as contributory infringement the importation, sale, or offer to sell a component of a claimed combination if the component is "especially made" for use in the patented combination (like the tubed structure depicted in the Oviatt patent) and not a "staple article or commodity of commerce suitable for substantial noninfringing use"[33] (such as a ping-pong ball). Originally, the law made no distinction between contributory infringement and inducement, and it is still useful to consider contributory infringement in the inducement context. The sale of a ping-pong ball could not, by itself, be legitimately regarded as an inducement to infringe the Oviatt patent, because the ping-pong ball could be used for something else. The sale of the single-purpose apparatus could, however, be viewed as an inducement to infringe, because the apparatus has no other plausible use.

The concept of a *staple article of commerce* most obviously applies to basic materials sold in large quantities and useful in numerous applications. Ordi-

---

[31] Although it is not apparent on the face of the statute, contributory infringement requires both knowledge that the component is adapted to a particular use and knowledge of the patent that proscribes that use. Hewlett-Packard Co. v. Bausch & Lomb Inc., 909 F.2d 1464, 1469 (Fed. Cir. 1990). Someone who is not aware of a patent cannot be a contributory infringer, at least until notified that the patent exists. However, in contrast to inducement, contributory infringement does not require intent to cause the infringing acts. *See id.* Although the courts have drawn these distinctions, it remains conceptually difficult to separate *knowledge* of the infringing acts, *intent* to cause the infringing acts, and *intent to infringe*.

[32] *See* Section 10.5.

[33] 35 U.S.C. § 271(c).

nary nuts and bolts and common chemicals would be considered staples, and their sale would not trigger contributory infringement.[34] But in this context "staple" also applies to goods having even one substantial noninfringing use.[35] If it did not, in practical effect the patentee's monopoly would extend to unpatented uses and combinations. If Oviatt could prevent the unlicensed sale of ping-pong balls, he would have an effective monopoly not only on his own invention, but also on the game of ping-pong.

Issues of contributory infringement often arise in the context of replacing worn or broken parts in a patented device. One who obtains a patented device from a legitimate source is permitted to repair that device, or replace a broken or exhausted part, without further obligation to the patent owner.[36] On the other hand, one cannot *reconstruct* the patented device to such an extent that one is, in effect, building a new and unlicensed device.[37] If the substitution of a part effects a reconstruction rather than a repair of the patented device, that reconstruction can constitute an infringement, and whoever supplied the part may be found liable as a contributory infringer.[38]

The line between *repair* and *reconstruction* is a difficult one to draw,[39] but courts generally have taken a broad view of what it is permissible to repair or replace.[40] If it is simply a matter of replacing a spent and easily replaceable component, the replacement will probably not be considered an

---

[34] There might be a legitimate claim of inducement, however, if the sale were accompanied by instructions telling the purchaser how to use the goods in an infringing manner.

[35] *See* Preemption Devices, Inc. v. Minnesota Mining & Mfg. Co., 803 F.2d 1170, 1174 (Fed. Cir. 1986) (a nonstaple article is one that has no substantial noninfringing use).

[36] *See Husky*, 291 F.3d at 785–86, Surfco Hawaii v. Fin Control Sys., Ltd., 264 F.3d 1062, 1065 (Fed. Cir. 2001). This is true whether or not the replaced part is one "essential" to the combination and whether or not the replaced part is the thing that distinguished the invention from the prior art. *See Husky*, 291 F.3d at 786–87; Porter v. Farmers Supply Service, Inc., 790 F.2d 882, 885–86 (Fed. Cir. 1986). Parts can also be exchanged to *modify* the patented combination for reasons other than extending its useful life. *See Husky*, 291 F.3d at 786, 788 (modifications that are "kin to repair," involving a substitution for an easily replaceable part, are permitted); *Surfco*, 264 F.3d at 1065–66 (owner may replace fins on a surfboard, even though fins are not worn out, in order to make the surfboard safer).

[37] *See* Aro Mfg. Co. v. Convertible Top Replacement Co., 365 U.S. 336, 346 (1961).

[38] *See* FMC Corp. v. Up-Right, Inc., 21 F.3d 1073, 1076 (Fed. Cir. 1994).

[39] *See Husky*, 291 F.3d at 784–85 (the courts "have struggled for years to appropriately distinguish between repair of a patented machine and reconstruction"). One court, in a passage cited with approval by the Federal Circuit, declined to adopt any bright-line test to distinguish between repair and reconstruction, placing its reliance instead on "'the exercise of sound common sense and an intelligent judgment.'" *FMC*, 21 F.3d at 1079 (quoting Goodyear Shoe Machinery Co. v. Jackson, 112 F. 146, 150 (1st Cir. 1901)); *see also* Bottom Line Management, Inc. v. Pan Man, Inc., 228 F.3d 1352, 1355 (Fed. Cir. 2000) (no "bright line test"). The Federal Circuit has suggested a "concept of proportionality inherent in the distinction between repair and reconstruction." *Husky*, 291 F.3d at 786–87. Such proportionality would lead one to distinguish between replacing the spark plugs on a vehicle (a permissible repair) and replacing the rest of the vehicle at a single stroke, retaining *only* the spark plugs (an impermissible reconstruction). *Id.* Of course, few cases will be so easy to categorize.

[40] Sage Prods., Inc. v. Devon Indus., Inc., 45 F.3d 1575, 1578 (Fed. Cir. 1995).

infringement, as long as the component is not the subject of a patent in its own right.[41] For example, the Federal Circuit held that supplying replacement liners for a biohazard disposal system was not an infringement of the related patent because the liners, only a component of the patented combination, were meant to be replaced after a single use.[42] In fact, although it defies logic, one may be allowed to replace an entire device over a period of time, by the successive replacement of worn out or spent parts, as long as in no single instance are the replacements so extensive that they amount to reconstruction.[43] On the other hand, if the entire product is spent, as a patented torpedo would be spent following its explosion,[44] construction of a new item from what remains would not be permitted. Also, the courts have sometimes balked at the replacement of a component clearly not meant to be, nor customarily considered to be, replaceable.[45]

10.5 LITERAL INFRINGEMENT

Determining whether a patent is infringed is a two-step process.[46] First, one must examine the language of the claims at issue and decide what they mean. This step, referred to as *claim construction* or *claim interpretation*, proceeds according to the rules discussed in Chapter 7. Although it is a principle difficult to apply in practice, claims are supposed to be construed without any reference to the thing that has been accused of infringing.[47] Once the claims have been properly construed, they must be compared to the accused product or method to see if the claims are infringed. A patent is said to be *literally*

---

[41] Although the distinction between replacement and repair is difficult to draw, the Federal Circuit has recently implied that the substitution of a new part for one that is "readily replaceable" is conduct within a "safe harbor." *See Husky*, 291 F.3d at 787. Consequently, the difficult cases involve parts that are *not* easily replaced. *See, e.g.,* Jazz Photo Corp. v. International Trade Comm'n, 264 F.3d 1094, 1107 (Fed. Cir. 2001) (replacement of film in a single-use camera is not impermissible reconstruction, even though the manufacturer of the camera did not intend for the camera to be reused); *Bottom Line*, 228 F.3d at 1356 (refurbishment of cooking surfaces with worn Teflon coatings was not impermissible reconstruction, even though removing the surfaces meant breaking welds).

[42] *Sage Prods.*, 45 F.3d 1575 (Fed. Cir. 1995).

[43] *See Husky*, 291 F.3d at 786; *FMC*, 21 F.3d at 1077.

[44] *See Husky*, 291 F.3d at 785.

[45] In *Sandvik Aktiebolag v. E.J. Co.*, 121 F.3d 669 (Fed. Cir. 1997), the Federal Circuit held that replacement of a carbide drill tip constituted reconstruction of the patented drill, rather than repair, even though the tip was only a component of the claimed combination. A number of factors influenced the court, including the elaborate procedures necessary to replace the tip, the long useful life of the tip compared to other components of the drill, the lack of any substantial market in replacement tips, and the lack of any evidence that the patentee intended for the drill tip to be replaced. *Id.* at 673.

[46] RF Delaware, Inc. v. Pacific Keystone Technologies, Inc., 326 F.3d 1255, 1266 (Fed. Cir. 2003); Apex, Inc. v. Raritan Computer, Inc., 325 F.3d 1364, 1370 (Fed. Cir. 2003).

infringed if the claims literally or "exactly" describe the thing accused of infringement.[48]

A claim cannot be literally infringed if any claim element is missing entirely from the accused product.[49] This is so even if the missing element seems insignificant in comparison to the invention as a whole. If a mouse-trap claim refers to a hook for hanging the trap on a wall when the trap is not in use, a trap that has no hook does not literally infringe. This principle is often called the *all-elements* rule. It can be helpful to think of a patent claim as a kind of checklist of features, every one of which must be found in the accused product in order for the claim to be infringed.

On the other hand, infringement is not avoided by adding things that are not described in the claim.[50] Suppose, for example, that a first inventor claimed a mousetrap comprising the combination of a spring, a latch, a mouse-trapping jaw, and a trigger that, when disturbed by the mouse, releases the latch and closes the jaw. A later inventor improves the combination by adding an audible alarm that sounds when the trap has sprung. The

[47] SRI Int'l v. Matsushita Electric Corp., 775 F.2d 1107, 1118 (Fed. Cir. 1985) (en banc) ("[C]laims are not construed 'to cover' or 'not to cover' the accused device. That procedure would make infringement a matter of judicial whim. It is only *after* the claims have been *construed without reference to the accused device* that the claims, as so construed, are applied to the accused device to determine infringement." (emphasis in original)). *But see* Vivid Technologies, Inc. v. American Science & Eng'g, Inc., 200 F.3d 795, 803 (Fed. Cir. 1999) ("although the claims are construed objectively and without reference to the accused device, only those terms need be construed that are in controversy, and only to the extent necessary to resolve the controversy"); Scripps Clinic & Research Found. v. Genentech, Inc., 927 F.2d 1565, 1580 (Fed. Cir. 1991) ("Of course the particular accused product (or process) is kept in mind, for it is efficient to focus on the construction of only the disputed elements or limitations of the claims.").

[48] DeMarini Sports, Inc. v. Worth, Inc., 239 F.3d 1314, 1331 (Fed. Cir. 2001); General American Transportation Corp. v. Cryro-Trans, Inc., 93 F.3d 766, 770 (Fed. Cir. 1996); Southwall Technologies, Inc. v. Cardinal IG Co., 54 F.3d 1570, 1575 (Fed. Cir. 1995).

[49] *See* Techsearch, L.L.C. v. Intel Corp., 286 F.3d 1360, 1371 (Fed. Cir. 2002) ("To establish literal infringement, all of the elements of the claim, as correctly construed, must be present in the accused system."); Network, LLC v. Centraal Corp., 242 F.3d 1347, 1353 (Fed. Cir. 2001); Signtech USA, Ltd. v. Vutek, Inc., 174 F.3d 1352, 1358 (Fed. Cir. 1999).

[50] *See* Suntiger, Inc. v. Scientific Research Funding Gp., 189 F.3d 1327, 1336 (Fed. Cir. 1999) ("It is fundamental that one cannot avoid infringement merely by adding elements if each element recited in the claims is found in the accused device.'"); Northern Telecom, Inc. v. Datapoint Corp., 908 F.2d 931, 945 (Fed. Cir. 1990) ("Nor is infringement avoided if a claimed feature performs not only as shown in the patent, but also performs an additional function."). The principle applies to method claims. *See* Smith & Nephew, Inc. v. Ethicon, Inc., 276 F.3d 1304, 1311 (Fed. Cir. 2001) ("Infringement arises when all of the steps of a claimed method are performed, whether or not the infringer also performs additional steps."). There is an exception if the claim is limited by its terms to the recited elements *and no others. See Suntiger*, 189 F.3d at 1336 ("If a claim is specific as to the number of elements and the addition of an element eliminates an inherent feature of the claim, then that additional element will prevent a finding of literal infringement."). When a claim preamble ends with the words *consisting of* (rather than the more common *comprising*), the claim is understood to be limited to *only* the elements recited. See Section 7.6.

improved trap would still literally infringe, as long as it had the spring, latch, jaw, and trigger claimed.

Some accused infringers mistakenly believe that if they have obtained a patent covering their own product, they are immune from charges of infringing another patent. This is simply not the case. A patent only conveys the right to *exclude others*; it does not convey a right to produce or sell the invention claimed.[51] Even if the inventor of the trap-with-alarm had obtained a patent on the improvement (which is perfectly proper as long as the improvement is nonobvious), the product would still infringe.[52] However, the new patent would prevent the first inventor from adding an alarm to his invention, without a license from the second inventor.

The concept of literal infringement is relatively straightforward—a patent is literally infringed if the accused product is exactly what the claims describe. But this is not the end of the infringement inquiry. Even if the accused product is *not* exactly what the claims describe, it can still be found infringing under the doctrine of equivalents. Alternatively, if an accused product *is* exactly what the claims describe, it can still theoretically be found noninfringing under the reverse doctrine of equivalents. These doctrines are discussed in the sections that follow.

10.6 THE DOCTRINE OF EQUIVALENTS

The *doctrine of equivalents* is one of the most important doctrines in patent law, and one of the most perplexing. It is not based on the patent statutes passed by Congress, but is entirely a product of judicial reasoning. Some critics view the doctrine as inconsistent with other fundamental principles of patent law. However, the doctrine has a long history, and, having survived recent criticisms, it is clearly here to stay.

10.6.1 *Winans v. Denmead*

Winans v. Denmead,[53] an ancient but important case in the evolution of the doctrine of equivalents, provides a useful introduction. Winans obtained a

---

[51] Bio-Technology General Corp. v. Genentech, Inc., 80 F.3d 1553, 1559 (Fed. Cir. 1996) ("'[T]he existence of one's own patent does not constitute a defense to infringement of someone else's patent. It is elementary that a patent grants only the right to *exclude others* and confers no right on its holder to make, use, or sell.'" (emphasis in original)); Atlas Powder Co. v. E.I. Du Pont de Nemours & Co., 750 F.2d 1569, 1580 (Fed. Cir. 1984).

[52] *See Atlas Powder*, 750 F.2d at 1580 ("if Atlas patents A+B+C and Du Pont then patents the improvement A+B+C+D, Du Pont is liable to Atlas for any manufacture, use, or sale of A+B+C+D because the latter directly infringes claims to A+B+C"). Note, however, that a second patent can bear on whether an improvement is "equivalent" to the original, if there is no literal infringement. See Section 10.6.

[53] 56 U.S. 330 (1853).

patent on a coal-carrying railroad car shaped like the base (or frustum) of a cone, with the smaller end extending below the level of the axles. The circular cross section and tapered dimensions of the car equalized the pressures on the load-bearing surfaces, with the result that a lighter car could carry a relatively larger burden without damage. Winans' patent claim specifically referred to a car "in the form of a frustum of a cone." The car accused of infringing Winans' patent was similarly tapered, but it had an octagonal rather than a circular cross section. Rather than the "frustum of a cone," the shape of the car was closer to an octagonal pyramid. The accused car did not fall within the literal language of the claim, but it provided similar (though reduced) benefits in equalizing the pressures exerted by the load.

Even though the accused car was outside of the literal language of the claim, the court found that it employed the principle of Winans' invention. The differences were merely differences of "form," and the court held these differences insufficient to avoid infringement.

> The exclusive right to the thing patented is not secured, if the public are at liberty to make substantial copies of it, varying its form or proportions. And, therefore, the patentee, having described his invention, and shown its principles, and claimed it in that form which most perfectly embodies it, is, in contemplation of law, deemed to claim every form in which his invention may be copied, unless he manifests an intention to disclaim some of those forms.[54]

A dissenting justice rejected this "substance over form" approach to infringement and emphasized the importance of definite claims in informing the public of the limits of the patentee's monopoly. A patentee, he felt, should be held to the limitations made explicit in the claims. He also warned that nothing could be "more mischievous, more productive of oppressive and costly litigation, or exorbitant and unjust pretensions and vexatious demands" than relaxation of the requirement that patentees be bound by definite claims.[55]

10.6.2 *Graver Tank*

The modern history of the doctrine of equivalents begins in 1950 with *Graver Tank & Mfg. Co. v. Linde Air Prods. Co.*[56] The patent at issue claimed a material to be used in an electric welding process, including as a principal ingredient an "alkaline earth metal" such as magnesium. The accused product used manganese instead of magnesium, and although the names of the ingredients are nearly the same, manganese is *not* an alkaline earth metal as specifically required by the patent claims. Nevertheless, invoking the doc-

---

[54] *Winans*, 56 U.S. at 343.
[55] *Winans*, 56 U.S. at 347 (Campbell, J., dissenting).
[56] 339 U.S. 605 (1950).

trine of equivalents as expressed in *Winans v. Denmead*, the court found the
patent infringed. The following paragraph summed up the majority's support for the doctrine:

> [T]o permit imitation of a patented invention which does not copy every literal
> detail would be to convert the protection of the patent grant into a hollow and use-
> less thing. Such a limitation would leave room for—indeed encourage—the unscrupu-
> lous copyist to make unimportant and insubstantial changes and substitutions in the
> patent which, though adding nothing, would be enough to take the copied matter
> outside the claim, and hence outside the reach of law. . . . Outright and forthright
> duplication is a dull and very rare type of infringement. To prohibit no other would
> place the inventor at the mercy of verbalism and would subordinate substance to
> form.[57]

The court declined to establish any definite test of whether something outside of the literal scope of a patent claim is still equivalent. "Equivalence," said
the court, "is not the prisoner of a formula."[58] Rather, the judgment must be
made in the context of the particular invention, the functions performed by
the claimed and the substituted element, and the knowledge available to
those skilled in the art. In addition, "[a]n important factor is whether persons
reasonably skilled in the art would have known of the interchangeability of an
ingredient not contained in the patent with one that was."[59] The court also
referred to an earlier case inquiring whether the accused product performs
"'substantially the same function in substantially the same way to obtain the
same result,'"[60] reasoning that "'if two devices do the same work in substantially the same way, and accomplish substantially the same result, they are the
same, even though they differ in name, form or shape.'"[61]

Applying these principles to the case before it, the court found the patent
infringed, even though the accused welding material did not include the alkaline earth metal apparently required by the claim. The manganese served the
same purpose as an alkaline earth metal, and persons skilled in the art knew
the two ingredients to be interchangeable. The substitution was nothing more
than a slight and obvious variation of the invention literally described.[62]

10.6.3 Challenges to the Doctrine

The doctrine of equivalents is intended to free the infringement inquiry
from excessive literalism and elevate substance over form.[63] From that

---

[57] *Graver Tank*, 339 U.S. at 607.

[58] *Graver Tank*, 339 U.S. at 609.

[59] *Graver Tank*, 339 U.S. at 609.

[60] *Graver Tank*, 339 U.S. at 608 (quoting Sanitary Refrigerator Co. v. Winters, 280 U.S. 30, 42 (1929)).

[61] *Graver Tank*, 339 U.S. at 608 (quoting Union Paper-Bag Machine Co. v. Murphy, 97 U.S. 120, 125 (1877)).

[62] *Graver Tank*, 339 U.S. at 612.

perspective, the doctrine seems an enlightened policy. However, the doctrine is at odds with the requirement of claims "particularly pointing out and distinctly claiming the subject matter which the applicant regards as his invention."[64] Ideally, claims notify the public of what can or cannot be done without risk of infringing the patent.[65] But when the doctrine of equivalents is applied, claims can be positively misleading, by seeming to include restrictions that, in the end, a court will disregard. By attempting to honor the "competitor's need for precise wording as an aid in avoiding infringement," while avoiding "the risk of injustice that may result from a blindered focus on words alone,"[66] *Graver Tank* committed courts to a narrow and difficult path.

Recognizing the tension between the doctrine of equivalents and fair notice to potential infringers, the Federal Circuit has warned that

[a]pplication of the doctrine of equivalents is the exception . . . not the rule, for if the public comes to believe (or fear) that the language of patent claims can never be relied on, and that the doctrine of equivalents is simply the second prong of every infringement charge, regularly available to extend protection beyond the scope of the claims, then claims will cease to serve their intended purpose. Competitors will never know whether their actions infringe a granted patent.[67]

Yet in practice, allegations of infringement under the doctrine of equivalents have become the rule, not the exception. Wherever there is any doubt as to literal infringement, the doctrine of equivalents is routinely invoked as a fallback position. Indeed, attorneys representing patent owners would be remiss if they failed to take advantage of the opportunities the doctrine provides. The principle that "the protected invention is what the claims say it is,"[68] appears increasingly "utopian."[69]

Eventually, critics began to suggest ways in which application of the doctrine of equivalents might be limited. For example, because *Graver Tank* had alluded to the "pirating" of an invention, or a "fraud on the patent" by an "unscrupulous copyist," some critics suggested that the doctrine of equiva-

63 "Unfortunately, the nature of language makes it impossible to capture the essence of a thing in a patent application. . . . If patents were always interpreted by their literal terms, their value would be greatly diminished. Unimportant and insubstantial substitutes for certain elements could defeat the patent, and its value to inventors could be destroyed by simple acts of copying." Festo Corp. v. Shoketsu Kinzoku Kogyo Kabushiki Co., 535 U.S. 722, 731 (2002).
64 35 U.S.C. § 112.
65 *See* Slimfold Mfg. Co., Inc. v. Kinkead Indus., Inc., 932 F.2d 1453, 1457 (Fed. Cir. 1991) ("Inherent in our claim-based patent system is also the principle that the protected invention is what the claims say it is, and thus that infringement can be avoided by avoiding the language of the claims.").
66 Laitram Corp. v. Cambridge Wire Cloth Co., 863 F.2d 855, 856–57 (Fed. Cir. 1988).
67 London v. Carson Pirie Scott & Co., 946 F.2d 1534, 1538 (Fed. Cir. 1991).
68 *Slimfold,* 932 F.2d at 1457.
69 Paper Converting Machine Co. v. Magna-Graphics Corp., 745 F.2d 11, 19 (Fed. Cir. 1984).

lents ought to be applied only in such egregious circumstances.[70] Had this approach been adopted, it would have significantly changed the prevailing practice of applying the doctrine even against "innocent infringers."

However, in *Warner-Jenkinson Co. v. Hilton Davis Chemical Co.,*[71] the Supreme Court entered the debate for the first time since *Graver Tank.* Although the court "share[d] the concern . . . that the doctrine of equivalents . . . has taken on a life of its own, unbounded by the patent claims,"[72] it declined the invitation to abolish the doctrine of equivalents or limit it to "unscrupulous copyists."[73] Instead, it reaffirmed the principles of *Graver Tank* and the generalized application of the doctrine, with some refinements discussed below. Unless Congress enacts new legislation, which seems very unlikely, the doctrine of equivalents will be with us for the foreseeable future.[74]

10.6.4 Tests of Equivalence

One of the most intractable problems raised by the doctrine of equivalents is that of how a court, or in many cases a jury, can decide what is equivalent and what is not. Fulfilling the prophecy of the dissenting justice in

---

[70] *See, e.g.,* International Visual Corp. v. Crown Metal Mfg. Co., 991 F.2d 768, 773–75 (Fed. Cir. 1993) (Lourie, J., concurring). Note, however, that one person's "piracy" is another person's "designing around" a patent claim. The latter, which refers to the deliberate avoidance of a patent claim when engineering a product, is encouraged as a means of furthering the useful arts promoted by patent law. *See* State Indus., Inc. v. A.O. Smith Corp., 791 F.2d 1226, 1235–36 (Fed. Cir. 1985) ("One of the benefits of a patent system is its so-called 'negative incentive' to 'design around' a competitor's products, even when they are patented, thus bringing a steady flow of innovations to the marketplace."). As the Supreme Court remarked in rejecting an equitable distinction, "one wonders how ever to distinguish between the intentional copyist making minor changes to lower the risk of legal action, and the incremental innovator designing around the claims, yet seeking to capture as much as is permissible of the patented advance." Warner-Jenkinson Co. v. Hilton Davis Chemical Co., 520 U.S. 17, 36 (1997).

[71] 520 U.S. 17 (1997).

[72] *Warner-Jenkinson,* 520 U.S. at 28–29.

[73] *Warner-Jenkinson,* 520 U.S. at 34–36.

[74] In 2002, the Supreme Court reaffirmed the doctrine of equivalents, while taking note of the usual arguments against it. As the court explained,

It is true that the doctrine of equivalents renders the scope of patents less certain. It may be difficult to determine what is, or is not, an equivalent to a particular element of an invention. If competitors cannot be certain about a patent's extent, they may be deterred from engaging in legitimate manufactures outside its limits, or they may invest by mistake in competing products that the patent secures. In addition the uncertainty may lead to wasteful litigation between competitors, suits that a rule of literalism might avoid. These concerns with the doctrine of equivalents, however, are not new. Each time the Court has considered the doctrine, it has acknowledged this uncertainty as the price of ensuring the appropriate incentive for innovation, and it has affirmed the doctrine over dissents that urged a more certain rule.

Festo, 535 U.S. at 732.

Winans v. Denmead, the issue of equivalence has been as "productive of oppressive and costly litigation" as any other, primarily because the results are unpredictable.[75] In virtually any case where literal infringement is absent, the patentee can produce evidence of similarities between what is literally described by the patent claims and what is found in the accused product, seemingly leading to a conclusion of equivalence. At the same time, the defendant can produce evidence of dissimilarities, seemingly leading to a conclusion of nonequivalence. How is a judge or jury to decide? What Justice Story observed as long ago as 1818 remains true today:

> In all my experience I can scarcely recollect a single instance, in which the general question, whether the principles of two machines were the same or different, has not produced from different witnesses, equally credible and equally intelligent, opposite answers.[76]

Although the *Graver Tank* court declined to reduce equivalence to a formula, its reference to equivalence based on performing "substantially the same function in substantially the same way to obtain the same result" was adopted in many subsequent decisions as the touchstone of infringement.[77] Indeed, this function-way-result test of equivalence (also referred to as the *three-prong* test or *triple identity* test of equivalence) took on a significance that the *Graver Tank* court may not have intended or foreseen. The Federal Circuit went so far as to require that a patentee produce independent evidence on *each* part of the three-prong test—in other words, evidence that the substituted ingredient or apparatus (1) performs substantially the same function, in (2) substantially the same way, to (3) achieve substantially the same result as that which is literally claimed.[78] Without such close adherence to the three-prong test, it was feared that juries would be "put to sea without guiding charts."[79] Still, the debate commonly boils down to the second prong of the test—whether the accused product and the claimed invention function in "substantially the same way"[80]—and the answer to that question is rarely straightforward.

Another important consideration is whether the item found in the accused product is known to be interchangeable with the item literally claimed.[81] This is not a definitive test of equivalence.[82] Things may be interchangeable in the broadest sense if they produce similar results, but still

[75] *See* Paper Converting Machine Co. v. Magna-Graphics Corp., 745 F.2d 11, 19 (Fed. Cir. 1984) ("In view of [the doctrine of equivalents], a copier rarely knows whether his product 'infringes' a patent or not until a district court passes on the issue.").

[76] Barrett v. Hall, 2 F. Cas. 914, 923 (C.C.D. Mass. 1818).

[77] *See, e.g.,* Malta v. Schulmerich Carillons, Inc., 952 F.2d 1320, 1327 (Fed. Cir. 1991); Lear Siegler, Inc. v. Sealy Mattress Co., 873 F.2d 1422, 1425 (Fed. Cir. 1989).

[78] *See Malta*, 952 F.2d at 1327; *Lear Siegler*, 873 F.2d at 1425.

[79] *Lear Siegler*, 873 F.2d at 1426–27.

[80] *See* Slimfold Mfg. Co., Inc. v. Kinkead Indus., Inc., 932 F.2d 1453, 1457 (Fed. Cir. 1991).

operate in substantially different ways. A word processor may be inter-changeable with a ballpoint pen for the purpose of preparing a grocery list, but the two are unlikely to be considered equivalent in an infringement analysis.[83] On the other hand, a physical incompatibility that would compli-cate the substitution of one thing for another (e.g., putting instant film in a 35 mm camera) does not, necessarily, prevent those things from being equiva-lent in a more conceptual sense.[84]

In recent years, the trend has been to downplay the function-way-result test as the conclusive test of equivalency.[85] Instead, the three-prong test has been described as just one approach to the fundamental inquiry, which is whether the differences between the claimed and the accused product are "insubstantial."[86] Yet to ask whether a difference is "insubstantial" seems a rephrasing of the equivalence question, more than a clarification.[87] For its part, the Supreme Court in *Warner-Jenkinson* declined to endorse any partic-ular "linguistic framework" for deciding the ultimate question of equiva-

[81] *See Graver Tank*, 339 U.S. at 609; Vulcan Eng'g Co. v. Fata Aluminium, Inc., 278 F.3d 1366, 1374 (Fed. Cir. 2002) ("Known interchangeability is an important factor in determining equivalence.").

[82] *See* Warner-Jenkinson Co. v. Hilton Davis Chemical Co., 520 U.S. 28, 37 (1997) (known in-terchangeability "is not relevant for its own sake, but rather for what it tells the fact-finder about the similarities or differences between those elements"); Key Mfg. Gp., Inc. v. Micro-dot, Inc., 925 F.2d 1444, 1449 (Fed. Cir. 1991) ("an interchangeable device is not necessarily an equivalent device"); Perkin-Elmer Corp. v. Westinghouse Electric Corp., 822 F.2d 1528, 1535 (Fed. Cir. 1987) (interchangeable devices "still must perform substantially the same function in substantially the same way to obtain the same result").

[83] *See Perkin-Elmer*, 822 F.2d at 1535 (devices were "interchangeable" only in "entirely different and unrelated environments" and were not interchangeable for performing certain functions).

[84] *See* Interactive Pictures Corp. v. Infinite Pictures, Inc., 274 F.3d 1371, 1383 (Fed. Cir. 2001) ("Rather than focusing on physical or electronic compatibility, the known interchangeability test looks to the knowledge of a skilled artisan to see whether that artisan would contemplate the interchange as a design choice.").

[85] *See Warner-Jenkinson*, 520 U.S. at 39–40 ("[W]hile the triple identity test may be suitable for analyzing mechanical devices, it often provides a poor framework for analyzing other prod-ucts or processes. . . . In our view, the particular linguistic framework used is less important than whether the test is probative of the essential inquiry: does the accused product or pro-cess contain elements identical or equivalent to each claimed element of the patented inven-tion?"); Toro Co. v. White Consolidated Indus., Inc., 266 F.3d 1367, 1370 (Fed. Cir. 2001) ("In appropriate cases the function-way-result test offers additional guidance on the question of equivalence."); Telemac Cellular Corp. v. Topp Telecom, Inc., 247 F.3d 1316, 1330 (Fed. Cir. 2001) (three-prong test is "[o]ne method for finding infringement under the doctrine of equivalents"); Upjohn Co. v. Mova Pharmaceutical Corp., 225 F.3d 1306, 1309 (Fed. Cir. 2000) (three-prong test is "[t]he usual test of the substantiality of the differences").

[86] *See Toro*, 266 F.3d at 1370 ("To determine whether the accused device includes equivalents for a claim limitation, this court applies the 'insubstantial differences' test."); Viskase Corp. v. American National Can Co., 261 F.3d 1316, 1324 (Fed. Cir. 2001) (question is "whether the accused composition is only insubstantially changed from what is claimed"). As one court explained the test, an equivalent is "an insubstantial change which, from the perspective of one of ordinary skill in the art, adds nothing of significance to the claimed invention." Val-mont Indus., Inc. v. Reinke Mfg. Co., 983 F.2d 1039, 1043 (Fed. Cir. 1993).

lence.[88] In short, the question of equivalence is likely to remain a perennial source of confusion and difficulty.

10.6.5 Improvements

Equivalency is measured from the perspective of one of ordinary skill in the art *at the time of the alleged infringement.*[89] As a result, variations that the patentee had not even imagined, much less enabled, can be held infringing under the doctrine of equivalents. For example, if a transistor were substituted for a vacuum tube referenced in a patent claim, that claim might still be infringed under the doctrine of equivalents even if, when the patent application was filed, transistors had not been invented yet. If the rule were otherwise, technological advancements would allow competitors to take the substance of an invention but still avoid infringement. This does not mean, however, that technological advancements are irrelevant when judging equivalency. A transistor might be such an advancement over a vacuum tube that, in the context of a particular invention, the differences between the two would be thought substantial even at the time of infringement.

One factor that bears on whether an improvement is still an equivalent is whether the improvement is itself the subject of a patent. If equivalence is limited to "insubstantial variations," a change worthy of its own patent would seem beyond reach. However, although it is a factor to be considered and given "due weight,"[90] it cannot be said categorically that a patented improvement is never equivalent.[91]

Texas Instruments, Inc. v. U.S. Int'l Trade Comm'n[92] is a case that illustrates the difficulty of applying the concept of equivalency in fields subject to rapid

---

[87] *See Warner-Jenkinson,* 520 U.S. at 40 ("the insubstantial differences test offers little additional guidance as to what might render a given difference 'insubstantial'"); *Toro,* 266 F.3d at 1370. However, "[i]n some cases, the change in the accused device is so facially 'unimportant and insubstantial' that little additional guidance is needed." *Toro,* 266 F.3d at 1370.

[88] *Warner-Jenkinson,* 520 U.S. at 40.

[89] *Warner-Jenkinson,* 520 U.S. at 37 ("[T]he proper time for evaluating equivalency—and thus knowledge of interchangeability between elements—is at the time of infringement, not at the time the patent was issued."); Texas Instruments, Inc. v. United States Int'l Trade Comm'n, 805 F.2d 1558, 1563 (Fed. Cir. 1986).

[90] National Presto Indus., Inc. v. West Bend Co., 76 F. 3d 1185, 1192 (Fed. Cir. 1996); *see also* Zygo Corp. v. Wyko Corp. 79 F.3d 1563, 1570 (Fed. Cir. 1996) ("The nonobviousness of the accused device, evidenced by the grant of a United States patent, is relevant to the issue of whether the change therein is substantial.").

[91] Fiskars, Inc. v. Hunt Mfg. Co., 221 F.3d 1318, 1324 (Fed. Cir. 2000) ("it is well established that separate patentability does not avoid equivalence as a matter of law"); *National Presto,* 76 F.3d at 1192; Atlas Powder Co. v. E.I. Du Pont de Nemours & Co., 750 F.2d 1569, 1580 (Fed. Cir. 1984). Note that just as an improvement is sometimes still an equivalent, the same is true of an inferior variation of the invention literally claimed. As the Federal Circuit has observed, "inferior infringement is still infringement." Whapeton Canvas Co. v. Frontier, Inc., 870 F.2d 1546, 1548 n.2 (Fed. Cir. 1989). The question, as before, is whether or not the differences are substantial.

technological change.[93] Texas Instruments obtained the first patent ever issued on a pocket calculator. The court acknowledged it as a "pioneering invention"[94] and noted that the prototype had become part of the permanent collection at the Smithsonian's Museum of History and Technology. In essence, the claims of the patent called for the basic combination of a keyboard, a processing circuit, a memory, and a display, but because the claims were drafted in means-plus-function format,[95] the claims literally incorporated only the particular keyboard, processing circuit, memory, and display described in the patent specification, and their equivalents.

About 17 years after its patent application was filed, and 10 years after the patent issued, Texas Instruments brought an action to prevent the importation of pocket calculators by foreign manufacturers. During those years, the field had advanced in significant ways. MOS transistors had replaced bipolar transistors, liquid crystal displays had replaced thermal printer displays, and so forth. The Federal Circuit found that each substitution, by itself, might be considered the substitution of an equivalent, but when considered *as a whole*, all of the technological changes were sufficient to take the accused devices beyond the protection of the doctrine of equivalents.[96] The decision was a controversial one, even among the judges of the Federal Circuit.

Years later, and in spite of the result in *Texas Instruments*, the Federal Circuit announced in *Chiuminatta Concrete Concepts, Inc. v. Cardinal Indus., Inc.*,[97] that the unpredictability of technological developments is the primary reason, perhaps the *only* reason, to invoke the doctrine of equivalents. "The doctrine of equivalents is necessary," the court observed, "because one cannot predict the future."[98] If the unclaimed equivalent was known to the applicant (i.e., "technology that predates the invention itself"), and therefore *could* have been claimed in the patent, the court could see "no policy-based reason why a patentee should get two bites at the apple."[99] In other words, unless the failure to claim the full scope of the invention explicitly can be excused by historical necessity, the court may refuse to apply the doctrine of equivalents.

---

[92] 805 F.2d 1558 (Fed. Cir. 1986). Also see the opinion on denial of rehearing en banc, 846 F.2d 1369 (Fed. Cir. 1988).

[93] The opinion deals with equivalence under 35 U.S.C. § 112, ¶ 6, discussed in Section 10.7, and under the doctrine of equivalents. At the time the court treated the analysis as essentially the same. *See Texas Instruments*, 805 F.2d at 1571. More recently, the court has suggested a difference—confining § 112, ¶ 6 equivalence to structures that existed in the art when the patent was filed, and equivalence under the doctrine of equivalents to later-developed structures. See Section 10.7.

[94] *See* Section 10.6.7.

[95] *See* Section 7.7.4.

[96] *Texas Instruments*, 805 F.2d at 1570–72.

[97] 145 F.3d 1303 (Fed. Cir. 1998).

[98] *Chiuminatta*, 145 F.3d. at 1310.

[99] *Chiuminatta*, 145 F.3d. at 1311.

Chiuminatta's emphasis on later-developed technology may be over-done.[100] The Supreme Court has justified the doctrine of equivalents, at least in part, by reference to the inherent imprecision of language[101]—a problem that is broader than that of advancing technologies. *Graver Tank* itself dealt with an equivalent known at the time the patent application was filed. Later cases have interpreted *Chiuminatta*'s "two bites at the apple" reasoning as applying only to means-plus-function claims, where equivalence of structure is already an issue for literal infringement.[102] Except in those cases, "the mere fact that the asserted equivalent structure was preexisting technology does not foreclose a finding of infringement under the doctrine of equivalents."[103] The rhetoric of *Chiuminatta* is, however, representative of recent efforts by the Federal Circuit to confine the doctrine of equivalents to situations where the uncertainty it creates is easiest to justify.[104]

10.6.6 The Impact of the All-Elements Rule on Equivalence

One of the most important refinements of the principles announced in *Graver Tank* involves the *all-elements* rule, which states that each and every element of the claimed invention must be found in an infringing product.[105] In *Pennwalt Corp. v. Durand-Wayland, Inc.*,[106] the Federal Circuit, in the form of an expanded en banc panel, considered whether the doctrine of equivalents could be applied if the claimed invention and the accused product were similar *as a whole*, even though individual claim elements were entirely absent in the accused product.

The invention in *Pennwalt* was a machine used to sort fruit by color and weight. One of the claimed components of the machine was a "position indi-cating means," which kept track of the physical location of a piece of fruit as it passed through the sorter. The accused product was also a sorting device, and it produced comparable results. However, it did so without any means for keeping track of the physical location of a piece of fruit. Although a num-ber of judges dissented, the majority held that an accused product cannot

---

[100] The paragraphs discussing the "after-developed technology" rationale for the doctrine of equivalents are uncharacteristically free of citations to precedent. *See Chiuminatta*, 145 F.3d at 1310–13.

[101] "[T]the nature of language makes it impossible to capture the essence of a thing in a patent application." Festo Corp. v. Shoketsu Kinzoku Kogyo Kabushiki Co., 535 U.S. 722, 731 (2002).

[102] See Section 10.7.

[103] Kraft Foods, Inc. v. International Trading Co., 203 F.3d 1362, 1373 (Fed. Cir. 2000).

[104] A more specific application of the *Chiuminatta* reasoning is the Federal Circuit's refusal to recognize equivalents that were actually *disclosed* in the application, without being explicitly claimed. See Section 10.6.9.

[105] *See* Forest Labs., Inc. v. Abbott Labs., 239 F.3d 1305, 1310 (Fed. Cir. 2001) ("A patentee claiming infringement must present proof that the accused product meets each and every claim limitation.").

[106] 833 F.2d 931 (Fed. Cir. 1987) (en banc).

infringe a claim under the doctrine of equivalents unless each and every claim element, or its equivalent, can be found in the accused product. Overall similarity is insufficient if any claim element is entirely missing.[107] In *Warner-Jenkinson*, the Supreme Court reaffirmed the rule established in *Pennwalt*, stating that a strict, element-by-element application of the doctrine would ensure fair notice to potential infringers.[108]

As a corollary to the all-elements rule, courts resist any argument, even couched in terms of equivalence, that seems to ignore completely a very clear claim limitation.[109] As the Supreme Court stated, "[i]t is important to ensure that the application of the doctrine, even as to an individual element, is not allowed such broad play as to effectively eliminate that element in its entirety."[110] When a claim limitation specifically excludes an alternative, a court may refuse to find them equivalent.[111] For example, in *Moore U.S.A.,*

[107] *Pennwalt*, 833 F.2d at 935, 939; *see also* Bell Atlantic Network Services, Inc. v. Covad Communications Gp., Inc., 262 F.3d 1258, 1279 (Fed. Cir. 2001) ("under the 'all elements rule,' there can be no infringement under the doctrine of equivalents if even one element of a claim or its equivalent is not present in the accused device"); De Marini Sports, Inc. v. Worth, Inc., 239 F.3d 1314, 1331 (Fed. Cir. 2001) ("Infringement under the doctrine of equivalents requires that each accused product contain each limitation of the claim or its equivalent."). However, there need not be a "one-to-one correspondence" between the claim and the accused product. A single component of an accused product can perform the functions of several components described in the claim, and the single component can be considered the equivalent of *each* claimed component. Dolly, Inc. v. Spalding & Evenflo Co., 16 F.3d 394, 398 (Fed. Cir. 1994); Sun Studs, Inc. v. ATA Equipment Leasing, Inc., 872 F.2d 978, 989 (Fed. Cir. 1989) ("elements or steps may be combined without *ipso facto* loss of equivalency"). This principle allows somewhat greater flexibility in applying the doctrine of equivalents than the all-elements rule might suggest.

[108] Warner-Jenkinson Co. v. Hilton Davis Chemical Co., 520 U.S. 17, 29–30 (1997) ("Each element in a patent claim is deemed material to defining the scope of the patented invention, and thus the doctrine of equivalents must be applied to individual elements of the claim, not to the invention as a whole."). Interestingly, the Supreme Court did not mention *Pennwalt*, and discussed the all-elements approach as though it were a newly discovered compromise solution to the problems posed by the doctrine of equivalents.

[109] *See* Athletic Alternatives, Inc. v. Prince Mfg., Inc., 73 F.3d 1573, 1582 (Fed. Cir. 1996) (specific exclusion rule as a "corollary to the 'all limitations' rule").

[110] *Warner-Jenkinson*, 520 U.S. at 29; *see also* Scimed Life Sys., Inc. v. Advanced Cardiovascular Sys., Inc., 242 F.3d 1337, 1346 (Fed. Cir. 2001) ("the doctrine of equivalents cannot be employed in a manner that wholly vitiates a claim limitation"); Lear Siegler, Inc. v. Sealy Mattress Co., 873 F.2d 1422, 1425 (Fed. Cir. 1989) ("'a court may not, under the guise of applying the doctrine of equivalents, erase a plethora of meaningful structural and functional limitations of the claims[s] on which the public is entitled to rely in avoiding infringement.'").

[111] *See Scimed*, 242 F.3d at 1345 ("Having specifically identified, criticized, and disclaimed the dual lumen configuration, the patentee cannot now invoke the doctrine of equivalents to 'embrace a structure that was specifically excluded from the claims.'"); Weiner v. NEC Electronics, Inc., 102 F.3d 534, 541 (Fed. Cir. 1996) ("even under infringement by equivalents . . . the protection of a patent may not 'embrace a structure that is specifically excluded from the scope of the claims.'"); *Athletic Alternatives*, 73 F.3d at 1582 (arrangement of strings in accused sports racket was nonequivalent because "'specifically excluded from the scope of the claims'").

Inc. v. Standard Register Co.,[112] the patent claims described a "business type mailer form" having adhesive strips extending "the majority of the lengths" of the margins.[113] The accused product had adhesive strips that covered only a minority of the margins, but the plaintiff argued that the product was still equivalent. The court rejected that argument, in part because "it would defy logic to conclude that a minority–the very antithesis of a majority– could be insubstantially different from a claim limitation requiring a majority."[114] Of course, whether something is an opposite or "antithesis" as opposed to an insignificant difference is sometimes a matter of perspective. "Majority" seems the opposite of "minority," but, as a dissenting justice in *Moore* pointed out, just under 50 percent might differ insubstantially from just over 50 percent.[115]

10.6.7 The Impact of the Prior Art on Equivalence

Another limitation on the doctrine of equivalents is imposed by the prior art.[116] The doctrine of equivalents cannot expand the scope of a claim so far that it encompasses the prior art.[117] One method of analyzing the problem (though it is not an exclusive method) is to imagine a *hypothetical claim* that would be *literally* infringed by the product at issue.[118] If no such claim could have been validly obtained from the Patent Office, because it would have been anticipated by the prior art or rendered obvious,[119] then the accused product cannot be held to infringe under the doctrine of equivalents. The purpose of this limitation is to ensure that patentees do not achieve indirectly, through the doctrine of equivalents, a monopoly that could not have been obtained directly by prosecution of a broader claim.[120]

---

[112] 229 F.3d 1091 (Fed. Cir. 2000).
[113] *Moore*, 229 F.3d at 1095.
[114] *Moore*, 229 F.3d at 1106.
[115] *See Moore*, 229 F.3d at 1119 (Newman, J., concurring-in-part and dissenting-in-part).
[116] The concept of prior art is discussed in Section 8.9.
[117] Tate Access Floors, Inc. v. Interface Architectural Resources, Inc., 279 F.3d 1357, 1367 (Fed. Cir. 2002); Interactive Pictures Corp. v. Infinite Pictures, Inc., 274 F.3d 1371, 1380 (Fed. Cir. 2001) ("It is well settled law that a patentee cannot assert a range of equivalents that encompasses the prior art.").
[118] Abbott Labs. v. Dey, L.P., 287 F.3d 1097, 1105 (Fed. Cir. 2002); *Interactive Pictures*, 274 F.3d at 1380; Wilson Sporting Goods Co. v. David Geoffrey & Assoc., 904 F.2d 677, 684 (Fed. Cir. 1990).
[119] *See* Sections 8.9.5–8.9.6.
[120] *See Tate Access Floors*, 279 F.3d at 1367 ("the doctrine of equivalents is an equitable doctrine and it would not be equitable to allow a patentee to claim a scope of equivalents encompassing material that had been previously disclosed by someone else, or that would have been obvious in light of others' earlier disclosures"); *Wilson Sporting Goods*, 904 F.2d at 684 ("The doctrine of equivalents exists to prevent fraud on a patent . . . *not* to give a patentee something which he could not lawfully have obtained from the PTO had he tried.").

The restrictions imposed by the prior art create, in effect, a safe harbor insofar as the doctrine of equivalents is concerned, if the accused product in all relevant respects is identical to an invention in the prior art. No hypothetical claim could encompass such a product yet avoid invalidity. The restriction applies only to the claim as a whole, so there is no immunity from infringement by equivalence unless all of the relevant features of the accused product are found in the prior art, either in one reference or in several that, together, made the combination obvious. Because patents are often granted to novel combinations of known elements, one cannot escape infringement, either literal or under the doctrine of equivalents, merely by identifying isolated features of the accused product in the prior art.[121]

The prior art also influences the doctrine of equivalents in a subtler fashion through the concept of the *pioneer patent*. Whereas most patents are granted to incremental improvements of inventions that have gone before, a pioneer patent is one that breaks with the past so distinctly that it creates an entirely new field. Patents such as Bell's on the telephone, or the Texas Instruments calculator patent, have staked claims to pioneering status. Some cases have held that a pioneer patent, as a very basic advancement in technology, should be given a correspondingly broad scope of equivalence. A patent on a narrow improvement, on the other hand, should be held more strictly to the language of the claims.[122] Of course, whether or not a patent deserves to be called pioneering will often be a subject for debate.[123]

For the most part, the Federal Circuit has declined to divide patents into pioneer and nonpioneer categories. Instead, it has treated pioneer patents as just one end of a spectrum that embraces various degrees of inventiveness.[124] Moreover, it has emphasized that pioneer patents are not subject to different legal standards than other patents, as a reward for merit or otherwise.[125] A pioneer patent merely enjoys a potentially broader scope of

---

[121] *See Abbott Labs.*, 287 F.3d at 1106; Corning Glass Works v. Sumitomo Electric U.S.A., Inc., 868 F.2d 1251, 1261 (Fed. Cir. 1989).

[122] *See* Sun Studs, Inc. v. ATA Equipment Leasing, Inc., 872 F.2d 978, 987 (Fed. Cir. 1989) ("The concept of the 'pioneer' arises from an ancient jurisprudence, reflecting judicial appreciation that a broad breakthrough invention merits a broader scope of equivalents than does a narrow improvement in a crowded technology.").

[123] "That an improvement enjoys commercial success and has some industry impact, as many do, cannot compel a finding that an improvement falls within the pioneer category." Perkin-Elmer Corp. v. Westinghouse Electric Corp., 822 F.2d 1528, 1532 (Fed. Cir. 1987). Even the pioneering status of Texas Instruments' calculator patent was challenged. *See* Texas Instruments, Inc. v. U.S. Int'l Trade Comm'n, 846 F.2d 1369, 1370 (Fed. Cir. 1988).

[124] *See Sun Studs*, 872 F.2d at 987 ("[T]he 'pioneer' is not a separate class of invention, carrying a unique body of law. The wide range of technological advance between pioneering breakthrough and modest improvement accommodates gradations in scope of equivalency."); *Texas Instruments*, 846 F.2d at 1370 ("[t]here is not a discontinuous transition from 'mere improvement' to 'pioneer'").

[125] *See* Augustine Medical, Inc. v. Gaymar Indus., Inc., 181 F.3d 1291, 1301 (Fed. Cir. 1999) ("no objective legal test separates pioneers from non-pioneers").

equivalence because it is not hemmed in by large numbers of similar inventions in the prior art, as is generally true of an incremental improvement in an already crowded field.[126]

10.6.8 Prosecution History Estoppel

One of the most important limitations of the doctrine of equivalents is the doctrine of prosecution history estoppel. The prosecution history is the written record of an applicant's dealings with the Patent Office, including any actions taken by the examiner, and any statements, arguments, or modifications of the claims made by the applicant.[127] Estoppel means a claim is barred because the claimant's prior actions are inconsistent with that claim. Simply put, prosecution history estoppel prevents a patent owner from contradicting the prosecution history by claiming as an equivalent subject matter that was *given up* during prosecution in order to obtain the patent.[128]

Brenner v. United States[129] supplies a good example of prosecution history estoppel. The patented invention concerned a system for coding and sorting mail. The claims described a means for applying a "codable" material, such as a magnetic strip, to an article of mail. The material would carry the information needed for the sorting. When the patent application was filed, the claims referred to a "coded" rather than "codable" material, implying that the information was encoded beforehand. However, the applicant changed the claim language to "codable," telling the examiner that the new language more accurately described the invention "since when the material is placed

---

[126] *See Abbott Labs.,* 287 F.3d at 1105 ("A pioneer patent by definition will have little applicable prior art to limit it, whereas an improvement patent's scope is confined by the existing knowledge on which the improvement is based."); *Augustine Medical,* 181 F.3d at 1301 ("Without extensive prior art to confine and cabin their claims, pioneers acquire broader claims than non-pioneers who must craft narrow claims to evade the strictures of a crowded art field."); *Texas Instruments,* 846 F.2d at 1370 (the "liberal" scope of equivalency afforded to pioneer patents "flows directly from the relative sparseness of prior art in nascent fields of technology").

[127] See Section 5.1.

[128] *See* Festo Corp. v. Shoketsu Kinzoku Kogyo Kabushiki Co., 535 U.S. 722, 733–34 (2002) (When . . . the patentee originally claimed the subject matter alleged to infringe but then narrowed the claim in response to a rejection, he may not argue that the surrendered territory comprised unforeseen subject matter that should be deemed equivalent to the literal claims of the issued patent."); General Electric Co. v. Nintendo Co., Ltd., 179 F.3d 1350, 1363 (Fed. Cir. 1999) ("'The essence of prosecution history estoppel is that a patentee should not be able to obtain, through the doctrine of equivalents, coverage of subject matter that was relinquished during prosecution to procure issuance of the patent.'"). Although the clearest cases of estoppel arise after a claim is narrowed by *amendment,* even where a claim is unchanged estoppel can result from an applicant's *arguments* in favor of a narrow claim interpretation. *See* Allen Eng'g Corp. v. Bartell Indus., Inc., 299 F.3d 1336, 1350 (Fed. Cir. 2002). As the Supreme Court recently held, "the doctrine of equivalents is premised on language's inability to capture the essence of innovation"–a premise that is undercut when the applicant specifically abandoned material now urged to be equivalent. *Festo,* 535 U.S. at 734.

[129] 773 F.2d 306 (Fed. Cir. 1985).

on the mail it is not yet coded."[130] When compelled to distinguish certain prior art, the applicant stressed this distinction and also emphasized that the material could be erased after encoding.

The system accused of infringing used an ink jet printer to spray bar codes directly on the mail to be sorted. The only article applied to the mail was the ink itself, and the ink was not codable. By the time the ink hit the paper, it was fixed in a predetermined pattern, and it could not be altered or erased afterward. The trial court, affirmed by the Federal Circuit, found that the accused system could not be held equivalent to the system claimed because the applicant, during prosecution, had clearly limited the invention to "codable material."[131]

Prosecution history estoppel checks the inclination of some patent owners to treat claims as a "nose of wax," to be twisted in one direction to avoid invalidity and another to ensure infringement. An applicant who represents the invention as one thing in prosecution must be prepared to live with that interpretation in litigation. There can be no "second bite at the abandoned apple."[132] The doctrine also provides better notice to a patentee's competitors of the scope of the patented invention, at least in those cases where the competitors have an opportunity to review the prosecution history.[133] Most importantly, the doctrine of prosecution history estoppel prevents applicants from circumventing the process of patent examination. If the scope of equivalence were not limited by the prosecution history, an applicant could narrow the claims as much as necessary to satisfy the examiner, while resorting to the doctrine of equivalents to preserve what amounts to a broader claim. Prosecution history estoppel helps to ensure that a patent claim is no broader in scope than the examiner understood it to be.[134]

In *Festo Corp. v. Shoketsu Kinzoku Kogyo Kabushiki Co.*,[135] the Federal Circuit, to the surprise of many patent attorneys, announced that if a claim element had been narrowed during prosecution, for reasons related to patentability, the doctrine of equivalents could not be applied to that element *at all* in any subsequent litigation.[136] Suppose, for example, that a claim to a mousetrap had originally called for "at least one spring," but the examiner had found the claim anticipated by a prior mousetrap with one spring.

[130] *Brenner*, 773 F.2d at 307.
[131] *Brenner*, 773 F.2d at 308.
[132] Lemelson v. General Mills, Inc., 968 F.2d 1202, 1208 (Fed. Cir. 1992).
[133] *See Lemelson*, 968 F.2d at 1208 ("Other players in the marketplace are entitled to rely on the record made in the Patent Office in determining the meaning and scope of the patent.").
[134] *See* Genentech, Inc. v. Wellcome Foundation Ltd., 29 F. 3d 1555, 1564 (Fed. Cir. 1994) ("An applicant should not be able deliberately to narrow the scope of examination to avoid during prosecution scrutiny by the PTO of subject matter . . . and then, obtain in court, either literally or under the doctrine of equivalents, a scope of protection which encompasses that subject matter.").
[135] 234 F.3d 558 (Fed. Cir. 2000) (en banc).
[136] *Festo*, 234 F.3d at 574.

The applicant might amend the claim to call for "two springs," perhaps pointing out how the two springs of the preferred embodiment produced nonobvious advantages compared to the one-spring prior art. According to *Festo*, the patentee could not argue afterwards that a trap with *three* springs infringed by equivalency, even though the difference between two and three springs might be insignificant. By specifically referring to "two springs," the applicant disclaimed anything else.[137] The majority of the court viewed this as the only "workable" approach, fostering predictability and respect for the notice function of claims.[138] However, the decision contradicted earlier cases promoting a more flexible brand of estoppel,[139] and it confounded the expectations of many patent attorneys who had routinely amended claims without being aware of the drastic effect it would have on the availability of the doctrine of equivalents.[140]

The Supreme Court accepted the appeal and reversed.[141] The court reaffirmed the principle of prosecution history estoppel[142] and held that the scope of equivalence could be limited by any claim amendment made in order to secure a patent (and not merely to avoid prior art).[143] On the other hand, the court rejected the notion that a claim amendment leads automatically to a complete bar on equivalents:

> By amending the application, the inventor is deemed to concede that the patent does not extend as far as the original claim. It does not follow, however, that the amended claim becomes so perfect in its description that no one could devise an equivalent. After amendment, as before, language remains an imperfect fit for invention. The narrowing amendment may demonstrate what the claim is not; but it may still fail to capture precisely what the claim is. There is no reason why a narrowing amendment should be deemed to relinquish equivalents unforeseeable at the time of the amendment and beyond a fair interpretation of what was surrendered. Nor is there any call to foreclose claims of equivalence for aspects of the invention that have only a peripheral relation to the reason the amendment was submitted.

Consequently, one must consider the amendment carefully and determine whether what the patentee now claims as an equivalent is precisely what the patentee surrendered. One would have to determine, for example, whether changing "at least one spring" to "two springs" in order to avoid the one-spring prior art could be interpreted as surrendering the three-spring mousetrap.

---

[137] *Festo*, 234 F.3d 575 ("By narrowing his claims, a patentee disclaims subject matter encompassed by the original claims.").

[138] *Festo*, 234 F.3d at 575–577.

[139] *See, e.g.,* Insta-Foam Prods., Inc. v. Universal Foam Sys., Inc., 906 F.2d 698, 703 (Fed. Cir. 1990) ("'Depending on the nature and purpose of an amendment it may have a limiting effect within a spectrum ranging from great to small to zero.'").

[140] *See Festo*, 234 F.3d at 638 (Newman, J., concurring-in-part and dissenting-in-part).

[141] 535 U.S. 722 (2002).

[142] 535 U.S. at 733–34.

[143] 535 U.S. at 736–37.

The more subtle approach breeds uncertainty, but this is alleviated, to some degree, by the Supreme Court's assignment of the burden of proof. First, one must *presume* that a narrowing claim amendment offered during prosecution was occasioned by a "substantial reason related to patentability."[144] The burden is on the patent owner to rebut that presumption by showing that the amendment had another explanation "sufficient to overcome prosecution history estoppel."[145] It might have been, for example, a "truly cosmetic"[146] or clarifying amendment, having no impact on the scope of the claim. Second, if the amendment was related to patentability, the patentee also "bear[s] the burden of showing that the amendment [did] not surrender the particular equivalent in question."[147] If the patentee cannot meet that burden, a court will presume that the patentee gave up, irretrievably, all of the subject matter excluded from the claim due to the amendment—like the three-spring mousetrap encompassed, in our hypothetical, by the original claim language.[148]

After remand from the Supreme Court, the Federal Circuit explained that the presumption of surrender can be rebutted in three ways. First, the patentee can show that "the rationale underlying the amendment [bore] no more than a tangential relation to the equivalent in question."[149] If the amendment in our example had depended on a fundamental distinction between a single spring and multiple springs (perhaps it had been questioned whether any single spring could generate the force required), the patentee might argue that the one-spring-versus-two-spring rationale had been, at best, tangential to the issue of equivalence between two springs and three.[150] Second, the patentee can demonstrate that the alleged equivalent was unforeseeable at the time of the amendment. If a three-spring mousetrap had been inconceivable, perhaps because of some technical barrier in the art that no one

---

[144] Warner-Jenkinson, Inc. v. Hilton Davis Chemical Co., 520 U.S. 17, 33 (1997).

[145] *Warner-Jenkinson*, 520 U.S. at 33. Alternative reasons for claim amendment should be demonstrated by evidence in the prosecution history, not by an after-the-fact declaration of the patentee's intentions. *See* Pioneer Magnetics, Inc. v. Micro Linear Corp., 330 F.3d 1352, 1356 (Fed. Cir. 2003) (rejecting patent attorney's contention that a narrowing amendment had been made "through sheer inadvertence").

[146] 535 U.S. at 736–37.

[147] *Festo*, 535 U.S. at 740.

[148] If the applicant adds a narrowing limitation to one claim, and that same term was already present in another claim, the estoppel may limit the range of equivalents available to *both* claims, a phenomenon dubbed "infectious estoppel" by one litigant. *See* Glaxo Wellcome Inc. v. Impax Labs. Inc., 356 F.3d 1348, 1356 (Fed. Cir. 2004) ("[S]ubject matter surrendered via claim amendments during prosecution is also relinquished for other claims containing the same limitation. . . . This court follows this rule to ensure consistent interpretation of the same claim terms in the same patent.").

[149] Festo Corp. v. Shoketzu Kinzoku Kogyo Kabushiki Co., 344 F.3d 1359, 1365 (Fed. Cir. 2003) (quoting *Festo*, 535 U.S. at 740).

[150] If this were the case, however, one could certainly question why the applicant had not simply changed the language to "at least two springs."

expected to overcome, the applicant could not have anticipated the limiting effect of the amendment, nor might on objective observer, equally skilled in the art, have expected such an effect.[151] Generally, if the alleged equivalent embodies technology unknown in the art at the time of the claim amendment–for example, a variant with transistors unforeseeable when vacuum tubes were the state of the art–the equivalent will be considered unforeseeable. Old technology, particularly if found in prior art in the field of the invention, is likely to be considered foreseeable.[152] Finally, the patentee may rebut the presumption by showing "some other reason" why it could not have been expected to express the claim amendment in such a way as to still include what is now argued as an equivalent.[153] This catch-all category is necessarily vague, but it might include arguments based on "the shortcomings of language."[154] Whether the patentee has met its burden of proof will be determined by the judge as a matter of law, not by the jury.[155]

If *Festo* is not the watershed it might have been, had the original Federal Circuit decision been allowed to stand, it does at least promise a more predictable analysis for prosecution history estoppel. The focus on foreseeability recognizes both the difficulties of patent applicants, who hope to reap the rewards of their efforts for years to come, and the interests of potential infringers, who deserve fair warning of prohibited conduct.

10.6.9 The Disclosure of Unclaimed Embodiments

Sometimes the variation claimed as an equivalent by the patentee is discussed in the patent specification, even though it is beyond the literal scope of the claims. In some ways this seems to bolster the patentee's argument in favor of equivalence. At least it shows that the patentee was aware of the alleged equivalent, and it suggests the possibility of substituting that equivalent for the matter literally claimed. But the effect of the disclosure can be quite the opposite, as illustrated in the case of *Maxwell v. J. Baker, Inc.*[156]

Maxwell was a store employee who invented a system for tying together pairs of shoes for display. Previous systems had relied on plastic filaments strung through the eyelets of the shoes, but this only worked for shoes that *had* eyelets. This led some retailers to puncture holes in the shoes, just to provide a way of tying them together. Maxwell's idea was to anchor plastic

---

[151] "This criterion presents an objective inquiry, asking whether the alleged equivalent would have been unforeseeable to one of ordinary skill in the art at the time of the amendment." *Festo*, 344 F.3d at 1369.

[152] *Festo*, 344 F.3d at 1369. Expert testimony may be useful in determining what would have been foreseeable at the time of the claim amendment. *See id.*

[153] Festo, 344 F.3d at 1370.

[154] *Festo*, 344 F.3d at 1370. The Federal Circuit cautioned that this third category of excuse "must be a narrow one." *Id.*

[155] *Festo*, 344 F.3d at 1369.

[156] 86 F.3d 1098 (Fed. Cir. 1996).

tabs inside the shoes and use holes or loops in the tabs as the attachment point for the filament. The figures in Maxwell's patent specification showed the tabs anchored between the inner and outer soles of the shoes, and the claims explicitly referred to this construction, but the specification also observed that the tabs could be stitched into the lining of the shoes. The court held that shoes having tabs sown into the lining did not infringe Maxwell's patent under the doctrine of equivalents, precisely because that option had been disclosed, but *not claimed,* in Maxwell's patent. Such unclaimed disclosures are "dedicated to the public," and cannot be recaptured through the doctrine of equivalents.[157]

The court's position tends to penalize applicants for making their disclosures more thorough and informative. If Maxwell had kept silent about the unclaimed alternative, it might well have been found infringing. On the other hand, if viewed from the perspective of a competitor trying to determine what would infringe, it might be reasonable to conclude that things discussed in the patent, but specifically excluded from the claims, were not meant to be covered by the patent. In addition, the Supreme Court has stressed the inability of language to capture the essence of an invention as the rationale for the doctrine of equivalents.[158] If an alleged equivalent was described in the specification, the patentee can hardly claim that he "lacked the words to describe the subject matter in question."[159] Finally, the dedication to the public of unclaimed embodiments forces applicants to subject to the rigors of PTO examination claims as broad as the monopoly they ultimately attempt to enforce.

For a time, it was uncertain whether the principle of *Maxwell* would find broad application,[160] but in 2002, the Federal Circuit's en banc opinion in *Johnson & Johnston Assoc., Inc. v. R.E. Service Co.,*[161] reaffirmed the rule that "when a patent drafter discloses but declines to claim subject matter . . . this action dedicates that unclaimed subject matter to the public."[162] In this case, the patentee whose claims called for an "aluminum sheet" could not argue

---

[157] *Maxwell,* 86 F.3d at 1106–7; *see also* Unique Concepts, Inc. v. Brown, 939 F.2d 1558, 1562–63 (Fed. Cir. 1991).

[158] *See* Festo Corp. v. Shoketsu Kinzoku Kogyo Kabushiki Co., 535 U.S. 722, 734–38 (2002).

[159] *Festo,* 535 U.S. at 734 (applying the same reasoning where claims were narrowed to exclude the alleged equivalent).

[160] *See* YBM Magnex, Inc. v. Int'l Trade Comm'n, 145 F.3d 1317 (Fed. Cir. 1998) (holding that *Maxwell* creates no "blanket rule" regarding disclosed but unclaimed embodiments, but offering little to clarify the limits of the *Maxwell* principle).

[161] 285 F.3d 1046 (Fed. Cir. 2002).

[162] *Johnson & Johnston,* 285 F.3d at 1054; *see also* PSC Computer Prods. Inc. v. Foxconn Int'l Inc., 355 F.3d 1353, 1357–60 (Fed. Cir. 2004). Although in the landmark Supreme Court case of *Graver Tank* the equivalent alternative of manganese was disclosed in the specification, the Federal Circuit distinguished that case as one in which the applicant at least *tried* to obtain the broader claim, though it failed when the PTO rejected it. That reasoning presents some difficulties, but at least the *Graver Tank* situation is less likely an instance of a patentee attempting to "game the system." *See Johnson & Johnston,* 285 F.3d at 1060 (Dyk, J., concurring).

that a steel sheet was equivalent, when the patent specifically disclosed, without claiming, the steel alternative.[163] The court cited the usual concerns regarding the primacy of claims and the desirability of fair notice to the public.[164] Like its attempt in *Festo*,[165] *Johnson & Johnston* can be seen as another effort by the Federal Circuit to rein in the doctrine of equivalents and restore some certainty to the patent system.

10.7 EQUIVALENCE IN THE CONTEXT OF MEANS-PLUS-FUNCTION CLAIMS

Patent law would be less confusing if equivalence were an issue arising solely in connection with the doctrine of equivalents, but in fact equivalence is an issue affecting *literal* infringement if the claim is a means-plus-function claim drafted in accordance with ¶ 6 of 35 U.S.C. § 112.[166] Means-plus-function claims are discussed in Section 7.7.4, but to summarize, a claim element described as a *means* for performing a specific function is literally infringed only if (1) the accused product performs that function, and (2) the function is performed by a structure that is identical or equivalent to the corresponding structure disclosed in the patent specification.[167]

Suppose that a claim to a mousetrap had, as one claim element, a "means for snapping the trap shut," and in the patent specification the structure disclosed for performing that function was a steel spring. The first step in determining whether the claim was infringed would be to see if the accused mousetrap had *any* means for "snapping the trap shut." If that function was not performed by any component of the accused mousetrap, the claim would not be literally infringed.[168] If the accused mousetrap did have some

---

[163] *Johnson & Johnston*, 285 F.3d at 1055.

[164] *Johnson & Johnston*, 285 F.3d at 1052. In order to be "dedicated to the public," the unclaimed alternative must be described in the patent with sufficient specificity that it can be identified by a person of ordinary skill in the art as a variation disclosed but not claimed. *PSC*, 355 F.3d at 1360.

[165] *See* Section 10.6.8.

[166] "An element in a claim for a combination may be expressed as a means or step for performing a specified function without the recital of structure, material, or acts in support thereof, and such claim shall be construed to cover the corresponding structure, material or acts described in the specification and equivalents thereof."

[167] Overhead Door Corp. v. Chamberlain Gp., Inc., 194 F.3d 1261, 1273 (Fed. Cir. 1999); Cybor Corp. v. FAS Technologies, Inc., 138 F.3d 1448, 1457 (Fed. Cir. 1998); King Instruments Corp. v. Perego, 65 F.3d 941, 945–46 (Fed. Cir. 1995).

[168] One might inquire, however, whether it performed an equivalent function that might be sufficient for a finding of infringement under the doctrine of equivalents. *See* Interactive Pictures Corp. v. Infinite Pictures, Inc., 274 F.3d 1371, 1382 (Fed. Cir. 2001) ("[I]nfringement under the doctrine of equivalents may be premised on the accused and the patented component having *substantially* the same function, whereas structure corresponding to the disclosed limitation in a means-plus-function clause must perform the *identical* function." (emphasis in original)).

means for performing that function, one would then ask whether the structure performing that function was identical or equivalent to the steel spring. If the accused mousetrap used, for example, a rubber band to perform the same function, one would have to decide whether a rubber band and a steel spring were equivalent in the context of the invention.

Paradoxically, this is one case in which literal infringement is not based on taking the language of the claims literally. Literally, a claim requiring a "means for snapping the trap shut" would be satisfied by *any* means for snapping the trap shut. The compromise embodied in § 112, ¶ 6 is that patentees are allowed to express a claim element as a *means* (which otherwise might be considered indefinite), but literal infringement is restricted to equivalents of the corresponding structure shown in the specification.[169]

Equivalency for purposes of § 112, ¶ 6 should not to be confused with equivalency for purposes of the doctrine of equivalents. The contexts are different because the latter is a specialized subset of the *literal* infringement inquiry.[170] The basis for comparison is also different. Section 112, ¶ 6 requires comparison of the accused product to the structures disclosed in the *specification*, whereas the doctrine of equivalents requires comparison of the accused product to the *claims*.

The tests of equivalence are generally similar. Both "invoke[] the familiar concept of an insubstantial change which adds nothing of significance."[171] It is less clear whether the traditional function-way-result test of the doctrine of equivalents can also be applied to equivalence under § 112, ¶ 6. In the *Texas Instruments* case, the court stated that in either instance "the test is the same three-part test of history: does the asserted equivalent perform substantially the same function in substantially the same way to accomplish substantially the same result."[172] Later, the court held that "[a] determination of section 112 equivalence does not involve the . . . tripartite test of the doctrine of equivalents."[173] Perhaps the most that can really be said is that equivalence under § 112, ¶ 6, like the equivalence discussed in *Graver Tank*, is "not the prisoner of a formula," but depends on the circumstances of each case.[174]

---

[169] *See* Warner-Jenkinson Co. v. Hilton Davis Chemical Co., 520 U.S. 17, 28 (1997) (equivalence under §112, ¶ 6 is "an application of the doctrine of equivalents in a restrictive role, narrowing the application of broad literal claim elements"); Al-Site Corp. v. VSI Int'l, Inc.174 F.3d 1308, 1320 (Fed. Cir. 1999); Johnston v. IVAC Corp., 885 F.2d 1574, 1580 (Fed. Cir. 1989) (§ 112, ¶ 6 "operates to *cut back* on the types of *means* which could literally satisfy the claim language" (emphasis in original)).

[170] *See* Valmont Indus., Inc. v. Reinke Mfg. Co., 983 F.2d 1039, 1043 (Fed. Cir. 1993) ("The doctrine of equivalents has a different purpose and application than section 112.").

[171] *Valmont*, 983 F.2d at 1043; *see also* Chiuminatta Concrete Concepts, Inc. v. Cardinal Indus., Inc., 145 F.3d 1303, 1310 (Fed. Cir. 1998) (both forms of equivalency "protect the substance of a patentee's right to exclude by preventing mere colorable differences or slight improvements from escaping infringement," and they do so "by applying similar analyses of insubstantiality of the differences").

[172] Texas Instruments, Inc. v. United States Int'l Trade Comm'n, 805 F.2d 1558, 1571 (Fed. Cir. 1986).

In *Chiuminatta Concrete Concepts, Inc. v. Cardinal Indus., Inc.*,[175] the court distinguished between the rationales for the doctrine of equivalents and equivalency under § 112, ¶ 6. The reason for the doctrine of equivalents, the court said, is that unforeseen technological advances may allow minor variations in what the applicant has literally described.[176] It would not be fair to an applicant whose claims had required a vacuum tube to allow the substitution of its modern equivalent, the solid-state transistor.[177] In cases of newly developed technology, the court seemed willing to permit a broader range of equivalents than would be permitted under § 112, ¶ 6.[178] If, on the other hand, the alleged equivalent is "technology that predates the invention itself" rather than a newly developed variation, a finding of nonequivalence under 112, ¶ 6 should preclude a finding of equivalence under the doctrine of equivalents.[179]

The *Chiuminatta* opinion is not a model of clarity, and it seems to overstate the differences in rationale between the doctrine of equivalents and § 112, ¶ 6. Arguably, each is a remedy for the inherent inability of language to capture the essence of an invention, whether that inability is due to evolving technologies or to lack of foresight and suitable vocabulary.[180] Later interpretations of *Chiuminatta* suggest that an important difference is between equivalence of *structure*, where the issues of equivalence may merge, and equivalence of

[173] *Valmont*, 983 F.2d at 1043. The function-way-result test may be inappropriate to the literal infringement analysis under § 112, ¶ 6 because the function must be *identical*, not merely "substantially the same." *See* IMS Technology, Inc. v. Haas Automation, Inc., 206 F.3d 1422, 1435 (Fed. Cir. 2000) ("[A] reduced version of the well-known tripartite test for the doctrine of equivalents has been applied in the § 112, ¶ 6 context to determine if the differences are insubstantial, i.e., after determining that the accused device performs the identical function, as required by statute, whether it performs the function in substantially the same way to achieve substantially the same result.").

[174] *See IMS Technology*, 206 F.3d at 1436 ("the context of the invention should be considered when performing a § 112, ¶ 6 equivalence analysis just as it is in a doctrine of equivalents determination"); Intel Corp. v. U.S. Int'l Trade Comm'n, 946 F.2d 821, 842–43 (Fed. Cir. 1991) ("[A]ids for determining a structural equivalent to the structure disclosed in the patent specification are the same as those used in interpreting any other type of claim language, namely, the specification, the prosecution history, other claims in the patent, and expert testimony.").

[175] 145 F.3d 1303 (Fed. Cir. 1998).

[176] See Section 10.6.5.

[177] *See Chiuminatta*, 145 F.3d at 1310 ("Due to technological advances, a variant of an invention may be developed after the patent is granted, and that variant may constitute so insubstantial a change from what is claimed in the patent that it should be held to be an infringement.").

[178] *See Chiuminatta*, 145 F.3d at 1310 ("Even if [a later-developed] element is found not to be a § 112, ¶ 6, equivalent because it is not equivalent to the structure disclosed in the patent, this analysis should not foreclose it from being an equivalent under the doctrine of equivalents.").

[179] *Chiuminatta*, 145 F.3d at 1311.

[180] *See* Kraft Foods, Inc. v. International Trading Co., 203 F.3d 1362, 1372–73 (Fed. Cir. 2000) (except in the case of means-plus-function claims, where equivalent structures known at the time of the patent already literally infringe, infringement under the doctrine of equivalents is *not* limited to later-developed technologies).

function, where only the doctrine of equivalents is relevant.[181] This line of cases, however, has produced one important distinction, which may explain how the results could differ when the tests of equivalence seem to be identical. Under the doctrine of equivalents, equivalence is judged as of the date of the alleged infringement.[182] Equivalence under § 112, ¶ 6 is judged as of the date the patent issued because the literal meaning of a claim should be fixed at that time.[183] Accordingly, an alternative that a person skilled in the art might not have considered equivalent when the patent issued–perhaps because he had never heard of it–might be considered equivalent at a later date.

Another potential difference between § 112, ¶ 6 and the doctrine of equivalents noted by the Federal Circuit, though perhaps again overstated, involves the prior art. As discussed previously, the prior art limits the subject matter that a patentee can claim as equivalent under the doctrine of equivalents.[184] Otherwise a patentee could obtain, in effect, a broader claim than would have been allowed by the Patent Office. But in *Intel Corp. v. U.S. Int'l Trade Comm'n*,[185] the court held that "[i]t is not necessary to consider the prior art in applying section 112, paragraph 6."[186] Section 112, ¶ 6 applies only to individual claim *elements*, and such elements are often found in the prior art, without affecting the patentability of the claimed *combination*. To return to the mousetrap example, the existence of rubber bands in the prior art would not prevent the patentee from arguing that a rubber band is equivalent to a steel spring when employed as a "means for snapping the trap shut."

The distinction may have been overstated because the doctrine of equivalents also applies to claim elements–a point reemphasized in *Warner-Jenkinson*.[187] If a mousetrap claim explicitly referred to a "steel spring," one could conclude that a rubber band was an equivalent, even if rubber bands were found in the prior art. The prior art would prevent a finding of equivalence only if the *combination* of a rubber band with all of the other claim elements could be found in the prior art.[188] Conversely, one can conceive of a situa-

---

[181] *See Interactive Pictures*, 274 F.3d at 1381–82; WMS Gaming, Inc. v. International Game Technology, 184 F.3d 1339, 1353 (Fed. Cir. 1999). The later cases, however, still preserve the possibility of newly developed structure that is equivalent only under the doctrine of equivalents. *Interactive Pictures*, 274 F.3d at 1381; *Al-Site*, 174 F.3d at 1320 n.2 (because of the problem of unforeseeable technological change, "the doctrine of equivalents appropriately allows marginally broader coverage than § 112, ¶ 6").

[182] *Warner-Jenkinson*, 520 U.S. at 37.

[183] *Al-Site*, 174 F.3d at 1320.

[184] See Section 10.6.7.

[185] 946 F.2d 821 (Fed. Cir. 1991).

[186] *Intel*, 946 F.2d at 842; *see also* Applied Medical Resources Corp. v. U.S. Surgical Corp., 147 F.3d 1374, 1381 (Fed. Cir. 1998); Kearns v. Chrysler Corp., 32 F.3d 1541, 1547 n.7 (Fed. Cir. 1994).

[187] *See Warner-Jenkinson*, 520 U.S. at 29.

[188] *See* Corning Glass Works v. Sumitmo Electric U.S.A., Inc., 868 F.2d 1251, 1261 (Fed. Cir. 1989).

tion in which the only novelty to be found in a means-plus-function claim was derived from the unique structures disclosed in the specification.[189] If the accused product substituted other structures already known in the art, so that the accused product *as a whole* was indistinguishable from the prior art, then perhaps this fact ought to prevent a finding of equivalence under § 112, ¶ 6. However, this scenario does not appear to have arisen so far.

10.8 THE REVERSE DOCTRINE OF EQUIVALENTS

The doctrine of equivalents has a judicially devised counterpart known as the *reverse doctrine of equivalents*. The source of the reverse doctrine is the following language in *Graver Tank*:[190]

The wholesome realism of [the doctrine of equivalents] is not always applied in favor of a patentee but is sometimes used against him. Thus, where a device is so far changed in principle from a patented article that it performs the same or a similar function in a substantially different way, but nevertheless falls within the literal words of the claim, the doctrine of equivalents may be used to restrict the claim and defeat the patentee's action for infringement.

Thus, a product literally described by a claim can be held noninfringing, if it is "so far changed in principle" that it functions in a "substantially different way" when compared to what the patentee actually invented.

The language in *Graver Tank* suggests that the doctrine of equivalents is a two-way street, but in practice the reverse doctrine has proven to be far less potent than its counterpart. Cases won on the reverse doctrine of equivalents are exceedingly rare.[191] In 2002 the Federal Circuit observed that it had never, in its 20-year history, affirmed a finding of noninfringement based on the reverse doctrine.[192] Before the legislative adoption of means-plus-function claims and their explicit limitations, the judicially created

---

[189] This should not have been the case until recently because it was the practice of the Patent Office to ignore the structures disclosed in the specification when deciding whether a claim could be granted. In other words, the Patent Office would treat a means-plus-function claim element as though it covered *all* means for performing the specified function. Any novelty supporting patentability would have to be found in the claim itself. The Federal Circuit put a stop to this practice in *In re Donaldson Co.*, 16 F.3d 1189, 1193 (Fed. Cir. 1994). Now it is possible to allow a claim solely because the structures disclosed in the specification are novel.

[190] Graver Tank & Mfg. Co. v. Linde Air Prods. Co., 339 U.S. 605, 608–9 (1950); *see also* Scripps Clinic & Research Found. v. Genentech, Inc., 927 F.2d 1565, 1581 ("the purpose of the 'reverse' doctrine is to prevent unwarranted extension of the claims beyond a fair scope of the patentee's invention"); SRI Int'l v. Matsushita Electric Corp., 775 F.2d 1107, 1123 (Fed. Cir. 1985) (en banc).

[191] *See, e.g.,* Precision Metal Fabricators Inc. v. Jetstream Sys. Co., 6 U.S.P.Q.2d 1704 (N. D. Cal. 1988); Lesona Corp. v. United States, 530 F.2d 896, 905–06 (Ct. Cl. 1976).

[192] Tate Access Floors, Inc. v. Interface Architectural Resources, Inc., 279 F.3d 1357, 1368 (Fed. Cir. 2002).

reverse doctrine of equivalents may have served to restrict the scope of overly broad claims. Today, the court found, the strictures of § 112—including the definiteness, description, and enablement requirements—left the reverse doctrine an "anachronistic exception . . . long mentioned but rarely applied."[193] Absent a problem of enablement or description, it would be difficult to persuade a court that an accused product literally described by a patent claim was still so "changed in principle" as to avoid infringement.

10.9 THE EXPERIMENTAL USE EXCEPTION TO INFRINGEMENT

A rarely invoked defense to a charge of infringement is that the challenged activity was done for purposes of experimentation rather than profit. This defense finds some support in a number of older cases in which a patented device was constructed not to sell it, but to test its advantages. For example, in *Akro Agate Co. v. Master Marble Co.*,[194] the court held that the use of a patented machine to make glass marbles was not an infringement because the marbles had been made only as an experiment, the results were unsatisfactory, and the marbles themselves were not sold. In *Kaz Mfg. Co. v. Chesebrough-Ponds, Inc.*,[195] a patented vaporizer was constructed solely for the purpose of a television commercial in which the design was compared unfavorably to a rival (with the slogan "steam is dangerous"). The court did not view this as an infringement either.

The Federal Circuit has viewed the experimental use exception as a narrow one, applicable only when the experiments were conducted "solely for amusement, to satisfy idle curiosity, or for strictly philosophical inquiry."[196] In other words, a kitchen experimenter amusing himself on a rainy afternoon might practice a patent without infringing, but experiments conducted for commercial purposes are likely to violate a patent if they involve making or using the claimed invention.[197] Any use "in keeping with the legitimate business of the alleged infringer" fails to qualify for the limited exception,[198] including research undertaken by a university solely for purposes of education and discovery.[199]

---

[193] *Tate Access Floors*, 279 F.3d at 1368.

[194] 318 F. Supp. 305, 315, 333 (N.D.W. Va. 1937).

[195] 317 F.2d 679 (2d Cir. 1963).

[196] Madey v. Duke University, 307 F.3d 1351, 1362 (Fed. Cir. 2002); Embrex, Inc. v. Service Eng'g Corp., 216 F.3d 1343, 1349 (Fed. Cir. 2000).

[197] *See* Douglas v. United States, 181 U.S.P.Q. 170, 176–77 (Ct. Cl. 1974). In the former instance, the infringement is seemingly excused on the legal principle of *de minimis non curat lex*, or "the law does not concern itself with trifles." *But see Embrex*, 216 F.3d at 1352–53 (Rader, J., concurring) (arguing that patent law does not permit *de minimis* infringement; "the statute leaves no leeway to excuse infringement because the infringer only infringed a little").

[198] *Madey*, 307 F.3d at 1362.

In 35 U.S.C. § 271(e), Congress established a narrow experimental use exception to cover the testing of patented pharmaceuticals.[200] When a patent on a particular drug expires, rival manufacturers are, of course, permitted to market their own versions of the drug. But before this can happen, the new drug must undergo extensive government-required tests of safety and effectiveness. If manufacturing and using the drug for purposes of such tests were held to be an infringement, the tests could not *begin* until after the patent had expired. Consequently, there would be a considerable delay between the expiration of the patent and the opportunity to market a competitive drug. The patent owner would have, in effect, a patent of longer duration than the patent laws intend. Section 271(e) prevents this by allowing these tests to occur prior to the expiration of the patent, without fear of liability.

---

[199] *Madey*, 307 F.3d at 1362 ("[M]ajor research universities . . . often sanction and fund research projects with arguably no commercial application whatsoever. However, these projects unmistakably further the institution's legitimate business objectives, including educating and enlightening students and faculty participating in these projects. These projects also serve . . . to increase the status of the institution and lure lucrative research grants, students and faculty.").

[200] Although the statute is not clear on this point, it has been held to cover both drugs and *medical devices* that must undergo government-required tests. Eli Lilly & Co. v. Medtronic, Inc., 496 U.S. 661 (1990).

CHAPTER 11

Patent Litigation

A patent owner whose rights have been infringed can file a lawsuit in a Federal District Court.[1] If the suit is successful, the infringer can be compelled to stop its infringing activity and pay the patent owner for infringement that has already occurred. Litigation, or the threat of litigation, is what gives a patent its "teeth."

A typical lawsuit concerns three issues:

- Is the patent valid and enforceable?
- Are the claims infringed?
- If the claims are infringed, what relief should be awarded?

The patent owner can prevail only if the patent is valid *and* infringed. On occasion, the defendant[2] will concede that the patent is valid and challenge only the charge of infringement, or it will concede infringement and argue invalidity, but it is more common for the defendant to make war on both fronts. A patent suit may also involve other related claims (e.g., breach of contract, unfair competition, or antitrust claims) if they arise from the same factual situation.

---

[1] A suit for patent infringement cannot be filed in a state court, because the federal courts have exclusive jurisdiction. *See* 28 U.S.C. § 1338(a). If the infringing goods are being imported, it is possible to initiate a proceeding in the International Trade Commission in lieu of, or in addition to, a suit in a district court. *See* Section 11.9. Infringement suits against the U.S. government must be brought in the Court of Claims. *See* 28 U.S.C. § 1498.

[2] It is convenient to use the term *defendant* interchangeably with *accused infringer*, but in a declaratory judgment action (*see* Section 11.2) the accused infringer may technically be the plaintiff.

Infringement litigation is often a complicated, time-consuming, and costly process. Patent cases typically involve both subtle issues of law and complex questions of technology. In order to try such a case, both parties have to acquire a thorough understanding of, at a minimum, the patent and its prosecution history, the accused products, and any prior art that might be used to challenge the validity of the patent. As a result, just the *discovery* phase of the litigation (in which both parties gather the evidence needed to try the case) often takes more than a year. It is not unusual for an infringement suit to take several years from the day it is filed until the final disposition of the case, and worse examples can be found.[3]

Patent cases are difficult for courts and juries, both because the law is unfamiliar and because an understanding of complex technology is often critical to deciding the case. Imagine how difficult it would be for an average juror to determine, for example, whether one complex procedure in genetic engineering is equivalent to another. Simply mastering the vocabulary can be a daunting task. These difficulties contribute to a certain level of unpredictability in the outcome of patent litigation.

11.1 JURISDICTION AND VENUE

The geographical location where a suit for patent infringement must be filed (e.g., in the Northern District of California or in the Eastern District of New York) depends on the rules of *in personam jurisdiction* and *venue*. A federal court has in personam jurisdiction (or jurisdiction over the person) only if the individual or corporate defendant has had certain *"minimum contacts"* with the district in which that court resides.[4] If an accused infringer has had no contact whatsoever with, for example, the state of Florida, then suit cannot be filed there. The minimum contacts doctrine has constitutional origins in the due process clause. The rules are subtle and depend in part on the jurisdictional rules of the state where the court is located. If the accused infringer has an office in the district, or regularly transacts business in the district, or conducts infringing activity in the district, the minimum contacts test will likely

---

[3] For example, in March 1999 the Supreme Court denied the last appeal in *United States v. Hughes Aircraft Co.*, a case filed in 1973. *See* 525 U.S. 1177 (1999).

[4] *See* International Shoe Co. v. State of Washington, 326 U.S. 310, 316 (1945) (defendant must have "certain minimum contacts with [the forum] such that the maintenance of the suit does not offend 'traditional notions of fair play and substantial justice.'"). The defendant's contacts with the forum must be such that "he should reasonably anticipate being haled into court there." World-Wide Volkswagen Corp. v. Woodson, 444 U.S. 286, 297 (1980); LSI Indus. Inc. v. Hubbell Lighting, Inc., 232 F.3d 1369, 1375 (Fed. Cir. 2000). The emphasis is on deliberate or "purposeful" contacts rather than those that may occur by accident. *See* Beverly Hills Fan Co. v. Royal Sovereign Corp., 21 F.3d 1558, 1565 (Fed. Cir. 1994).

be satisfied.[5] It may even be sufficient that the infringer intended the accused products to enter the district via the *stream of commerce.*[6]

If a court has jurisdiction over the defendant, the next question is one of venue. The rules of venue create further restrictions on where suit can be filed. In a patent case, venue is appropriate in the following districts:

- Where the defendant "resides," *or*
- Where the defendant has committed acts of infringement *and* has a regular and established place of business.[7]

In 1988, the federal venue statutes were altered so that corporate defendants are held to reside in any district where the corporation is subject to in personam jurisdiction—in other words, wherever it has established "minimum contacts."[8] Since most patent cases are filed against corporations rather than against individuals or partnerships, the minimum contacts standard is generally the test of whether a suit can or cannot be filed in a particular judicial district.

Because a corporate defendant typically has minimum contacts with several states—possibly with all 50—patent owners may have a number of choices in deciding where to file suit. The choice is likely to be governed by factors such as geographical convenience, the experience of the court in dealing with patent litigation,[9] whether the court's docket permits a speedy trial, and any perceived home-field advantages. Within the limits set by the rules of jurisdiction and venue, the location of the lawsuit is generally within the control of the plaintiff. If, however, the defendant can show that another district would be more suitable (for the "convenience of parties and witnesses" and "in the interest of justice"[10]), the court in which the suit was filed

---

[5] If the accused infringer's contacts with the forum are "continuous and systematic," the court may have *general jurisdiction* concerning *any* matter involving the accused infringer. *See* Deprenyl Animal Health, Inc. v. University of Toronto Innovations Found., 297 F.3d 1343, 1350 (Fed. Cir. 2002). If the contacts are more sporadic, but relate specifically to the subject matter of the suit, the court may exercise *specific jurisdiction,* so long as that is consistent with "fair play and substantial justice." *See id.* at 1350–51; *LSI,* 232 F.3d at 1375.

[6] *See* Viam Corp. v. Iowa Export-Import Trading Co., 84 F.3d 424, 427-28 (Fed. Cir. 1996); *Beverly Hills Fan,* 21 F.3d at 1565 ("The allegations are that defendants purposefully shipped the accused fan into Virginia through an established distribution channel. The cause of action for patent infringement is alleged to arise out of those activities. No more is usually required to establish specific jurisdiction.").

[7] 28 U.S.C. § 1400(b).

[8] *See* 28 U.S.C. § 1391(c); VE Holding Corp. v. Johnson Gas Appliance Co., 917 F.2d 1574 (Fed. Cir. 1990).

[9] If suit is filed in, for example, the Northern District of California, there is a greater likelihood that the judge assigned to the case will have handled patent cases before, in comparison to locations where technology-driven businesses are less common.

[10] 28 U.S.C § 1404(a).

has the power to transfer the case to another district, if it is a district in which the suit could have been filed in the first instance.

11.2 DECLARATORY JUDGMENT

Patent cases generally arise when a patent owner files suit against a party it accuses of infringement. However, it is also possible for the accused infringer to launch a preemptive strike by filing suit against a patentee. A suit of this kind is called an action for *declaratory judgment* because it asks the court to declare that the party filing suit is *not* liable to the patent owner, either because the patent is invalid, or not infringed, or for some other reason.[11] The potential infringer, in such a case, is nominally the plaintiff and the patent owner is the defendant.[12]

If it were not for declaratory judgment actions, parties accused of infringement would have to wait until the patent owner chose to litigate before the dispute could be resolved. In the meantime, the accused infringer would have to give in to the patent owner's demands, or proceed as before with the risk that investments would be lost, and accumulated damages assessed, when the patent owner finally did sue.[13] A suit for declaratory judgment allows the potential infringer to bring matters to a head. It also gives the accused infringer more control over the forum in which the case will be heard.

Federal courts generally follow a *first-to-file* rule in deciding where a case will be tried.[14] Suppose that a patent owner in California accused a company in Illinois of infringement. For the sake of convenience, and possibly in the hope of sympathy from a hometown jury, the patent owner would likely prefer that any litigation take place in California, whereas the accused infringer, for the same reasons, would prefer Illinois. If the accused infringer sues for declaratory judgment in Illinois before the patent owner sues in California, the first-to-file rule generally means that the case will be heard in Illinois. The first-to-file rule is not absolute, however. An exception can be made if the interests of justice or expediency so require.[15]

A federal court can only try a case if there is a genuine dispute—a "case or controversy" in constitutional terms.[16] A potential infringer cannot file an action for declaratory judgment simply because there is a hypothetical possibility that a patent owner will allege infringement. The threat must be far

---

[11] *See* 22 U.S.C. § 2201 (Declaratory Judgment Act).

[12] Even if the patent owner initiates the lawsuit, the accused infringer may choose to file a *counterclaim* for declaratory judgment.

[13] *See* Cardinal Chemical Co. v. Morton Int'l, Inc., 508 U.S. 83, 95 (1993) (discussing the Declaratory Judgment Act as a cure for the "scarecrow patent").

[14] *See* Genentech, Inc. v. Eli Lilly & Co., 998 F.2d 931, 937 (Fed. Cir. 1993).

[15] *See* Serco Services Co. v. Kelley Co., 51 F.3d 1037, 1039 (Fed. Cir. 1995); *Genentech*, 998 F.2d at 937.

more immediate and concrete. The party filing for declaratory judgment must have acted, or prepared to act, in a potentially infringing manner, *and* the patent owner must have made an explicit accusation of infringement, or must at least have acted in such a way as to create a reasonable apprehension of litigation.[17]

A potential infringer might receive a letter from a patent owner advising the recipient (1) that the patent owner has an extensive patent portfolio and (2) that the recipient should discuss the terms of a license. This warning would likely be considered so general (not referring to a specific patent, a specific product, or a specific intention to file suit) that it would not create a *reasonable apprehension* of imminent litigation.[18] In fact, the patent owner may deliberately refrain from a more concrete warning, specifically to prevent the potential infringer from filing suit.

11.3 THE BURDEN OF PROOF

The patent owner has the burden of proving infringement by a *preponderance of the evidence*.[19] In other words, based on the evidence presented, it must be more likely than not that the patent is infringed. If the evidence on both sides is equally persuasive, the claim must fail.

If the accused infringer raises a defense of invalidity or unenforceability, the defendant bears the burden of proof with respect to that defense.[20] Moreover, the burden is one of *clear and convincing evidence*, a higher standard of proof than a mere preponderance of the evidence.[21] The evidence not only must favor the accused infringer's version of the facts, it must be sufficient to produce an "abiding conviction" that the facts are "highly probable."[22] The reason for this

---

[16] *See* Sandt Technology, Ltd. v. Resco Metal & Plastics Corp., 264 F.3d 1344, 1356 n.4 (Fed. Cir. 2001); Aqua Marine Supply v. Aim Machining, Inc., 247 F.3d 1216, 1220 (Fed. Cir. 2001).

[17] *See Sandt*, 264 F.3d at 1356 n.4; Phillips Plastics Corp. v. Kato Hatsujou K.K., 57 F.3d 1051, 1052 (Fed. Cir. 1995). "To invoke the court's declaratory judgment jurisdiction, a plaintiff must show 'more than the nervous state of mind or a possible infringer,' but does not have to show that the patentee is 'poised on the courthouse steps.'" Vanguard Research, Inc. v. Peat, Inc., 304 F.3d 1249, 1254–55 (Fed. Cir. 2002).

[18] *See Phillips*, 57 F.3d at 1053–54 (ongoing license negotiations were not sufficient to create a reasonable apprehension of litigation).

[19] Advanced Cardiovascular Sys., Inc. v. Scimed Life Sys., Inc., 261 F.3d 1329, 1336 (Fed. Cir. 2001); Bayer AG v. Elan Pharmaceutical Research Corp., 212 F.3d 1241, 1247 (Fed. Cir. 2000); Seal-Flex, Inc. v. Athletic Track & Court Construction, 172 F.3d 836, 842 (Fed. Cir. 1999).

[20] 35 U.S.C. § 282; Apotex USA, Inc. v. Merck & Co., 254 F.3d 1031, 1036 (Fed. Cir. 2001); Budde v. Harley-Davidson, Inc., 250 F.3d 1369, 1376 (Fed. Cir. 2001).

[21] *Apotex*, 254 F.3d at 1036; *Budde*, 250 F.3d at 1376.

[22] Am-Pro Protective Agency, Inc. v. United States, 281 F.3d 1234, 1239–40 (Fed. Cir. 2002) (also referring to the standard as one of "well-nigh irrefragable" proof); Price v. Symsek, 988 F.2d 1187, 1191 (Fed. Cir. 1993).

higher standard of proof is the presumption of validity discussed in Section 8.2. The heavier burden of proof for establishing invalidity, as compared to infringement, provides a tactical advantage to patent owners.

11.4 THE ROLE OF JUDGE AND JURY

Litigants in a patent case are entitled to trial by jury,[23] although this right can be waived, by consent of both parties, in favor of a bench trial in which all issues are left to the judge.[24] Even if the trial does involve a jury, the judge will still decide certain questions. Generally speaking, a judge decides *questions of law,* whereas the jury decides *questions of fact.*[25] In reality, most questions have a factual aspect and a legal aspect. For example, to decide if an accused product is equivalent to a claimed invention, one has to address questions of fact (how does the accused product differ from the claimed invention?) and questions of law (how much can the accused product differ from the claimed invention before the law no longer considers them equivalent?).

Because there is no practical way to separate every nuance of fact and law, certain issues have, somewhat arbitrarily, been deemed questions of law for the judge, and others questions of fact for the jury.[26] For example, anticipation is a question of fact for the jury,[27] but obviousness is a question of law for the judge.[28] Compliance with the enablement and definiteness requirements are questions of law;[29] compliance with the written description and utility requirements are questions of fact.[30] Claim interpretation is a question of law,[31] but infringement is a question of fact.[32] Some questions of law, such

---

[23] *See* Markman v. Westview Instruments, Inc., 517 U.S. 370, 377 (1996) ("there is no dispute that infringement cases today must be tried to a jury, as their predecessors were more than two centuries ago").

[24] *See* Rule 38 of the Federal Rules of Civil Procedure.

[25] *See* Jurgens v. McKasy, 927 F.2d 1552, 1557 (Fed. Cir. 1991) ("In a jury trial, there are two decisionmakers, the judge and the jury. In general, the judge decides issues of law and issues committed to his discretion, and the jury decides issues of fact that are material to the case and in genuine dispute.").

[26] The arbitrariness of the distinction is suggested by the frequent disagreements among the Federal Circuit judges as to whether an issue is really a question of law or a question of fact. *See, e.g., Markman,* 52 F.3d 967 (en banc panel split on whether claim interpretation is an issue of law decided by the judge alone); Lough v. Brunswick Corp., 103 F.3d 1517 (Fed. Cir. 1997) (Federal Circuit split on whether "experimental use" in the context of § 102(b) is a question of fact or law).

[27] Bowers v. Baystate Technologies, Inc., 320 F.3d 1317, 1323 (Fed. Cir. 2003).

[28] Mazzari v. Rogan, 323 F.3d 1000, 1005 (Fed. Cir. 2003); *Bowers,* 320 F.3d at 1323.

[29] Plant Genetic Sys., N.V. v. DeKalb Genetics Corp., 315 F.3d 1335, 1339 (Fed. Cir. 2003) (enablement); North American Vaccine, Inc. v. American Cyanamid Co., 7 F.3d 1571, 1579 (Fed. Cir. 1993) (definiteness).

[30] Enzo Biochem, Inc. v. Gen-Probe Inc., 296 F.3d 1316, 1323 (Fed. Cir. 2002) (written description); *In re* Swartz, 232 F.3d 862, 863 (Fed. Cir. 2000) (utility).

[31] *Markman,* 517 U.S. at 372; *Bowers,* 320 F.3d at 1323.

as obviousness, depend in part on underlying issues of fact, which can be submitted to the jury.[33]

In addition to questions of law, the judge also rules on equitable claims and defenses. In the eighteenth century, there were two varieties of court—courts of law and courts of equity—and they differed somewhat in the kinds of claims that could be heard and the remedies that could be granted. Only courts of law provided a right to a jury trial. In the United States, courts of law and equity were merged long ago, so the distinction would be little more than an historical curiosity if not for the language of the Seventh Amendment of the Constitution. In lieu of setting forth the right to a jury trial in explicit terms, the Seventh Amendment provides that "the right of trial by jury shall be *preserved*" as it was under English common law. To this day courts are required to examine claims from an historical perspective and try to determine whether, applying eighteenth-century standards, the claim is legal or equitable. If the latter, there is no right to a jury.[34]

For purposes of patent litigation, it is enough to know that a claim seeking *money damages* is a legal claim with a right to a jury trial, but a claim to an *injunction* is an equitable claim. In the rare instance that a patentee chooses to forgo damages and sue only for an injunction, neither party has a right to a jury trial.[35] Certain defenses are also equitable and reserved to the judge to decide. The most important of these are inequitable conduct[36] (discussed in Section 9.1), laches, and estoppel[37] (discussed in Sections 11.8.3.3–11.8.3.4). The Federal Circuit has held that infringement under the doctrine of equivalents (discussed in Section 10.6), often referred to as the "equitable doctrine of equivalents," is in fact a matter for decision by a jury.[38]

In spite of the latter development, there may be a trend toward assigning more decision-making responsibility to judges and less to juries. At least certain disapproving Federal Circuit judges perceive such a trend.[39] This shift,

---

[32] Amgen Inc. v. Hoechst Marion Roussel, Inc., 314 F.3d 1313, 1339 (Fed. Cir. 2003); Middleton, Inc. v. Minnesota Mining & Mfg. Co., 311 F.3d 1384, 1387 (Fed. Cir. 2002).

[33] *See* Mycogen Plant Science, Inc. v. Monsanto Co., 243 F.3d 1316, 1331 (Fed. Cir. 2001) (questions of law with underlying issues of fact can be submitted to the jury, accompanied by appropriate instructions on the law).

[34] *See* Tegal Corp. v. Tokyo Electron America, Inc., 257 F.3d 1331, 1339 (Fed. Cir. 2001).

[35] *See Tegal,* 257 F.3d at 1341.

[36] *See* Kingsdown Medical Consultants, Ltd. v. Hollister, Inc., 863 F.2d 867, 876 (Fed. Cir. 1988) ("the ultimate question of whether inequitable conduct occurred is equitable in nature").

[37] *See* A.C. Aukerman Co. v. R.L. Chaides Construction Co., 960 F.2d 1020, 1028 (Fed. Cir. 1992).

[38] *See* Interactive Pictures Corp. v. Infinite Pictures, Inc., 274 F.3d 1371, 1376 (Fed. Cir. 2001); CAE Screenplates Inc. v. Heinrich Fiedler GmbH, 224 F.3d 1308, 1319 (Fed. Cir. 2000).

[39] *See* Judge Newman's dissent in *Lough,* 103 F.3d at 1519 ("In converting the factual question of experimental purpose into a matter of law, our court has cut another notch in the removal of patent issues from the trier of fact.").

if there is one, may reflect a feeling that juries are overmatched by the complex and difficult issues often presented in patent cases.

11.5 BIFURCATION

Patent cases are often tried in phases rather than all at once. A trial divided into two phases is *bifurcated,* but division into three or more phases is also possible. The purpose of holding trial in stages is to focus the issues, avoid confusion, and save unnecessary effort.

One common practice is to hold separate trials on liability and damages. If the infringer is not found liable, there is no need to proceed with the damages phase. Another option is to hold a preliminary bench trial on those issues that do not require fact-finding by the jury. For example, if a patent has been challenged on grounds of inequitable conduct (an equitable defense reserved to the judge), that part of the case can be tried before any jury has been selected.

When the Supreme Court held in *Markman v. Westview Instruments*[40] that claim interpretation is a matter within the province of the judge rather than the jury, a question was raised as to how and when a judge should decide questions of claim interpretation and how the judge should communicate his findings to the jury. Many courts have responded by scheduling a *Markman hearing* before the jury trial.[41] During the hearing, the court may receive evidence and argument from all parties regarding their proposed claim interpretations. The judge's findings can then be incorporated into the jury instructions.

11.6 PRELIMINARY INJUNCTIONS

Patent litigation often begins with a motion for a *preliminary injunction.*[42] A preliminary injunction is a court order preventing the accused infringer from making, using, selling, offering to sell, or importing the accused product until the case has been decided. In effect, it forces the accused infringer to put its activities on hold. On occasion, the Federal Circuit has characterized a preliminary injunction as "a drastic and extraordinary remedy that is not to be routinely granted."[43]

---

[40] 517 U.S. 370, 372 (1996).
[41] *See, e.g.,* Eaton Corp. v. Rockwell Int'l Corp., 323 F.3d 1332, 1337–38 (Fed. Cir. 2003); Amgen Inc. v. Hoechst Marion Roussel, Inc., 314 F.3d 1313, 1323 (Fed. Cir. 2003); Ecolab, Inc. v. Paraclipse, Inc., 285 F.3d 1362, 1367–68 (Fed. Cir. 2002).
[42] *See* 35 U.S.C. § 283.
[43] Intel Corp. v. ULSI Sys. Technology, Inc., 995 F.2d 1566, 1568 (Fed. Cir. 1993).

A motion for a preliminary injunction is made to the judge, and the decision to grant or deny the motion is generally based on the following factors:[44]

- The likelihood that the patent owner will ultimately prevail in the litigation—in other words, the likelihood that the patent will be held valid, enforceable, and infringed. This requires the judge to make a preliminary assessment of the evidence, including any defenses that may be raised by the accused infringer.

- Whether the patent owner would suffer *irreparable harm* if the injunction were denied.[45] Irreparable harm is harm that cannot be cured by the eventual payment of money damages. If the only harm to the patentee is a temporary loss of royalty income pending trial, this loss is one that probably can be made up, with interest, when damages are ultimately awarded. However, the harm might be irreparable if, for example, the accused infringer would not have the funds to pay damages after trial, or if sales of infringing articles would create some form of intangible harm. For example, if the patent owner himself sold an article within the scope of the patent, the infringer's sales of an inferior product pending trial might injure the patent owner's reputation and market share in ways that would be difficult to translate into a payment of money. Note that if the patent owner fails to seek a preliminary injunction at the first opportunity, it may be difficult to convince the court that there is a threat of immediate harm.[46]

- The balance of hardships if the motion is granted or denied. In other words, would the harm to the patent owner if the injunction were denied outweigh the harm to the accused infringer if the injunction were granted? The harm to the accused infringer is often more tangible and immediate. If the accused product accounts for a substantial portion of the accused infringer's business, the loss of that business pending trial could result in diminished profits, employee layoffs, or even bankruptcy. A court is unlikely to grant an injunction with such severe consequences unless it is very clear that the patent owner will prevail on the merits.

- The public interest. A court may hesitate to grant an injunction that would deny the public an important product—for example, a drug or medical device—even temporarily.[47] On the other hand, the enforcement of valid patents ultimately benefits the public by encouraging innovation.

---

[44] *See* Anton/Bauer, Inc. v. Pag, Ltd., 329 F.3d 1343, 1348 (Fed. Cir. 2003); Jack Guttman, Inc. v. Kopykake Enterprises, Inc., 302 F.3d 1352, 1356 (Fed. Cir. 2002); Tate Access Floors, Inc. v. Interface Architectural Resources, Inc., 279 F.3d 1357, 1362 (Fed. Cir. 2002).

[45] A strong likelihood of success on the merits leads to a rebuttable presumption that, if the preliminary injunction is denied, the patentee will be irreparably harmed. *Kopykake*, 302 F.3d at 1356.

[46] *See, e.g.,* High Tech Medical Instrumentation, Inc. v. New Image Indus., Inc., 49 F.3d 1551, 1557 (Fed. Cir. 1995) ("Absent a good explanation, not offered or found here, 17 months is a substantial period of delay that militates against the issuance of a preliminary injunction by demonstrating that there is no apparent urgency to the request for injunctive relief.").

[47] *See* Hybritech Inc. v. Abbott Labs., 849 F.2d 1466, 1458 (Fed. Cir. 1988).

A court must weigh each of these factors and determine whether a pre-liminary injunction is appropriate. The stronger the patent owner's case, the lesser the showing of irreparable harm necessary to justify an injunction.[48]

11.7 SUMMARY JUDGMENT

Sometimes the merits of a case are so clear that it is unnecessary to con-duct a full-blown jury trial. The mechanism for cutting short such a case is known as *summary judgment.* Summary judgment is granted if a judge finds that there is no "genuine issue of material fact" for decision by a jury.[49] In other words, the evidence is so one-sided that the outcome of the case can-not be reasonably disputed, and no reasonable jury could reach a contrary decision.[50] Either party to a patent infringement suit may bring a motion for summary judgment, supported by evidence in its favor (usually in the form of documents and sworn testimony), or pointing out the absence of evidence supporting claims on which the other party bears the burden of proof.[51] The opposing party naturally submits its own evidence in an attempt to convince the judge that there is, at least, a "genuine issue of material fact" to be decided.

An entire matter may be decided by summary judgment, or the judge may determine that individual questions raise no genuine issue of fact, even if they do not resolve the entire case.[52] For example, a court might grant summary judgment (or *summary adjudication*), finding that a particu-lar invention predates the patentee's invention, and leave to the jury the genuinely disputed question of whether the prior invention anticipates the claims at issue. It is only on rare occasions that courts grant summary judg-

---

[48] *See* New England Braiding Co. v. A.W. Chesterton Co., 970 F.2d 878, 883 n.5 (Fed. Cir. 1992).

[49] Rule 56(c) of the Federal Rules of Civil Procedure states that summary judgment "shall be rendered forthwith if the pleadings, depositions, answers to interrogatories, and admissions on file, together with the affidavits, if any, show that there is no genuine issue as to any ma-terial fact and that the moving party is entitled to a judgment as a matter of law." Summary judgment is not precluded by a genuine dispute as to an *immaterial fact*–that is, one that need not be decided to render a judgment. *See* Techsearch, L.L.C. v. Intel Corp., 286 F.3d 1360, 1369 (Fed. Cir. 2002); Telemac Cellular Corp. v. Topp Telecom, Inc., 247 F.3d 1316, 1323 (Fed. Cir. 2001). "A disputed fact is material to the outcome of the suit if a finding of that fact is necessary and relevant to the proceeding." Madey v. Duke University, 307 F.3d 1351, 1358 (Fed. Cir. 2002).

[50] *See Madey,* 307 F.3d at 1358 ("Issues of fact are genuine only 'if the evidence is such that a reasonable jury could return a verdict for the nonmoving party.'").

[51] *See* Golan v. Pingel Enterprise, Inc., 310 F.3d 1360, 1367–68 (Fed. Cir. 2002); Biotec Biolo-gische Naturverpackungen GmbH v. Biocorp, Inc., 249 F.3d 1341, 1353–54 (Fed. Cir. 2001); Celotex Corp. v. Catrett, 477 U.S. 317, 325 (1986). The party opposing the motion "must show more than a mere metaphysical doubt regarding the material facts" and must produce more than "a mere scintilla of evidence." *Golan,* 310 F.3d at 1368.

[52] *See* Rule 56(d) of the Federal Rules of Civil Procedure.

ment that a patent is infringed.[53] Usually the accused infringer can at least raise a genuine issue of fact regarding alleged differences between the accused product and the claimed invention. More frequently, a patent is held *not* infringed on summary judgment,[54] often because infringement is precluded by the principle of prosecution history estoppel.[55] Sometimes courts grant summary judgment that patents are invalid or unenforceable.[56] Because liability can be found only if a patent is valid, enforceable, *and* infringed, a negative judgment on one of these issues can dispose of the entire case.

11.8 REMEDIES

When a court, with or without a jury, finds a patent both valid and infringed, then it must decide what remedies to grant the patentee. A permanent injunction against further infringement is one remedy that is granted almost routinely.[57] This is simply a court order that describes in specific terms the activities that the infringer must henceforth avoid.[58] If the infringer does not abide by the terms of the injunction, it can be enforced by contempt proceedings.[59]

11.8.1 Damages

The other remedy available to a patentee is an award of money damages to compensate for past infringement. Although injunctions are a matter

---

[53] *See, e.g.,* Amgen Inc. v. Hoechst Marion Roussel, Inc., 314 F.3d 1313, 1351 (Fed. Cir. 2003) (affirming summary judgment that certain of the patentee's claims were infringed); McGinley v. Franklin Sports, Inc., 262 F.3d 1339, 1348–49 (Fed. Cir. 2001).

[54] *See, e.g., Techsearch,* 286 F.3d at 1363; *Telemac,* 247 F.3d at 1319; Glaverbel Societe Anonyme v. Northlake Marketing & Supply, Inc., 45 F.3d 1550, 1562 (Fed. Cir. 1995).

[55] *See* Section 10.6.8.

[56] *See, e.g.,* Scaltech, Inc. v. Retec/Tetra, L.L.C., 269 F.3d 1321 (Fed. Cir. 2001) (on-sale bar); Apple Computer, Inc. v. Articulate Sys., Inc., 234 F.3d 14 (Fed. Cir. 2000) (anticipation); United States Gypsum Co. v. Nat'l Gypsum Co., 74 F.3d 1209 (Fed. Cir. 1996) (best mode); Quantum Corp. v. Rodime, PLC, 65 F.3d 1577 (Fed. Cir. 1995) (claims improperly broadened during reexamination); Paragon Podiatry Lab., Inc. v. KLM Labs., Inc., 984 F.2d 1182 (Fed. Cir. 1993) (on-sale bar and inequitable conduct).

[57] *See* Richardson v. Suzuki Motor Co., 868 F.2d 1226, 1246–47 (Fed. Cir. 1989) ("Infringement having been established, it is contrary to the laws of property, of which the patent law partakes, to deny the patentee's right to exclude others from use of his property. . . . It is the general rule that an injunction will issue when infringement has been adjudged, absent a sound reason for denying it."). A rare exception might be granted if an injunction would deny the public a product essential to health or safety. *See* Rite-Hite Corp. v. Kelley Co., 56 F.3d 1538, 1547–48 (Fed. Cir. 1995) (en banc). Also, no injunction would normally issue if the patent had already expired. *See* Kearns v. Chrysler Corp., 32 F.3d 1541, 1549–50 (Fed. Cir. 1994).

[58] The injunction should be more specific than simply prohibiting any further infringement. *See* Additive Controls & Measurement Sys., Inc. v. Flowdata, Inc., 986 F.2d 476, 479–80 (Fed. Cir. 1993) (injunction must give fair warning of the specific conduct that is enjoined).

[59] *See* Arbek Mfg., Inc. v. Moazzam, 55 F.3d 1567, 1569–70 (Fed. Cir. 1995).

within the discretion of the judge, the calculation of damages is a question of fact for the jury.[60] A patentee can elect to pursue damages in either of two forms. One is *lost profits* attributable to the infringement.[61] This form of recovery is appropriate if the infringer competed with the patentee in the marketplace, and it can be shown that sales made by the infringer were sales lost to the patentee.[62] The standard of proof is one of "reasonable probability."[63]

The calculation of lost profits is often complicated by disputes over collateral sales that the patentee might have lost, together with sales of the patented item. Suppose, for example, that the patent covered a component of a larger item—perhaps an improved lens for a flashlight. The patentee would demand the profits that could have been made from the sale of *flashlights* if the infringer had not misappropriated the lens design. The infringer, on the other hand, might attempt to apportion the profits in some way so that only profits from the *lens* could be recovered. At the same time, the patentee might argue that lost flashlight sales also resulted in lost sales of accessories and spare parts—for example, spare bulbs, batteries, and so forth. The infringer would likely attempt to exclude these from the calculation.

These disputes are resolved by the *entire market value rule*. The entire market value rule allows recovery for profits from patented *and* unpatented items if together they are "components of a single assembly or parts of a complete machine," or if together they constitute "a single functioning unit."[64] However, the patented component should contribute substantially to the demand for the entire unit.[65] Recovery cannot be had

---

[60] Micro Chemical, Inc. v. Lextron, Inc., 317 F.3d 1387, 1394 (Fed. Cir. 2003); Oiness v. Walgreen Co., 88 F.3d 1025, 1029 (Fed. Cir. 1996). "A court is not at liberty to supplant its own judgment on the damages amount for the jury's findings." *Oiness,* 88 F.3d at 1030. The award can be rejected by the court only if "the amount is 'grossly excessive or monstrous,' clearly not supported by the evidence, or based only on speculation or guesswork." Biotec Biologische Naturverpackungen GmbH v. Biocorp, Inc., 249 F.3d 1341, 1355 (Fed. Cir. 2001). This is assuming that the case was tried to a jury. If the parties waived their right to a jury trial, the judge would determine all issues of fact, including the amount of damages.

[61] The infringer cannot be compelled to turn over *its* profits in lieu of calculating the *patentee's* lost profits, except where the infringed patent is a design patent. *See* 35 U.S.C. § 289.

[62] *See* Stryker Corp. v. Intermedics Orthopedics, Inc., 96 F.3d 1409, 1417 (Fed. Cir. 1996). Lost profits are most easily proven in a two-supplier market, but they can also be based on suppositions relating to market share. *See* King Instruments Corp. v. Perego, 65 F.3d 941, 953 (Fed. Cir. 1995). In the two-supplier situation (the two suppliers being the patentee and the infringer), proof of lost profits typically focuses on the following factors: (1) the demand for the patented product; (2) the absence of acceptable substitutes; (3) the capacity of the patentee to exploit the demand had there been no infringement (e.g., did the patentee have the manufacturing capacity to make the sales that the infringer made?); and (4) the amount of profit the patentee would have made if the patentee, rather than the infringer, had made the sales. *See Stryker,* 96 F.3d at 1418.

[63] *See* Grain Processing Corp. v. American Maize-Prods. Co., 185 F.3d 1341, 1349 (Fed. Cir. 1999).

[64] Rite-Hite Corp. v. Kelley Co., 56 F.3d 1538, 1550 (Fed. Cir. 1995) (en banc).

for unpatented items that "have essentially no functional relationship to the patented invention" but that "may have been sold with an infringing device only as a matter of convenience or business advantage."[66] Returning to the example, the entire flashlight would likely be held the appropriate base for calculating lost profits because the patented lens, together with the unpatented bulb and housing, form a single functioning unit. If the flashlights were sold as part of a tool kit, however, the other tools would likely be excluded from the calculation of lost profits because their use and function are unrelated to the patented lens.[67]

Another issue is whether a patentee can recover profits lost on sales of an *unpatented* item that competes with sales of an *infringing* item. Suppose, for example, that the inventor of the improved flashlight lens decided, for whatever reason, to market only flashlights that are *not* covered by the patent. Meanwhile, the infringer marketed flashlights that *are* covered by the patent. Can the patentee recover the profits that it would have made on unpatented flashlights if not for the sales of the infringing ones? According to the Federal Circuit, those profits can be recovered, as long as it can be shown that the sales of the unpatented flashlights would have been made if not for the infringement.[68]

In many cases lost profits are difficult to calculate, or the patentee did not lose any profits through competition because the patentee did not sell a product of its own. In these situations, the patentee may choose to pursue a *reasonable royalty* as the measure of damages. This is, by statute, the minimum that a patentee can be awarded.[69] A reasonable royalty is the amount that the infringer would have paid the patentee if, instead of infringing the patent, it had negotiated a license. This is generally assessed as a percentage of the sales price of the infringing goods, multiplied by total sales.

---

[65] *See* Bose Corp. v. JBL, Inc., 274 F.3d 1354, 1361 (Fed. Cir. 2001); *Rite-Hite*, 56 F.3d at 1549. *Bose* illustrates the use of the entire market value rule in calculating a *reasonable royalty*, the alternative remedy discussed below. In *Bose*, the invention concerned a particular kind of loudspeaker port, but the invention improved the performance of the loudspeaker as a whole, increasing demand for the entire unit.

[66] *Rite-Hite*, 56 F.3d at 1550.

[67] The flashlight *batteries* might be a close call. They are a necessary part of a functioning flashlight but are often sold separately. The infringer might argue that when batteries are sold with a flashlight, it is done only as a matter of "convenience and business advantage." Alternatively, a distinction might be drawn between the original batteries, which are sold as a part of the flashlight, and replacement batteries, which the patentee could not have expected to sell. *See* Kaufman Co. v. Lantech, Inc., 926 F.2d 1136, 1144 (Fed. Cir. 1991) (whether "accessories" should be included in the calculation of lost profits depends on whether there is a reasonable probability that the patentee would have made the sale if not for the infringement).

[68] *Rite-Hite*, 56 F.3d at 1548–49.

[69] 35 U.S.C. § 284 ("Upon finding for the claimant the court shall award the claimant damages adequate to compensate for the infringement, but in no event less than a reasonable royalty for the use made of the invention by the infringer, together with interest and costs as fixed by the court.").

The best guide to calculating a reasonable royalty is evidence of an established royalty.[70] If, for example, the patentee has already licensed the patent to others at a standard of royalty of 3 percent, then 3 percent appears to be an amount that the market will bear, and that is adequate to satisfy the patentee. If there is no established royalty, then a reasonable royalty must be determined through a difficult mental exercise. One must imagine what would have occurred if, at the time the infringement began, the patentee and the infringer sat down together and negotiated the terms of a patent license. The amount that the patentee would have been willing to accept, and that the infringer would have been willing to pay, is the amount of a reasonable royalty.[71]

The courts have identified a number of factors that should be considered in the context of this "hypothetical negotiation." These are commonly known as *Georgia-Pacific factors*—a reference to one of the first opinions to set them down.[72] The Georgia-Pacific factors include the following:[73]

- Any evidence of an established royalty rate
- Rates paid by the infringer for rights to similar patents
- Whether the patentee had a policy of refusing licenses
- Whether the patentee and the infringer were competitors
- Whether sales of the patented item would generate (for the infringer or the patentee) additional sales of nonpatented items, including such things as accessories and spare parts (these additional sales are known as *convoyed sales* or *derivative sales*)
- The time remaining before the patent expired
- The established success and profitability of items within the scope of the patent
- The advantages of the patented invention over available substitutes
- The portion of both selling price and profits that could be attributed to the patented invention rather than to other product components or features

The hypothetical negotiation exercise is difficult and imprecise, in part because it requires the jury (or the judge in a bench trial) to imagine the state of affairs as they existed when the infringement began, putting aside knowledge of subsequent events.[74] It also requires that the patentee and the

---

[70] Nickson Indus., Inc. v. Rol Mfg. Co., 847 F.2d 795, 798 (Fed. Cir. 1988) ("Where an established royalty exists, it will usually be the best measure of what is a 'reasonable' royalty.").

[71] *See* Integra Life Sciences I, Ltd. v. Merck KgaA, 331 F.3d 860, 869 (Fed. Cir. 2003); *Rite-Hite,* 56 F.3d at 1554.

[72] Georgia-Pacific Corp. v. United States Plywood Corp., 318 F. Supp. 1116 (S.D.N.Y. 1970); *see also Micro-Chemical,* 317 F.3d at 1393 (approving *Georgia-Pacific* factors for calculating a reasonable royalty); Interactive Pictures Corp. v. Infinite Pictures, Inc., 274 F.3d 1371, 1385–86 (Fed. Cir. 2001).

[73] *See Georgia-Pacific,* 318 F. Supp. at 1120.

infringer be pictured as a willing licensor and a willing licensee, respectively, when the reality may have been very different.[75]

Even if the hypothetical negotiation could be imagined perfectly, basing a damages figure on the result would seem to make infringement a "no-lose" proposition.[76] The potential infringer who would otherwise pay for a license might decide to take its chances, knowing that, at worst, it would be forced to pay after litigation no more than would have been required for a license. In reality, things are not so easy for the would-be infringer. First, courts recognize that the hypothetical negotiation is only a mental exercise. In the end, an infringer may be compelled to pay more than an actual licensee would have paid.[77] More importantly, if the infringement was *willful*, damages can be increased as a punishment.

11.8.2 Willful Infringement

Although unintentional infringement is still infringement, the law recognizes a difference in culpability between the infringer who was unaware of its trespass, and the infringer who acted deliberately. A court can as much as triple the damages assessed against a willful infringer.[78] Willfulness is a question of fact, and the standard of proof is one of clear and convincing evidence.[79] If infringement is found to be willful, whether or not to increase the damages, and by how much, is a decision left to the discretion of the judge.[80] The test of willfulness is whether, under all of the circumstances, a reason-

---

[74] *See* Unisplay, S.A. v. American Electronic Sign Co., 69 F.3d 512, 518 (Fed. Cir. 1995); Hanson v. Alpine Ski Area, Inc., 718 F.2d 1075, 1079 (Fed. Cir. 1983) ("'The key element in setting a reasonable royalty . . . is the necessity for return to the date when the infringement began.'"). In seeming contradiction to this rule, some cases have approved the use of later information to suggest what a reasonable royalty might have been. *See* Fromson v. Western Litho Plate & Supply Co., 853 F.2d 1568, 1575 (Fed. Cir. 1988) (the law "permits and often requires a court to look to events and facts that occurred thereafter and that could not have been known to or predicted by the hypothesized negotiators").

[75] *See Rite Hite*, 56 F.3d at 1554 n.13 (imagining the patentee as a willing licensor is "inaccurate, and even absurd").

[76] *See Fromson*, 853 F.2d at 1574–75.

[77] *See King Instruments*, 65 F.3d at 951 n.6; *Fromson*, 853 F.2d at 1575 n.11 ("Courts have on occasion recognized the need to distinguish between royalties payable by infringers and non-infringers.").

[78] *See* 35 U.S.C. § 284 ("the court may increase the damages up to three times the amount found or assessed"). Although the statute does not specify the circumstances under which damages may be increased, the courts have held that "enhancement of damages must be premised on willful infringement or bad faith." Sensonics, Inc. v. Aerosonic Corp., 81 F.3d 1566, 1574 (Fed. Cir. 1996).

[79] Biotec Biologische Naturverpackungen GmbH v. Biocorp, Inc., 249 F.3d 1341, 1356 (Fed. Cir. 2001) (willful infringement "is quintessentially a question of fact, for it depends on findings of culpable intent and deliberate or negligent wrongdoing"); Embrex, Inc. v. Service Eng'g Corp., 216 F.3d 1343, 1350 (Fed. Cir. 2000) (clear and convincing evidence standard); Johns Hopkins University v. Cellpro, Inc., 152 F.3d 1342, 1363-64 (Fed. Cir. 1998).

ably prudent person would have continued the challenged activity with any confidence that the patent would, in the end, be held invalid or not infringed.[81] Willfulness depends on the state of mind of the infringer but is judged from the standpoint of objectively reasonable behavior. Until the infringer is aware of the patent, the infringement cannot be willful.[82]

Because willfulness is only an issue after a court has held a patent valid and infringed, any conviction that the infringer held to the contrary was obviously mistaken. The question is not whether the infringer's point of view was correct, but whether it was reasonable and maintained in good faith. Although willfulness is judged under the totality of the circumstances,[83] a dominant consideration is whether the infringer, when made aware of the possibility of a claim, sought out and relied on competent advice of counsel. There is no absolute requirement that an accused infringer seek legal advice, but it is normally expected as part of the accused infringer's duty of due care.[84] Accordingly, any potential infringer is well-advised to seek competent legal advice at the first opportunity.

If the accused infringer failed to seek advice of counsel, this goes a long way toward proving willful infringement. On the other hand, an accused infringer who *does* seek advice of counsel is not guaranteed immunity.[85] In order for an accused infringer to reasonably rely on it, the advice of counsel must be competent.[86] In other words, it must come from an attorney who is qualified to render an opinion, it must show that the advice is based on a

[80] *See* Electro Scientific Indus., Inc. v. General Scanning Inc., 247 F.3d 1341, 1353 (Fed. Cir. 2001) ("A finding of willfulness does not mandate enhanced damages."); Graco, Inc. v. Binks Mfg. Co., 60 F.3d 785, 792 (Fed. Cir. 1995).

[81] *See* Hall v. Aqua Queen Mfg., Inc., 93 F.3d 1548, 1555 (Fed. Cir. 1996); State Indus., Inc. v. Mor-Flo Indus., Inc., 883 F.2d 1573, 1581 (Fed. Cir. 1989).

[82] Gustafson, Inc. v. Intersystems Industrial Prods., Inc., 897 F.2d 508, 511 (Fed. Cir. 1990) ("a party cannot be found to have 'willfully' infringed a patent of which the party had no knowledge").

[83] Advanced Cardiovascular Sys., Inc. v. Medtronic, Inc., 265 F.3d 1294, 1309 (Fed. Cir. 2001) ("a willfulness finding must be based on all relevant circumstances, also referred to as the totality of the circumstances").

[84] *See* LNP Eng'g Plastics, Inc. v. Miller Waste Mills, Inc., 273 F.3d 1347, 1357 (Fed. Cir. 2001) ("Usually [the] duty of due care requires a potential infringer to obtain competent legal advice before continuing its potentially infringing activities."); Comark Communications, Inc. v. Harris Corp., 156 F.3d 1182, 1190 (Fed. Cir. 1998); Ortho Pharmaceutical Corp. v. Smith, 959 F.2d 936, 944 (Fed. Cir. 1992).

[85] Willful infringement may occur where the potential infringer "obtains incompetent, conclusory opinions of counsel only to use as a shield against a later charge of willful infringement, rather than in a good faith attempt to avoid infringing another's patent." Jurgens v. CBK, Ltd., 80 F.3d 1566, 1571 (Fed. Cir. 1996).

[86] *See Comark,* 156 F.3d at 1191 ("[T]he legal opinion must be 'competent' or it is of little value in showing the good faith belief of the infringer.... [B]efore we may consider the exculpatory value of an opinion of counsel, the legal advice contained therein must be found on the totality of the circumstances to be competent such that the client was reasonable in relying upon it.").

thorough investigation, and it must explain its conclusions in reasonable detail.[87] Needless to say, the opinion also must be favorable to the accused infringer's position. An opinion of counsel supporting the view that the patent is valid and infringed only makes willfulness more apparent if the advice was ignored.

Normally, communications between attorney and client are privileged. However, if an accused infringer chooses to rely on an opinion of counsel to refute allegations of willful infringement, that privilege must be waived. This can create a dilemma for an accused infringer. If it decides to maintain the privilege by not disclosing the opinion (as it has every right to do), the court may infer that no advice of counsel was received, or that if it was received it was unfavorable.[88] On the other hand, if the accused infringer chooses to rely on the opinion, then it must disclose *all* communications from counsel related to the same subject matter, which may mean disclosing some information that the accused infringer would rather keep under wraps. The accused infringer cannot disclose only so much of the advice as favors its position, while maintaining in confidence the rest. It is all or nothing.[89]

In addition to advice of counsel, or the lack of it, a court may consider as evidence of willfulness whether the infringer deliberately set out to copy the patentee's invention.[90] On the other hand, an attempt to design around the claims of the patent (in other words, to make any changes necessary to avoid the scope of the claims) may be viewed as evidence of good faith.[91] Some courts have suggested that the conduct of the infringer during litigation, and

---

[87] *See* Johns Hopkins University v. Cellpro, Inc., 152 F.3d 1342, 1364 (Fed. Cir. 1998); *Graco*, 60 F.3d at 793–94; BIC Leisure Prods., Inc. v. Windsurfing Int'l, Inc., 1 F.3d 1214, 1223 (Fed. Cir. 1993); Minnesota Mining & Mfg. Co. v. Johnson & Johnson Orthopaedics, Inc., 976 F.2d 1559, 1580 (Fed. Cir. 1992); *Ortho*, 959 F.2d at 944; Read Corp. v. Portec, Inc., 970 F.2d 816, 829 (Fed. Cir. 1992); Underwater Devices Inc. v. Morrison-Knudsen Co., 717 F.2d 1380, 1390 (Fed. Cir. 1983). An opinion obtained from an outside counsel is generally afforded more weight than one obtained from a presumably less objective in-house counsel. *See Underwater Devices,* 717 F.2d at 1390; *but c.f.,* SRI Int'l, Inc. v. Advanced Technology Labs., Inc., 127 F.3d 1462, 1467 (Fed. Cir. 1997) ("there is no rule excluding reliance on house counsel opinions"). Also, written opinions are generally considered more favorably than oral opinions because the latter can be difficult to reconstruct. *See Minnesota Mining & Mfg.,* 976 F.2d at 1580. It does not, however, matter that the advice ultimately proved incorrect. If it had been correct, the issue of willfulness would never have arisen. *See Ortho,* 959 F.2d at 944.

[88] *See* Electro Medical Sys., S.A. v. Cooper Life Sciences, Inc., 34 F.3d 1048, 1056 (Fed. Cir. 1994); L.A. Gear, Inc. v. Thom McAn Shoe Co., 988 F.2d 1117, 1126 (Fed. Cir. 1993). On the other hand, the negative inference does not foreclose consideration of other circumstances that might still establish the infringer's good faith. *See Electro Medical,* 34 F.3d at 1056–57 (presumption is not irrebuttable).

[89] *See* McCormick-Morgan Inc. v. Teledyne Indus. Inc., 21 U.S.P.Q.2d 1412, 1416 (N.D. Cal. 1991) ("The law is clear: [an accused infringer] cannot waive the attorney-client privilege as to certain communications regarding infringement, validity, and unenforceability, but not others.").

[90] *See* Crystal Semiconductor Corp. v. Tritech Microelectronics Int'l, Inc., 246 F.3d 1336, 1352 (Fed. Cir. 2001); *Read,* 970 F.2d at 827.

the closeness of the questions decided against it, also may be weighed in the balance.[92]

Another potential remedy against a willful infringer is an award of reasonable attorneys' fees. The general rule in the United States is that each litigant must bear its own legal costs, regardless of the outcome of the case, but 35 U.S.C. § 285 provides for an award of attorneys' fees in an "exceptional case." Willful infringement may be found to create such an exceptional case,[93] though it is still a matter for the judge's discretion.[94] On occasion, attorneys' fees are awarded to an accused infringer who prevails in the litigation, generally when the patentee committed inequitable conduct in prosecuting the patent or the claim of infringement was frivolous.[95] It is by no means proper to award attorneys' fees to the prevailing party as a matter of routine.[96]

11.8.3 Limitations

Recovery of damages for patent infringement can be limited under certain circumstances. The most important limiting factors are the statute of limitations, failure to properly mark products or give notice of infringement, laches, and equitable estoppel.

---

[91] *See* Westvaco Corp. v. International Paper Co., 991 F.2d 735, 745 (Fed. Cir. 1993); Rolls-Royce Ltd. v. GTE Valeron Corp., 800 F.2d 1101, 1109–10 (Fed. Cir. 1986). Often, however, it is difficult to distinguish between designing around a patent claim and introducing an insubstantial variation which subjects the potential infringer to liability under the doctrine of equivalents. See Section 10.6.3.

[92] *Read*, 970 F.2d at 827.

[93] *See* Tate Access Floors, Inc. v. Maxcess Technologies, Inc., 222 F.3d 958, 972 (Fed. Cir. 2000); *L.A. Gear*, 988 F.2d at 1128. Even if the infringement was not willful, "vexatious conduct" by the infringer in the course of the litigation may be held sufficient to make an exceptional case and justify an award of attorneys' fees. *See* Beckman Instruments, Inc. v. LKB Produkter AB, 892 F.2d 1547, 1551–52 (Fed. Cir. 1989).

[94] Odetics, Inc. v. Storage Technology Corp., 185 F.3d 1259, 1274 (Fed. Cir. 1999). Where the jury has found willful infringement, a judge's *unexplained* failure to treat the case as exceptional may be found an abuse of discretion. *See Tate Access Floors*, 222 F.3d at 972.

[95] *See* Yamanouchi Pharmaceutical Co. v. Danbury Pharmacal, Inc., 231 F.3d 1339, 1347 (Fed. Cir. 2000); Haynes Int'l, Inc. v. Jessop Steel Co., 8 F.3d 1573, 1579 (Fed. Cir. 1993) (a "frivolous" lawsuit justifying an award of attorneys' fees is one which "the patentee knew or, on reasonable investigation, should have known, was baseless"); Stevenson v. Sears Roebuck & Co., 713 F.2d 705, 713 (Fed. Cir. 1983) ("There must be some finding of unfairness, bad faith, or inequitable conduct on the part of the unsuccessful patentee."). A patentee's failure to investigate thoroughly before bringing an unsuccessful claim of infringement may lead to a finding that the case is exceptional. *See* Superior Fireplace Co. v. Majestic Prods. Co., 270 F.3d 1358, 1378 (Fed. Cir. 2001) ("From the record on appeal, it is unclear if Superior inspected the allegedly infringing products, prepared claim charts, construed the claims at issue, or even read those claims.").

[96] *See* Revlon, Inc. v. Carson Prods. Co., 803 F.2d 676, 679 (Fed. Cir. 1986).

11.8.3.1 Statute of Limitations

Section 286 of the Patent Act provides that no damages may be recovered for infringement that occurred more than 6 years prior to the filing of a claim. This statute of limitations is equivalent to those found in many other areas of the law, and the purpose is the usual one of encouraging the prompt disposition of potential claims. Note that § 286 does not prevent the filing of a suit, unless the only relief that could be granted is damages for infringement more than 6 years ago. If, for example, the defendant had infringed continuously for the past 10 years, the patentee could still sue to recover damages for the most recent 6 years of infringement and could obtain an injunction against future infringement.

11.8.3.2 Notice and Marking

Many manufactured articles bear markings referring to a specific patent or patents. These are the result of 35 U.S.C. § 287, which states that such markings provide "notice to the public" that the article is patented. They may not provide *actual notice* to a particular individual who has never seen the article, but the law considers them *constructive* notice to anyone.[97] If it is not practical to list patent numbers on the article itself, they can be listed on packaging.[98]

If a patent owner or licensee makes, sells, offers to sell, or imports into the United States articles covered by the patent but not marked in this fashion, no damages for infringement can be recovered until (1) such marking begins, or (2) the infringer receives from the patent owner *actual notice* of the infringement.[99] Imagine the following scenario: A patent issues on January 1, 2001. Between January 1, 2001, and January 1, 2002, the patent owner sells goods in the United States that are covered by the patent but not properly marked. An infringer also sells goods during that period, but the patent owner fails to provide actual notice of the infringement. On January 1, 2002, the patent owner begins to mark its goods as contemplated by § 287. If the patent owner files suit in 2003, damages can be recovered only on infringing sales that occurred after January 1, 2002. This limitation of damages provides an incentive to patent owners to mark their goods and provide at least that much notice to the public.[100]

The marking of goods must be "substantially consistent and continuous."[101] If a large shipment of unmarked goods is sold, this resets the dam-

---

[97] *See* Gart v. Logitech, Inc., 254 F.3d 1334, 1345 (Fed. Cir. 2001); American Medical Sys., Inc. v. Medical Eng'g Corp., 6 F.3d 1523, 1538 (Fed. Cir. 1993).

[98] 35 U.S.C. § 287(a).

[99] *See* 35 U.S.C. § 287(a); SRI Int'l, Inc. v. Advanced Technology Labs., Inc., 127 F.3d 1462, 1469 (Fed. Cir. 1997); Maxwell v. J. Baker, Inc., 86 F.3d 1098, 1111 (Fed. Cir. 1996).

[100] *See* Nike, Inc. v. Wal-Mart Stores, Inc., 138 F.3d 1437, 1443 (Fed. Cir. 1998).

[101] *Maxwell*, 86 F.3d at 1111; *American Medical*, 6 F.3d at 1537.

ages clock, so to speak. If only a few unmarked goods slip through, this may be overlooked. Note that the obligation to mark applies to goods made or sold by the patent owner *or* licensee (express or implied).[102] Patent owners therefore have to make sure that licensees are properly marking their goods, or the patent owner's ability to recover damages for infringement will be impaired.[103] Section 287 does not apply to patents with just method claims, for the simple reason that a method cannot be marked.[104] If a patent includes both method and apparatus claims, and the method is related to an apparatus that can be marked, such marking will likely be required, at least if both method and apparatus claims are infringed.[105] If neither the patent owner nor the patent owner's licensees have sold any products covered by the patent, no marking or other notice is required to begin the accumulation of damages for infringement.

If products have not been properly marked, the patentee can provide *actual notice* to the infringer. The notice can come in the form of a warning letter from the patentee, or without ceremony in the form of a suit for infringement.[106] Once such notice has been provided, damages with respect to that infringer can begin to accrue. The notice must come from the patent owner; it is not sufficient that the accused infringer discovered the infringement on its own or through a third party.[107] Moreover, the notice must identify the patent, and it must specifically charge the recipient with infringement of that patent.[108] In *Amstead Indus. Inc. v. Buckeye Steel Castings Co.*,[109] the infringer (Buckeye) received a form letter from the patent owner mentioning the patent and warning it not to infringe. The same letter had been sent to other companies throughout the industry. The court found that this was not actual notice of infringement to Buckeye because it did not specifically charge Buckeye with infringement, nor did it identify any infringing device.[110]

---

[102] *Maxwell*, 86 F.3d at 1111; Amstead Indus. Inc. v. Buckeye Steel Castings Co., 24 F.3d 178, 185 (Fed. Cir. 1994).
[103] This obligation is, however, subject to a "rule of reason," and "substantial compliance" may be held sufficient. *See Maxwell*, 86 F.3d at 1111–1112 (patentee's reasonable efforts were sufficient, even though a "numerically large number" of goods–still a small percentage of the total–were not properly marked).
[104] *American Medical*, 6 F.3d at 1538; *see also* Hanson v. Alpine Valley Ski Area, Inc., 718 F.2d 1075, 1083 (Fed. Cir. 1983).
[105] *See American Medical*, 6 F.3d at 1538–39.
[106] *See American Medical*, 6 F.3d at 1537.
[107] *See* Lans v. Digital Equipment Corp., 252 F.3d 1320, 1327 (Fed. Cir. 2001); *American Medical*, 6 F.3d at 1537 n.18.
[108] It is immaterial whether the patent owner "threatens suit, demands cessation of infringement, or offers a license under the patent." *SRI*, 127 F.3d at 1470. The important thing is that "the recipient is notified, with sufficient specificity, that the patent holder believes that the recipient of the notice may be an infringer." *Id.*
[109] 24 F.3d 178, 185–87 (Fed. Cir. 1994).

11.8.3.3 **Laches**

The equitable principle of *laches* may also bar recovery of damages accrued before a suit was filed. As explained by the Federal Circuit in *A.C. Aukerman Co. v. R. L. Chaides Construction Co.*,[111] laches may bar the recovery of prefiling damages if (1) the patentee unreasonably and inexcusably delayed in filing suit, and (2) the accused infringer was materially harmed by the delay.[112] If the patentee delayed filing suit for more than 6 years, measured from the time it first knew or should have known of the alleged infringement,[113] laches is presumed, though that presumption can be overcome with the introduction of contrary evidence.[114]

The harm to the accused infringer can be either economic or evidentiary.[115] Economic harm means the loss of investments or the incurring of additional damages that could have been avoided if suit had been filed earlier. For example, during the period of delay the accused infringer might have made unrecoverable investments in a factory to manufacture the accused product. A patentee cannot delay unreasonably while such investments are made, nor can it "lie silently in wait watching damages escalate."[116] Evidentiary prejudice refers to the loss of evidence that the accused infringer might have used in its defense had the case been brought

---

[110] *Amstead,* 24 F.3d at 187. Somewhat clouding the picture, the Federal Circuit has recently stated that the notice of infringement must be specific, but not necessarily an "unqualified charge of infringement." *Gart,* 254 F.3d at 1344. Specific reference to the patent and the potentially infringing product, together with advice that the recipient seek an opinion of counsel to determine "whether a non-exclusive license under the patent is needed," is sufficient to warn the recipient that it is believed to infringe. *Id.*

[111] 960 F.2d 1020 (Fed. Cir 1992) (en banc).

[112] *Aukerman,* 960 F.2d at 1032; *see also* Wanlass v. General Electric Co., 148 F.3d 1334, 1337 (Fed. Cir. 1998); Gasser Chair Co. v. Infanti Chair Mfg. Corp., 60 F.3d 770, 773 (Fed. Cir. 1995); Meyers v. Asics Corp., 974 F.2d 1304, 1307 (Fed. Cir. 1993). Even if these facts are demonstrated, enforcement of the laches defense is still left to the judge's discretion and sense of fairness. *See Gasser,* 60 F.3d at 773. If the infringer itself has behaved unfairly (perhaps by deliberately copying the patentee's invention), the court may decline to exercise its equitable powers. *See id.*

[113] *See Wanlass,* 148 F.3d at 1337 ("The period of delay begins at the time the patentee had actual or constructive knowledge of the defendant's potentially infringing activities."). Because laches can arise based on what the patentee *should* have known, patentees are, in effect, required to "police their rights" by keeping themselves reasonably informed of potentially infringing activity. *Id.* at 1338. A patentee cannot remain "negligently or willfully oblivious," where the potentially infringing activity is so "pervasive, open, and notorious" that a reasonable patentee would investigate. *Id.*

[114] *Aukerman,* 960 F.2d at 1028, 1037–39; *Wanlass,* 148 F.3d at 1337 ("A delay of more than six years raises a presumption that it is unreasonable, inexcusable, and prejudicial.").

[115] *Aukerman,* 960 F.2d at 1033.

[116] *Aukerman,* 960 F.2d at 1033. The court must find that the potential infringer would have acted differently if the infringer had made its claim more promptly. In other words, the losses must have been *caused* by the delay. *See Gasser,* 60 F.3d at 775.

sooner. Such prejudice can arise where, for example, important documents have been lost, memories have faded, or witnesses have died.[117]

Laches is an equitable defense that depends on the exercise of the judge's discretion, in view of all the circumstances.[118] Those circumstances include the length of the delay and any excuses or justifications offered by the patentee. Excuses for delay that may be acceptable include the demands of other litigation, negotiations with the accused infringer, and disputes over ownership of the patent.[119] Fairness may sometimes require that the patentee notify the accused infringer of the reason for its delay.[120]

The effect of a successful laches defense is to bar recovery of damages incurred *before* the lawsuit was filed.[121] The patentee can still recover damages for subsequent infringement, as well as an injunction against future infringement.

Recently the Federal Circuit endorsed the concept of *prosecution laches*, which bars enforcement of a patent issuing after unreasonable and unexplained delays in prosecution, even though the applicant complied with the relevant PTO regulations.[122] The defense prevents an applicant from unreasonably delaying the issuance of a patent simply to put itself in a more advantageous position with respect to others, who, not knowing of the pending application, may be investing in infringing technology. In this instance, a successful laches defense appears to render the claims generally unenforceable.[123]

11.8.3.4 *Equitable Estoppel*

Equitable estoppel is an equitable defense similar to laches, but it depends on a somewhat different set of circumstances. In order for this defense to apply, the patentee must somehow have *communicated* to the potential infringer the idea that the patentee would not press a claim.[124] This communication can be in the form of words, conduct, or even silence if, under the circumstances, one would expect the patentee to voice any objections to the

---

[117] *Aukerman*, 960 F.2d at 1033.

[118] *Aukerman*, 960 F.2d at 1032.

[119] *Aukerman*, 960 F.2d at 1033. Poverty or inability to find an attorney willing to work for a contingent fee have not been recognized as valid excuses for delay. *See* Hall v. Aqua Queen Mfg., Inc., 93 F.3d 1548, 1554 (Fed. Cir. 1996).

[120] *See Aukerman*, 960 F.2d at 1033; Vaupel Textilmaschinen KG v. Meccanica Euro Italia S.P.A., 944 F.2d 870, 877 (Fed. Cir. 1991) (for the "other litigation" excuse to apply, the patentee must inform the accused infringer of the other litigation and of its intention to enforce the patent when the other litigation is concluded).

[121] Odetics, Inc. v. Storage Technology Corp., 185 F.3d 1259, 1272–73 (Fed. Cir. 1999); *Aukerman*, 960 F.2d at 1041.

[122] *See* Symbol Technologies, Inc. v. Lemelson Medical, 277 F.3d 1361, 1363–65 (Fed. Cir. 2002).

[123] *See Symbol Technologies*, 277 F.3d at 1364.

[124] A.C. Aukerman Co. v. R.L. Chaides Construction Co., 960 F.2d 1020, 1042 (Fed. Cir. 1992) (en banc).

potential infringer's activities.[125] In addition, the potential infringer must have *relied* on that communication and suffered material harm as a result of that reliance.[126] Equitable estoppel is most easily applied where, for example, the patentee told the potential infringer that it would not interfere with its activities, the potential infringer relied on that communication and invested in a new factory, and the patentee then reversed itself and filed suit.[127] The more difficult cases are those where the patentee did nothing, and the potential infringer interpreted that inaction as tacit permission.

As in applying the laches defense, the court must weigh all of the circumstances and determine what fairness dictates.[128] If the defense of equitable estoppel is held to apply, it bars *any* relief to the patentee.[129] In this respect, the consequences are more severe than those of the traditional laches defense, which prevents only the recovery of past damages.

11.9 THE INTERNATIONAL TRADE COMMISSION

If allegedly infringing products are being *imported* into the United States, a patent owner can request an investigation by the International Trade Commission (ITC). In many ways, an ITC investigation is similar to a suit for patent infringement in a district court, but there are important differences.

First, the matter will be handled by an Administrative Law Judge (ALJ) rather than a conventional judge or jury. The decision of the ALJ is reviewed by the ITC commissioners and, if an exclusion of infringing goods is ordered, by the president of the United States.[130] Second, the patent owner must demonstrate that importation of infringing articles threatens a *domestic industry* in those articles—in other words, there must be significant business activity in the United States, either underway or imminent, that will

---

[125] *Aukerman*, 960 F.2d at 1041–42. If the communication is in the form of inaction, then there must have been some contact or relationship with the patentee that would allow the inaction to be reasonably interpreted as a sign of abandonment. *Id.* at 1042. For example, the patentee might have threatened immediate enforcement of its patents and then failed to follow through, which could reasonably be interpreted as a change of heart. *See* Meyers v. Asics Corp., 974 F.2d 1304, 1309 (Fed. Cir. 1993). Ironically, the patentee who insists most emphatically that it will enforce its patent rights is the patentee most likely to be found to have abandoned those rights by its subsequent inaction.

[126] *Aukerman*, 960 F.2d at 1042–43. The accused infringer "must have knowledge of the patentee and its patent and must reasonably infer that the patentee acquiesced to the allegedly infringing activity for some time." Winbond Electronics Corp. v. International Trade Comm'n, 262 F.3d 1363, 1374 (Fed. Cir. 2001).

[127] Note that, unlike the laches defense, equitable estoppel does not require any element of delay. *Aukerman*, 960 F.2d at 1041–42.

[128] *Aukerman*, 960 F.2d at 1043.

[129] *Aukerman*, 960 F.2d at 1041.

[130] *See* 19 U.S.C. § 1337(c), (j).

be injured by the illicit competition of infringing goods.[131] Third, the ITC can award no money damages for past infringement. It can only order that the importation of infringing goods be stopped.[132] Finally, although an ITC investigation involves much of the same effort as a suit in a district court, the schedule is generally more compressed. An ITC investigation, from start to finish, is generally completed in little more than a year.

11.10 JUDGMENTS OF INVALIDITY

When a court has held a patent invalid, and all avenues of appeal have been exhausted, the patent cannot in the future be asserted against any potential infringer.[133] In a sense, a patent owner has only one chance to defend the validity of the patent. On the other hand, an unsuccessful attempt by one accused infringer to challenge the validity of a patent generally does not preclude another accused infringer from raising similar arguments.

---

[131] *See* 19 U.S.C. § 1337(a)(2)–(3).

[132] *See* 19 U.S.C. § 1337(d).

[133] Assuming that the patent owner had a "full and fair opportunity" to defend the patent. *See* Blonder-Tongue Labs., Inc. v. University of Illinois Foundation, 402 U.S. 313, 328 (1971).

CHAPTER 12

Special Topics

This final chapter covers a number of specialized topics outside the mainstream of patent law, but still worthy of discussion. These include design patents, plant patents, foreign patents, and the complex problem of extending patent protection to computer software.

12.1 DESIGN PATENTS

Throughout this book, the term *patent* generally refers to a utility patent. A *utility patent* is a patent on a device, method, or composition of matter having a practical use.[1] Most of the inventions one would commonly think of, from mousetraps to pharmaceuticals to communications satellites, are things properly the subject of a utility patent. However, the Patent Office also issues design patents. A *design patent* is a curious hybrid similar in some respects to an ordinary utility patent, but applied to the kinds of artistic (or at any rate decorative) expression that are also the subject of copyright or trademark protection.[2] Whereas utility patents exist to promote the "useful arts," design patents exist to promote the "decorative arts."[3]

Design patents are granted to new, original, and ornamental designs, as they are embodied in manufactured objects.[4] The design can be a surface ornament, such as a pattern on a cream pitcher, or it can derive from the shape and configuration of the object itself. If one conceived of a sleek new

---

[1] *Utility* is defined rather broadly, however, and can be applied to inventions such as toys that have minimal practical value. *See* Section 8.4.

[2] *See* Sections 2.1–2.2.

[3] Avia Group Int'l, Inc. v. L.A. Gear California, Inc., 853 F.2d 1557, 1563 (Fed. Cir. 1988).

[4] 35 U.S.C. § 171.

shape for a telephone, that shape could be the subject of a design patent. Copies of three design patents can be found at Appendix B. They depict a candle holder, a faucet, and an automobile tire, respectively.

A design patent cannot be awarded to an entirely abstract design not associated with any particular utilitarian object. One could not, for example, obtain a design patent on a painting of sunflowers.[5] One could, however, obtain a design patent on a vase that bears the same painting as a decoration. Although a design patent must claim an article of manufacture, the design cannot be dictated by functional considerations.[6] If the shape of a new tennis racket were dictated by a scheme to enlarge the "sweet spot," that shape should not be the subject of a design patent. Instead, the shape should be protected by a utility patent, assuming that it meets the criteria of patentability. One factor to consider in judging whether a design is functional or ornamental is whether the same functions could be accomplished by designs of significantly different appearance.[7]

Although neither the Patent Office nor the courts may be well suited to judge artistic merit, a design is required to be *ornamental* before it can be granted a design patent. The design need not be a fine example of artistic expression, but it must, in some way, appeal to the aesthetic sense. On occasion, design patents have been denied because the depicted article failed to meet this criterion.[8] On the other hand, design patents can be granted to numerous objects that would not ordinarily be thought of as having an ornamental aspect—for example, a hip prosthesis.[9] Apparently, a physician

---

[5] *See* M.P.E.P. § 1504.01A.

[6] *See* Door-Master Corp. v. Yorktowne, Inc., 256 F.3d 1308, 1312 (Fed. Cir. 2001) ("only 'the non-functional aspects of an ornamental design as shown in a patent' are proper bases for design patent protection"); L.A. Gear, Inc. v. Thom McAn Shoe Co., 988 F.2d 1117, 1123 (Fed. Cir. 1993); *Avia*, 853 F.2d at 1563.

[7] *See* Rosco, Inc. v. Mirror Lite Co., 304 F.3d 1373, 1378 (Fed. Cir. 2002) ("[I]f other designs could produce the same or similar functional capabilities, the design of the article in question is likely ornamental, not functional."); *L.A. Gear*, 988 F.2d at 1123 ("When there are several ways to achieve the function of an article of manufacture, the design on the article is more likely to serve a primarily ornamental purpose."); *Avia*, 853 F.2d at 1563. Note that even if every element of the design has a function, the overall configuration may be a matter of patentable aesthetic expression. *See L.A. Gear*, 988 F.2d at 1123; *Avia*, 853 F.2d at 1563.

[8] *See, e.g.,* Blisscraft of Hollywood v. United Plastics Co., 294 F.2d 694, 696 (2d Cir. 1961) (holding a design patent on a pitcher invalid because the pitcher was not sufficiently ornamental in design: "Plaintiff's pitcher has no particularly aesthetic appeal in line, form, color, or otherwise. . . . The reaction which the pitcher inspires is simply that of the usual, useful and not unattractive piece of kitchenware."). In the more recent cases, a design is not likely to be criticized on the grounds that it fails to appeal to the eye. Instead, the debate is likely to center on whether the form is dictated by aesthetic aspirations (however successful) or by functional necessity. *See* Seiko Epson Corp. v. Nu-Kote Int'l, Inc., 190 F.3d 1360, 1368 (Fed. Cir. 1999) ("Nor need the design be aesthetically pleasing. . . . The design may contribute distinctiveness or consumer recognition to the [product], but an absence of artistic merit does not mean that the design is purely functional.").

[9] *See In re* Webb, 916 F.2d 1553 (Fed. Cir. 1990).

selecting a hip prosthesis might be moved to select the one that appeals to the eye.

Because design patents are meant to protect a visually appealing design, objects that are hidden from view may be denied a design patent.[10] A vacuum cleaner bag, for example, has been denied a design patent on that ground.[11] Nevertheless, a design may be found sufficiently ornamental to warrant a design patent if its appearance is a "matter of concern" during some significant portion of its life cycle.[12] The hip prosthesis, for example, is not visible in use, but it is visible when displayed at a trade show or in advertising.

Where a utility patent generally has many pages describing the invention in words, a design patent usually includes little description apart from the drawings.[13] This is appropriate because the purpose of the patent is to protect a visual design. Where a utility patent can have many claims, a design patent can have only one,[14] typically in the form "The ornamental design for the [object] as shown."[15] The bracketed portion would name the kind of object depicted—for example, candleholder, faucet, or automobile tire.

A design patent carries no requirement of utility, but the design must be new and nonobvious.[16] Obviousness is inherently difficult to judge in aesthetic matters,[17] and the prior art available for the Patent Office to consult (primarily earlier design patents and utility patents) may barely scratch the surface. Nevertheless, a design patent, like a utility patent, carries a presumption of validity.

The term of a design patent is 14 years from the date of issue.[18] An object can infringe a design patent if it presents substantially the same appearance to an ordinary observer,[19] and if the accused product includes the aspects of the claimed design that distinguished it from the prior art.[20] Differences will

---

10 *See Door-Master*, 256 F.3d at 1312 ("generally concealed features are not proper bases for design patent protection because their appearance cannot be a 'matter of concern'"); *Webb*, 916 F.2d at 1557.

11 *See Ex Parte* Fesco, 147 U.S.P.Q. 74 (Pat. Off. Bd. App. 1965).

12 *See* Contessa Food Prods., Inc. v. Conagra, Inc., 282 F.3d 1370, 1379 (Fed. Cir. 2002) ("We have construed 'normal use' in the design patent context to extend over 'a period in the article's life, beginning after completion of manufacture or assembly and ending with the ultimate destruction, loss, or disappearance of the article.'"); Keystone Retaining Wall Sys., Inc. v. Westrock, Inc., 997 F.2d 1444, 1451 (Fed. Cir. 1993); *Webb*, 916 F.2d at 1557–58.

13 *See* Hupp v. Siroflex of America, Inc., 122 F.3d 1456, 1464 (Fed. Cir. 1997) ("A design patent contains no written description; the drawings are the claims to the patented subject matter.").

14 *See* 37 C.F.R. § 1.153.

15 *See* M.P.E.P. § 1503.03.

16 35 U.S.C. §§ 171, 103; *L.A. Gear*, 988 F.2d at 1124; *Avia*, 853 F.2d at 1563.

17 As in the case of a utility patent, the factors to consider include the scope and content of the prior art, the differences between the prior art and the claimed subject matter, the level of ordinary skill in the art, and secondary considerations such as commercial success or copying. *Avia*, 853 F.2d at 1564. *See* Section 8.9.6. In the case of a design patent, obviousness is to be judged from the perspective of a designer of ordinary capabilities. Litton Sys., Inc. v. Whirlpool Corp., 728 F.2d 1423, 1443 (Fed. Cir. 1984).

18 35 U.S.C. § 173.

not avoid infringement, if the patented design and the accused product are sufficiently similar overall.[21] It is not an infringement to copy only the functional aspects of a patented design.[22]

The patentee can recover the "entire profit" of an infringer who has sold an article covered by a design patent.[23]

12.2 PLANT PATENTS

A new plant variety can be the subject of a utility patent,[24] but only if the variety is nonobvious,[25] and only if the patent disclosure satisfies the usual requirements, such as the enablement and written description requirements.[26] These requirements are often problematic in the case of a plant variety. If, for example, the difference between a newly discovered rose and a known variety is a subtle difference in color and perfume, it is difficult to describe these differences in words and equally difficult to decide whether the differences are nonobvious. Congress addressed these difficulties by providing a special form of patent for plant varieties, thereby putting agriculture on a more even footing with industry when it comes to encouraging and rewarding innovation.

A plant patent can be granted to one who "invents or discovers and asexually reproduces any distinct and new variety of plant, including cultivated spores, mutants, hybrids, and newly-found seedlings, other than a tuber propagated plant or a plant found in an uncultivated state."[27] Asexual reproduction refers to reproduction by grafting, budding, and similar procedures

---

[19] "'[I]f, in the eye of an ordinary observer, giving such attention as a purchaser usually gives, two designs are substantially the same, if the resemblance is such as to deceive such an observer, inducing him to purchase one supposing it to be the other, the first one patented is infringed by the other.'" *Avia*, 853 F.2d at 1565; *see also Contessa*, 282 F.3d at 1377; Unidynamics v. Automated Prods. Int'l, Ltd., 157 F.3d 1311, 1323 (Fed. Cir. 1998). If the item is specialized, the court may adopt the perspective of an "ordinary purchaser" of such a specialized item. *See* Goodyear Tire & Rubber Co. v. Hercules Tire & Rubber Co., 162 F.3d 1113, 1117 (Fed. Cir. 1998). Note the similarity to the test of infringement for a trademark, discussed at Section 2.2. The proper comparison, however, is between the accused product and the design depicted in the patent, not between the accused product and the patentee's own commercial embodiment, which may include features not depicted in the patent. *See* Sun Hill Indus., Inc. v. Easter Unlimited, Inc., 48 F.3d 1193, 1196 (Fed. Cir. 1995).

[20] *See Contessa*, 282 F.3d at 1377 ("The 'point of novelty' test is distinct from the 'ordinary observer' test and requires proof that the accused design appropriates the novelty which distinguishes the patented design from the prior art."); *Unidynamics*, 157 F.3d at 1323; *Sun Hill*, 48 F.3d at 1197.

[21] *See Contessa*, 282 F.3d at 1376–78.

[22] *See* Lee v. Dayton-Hudson Corp., 838 F.2d 1186, 1189 (Fed. Cir. 1988).

[23] 35 U.S.C. § 289.

[24] J.E.M. AG Supply, Inc. v. Pioneer Hi-Bred Int'l, Inc., 534 U.S. 124, 127 (2001).

[25] *See* Section 8.9.6.

[26] *See* Sections 8.6.8 and 8.8.

that reproduce a genetically identical plant from a portion of the first plant or its progeny.[28] The "invention" is complete only when the new variety has been discovered, its distinguishing characteristics have been identified, and it has been asexually reproduced. If the asexually reproduced plant has the distinctive characteristics of its parent, this demonstrates that the characteristics likely represent a genetic rather than an environmental variation.

A patent cannot be granted for the discovery of a new plant in the wild—that is, in an "uncultivated state." However, patents can be granted for varieties that arise from unplanned sports or mutations of cultivated crops. *Imazio Nursery, Inc. v. Dania Greenhouses,*[29] for example, discusses a patented variety of heather discovered as a seedling in a cultivated field. This variety, dubbed "Erica Sunset," blooms during the Christmas season, much earlier than the ordinary heather from which it arose.

Plant patents have only one claim, which typically refers to the plant variety "shown and described" in the specification, usually with a brief recital of the characteristics that distinguish the new variety.[30] In contrast to a utility patent, a description found in a plant patent need only be "as complete as is reasonably possible."[31] Because of their function in identifying the patented variety, illustrations are an important part of a plant patent, and they must be "artistically and competently executed."[32]

A plant variety is patentable if it is "distinct and new"[33]—a threshold of novelty less demanding than nonobviousness. The patent confers the right to exclude others from asexually reproducing the claimed plant or from using or selling such a plant.[34] It is not an infringement of a plant patent to grow the claimed plant from seed. It is also not an infringement to develop independently a variety that is indistinguishable from the patented variety. An infringement occurs only if the accused variety is an *offspring* of the original, which means that an element of proving infringement is evidence that

[27] 35 U.S.C. § 161. According to the Manual of Patent Examining Procedure, tubers (such as potatoes) are excluded because "this group alone, among asexually reproduced plants, is propagated by the same part of the plant that is sold as food." M.P.E.P. § 1601. The term *plant* is used in its popular sense rather than a strict scientific sense, so species such as bacteria are also excluded. *Id.*

[28] *See* M.P.E.P. § 1601. The Plant Variety Protection Act, 7 U.S.C. § 2321 *et seq.*, provides similar legal protection for sexually reproduced plant varieties (e.g., plants grown from seed), but not as a part of the patent system. The Plant Variety Protection Act is administered by the Department of Agriculture.

[29] 69 F.3d 1560 (Fed. Cir. 1995).

[30] *See* 35 U.S.C. § 162 ("The claim in the specification shall be in formal terms to the plant shown and described.").

[31] 35 U.S.C. § 162.

[32] M.P.E.P. § 1606. Either drawings or color photographs are acceptable. *Id.* Examples of plant patents have been omitted from the appendices due to the difficulty of reproducing the illustrations.

[33] 35 U.S.C. § 161.

[34] 35 U.S.C. § 163.

the accused infringer had access to the original plant or its asexually reproduced progeny.[35] This is in contrast to the usual rule (applied to utility patents) that independent development is not a defense to infringement.

12.3 FOREIGN PATENTS

An inventor who wishes to protect an invention in a foreign country must
apply for a patent in that country.[36] Foreign patent systems generally convey
rights similar to those obtainable in the United States, but there are important differences.

Other countries award a patent to the *first person to file a patent application,*
whereas the United States awards a patent to the *first person to invent.* The
first-to-file system provides a far simpler way to resolve issues of priority,
which in the United States must be resolved by complex inquiries into conception, reduction-to-practice, and diligence.[37] It is often proposed that the
United States adopt the first-to-file rule in order to make its practice consistent with that of the rest of the world. Still, there is something to be said for
rewarding the person who is first to invent, rather than the person who wins
the "race to the Patent Office."

Many other countries allow a degree of public participation in the process of patent examination. In Japan, for example, applications are "laid
open"–that is, made public–18 months after a patent application is filed. At
this time, members of the public, most likely competitors of the applicant,
may submit prior art that bears upon the patentability of the claimed invention. If the Patent Office still determines that the patent should issue, the
public is notified again and anyone who opposes issuance of the patent is
allowed to file an opposition. This system ensures a more rigorous examination than typically occurs in the United States, where prosecution is often
conducted in secret and the government hears only from the applicant. As
discussed in Section 5.1, the recently enacted legislation allowing publication of United States patent applications under some circumstances does not
provide for any form of third-party opposition.

An applicant for a United States patent can take the benefit of an earlier filing date in most foreign countries, if the foreign application was filed no more
than 12 months before the U.S. filing date.[38] This earlier effective filing date
does not remove any statutory bar problems raised by 35 U.S.C. § 102(b).[39]

---

[35] *See Imazio Nursery,* 69 F.3d at 1569–70.

[36] Many countries, including the United States, are parties to a Patent Cooperation Treaty,
    which provides for a standardized patent application acceptable for filing in any of the par-
    ticipating countries. The patent laws of the participating countries differ, however, so an in-
    vention that is patentable in one country may be denied a patent in another.

[37] *See* Sections 8.9.2–8.9.3.

[38] *See* 35 U.S.C. § 119.

The foreign filing date can, however, be used to establish an earlier constructive reduction to practice,[40] possibly avoiding certain prior art references or improving the applicant's position in an interference contest.[41] On the other hand, an inventor who files an application in a foreign country should wait no longer than 12 months before filing in the United States. Otherwise, the foreign patent, if it issues before the United States application is on file, may constitute invalidating prior art under 35 U.S.C. § 102(d).[42]

12.4 PATENTING COMPUTER PROGRAMS

In recent years, one of the thorniest questions in patent law has been whether, and under what circumstances, a computer program can be patented. Because the issue is increasingly important as the number of software patents grows, and because the precedent is difficult to sort out, we will digress on this topic at some length.

At first blush, there may seem no reason to doubt that a computer program constitutes patentable subject matter. A program is, literally, a *process*– one of the categories of patentable subject matter set out in 35 U.S.C. § 101. A programmed computer might also be claimed as a "machine." Moreover, computer programs are undoubtedly *technological* in nature. Even though the process of writing a computer program involves a degree of personal expression, the purpose of the program is to control the operation of a physical device. Finally, from a constitutional perspective, there is no reason to suppose that progress in the art of computer programming is less dependent on patent protection than progress in the arts of circuit design, pharmaceuticals, or any other field in which patents are granted routinely. Why then have software patents met with resistance?

The source of the difficulty lies in two long-standing doctrines. The first is the unpatentability of *mathematical algorithms*. A mathematical algorithm is a series of precisely defined steps for performing a mathematical operation. The following is an example of a mathematical algorithm that begins with two quantities, a and b:

1. Raise a to the power 2, and call the result x.
2. Raise b to the power 2, and call the result y.

---

[39] "[B]ut no patent shall be granted on any application for patent for an invention which had been patented or described in a printed publication in any country more than one year before the date of the actual filing of the application in this country, or which had been in public use or on sale in this country more than one year prior to such filing." 35 U.S.C. § 119(a). The § 102(b) statutory bar provisions are discussed in Section 8.10.

[40] *See In re* Mulder, 716 F.2d 1542, 1544–45 (Fed. Cir. 1983). Constructive reduction to practice is discussed in Section 8.9.2.

[41] *See* Section 5.4.

[42] *See* Section 8.11.

3. Add *x* and *y*, and call the result *z*
4. Take the square root of *z*, and call the result *c*.

As we have seen, a patent cannot be granted on a "principle of nature" such as a mathematical formula. The truths of mathematics are considered beyond the possibility of ownership, even by the first person to discover those truths. Accordingly, Pythagoras could not have patented his famous theorem. When the mathematical truth expresses a relationship, as in the case of the Pythagorean theorem, the relationship also suggests a *process* by which one set of numbers can be converted, by mathematics, to another. As the reader may already have recognized, the algorithm set forth above is simply a sequence of steps, based on the relationship expressed in the Pythagorean theorem, by which one could derive the length (*c*) of the hypotenuse of a right triangle, given the lengths of the two sides (*a* and *b*).

If the formula itself cannot be patented, it seems to follow that an algorithm based on the formula cannot be patented either. If it were otherwise, only the patentee could *use* the formula, and the effect would be the same as if the patentee owned the formula itself.[43] Hence, courts have categorized mathematical algorithms as unpatentable subject matter, akin to principles of nature and abstract ideas.

Computers carry out their myriad functions by performing, at tremendously high speeds, a number of very fundamental mathematical and logical operations. These operations are controlled by a computer program, which dictates the sequence of steps that the computer is to perform. If expressed in slightly different terms, the algorithm set forth above could be made a computer program that would cause a computer to calculate, in an instant, the length of hypotenuse *c*. If a programmer attempted to patent such a program, the question would arise whether the program was a practical advancement in the technological art of computer programming or nothing more than an unpatentable mathematical algorithm.

The other source of doubt as the patentability of computer programs is the *mental steps doctrine*, which holds that a process is unpatentable if an essential step of the process requires human thought. In the past, this theory has been relied upon to deny the patentability of processes that called for human judgment, calculation, or perception. The rationale for the doctrine appears to be that human thought processes are too abstract, too remote from the technological useful arts, or too difficult to capture in terms of a patent disclosure, to be suitable for patent protection. One court simply pro-

---

[43] If various algorithms could be devised that would achieve the same mathematical result, one could argue that patenting one of those algorithms would not monopolize the underlying abstract principle. On the other hand, one could argue that algorithms associated with any mathematical relationship are themselves abstract ideas or fundamental truths, in which case they would also not be available for patenting.

nounced it "self-evident that thought is not patentable," perhaps inferring that exclusive rights to a mental process would impinge too greatly on human freedoms.[44] The doctrine is now discredited, or at least displaced by other debates, but the notion that a computer program is a mechanical analogue of human thought processes seems to account for some of the early hostility toward the patenting of computer software.

12.4.1 The Supreme Court Trilogy

Any discussion of the patentability of computer software must include the trilogy of Supreme Court cases decided in the 1970s and early 1980s: *Gottschalk v. Benson*,[45] *Parker v. Flook*,[46] and *Diamond v. Diehr*.[47]

12.4.1.1 Gottschalk v. Benson

The *Benson* case involved an attempt to patent a process for converting binary-coded decimal (BCD) numbers into pure binary numbers.[48] The method did not rely on a new kind of computer. It could be performed with any computer, then existing or yet to be invented. The Supreme Court held the claims unpatentable, on the ground that the claimed method embodied an abstract idea, or a mathematical truth, rather than the application of an idea to a specific technological end.

Regarding "process" claims in general, the court observed that "[t]ransformation and reduction of an article 'to a different state or thing' is the clue to the patentability of a process claim that does not include particular machines."[49] If this statement is taken at face value, it would appear that no computer program would be patentable as such because programs involve the manipulation of information, not the physical transformation of an article to "a different state or thing." Yet the court denied that it intended to bar the patentability of computer programs altogether. Instead, it focused on the preemptive effect of allowing an inventor to patent a method that is "not limited to any particular art or technology, to any particular apparatus or machinery, or to any particular end use:"[50]

---

[44] *In re* Abrams, 89 U.S.P.Q. 266, 269 (C.C.P.A. 1951).
[45] 409 U.S. 64 (1972).
[46] 437 U.S. 584 (1978).
[47] 450 U.S. 175 (1981).
[48] Binary numbers are expressed in base 2, rather than in the base 10 of the decimal system. The only numerals needed to represent binary numbers are 1 and 0. The number 13, for example, is expressed in binary as 1101. In binary-coded decimal notation, a binary number independently represents each base ten *digit.* In that notation, 13 would be expressed as 0001 0011—the binary equivalent of 1, followed by the binary equivalent of 3. Binary numbers are important because of their use in computing.
[49] *Benson*, 409 U.S. at 70.
[50] *Benson*, 409 U.S. at 64.

It is conceded that one may not patent an idea. But in practical effect that would be the result if the formula for converting BCD numerals to pure binary numerals were patented in this case. The mathematical formula involved here has no substantial practical application except in connection with a digital computer, which means that if [a patent were granted], the patent would wholly preempt the mathematical formula and in practical effect would be a patent on the algorithm itself.[51]

Although the reasoning of *Benson* has been debated by scholars, it seems to be as follows: (1) The conversion of BCD numerals to pure binary is an abstract idea, or a mathematical principle; (2) if Benson were allowed to patent his algorithm, the public, as a practical matter, would be denied all use of that principle, even in applications that had not yet been invented; (3) no process claim that denies the public all use of a mathematical principle can be considered within the realm of patentable subject matter under 35 U.S.C. § 101. *Benson* left open the question of whether one could patent a computer program embodying a mathematical algorithm if the use were limited to a particular technological application. This issue was presented in *Flook.*

12.4.1.2 *Parker v. Flook*

The claim at issue in *Flook* involved a method of updating an "alarm limit." An alarm limit is a number that is used to indicate an abnormal, or possibly dangerous, condition arising during the catalytic conversion of hydrocarbons. If temperature, pressure, or some other operating condition exceeds its respective alarm limit, the process is not going as planned. However, an alarm limit should not always be fixed; during certain stages of operation, the alarm limit needs to be adjusted or "updated." Flook's contribution was to devise an algorithm for updating an alarm limit.

As in *Benson*, the court held that the mathematical algorithm was unpatentable subject matter. Even though the algorithm was to be used only in connection with a catalytic conversion process, and even though a certain amount of specific "post-solution activity" followed the calculation (namely, the adjustment of the alarm limit), the court still found that patenting the process would be tantamount to patenting an abstract idea or phenomenon of nature. As a part of its analysis, the court adopted an odd mixture of the patentable subject matter standard of 35 U.S.C. § 101 and the standard of novelty under 35 U.S.C. § 102. The court found that if the algorithm were

---

[51] *Benson*, 409 U.S. at 71–72.

treated *as though it were already known,* the claim as a whole would describe no patentable invention.[52]

In some respects *Flook* is a troubling decision, because it seems to blur the distinction between principles of nature, which in the abstract are not patentable, and specific, technological applications of those principles, which seemingly should be patentable. Perhaps if the claim had been more specific as to how the alarm limit was to be used in the catalytic conversion process, the court would have regarded the claim as less of an abstraction.

12.4.1.3 Diamond v. Diehr

The Supreme Court revisited these issues in the *Diehr* case. Although the facts in *Diehr* are curiously similar to those in *Flook,* the result was different. Diehr's invention involved a process for curing rubber inside a molding press. In order to determine the proper time to open the press and remove the finished article, Diehr's method called for constant measurement of the temperature inside the press. This data was fed to a computer, which used the well-known Arrhenius equation to periodically recalculate the time necessary for the rubber to cure. When the calculated optimum and the actual curing time were the same, the computer would open the press automatically. This time, the court found that the use of the algorithm did not take the claims outside of the scope of patentable subject matter.

The *Diehr* case was decided not long after *Chakrabarty,*[53] and it reflects a similarly expansive interpretation of the Patent Act. The majority viewed the invention not as a mathematical algorithm per se, but as a method of curing rubber that happened to make use of a mathematical algorithm. Viewed in this light, Diehr's method was an industrial process for "transforming . . . an article . . . into a different state or thing"—the kind of process that has always been considered patentable.[54] The process was not made unpatentable simply because various steps of the process involved the use of an equation and a programmed computer.

As in *Benson,* the court referred to the issue of preemption, finding that Diehr did not seek a monopoly on the Arrhenius equation itself, but only on the use of that equation with other steps in a process for curing rubber.

---

[52] *Flook,* 437 U.S. at 594. The court apparently reasoned as follows: For a method to be a patentable invention, some part of that method must be outside of the public domain. Although a principle of mathematics may not be already known, it is in the public domain just as if it were. Hence, if the algorithm part of a method is in the public domain as a principle of mathematics, and the rest is in the public domain because it was already known, there is nothing about the method that can be the basis of a patent. Still, it could be argued that even if the algorithm and the remainder of the claim, individually, are in the public domain, the combination of the two, or the application of the algorithm to the known process steps, might be novel and not abstract.

[53] *See* Section 4.3.

[54] *Diehr,* 450 U.S. at 184.

Although *Flook* had seemingly dismissed "field of use" limitations as the key
to patentability, the *Diehr* court distinguished *Flook* as a case in which the
claimed method did nothing more than calculate a number, with hardly a
mention of the physical process steps associated with that calculation. The
implication is that if the claims in *Flook* had been drafted with additional references to the catalytic conversion process itself, the claims might have been
patentable as a catalytic conversion process, even if the only novel aspect of
the process had been the use of the mathematical algorithm.[55]

Diehr seems to mark a significant change in the Supreme Court's attitude
toward the patentability of computer software. However, because *Diehr* did
not overrule *Flook*, the lower courts, and the Federal Circuit in particular,
have been left with the difficult task of reconciling and applying the rules set
out in *Benson, Flook,* and *Diehr.*

12.4.2 The Federal Circuit Decisions

The application of patent law to computer software has provoked as
much dissension, and as many seemingly contradictory opinions, in the Federal Circuit Court of Appeals as in the Supreme Court. Nevertheless, one
can piece together from the case law at least some guidelines for determining whether a claim to a computer program, or a process involving a computer program, will be held patentable subject matter.

One approach adopted by the Federal Circuit is known as the *Freeman-
Walter-Abele* test, after a trio of cases that played a part in its evolution. The
court has characterized the test as the following:

> It is first determined whether a mathematical algorithm is recited directly or indi-
> rectly in the claim. If so, it is next determined whether the claimed invention as a
> whole is no more than the algorithm itself; that is, whether the claim is directed to a
> mathematical algorithm that is not applied to or limited by physical elements or pro-
> cess steps. Such claims are nonstatutory. However, when the mathematical algorithm
> is applied in one or more steps of an otherwise statutory process claim, or one or

---

[55] *Flook* had suggested that a method would be unpatentable if the only novel aspect of the
method were the use of a mathematical algorithm: "[Flook's] process is unpatentable under
§ 101, not because it contains an algorithm as one component, but because once that component is assumed to be within the prior art, the application, considered as a whole, contains no patentable invention." The *Diehr* court did not retract this statement, but it stressed
that claims must be viewed as a whole, and that even known elements in the combination
should not be ignored when addressing patentability under § 101. The *Diehr* opinion also
holds it "commonplace that the application of a law of nature or mathematical formula to
a known structure or process may be patentable," a statement that seems to contradict the
Flook approach. 450 U.S. at 187. Given that the *Diehr* court declined to contradict the comment in *Flook*, it is unfortunate that it did not provide a clearer statement of how it should
be interpreted.

more elements of an otherwise statutory apparatus claim, the requirements of section 101 are met.[56]

Thus, the Federal Circuit has distinguished between patent claims drawn to mathematical algorithms in the abstract, and claims that call for application of an algorithm to a *physical* process, or claims that call for a specific *machine* to perform the algorithm. For example, the Federal Circuit has rejected claims to a method of conducting an auction, where the mathematical algorithm was neither tied to specific computer hardware nor used to accomplish any physical transformation.[57] It has similarly denied a patent to an algorithm for constructing a "bubble hierarchy" to define the space around an object. This algorithm could be used to keep industrial robots from colliding with fixed objects, but, significantly, the challenged claims did not refer to this specific use.[58] On the other hand, the Federal Circuit held patentable an apparatus claim reciting various physical components, one of which used an "auto-correlation" algorithm to recognize patterns in signals (e.g., for voice recognition).[59]

The approach taken by the Federal Circuit raises two significant, but difficult, questions: (1) Does the inclusion in the claimed method of steps for *gathering data* to be processed by the algorithm and/or *displaying a result* provide sufficient connection with the physical world to make the algorithm more than an "abstract idea"? and (2) Can questions of patentability be avoided by the simple expedient of describing the invention as a *physical machine* (i.e., computer) for performing the mathematical algorithm?

The first question has no clear answer, as can be seen by comparing *In re Grams*[60] with *Arrhythmia Research Technology, Inc. v. Corazonix Corp.*[61] The former case concerned a method for diagnosing an abnormal condition in a patient, which depended on gathering data on a variety of patient "parameters," and processing this data by a mathematical algorithm to identify the possible cause of any unusual findings. The only physical process step involved data gathering. The court held that this did not bring the claim within the scope of patentable subject matter. Because a mathematical algorithm can be used only by plugging data into the equation, a patent claim that merely added to the algorithm a step for gathering data would be, in effect, the same as a patent on the algorithm itself.[62] The court declined to hold that a mathematical algorithm combined with data-gathering steps

---

[56] Arrhythmia Research Technology, Inc. v. Corazonix Corp., 958 F.2d 1053, 1058 (Fed. Cir. 1992).

[57] *In re* Schrader, 22 F.3d 290 (Fed. Cir. 1994).

[58] *In re* Warmerdam, 33 F.3d 1354 (Fed. Cir. 1994).

[59] *In re* Iwahashi, 888 F.2d 1370 (Fed. Cir. 1989).

[60] 888 F.2d 835 (Fed. Cir. 1989).

[61] 958 F.2d 1053 (Fed. Cir. 1992).

[62] "'If the steps of gathering and substituting values were alone sufficient, every mathematical equation, formula, or algorithm having any practical use would be per se subject to patenting as a 'process' under § 101.'" *Grams*, 888 F.2d at 839.

would always be unpatentable, but it noted that in this case there was little specific disclosure relating to the data-gathering steps, leading to the impression that "applicants are, in essence, claiming the mathematical algorithm, which they cannot do under *Gottschalk v. Benson.*"[63]

The patentee in *Arrhythmia* claimed a method of analyzing electrocardiographic signals in order to detect dangerous heart conditions. The method involved a mathematical algorithm to be performed by a computer. As in *Grams*, the method consisted essentially of gathering data from a patient and using an algorithm to detect an abnormality. However, this time the court held the method to be patentable. According to the court, the signals analyzed by the process were "not abstractions" because they were "related to the patient's heart function," and "the resultant output is not an abstract number, but is a signal related to the patient's heart activity."[64] In addition, the processing of the data involved "physical process steps that transform one physical, electrical signal to another."[65] Thus, the claimed method was not an algorithm in the abstract, but the specific application of an algorithm to a process for analyzing electrocardiographic signals.

Grams and *Arrhythmia* are difficult to reconcile. Although the data analyzed in *Arrhythmia* represented the functioning of an actual human heart, the data analyzed in *Grams* represented the condition of an actual human patient. In *Arrhythmia* the data processing involved the transformation of "one physical, electrical signal into another," but the same might be said of the data processing in *Grams*. In fact, computerized data processing always involves some manipulation of "physical, electrical signals."[66] Comparing *Grams* with *Arrhythmia*, the most one can conclude with any confidence is that if a claim is limited to a specific application, and if it includes disclosure of physical process steps or manipulation of physical signals, it is more likely to be found patentable subject matter.

The question of whether one can avoid the patentability issue merely by claiming a physical apparatus (i.e., computer) to perform the algorithm is also a troubling one. In *In re Warmerdam*, the court rejected the bubble hierarchy *method* claims, but as to the *apparatus* claim the court merely stated that "[c]laim 5 is for a machine, and is clearly patentable subject matter."[67] Yet the claim required nothing more than "[a] machine having a memory

---

63 *Grams*, 888 F.2d at 840.

64 *Arrhythmia*, 958 F.2d at 1059.

65 *Arrhythmia*, 958 F.2d at 1059.

66 The courts have seemed more willing to accept as patentable algorithms that analyze a "signal," as opposed to algorithms that derive a result based on discrete values. *Arrhythmia* is one example, as is *In re Taner*, 681 F.2d 787 (C.C.P.A. 1982), where the signal analyzed (*converted*, in the court's terminology) by the algorithm was a seismic energy wave generated to explore geologic strata. It is difficult to see why processing a stream of data in the form of a signal should be treated differently in terms of patentability than processing discrete data values, where both are obtained by measuring physical properties or conditions.

67 *Warmerdam*, 33 F.3d at 1360.

which contains data representing a bubble hierarchy generated by the method of any of [unpatentable] Claims 1 through 4."

In *In re Alappat*,[68] the Federal Circuit considered whether the Patent Office had properly rejected Alappat's claims to an improved rasterizer for an oscilloscope display, which used a software algorithm to make jagged lines appear smoother. The claims called for an apparatus comprising a combination of means to perform the necessary functions of calculation and display.[69] The majority of the court held the claims patentable, stressing the disclosure of specific memory and logic circuits to perform the functions recited in the claims: "This is not a disembodied mathematical concept which may be characterized as an 'abstract idea,' but rather a specific machine to produce a useful, concrete, and tangible result."[70] Moreover, because the claim to the machine required specific hardware, it would not "wholly pre-empt" the use of the formula.

Two of the dissenting judges in *Alappat* complained that the apparatus on which the majority relied was nothing more than conventional computer hardware, and the only thing that Alappat had invented (or discovered) was a mathematical operation. In the dissenters' view, Alappat's choice to describe the invention not as mathematics per se, but as conventional hardware to perform the mathematics, should not have determined the question of whether the invention was patentable subject matter.

Alappat suggests that virtually any software invention can be patented, as long as it is claimed in terms of a *machine* to perform the necessary functions, and the corresponding circuitry is disclosed in the specification. This is so even if the circuitry is nothing more than what one would find in any run-of-the-mill computer. In the majority's view, "[new] programming creates a new machine, because a general-purpose computer in effect becomes a special purpose computer once it is programmed to perform particular functions pursuant to instructions from program software."[71] On the other hand, some judges may persist in the view that such claim-drafting choices are matters of form rather than substance, and the question of patentability runs deeper than superficial questions of claim drafting. Even *Alappat* suggests that an apparatus claim can be only a "guise."[72]

Today many software patents involve methods of doing business, and for that reason lack the technological context of *Diehr* or *Alappat*. The patent discussed in *State Street Bank & Trust Co. v. Signature Financial Gp.*,[73] for example, includes only a cartoonish representation of a computer system; its innovation lies in the inherently abstract realm of manipulating money and avoiding

---

[68] 33 F.3d 1526 (Fed. Cir. 1994) (en banc).
[69] *See* the discussion of means-plus-function claims at Section 7.7.4.
[70] *Alappat*, 33 F.3d at 1544.
[71] *Alappat*, 33 F.3d at 1545.
[72] *Alappat*, 33 F.3d at 1541.
[73] 149 F.3d 1368 (Fed. Cir. 1998).

taxes. As discussed in Section 4.6, methods of doing business raise difficult questions under §101, which defines patentable subject matter, as well as the useful arts clause of the constitution. Even here, however, the Federal Circuit has held that a vaguely described computer system manipulating figures representing wealth produces the "useful, concrete and *tangible* result"[74] necessary to distinguish the invention from a mathematical abstraction.

The subject of software patentability continues to be a controversial one, so it would be foolish to conclude that the current state of the law is necessarily the last word on the subject. The Supreme Court, or Congress, may have more to contribute to the debate. For now the Patent Office has adopted the liberal view reflected in *Alappat.* Its guidelines require a patent examiner to presume that a programmed computer is a statutory machine, a computer-readable memory used to store a computer program is a statutory manufacture, and a series of steps to be performed by a computer (i.e., a program) is a statutory process.[75] Although these are only presumptions, they represent a dramatic change in attitude toward the acceptance of computer programs as suitable material for patent protection. As a result, software developers are more than ever looking to patents as a means to protect their creations.

---

[74] "Today, we hold that the transformation of data, representing discrete dollar amounts, by a machine through a series of mathematical calculations into a final share price, constitutes a practical application of a mathematical algorithm, formula, or calculation, because it produces 'a useful, concrete and tangible result'–a final share price momentarily fixed for recording and reporting purposes and even accepted and relied upon by regulatory authorities and in subsequent trades." *State Street,* 149 F.3d at 1373.

[75] M.P.E.P. § 2106.

Note on Sources

In any area of the law, there is no substitute for the original sources. In the specific case of patent law, the primary source is Title 35 of the United States Code, known as the Patent Act. Several one-volume references reproduce the Patent Act and other selected legislation concerning copyright and trademark law. A good example is *Selected Statutes and International Agreements on Unfair Competition, Trademark, Copyright and Patent,* edited by Paul Goldstein and Edmund W. Kitch and published by Foundation Press. Rules and regulations specifically relating to patent applications and prosecution can be found in Title 37 of the Code of Federal Regulations, published by the Office of the Federal Register, National Archives and Records, and the Manual of Patent Examining Procedure (or MPEP), published by the Department of Commerce. All of these materials can now be conveniently located online at the Patent and Trademark Office (PTO) Web site: http://www.uspto.gov/main/patents.htm.

Judicial opinions cited in this book can be found in any good law library or through electronic resources such as Lexis or Westlaw. Supreme Court decisions are found in the *United States Reports* (abbreviated in case citations as U.S.) published by West Publishing Co. Published decisions of the Federal Circuit Court of Appeals are found in West's *Federal Reporter* (F.2d or F.3d). District Court opinions are found in West's *Federal Supplement* (F. Supp.), or BNA's *United States Patent Quarterly* (U.S.P.Q. or U.S.P.Q.2d).

Several multivolume treatises provide very detailed surveys of United States patent law, including its historical development. The one the author turns to most frequently is Professor Donald S. Chisum's *Chisum on Patents,* published by Matthew Bender. Ernest Bainbridge Lipscomb's *Lipscomb's Walker on Patents,* published by Clark Boardman Callaghan, is also a valuable resource. Robert L. Harmon's *Patents and the Federal Circuit*, published by BNA Books, is a work that concentrates on the development of the law in the Federal Circuit Court of Appeals. Any of these works would be a useful supplement to this book when greater detail is required.

Sample Utility
Patents

US005502918A

United States Patent [19]

Oviatt

[11] **Patent Number:** 5,502,918

[45] **Date of Patent:** **Apr. 2, 1996**

[54] **MOUSETRAP FOR CATCHING MICE LIVE**

[76] Inventor: **Bill Oviatt**, 1375 Highway 71 North, Springdale, Ark. 72764

[21] Appl. No.: **347,890**

[22] Filed: **Dec. 1, 1994**

[51] **Int. Cl.⁶** **A01M 23/02**
[52] **U.S. Cl.** **43/61**; 43/60; 43/66
[58] **Field of Search** 43/66, 67, 61, 43/60, 58, 75

[56] **References Cited**

U.S. PATENT DOCUMENTS

944,926 12/1909 Turnbo 43/66

1,226,641 5/1917 Cushing 43/60
4,768,305 9/1988 Sackett 43/61

Primary Examiner—Kurt Rowan
Attorney, Agent, or Firm—Rick Martin

[57] **ABSTRACT**

A "Y" shaped mousetrap lures a mouse into an open end of the "Y" by means of smelly bait located at a closed end of the bottom of the "Y". The "Y" is pivotally supported horizontally by a stand. As the mouse walks past the pivot point, a ping pong ball rolls from the opposite short "Y" tube member and down to the entrance of the open ended tube member. The mouse is trapped alive and can be drowned by immersing the mousetrap.

8 Claims, 3 Drawing Sheets

FIG. 1

FIG. 2

FIG. 3

FIG. 4

FIG. 6

FIG. 7

FIG. 5

FIG. 8

FIG. 9

217

1

MOUSETRAP FOR CATCHING MICE LIVE

FIELD OF INVENTION

The present invention relates to a better mousetrap.

BACKGROUND OF THE INVENTION

Mice can be a nuisance and/or a health menace. Traditional mousetraps are comprised of either a mechanical or chemical killing means. When a mouse is killed in a household, many health problems can arise. These health problems include the release of body fluids containing viruses inside the household. Parasites including worms or lice can be released. Decomposition bacteria will cause odors and cause injury to pets or children who ingest them.

The present invention eliminates these hazards by catching the mouse alive. A simple, cylindrical, teeter-totter contains bait at a closed end of the cylinder. The mouse enters the open end of the cylinder and walks toward the bait. As the mouse passes a fulcrum the cylinder tilts the bait end of the cylinder downward. The mouse becomes trapped by a downward rolling ping pong ball. The trap containing the trapped mouse can be brought outside where the entire trap can be thrown in a bucket to drown the mouse.

SUMMARY OF THE INVENTION

The main object of the present invention is to trap a mouse alive.

Another object of the present invention is to provide an inexpensive trap.

Yet another object of the present invention is to allow the trap to be easily dropped into a bucket of water to drown the mouse.

Still yet another object of the present invention is to reuse the trap.

Other objects of this invention will appear from the following description and appended claims, reference being had to the accompanying drawings forming a part of this specification wherein like reference characters designate corresponding parts in the several views.

BRIEF DESCRIPTION OF THE DRAWINGS

FIG. 1 is a top perspective view of the preferred embodiment.

FIG. 2 is a front plan view of the preferred embodiment shown in FIG. 1.

FIG. 3 is a longitudinal sectional view taken along line 3—3 of FIG. 2.

FIG. 4 is a side plan view with a partial cut-away showing the mouse of FIG. 3 trapped.

FIG. 5 is a top perspective view of an alternate embodiment.

FIG. 6 is a front plan view of the retaining ring of FIG. 5.

FIG. 7 is a front plan view of the pivot stand of FIG. 5.

FIG. 8 is a longitudinal partial sectional view of the embodiment of FIG. 5 in the process of trapping a mouse.

FIG. 9 is a partial cut-away of the embodiment shown in FIG. 8 having caught the mouse.

Before explaining the disclosed embodiment of the present invention in detail, it is to be understood that the invention is not limited in its application to the details of the particular arrangement shown, since the invention is capable

2

of other embodiments. Also, the terminology used herein is for the purpose of description and not of limitation.

DESCRIPTION OF THE PREFERRED EMBODIMENT

Referring first to FIG. 1 the trap 1 is comprised of a support stand 2 preferably made of wire. Support stand 2 has wire ends 3, 4 which form a fulcrum for the main tube 5. Main tube 5 preferably is a plastic cylinder having holes 6, 60, 61. Holes 60, 61 removably attach to the wire ends 3, 4 thereby permitting the main tube 5 to teeter-totter around the fulcrum F. Holes 6 also provide an entrance for water when the trap 1 is immersed to kill a mouse.

A pair of removable end caps 7, 8 seal the ends of main tube 5. Before the end caps 7, 8 are secured to main tube 5, the bait 10 and the ping pong ball 9 are inserted as shown at bait end 100 and ball end 90.

An entrance tube 11 forms a "Y" with the main tube 5. Entrance tube 11 depends downward from main tube 5 and points away from the bait end 100.

FIG. 2 shows a mouse eye view of the trap 1. The lure of the bait 10 emanates from entrance E. In FIG. 3 the mouse M is entering entrance E of entrance tube 11. The main tube 5 is in the loaded position which is horizontal. Thus, the ping pong ball 9 rests at ball end 90.

Referring next to FIG. 4 the mouse M has had it. He's eating the bait 10. But as he walked past the fulcrum F his weight caused the main tube 5 to pivot around fulcrum F so that the bait end 100 fell down in direction D and the ball end 90 rose up in direction U. The ping pong ball 9 urged by gravity rolled in path C to close the entrance E. A rim 13 prevents the ping pong ball 9 from rolling past the entrance E.

When finished eating mouse M will turn around and walk past fulcrum F. Main tube 5 will teeter back to a horizontal position. However, ping pong ball 9 will prevent the egress of mouse M out of entrance E. All mouse M can do is travel back and forth in main tube 5 and entrance tube 11, thereby causing the trap 1 to teeter-totter around fulcrum F. Trap 1 can then be immersed in water to drown mouse M or opened at end caps 7, 8 to release mouse M. Of course, in an alternate use one could kill mouse M with poison bait and trap him in the same manner.

Referring next to FIGS. 5, 6, 7a trap 50 is shown. FIG. 5 shows the trap 50 in the horizontal loaded position. In this alternate embodiment a main tube 51 teeter-totters around fulcrum FF. Preferably a plastic ring 70 has a flat base 71 which acts as fulcrum FF. The entrance EE is at the entrance end 610 of the main tube 51. A removable cap 52 seals the bait end 609 of the main tube 51. Holes 66 can allow water to enter main tube 51 during immersion.

The trapping mechanism is comprised of a retaining tube 59 forming a "Y" with the main tube 51. Retaining tube 59 rises obliquely from main tube 51 away from the bait end 609 of the main tube 51. The ping pong ball 53 is held up in the load position by retaining prong 57 of swivel ring 56.

Referring last to FIGS. 8, 9 mouse M is first entering in FIG. 8 entrance EE. The swivel ring 56 is resting on the ground in the cocked position. The retaining prong 57 is pivotally supported in hole 67. Retaining prong 57 is holding up the ping pong ball 53.

When the mouse M passes the fulcrum FF he becomes trapped. The main tube 51 teeters so that the bait end 609 falls in direction D, and the entrance end 610 rises in

3

direction U. The swivel ring **56** pivots in direction T because the prong **57** is urged downward by ping pong ball **53**. Hole **67** acts as a fulcrum. The ping pong ball **53** is restrained from exiting entrance EE by rim **54**. End caps **52**, **55** prevent the mouse's egress.

Although the present invention has been described with reference to preferred embodiments, numerous modifications and variations can be made and still the result will come within the scope of the invention. No limitation with respect to the specific embodiments disclosed herein is intended or should be inferred.

I claim:

1. A mousetrap comprising:

a main tube having a central fulcrum means, a bait end, and a ball end;

a base stand having a means to support the main tube at the fulcrum;

said bait end further comprising mouse bait and a main tube closure;

said ball end further comprising a ball and a main tube closure;

an entrance tube depending down from the main tube at the central fulcrum means, and angled toward the ball end;

said entrance tube having a mouse entrance adjacent a supporting surface for the base stand; and

said main tube having a horizontal load position wherein said ball rests at the ball end, wherein a mouse enters the mouse entrance, walks toward the bait up the entrance tube, and passes the fulcrum means, thereby causing the main tube to teeter down at the bait end, and cause the ball to roll down the main tube then down the entrance tube, functioning to block an egress of the mouse out the mouse entrance.

2. The mousetrap of claim 1 wherein said central fulcrum means further comprise holes in the main tube.

3. The mousetrap of claim 2 wherein said means to support further comprises a pair of prong ends fittingly engaged in the holes in the main tube.

4. The mousetrap of claim 1 wherein the ball further comprises a ping pong ball.

4

5. The mousetrap of claim 3 wherein said central fulcrum means further comprises a support stand depending from the main tube.

6. A mousetrap comprising:

a main tube having a closed bait end, a mouse entrance end, and a central fulcrum means supporting the main tube on a support surface;

a ball tube angularly rising from the main tube;

said ball tube further comprising a closure, a ball, and a ball support means, functioning to hold the ball against the closure when the main tube is teetered in a cocked position;

a bait in the bait end, functioning to lure a mouse into the mouse entrance, past the central fulcrum means, thereby causing the main tube to teeter downward at the bait end, and causing the ball support means to release the ball to roll into the main tube and thereby block an egress of the mouse out the mouse entrance.

7. The mousetrap of claim 5 wherein said ball support means further comprises a swivel ring suspended from a hole in the ball tube by a prong, wherein said prong swings away from the ball, thereby releasing it when the main tube is teetered downward at the bait end.

8. A mousetrap comprising:

a "Y" shaped tube pivotally supported at a center point by a stand;

said "Y" shaped tube having a straight tube closed at both ends, and having bait at one end, and a ball at an opposing ball end, said ball end being adjacent to an open tube member;

said open tube member depending from the straight tube so as to form a mouse entrance when the straight tube is suspended horizontally, whereby a mouse attracted by a bait at the bait end passes the center point and causes the straight tube to teeter with the bait end down, thereby causing the ball to travel to the open tube member, thus trapping the mouse.

* * * * *

United States Patent [19]

Fisher

[11] Patent Number: **4,662,101**

[45] Date of Patent: **May 5, 1987**

[54] **RAT OR MOUSE TRAP**

[76] Inventor: **Harry L. Fisher**, 9336 S. 208th St., Kent, Wash. 98031

[21] Appl. No.: **880,285**

[22] Filed: **Jun. 30, 1986**

[51] Int. Cl.⁴ A01M 23/04
[52] U.S. Cl. 43/69
[58] Field of Search 43/69

[56] **References Cited**

U.S. PATENT DOCUMENTS

121,608	12/1871	Francisco	43/69
290,580	12/1883	Harwell	43/69
1,208,206	12/1916	Poynter	43/69
1,525,349	2/1925	Yamasaki	43/69

FOREIGN PATENT DOCUMENTS

81327 8/1934 Sweden 43/69

Primary Examiner—Gene P. Crosby
Attorney, Agent, or Firm—Bruce A. Kaser

[57] **ABSTRACT**

A mousetrap (10) is made of a pivoting platform (12) suspended over a pitfall (14). The platform (12) is balanced in a manner such that it normally assumes a horizontal position, thus giving a mouse an appearance of a stable bridge over the pitfall. When the mouse (42) steps onto the platform (12) for the purpose of obtaining bait placed thereon, however, the platform (12) spins and dumps the mouse into the pitfall thereby trapping it.

1 Claim, 5 Drawing Figures

Fig.1

Fig.2

𝕱𝖎𝖌.3

𝕱𝖎𝖌.4

𝕱𝖎𝖌.5

RAT OR MOUSE TRAP

TECHNICAL FIELD

This invention relates to animal traps, and in particular, traps for rats, mice and/or similar vermin.

BACKGROUND ART

The damage caused by rats and mice to agricultural products is well known. Every year these pests cause incalculable damage to crops, whether they be in the field or stored, and other foodstuffs of a similar nature. Further, the problems associated with rat or mice infestation of domestic household environments are well known.

Man has continuously engaged in war with these pests and has engaged in various attempts at eradicating and/or controlling them. The present invention provides yet another attempt which has certain advantages over previous ones. As will become apparent, the present invention is, quite literally, the better mousetrap.

DISCLOSURE OF THE INVENTION

The present invention provides a trap for rats, mice and similar vermin. This invention employs a pit or pitfall into which these pests fall and are trapped. Once there, they may be either killed or maintained in a live condition.

A platform is suitably supported over the pitfall in a manner such that the platform can freely turn or pivot about a center line axis. The platform is balanced in a manner such that it normally assumes a horizontal position thereby giving a vermin an appearance of providing a secure supporting surface over the pitfall. The vermin can access the platform from the edge of the pitfall, and when the vermin moves onto the platform, the vermin's weight causes the platform to become unbalanced and turn, thus causing the vermin to fall into the pitfall. Of course, the vermin would be enticed onto the platform by a suitable bait placed on the platform but out of reach from the edge of the pitfall's opening.

Preferably, the pitfall is made of a bucket or another suitable container of like nature. The platform is supported over the bucket's opening by a pair of supporting members hooked to the bucket's rim. One supporting member is positioned directly across the bucket's opening from the other.

The platform comprises a generally rectangular sheet of material which spans the distance between the supporting members, with each end of the platform being pivotally connected to the end's respective adjacent supporting member. These connections are symmetrical, that is, the mid-point of each end of the rectangular platform is pivotally connected to a supporting member. This makes a pair of pivot points which define the center line axis, such axis extending generally horizontally across the bucket or pitfall's opening and about which the platform is free to turn.

The rectangular platform is curved sufficiently that its center of gravity is offset from the center line axis. Since the platform can freely turn, this causes the platform to normally assume the above-mentioned horizontal position. After the weight of a mouse or rat on the platform unbalances it, causing it to turn, the platform naturally turns back to the horizontal position after the mouse or rat falls off.

Each supporting member may have an inwardly projecting ledge from the rim or edge of the bucket or pitfall which provides vermin-access onto the platform. Swivel members are provided for making the pivotal connection between each ledge and the ends of the platform.

An advantage to the present invention is that it is effective in controlling vermin without using poison. Poison, of course, has been known to be one of the most effective methods of controlling vermin. However, it is undesirable to use poison in situations where the poison may get mixed into foodstuffs that are eventually to be consumed by humans. This invention is ideally suited for use in these kinds of situations.

Another advantage to the present invention is that it may be used as a live trap, or otherwise, if so desired. The bottom of the bucket may be filled with a few inches of water into which a mouse or rat will fall after being dumped by the platform. Eventually, the mouse or rat drowns. However, by leaving the bucket empty, they may be trapped alive.

BRIEF DESCRIPTION OF THE DRAWINGS

In the drawings, like reference numerals and letters refer to like parts throughout the various views, and wherein:

FIG. 1 is a pictorial view of a preferred embodiment of the invention, and shows a curved rectangular platform pivotally supported over the opening of a bucket;

FIG. 2 is an enlarged fragmentary pictorial view showing a swivel member which connects the platform shown in FIG. 1 to a supporting member connected to the rim of the bucket;

FIG. 3 is a side elevational view of the platform shown in FIG. 1;

FIG. 4 is a view like FIG. 3 but shows the platform in a pivoting or turned condition; and

FIG. 5 is a view like FIG. 2 but shows an alternative embodiment for connecting the rectangular platform in FIGS. 1, 3 and 4 to a supporting member on the bucket's rim.

BEST MODE FOR CARRYING OUT THE INVENTION

Referring now to the drawings, and first to FIG. 1, therein is shown at 10 a preferred embodiment of the invention. The invention includes a rectangular platform 12 which is suspended over the upwardly directed opening of a bucket 14. The platform 12 is attached to the bucket 14 by a pair of supporting members 16, 18. Each supporting member has a hook portion 20 that is attached to the bucket's rim 22. Further, each member 16, 18 has an inwardly projecting ledge portion 24 that provides vermin-access from the edge of the bucket 22 onto the platform 12.

The platform 12 is pivotally connected at each of its ends 27, 29 to respective adjacent supporting members 16, 18 as shown at 26, 28. These connections are better illustrated in FIG. 2 which shows a swivel member 30 interconnecting a first member 32 and a second member 34. The swivel member 30 is connected to the two members 32, 34 by rivets 36, 38, or other suitable means, and permits the first member 32 to pivot relative to the second member 34.

Referring back to FIG. 3, each swivel member 26, 28 connects the approximate center point of the platform's ends 27, 29 to the supporting members 16, 18. The swivel members 26, 28 thus define two points through which a horizontal center line axis 40 passes. The plat-

3

form 12 is free to turn about this axis 40 and is curved slightly so that its center of gravity is offset from the axis. This offset causes the platform 12 to be normally balanced in the horizontal position shown in FIGS. 1 and 3.

Referring again to FIG. 1, therein is shown a mouse 42 poised on the rim 22 of the bucket 14. A suitable bait 44 is positioned on the center of the platform 12 and attracts the mouse 42. It should be understood that a suitable ramp or similar structure would be provided to permit the mouse 42 to access the bucket's rim 22. This is not shown in the drawings, however. The bait 44 would, of course, be positioned on the center of the platform 12 so that its weight would not unbalance the platform.

The horizontal position of the platform 12 gives the mouse 42 the appearance that the platform provides a bridge across the opening of the bucket 14. However, when the mouse 14 steps onto the platform 12, in its desire to obtain the bait 44, the mouse's weight unbalances the platform, causing it to turn as shown in FIG. 4, and thus dumps the mouse 42 into the bucket 14. The offset center of gravity of the platform 12 then causes the platform to return to the horizontal position after the mouse falls therefrom.

It should be appreciated that the above-described curved platform 12 could be replaced by a straight platform having a suitable counterweight attached thereto. This would not be a preferred embodiment, however.

The bottom of the bucket 14 may be filled with a few inches of water as indicated by the dashed lines 46. The mouse 42 may be able to swim in the water for a certain period of time but will eventually become tired and drown as shown at 48.

FIG. 5 shows an alternative embodiment of the swivel member 30 shown in FIG. 2. This embodiment may be used if it is desired to adapt the platform 12 to a bucket or other container having a different diameter. In this embodiment, the swivel member 30 comprises a plurality of swivel links as indicated at 50a, 50b, and 50c. The length of this alternative swivel member 30 is therefore adjustable by catching and releasing the links

4

50a, 50b, 50c from a link-catch 52 which is suitably connected to member 32.

The above description is presented for exemplary purposes only. This description is not meant to limit patent protection insofar as it is understood that certain departures may be taken from the above-described embodiments without departing from the overall spirit and scope of the invention. With regard to patent protection, the invention is to be limited not by the above description but only by the subjoined patent claims, in accordance with the well-established legal doctrines of patent claim interpretation.

What is claimed is:

1. A trap for mice, rats or vermin of a similar nature, and for use in connection with a pitfall having an upwardly directed opening, comprising:

a generally rectangular platform having a top surface and a bottom surface, and having a thin cross section;

a pair of platform supporting members, each of which is connected to the edge of said pitfall's opening, wherein one of said supporting members is positioned across said opening from the other, and wherein said platform substantially spans the distance between said supporting members, with a first end of said rectangular platform being pivotally connected to one of said members, and with a second end of said platform being pivotally connected to the other of said members, wherein such connections generally define a pair of points through which a center line axis extends across said pitfall's opening, said center line axis being an axis of symmetry for said platform and said platform being freely pivotably about said center line axis, and wherein

said platform's cross section is curved so that said top surface is concave and said bottom surface is convex, to cause said platform's center of gravity to be slightly offset from said center line axis, and to cause said platform to normally pivot into a position where said center of gravity is positioned below said center line axis, so that said platform is balanced in a manner that said platform's top surface provides said vermin with an appearance of a bridge across said pitfall.

* * * * *

50

55

60

65

United States Patent [19]

Fodor

[11] Patent Number: 4,819,368

[45] Date of Patent: Apr. 11, 1989

[54] **DISPOSABLE MOUSETRAP**

[76] Inventor: **John Fodor**, 13 Village Park Cir., Morgantown, W. Va. 26505

[21] Appl. No.: **552,153**

[22] Filed: **Nov. 14, 1983**

[51] Int. Cl.⁴ **A01M 23/18; A01M 23/02**

[52] U.S. Cl. **43/61**

[58] Field of Search 43/61, 60, 62, 67, 70

[56] **References Cited**

U.S. PATENT DOCUMENTS

2,573,228	10/1951	Slauth	43/61
2,598,007	5/1952	McCormick	43/61
3,729,852	5/1973	Holmes	43/61
3,823,504	7/1974	Dosch	43/61
4,142,320	3/1979	Marcolina	43/61
4,231,180	11/1980	Bare	43/61
4,232,472	11/1980	Muelling	43/61
4,238,902	12/1980	Holl et al.	43/61

Primary Examiner—Kurt Rowan
Attorney, Agent, or Firm—Mason, Fenwick & Lawrence

[57] **ABSTRACT**

A disposable rodent trap is formed of an aluminum beverage can comprising an internal chamber, a bottom end wall with an opposite end wall including an entry opening therein of sufficient size to permit a rodent to pass into the internal chamber. A door member in the form of a can end is positioned externally of said end wall and movable into a closed position covering and blocking the entry opening by a rubber band. A latch means normally holds the door open by engagement with an edge surface of the entry opening but is movable by rodent contact inside the chamber to unlatched position to permit the rubber band to move the door member to its closed postion to trap the rodent in said internal chamber.

15 Claims, 2 Drawing Sheets

FIG. 1

FIG. 2

FIG. 3

FIG. 4

FIG. 7

FIG. 5

FIG. 6

1

DISPOSABLE MOUSETRAP

BACKGROUND OF THE INVENTION

The present invention is in the field of animal trapping devices and is more specifically directed to a unique disposable rodent trap of particular value for capturing mice.

Numerous devices have evolved over the years for either capturing or killing mice. Many of the known devices have suffered from a number of shortcomings such as failing to operate properly and being overly expensive to fabricate. The most relevant prior known U.S. Patents comprise U.S. Pat. Nos. 100,986; 924,237; 1,261,189; 1,326,662; 1,372,663; 1,415,093; 1,861,478; 2,087,646; 2,434,031; 2,437,020; 2,573,228; 2,608,018; 3,426,470; 3,729,852; 3,733,735; 3,992,802. The present invention overcomes the shortcomings of the foregoing patents in providing a fool-proof functionally operational device that is quick and effective for capturing mice or other rodents and which is economical to fabricate and assemble due to the use of well-known widely available materials many of which are presently thrown away as scrap. It is consequently possible to simply dispose of the subject invention following the capture of a mouse or other rodent.

Therefore, it is the primary object of the present invention to provide a new and improved rodent trap which is functionally more effective than prior known rodent traps and is also economical to fabricate and assemble.

SUMMARY OF THE INVENTION

Achievement of the foregoing objects is enabled by the preferred embodiment of the invention in a remarkably effective manner. More specifically, the preferred embodiment of the invention comprises a container in the form of an aluminum beverage can of the type normally used for beer, soft drinks or the like. Such cans comprise a cylindrical wall member having a bottom end wall and a dispensing end wall with the dispensing end wall of the can used in the present invention including an elongated transverse entry opening of sufficient size to permit the passage of a rodent into the interior of the can.

A movable door is positioned adjacent the dispensing end wall of the can and is connected to an elongated latch member comprising an elongated tubular rod which extends into the interior of the can. Also, a rubber band extends from the bottom wall of the can through the length of the can outwardly through an opening provided in the dispensing end wall and is connected to the movable door member so as to urge the movable door member toward a closed position in which it overlies the entry opening and completely blocks same. The latch member includes a transverse surface engagable with a catch surface adjacent the edge of the entry opening so as to hold the door member in an open position against the urging of the elastic rubber band member. A tubular metal sheath encloses the rubber band member across the span between the dispensing end wall and the bottom end wall of the can so as to prevent any captured rodent from gnawing through the rubber band to permit the door to then open.

The inner end of the tubular latch member is provided with means for retaining bait on the inner end of the latch member for the purpose of attracting mice or

2

other rodents so as to cause them to enter the interior of the can. When such a mouse has entered the can, he will attempt to eat the bait and will dislodge the tubular latch member from engagement with the catch surface so that the elastic rubber band member immediately snaps the door closed and the rodent is consequently entrapped within the confines of the can. Additionally, the latch member is also provided with a lock latch surface which engages a second catch surface along the inside edge of the entry opening upon closure of the door member so as to lock the door member in closed position. Thus, the operation of the elongated elastic rubber band member and the lock surface provides a dual locking function to preclude escape of a captured rodent. In one embodiment of the invention the latch tube receives the bait member in an open-ended recess adjacent the end of the latch member with a transverse bore opening being provided on opposite sides of the opening so as to permit impalement of the bait by a retaining pin extended therethrough. In a second embodiment the bait is retained on the end of the latch member by a wire clip or the like extending through openings provided in a flattened end of the latch member.

BRIEF DESCRIPTION OF THE DRAWING

FIG. 1 is a perspective view of the preferred embodiment of the invention illustrating the door member in open position;

FIG. 2 is an exploded perspective view of the embodiment of FIG. 1;

FIG. 3 is a sectional view taken along lines 3—3 of FIG. 1 and illustrating the door in an opened condition;

FIG. 4 is a sectional view similar to FIG. 3 but illustrating the door in the closed position for imprisoning a rodent;

FIG. 5 is a sectional view taken along lines 5—5 of FIG. 3;

FIG. 6 is a side elevation view of a second embodiment with portions removed for the sake of illustration; and

FIG. 7 is a perspective view of a second embodiment of tubular latch means employed in the invention.

DESCRIPTION OF THE PREFERRED EMBODIMENTS

The preferred embodiment of the invention as illustrated in FIGS. 1 etc. comprises a disposable rodent trap including a container 10 in the form of a disposable aluminum beverage container having a cylindrical body wall 12, a bottom end wall 14 and a dispensing end wall 16. It should be observed that the bottom end wall 14 is normally the "bottom" wall when the beverage can is used for its original purpose whereas the dispensing end wall 16 is the end from which the beverage contained within the container is dispensed. Dispensing end wall 16 includes an opening 17 of sufficient size to permit the passage of a rodent therethrough so as to enter the interior of the container can 10 and also includes a peripheral flange 19. A stabilizer tab 18 extends through slots 20 provided in the cylindrical body wall 12 as best shown in FIG. 2. Stabilizer tab 18 prevents the can from rolling on a supporting surface in an obvious manner.

A floating door 22 comprising an end wall from a similar can is positioned adjacent and in contact with the dispensing end wall 16. Floating door 22 is provided with an upper circular opening 24 and a lower slot 26.

The upper circular opening 24 is in general alignment with an opening 28 in the dispensing end wall 16. The bottom end wall 14 is provided with an opening 30 in alignment with the opening 28 of the dispensing end wall. Biasing means in the form of an elastic rubber band member 32 extends through the openings 28 and 30 with the end of the biasing elastic rubber band member 32 adjacent the bottom wall 14 being anchored by a tubular anchor lug 34 while the opposite end of the rubber band member which extends through openings 28 and 24 is anchored by a similar lug 36. The lug members 34 and 36 can for example be formed of rolled pieces of aluminum scrap or the like. Thus it will be seen that the tension in rubber band 32 tends to move the floating door member 22 toward a closed position. A protective sheath 38 formed of metal in the form of aluminum or the like extends between the bottom wall 14 and the dispensing end wall 16 to fully enclose the rubber band 32 to prevent any rodent on the interior of the can from gnawing or eating through the band so as to cause its failure.

An elongated tubular latch member 40 is provided internally of the container can 10 and includes a flat outer end 42 which extends through the slot 26 and is held in position by an outer keeper pin 44 and an inner keeper pin 46 which are respectively on opposite sides of the floating door member 22. The inner end of the elongated tubular latch member 40 is provided with a pair of openings 48 through which a bait retention loop or wire or the like 50 extends so as to permit the attachment of bait 52 to the end of the latch member. Latch member 40 includes a first transverse latch surface 54 and a second transverse oppositely facing lock surface 56.

When the floating door 22 is in its open position the latch surface 54 is engaged with an upper external catch surface 60 extending along entry opening 17 in the dispensing end wall 16. Thus, the latch retains the floating door in its open position. A mouse or other rodent can enter the opening 17 and upon attempting to eat the bait 52 will effect dislodging of the latch surface 54 from the catch surface 60 to immediately result in a rapid and quick movement of the door member 22 from the open position of FIG. 3 to the closed position of FIG. 4. The rodent on the interior of the container will consequently be imprisoned. Moreover, movement of the floating door 22 to the closed position immediately results in the lock surface 56 becoming engaged with a lower catch inside surface 62 as shown in FIG. 4. Thus, the floating door member 22 will be held in closed position by operation of the lock surface 56 as well as the elastic urgings of the rubber band 32.

FIG. 6 illustrates a slightly simplified embodiment in which the protective sheath 38 is dispensed with and the bare rubber band extends between the bottom wall 14 and the dispensing wall 16. The advantage of this embodiment is that it is slightly easier to manufacture. Additionally, the embodiment of FIG. 6 is illustrated with a second embodiment latch member 40' which is basically identical to the first latch member with the exception of the manner in which the bait 52 is connected to the inner end of the latch member. More specifically, the inner end of the latch member 40' includes an open end chamber or cavity 70 through which diametric openings 72 extend with the chamber or cavity 70 being of sufficient size to receive the bait 52. A retention pin 75 extends through the opening 72 and the bait 52 to retain the bait 52 in the end of the

latch member in the manner shown in FIG. 6. Otherwise, the second embodiment operates in exactly the same manner as the first embodiment.

It should be understood that, while preferred embodiments of the invention are illustrated herein, numerous modifications of the disclosed embodiments will undoubtedly occur to those of skill in the art. For example, practice of the invention is not limited to the use of beverage cans and other type cans or containers of larger sizes could be employed. In fact, it would even be possible to practice the present invention by the use of such large containers as oil drums or the like for use in capturing larger animals. Consequently, the use of the term "rodent" as discussed herein and as set forth in the claims should be broadly interpreted to include other types of animals. For these reasons, the spirit and scope of the invention should be broadly interpreted.

I claim:

1. A disposable rodent trap comprising a container defining an internal chamber, an end wall having an entry opening therein of sufficient size to permit a rodent to pass therethrough so as to enter said internal chamber, a door member provided externally of said end wall and movable from an open position toward said end wall into a closed position covering and blocking said entry opening, biasing means comprising a rubber band for urging said door member toward its closed position, latch means having a portion inside said chamber and extending between said door member and a catch surface on, and forming part of, said end wall comprising an edge surface adjacent said entry opening for normally holding said door member in its open position but being movable by rodent contact inside said chamber out of contact with said catch surface to permit said biasing means to move said door member to its closed position to entrap the rodent in said internal chamber and wherein said container is a disposable beverage can having a cylindrical body wall, a bottom end wall and a dispensing end wall with said entry opening being provided in said dispensing end wall which comprises a wall from which beverage would normally be dispensed during usage of said beverage container for its original purpose.

2. The invention of claim 1 wherein said latch member comprises an elongated tube connected at one end to said door member and having a transverse latch surface medially of its length for engaging said catch surface adjacent one edge of said entry opening and further including a lock latch surface extending transversely of said tubular member at a location near the door member for engaging an inner edge surface of said entry opening for latching said door member in said closed position.

3. A rodent trap as recited in claim 2 additionally including a tubular sheath extending between said bottom end wall and said opening in said dispensing end wall for enclosing said rubber band portion inside said internal chamber for preventing any rodent in said chamber from chewing on said rubber band.

4. A disposable rodent trap as recited in claim 3 wherein said door member comprises a can end from a similar can which has one end engaged with said dispensing end wall, said dispensing end wall including a peripheral flange surface which retains said door member in position.

5. A rodent trap as recited in claim 4 wherein said latch member includes means on its end opposite its end connected to said door member for retaining rodent attracting means thereon.

5

6. A rodent trap as recited in claim 5 additionally including transversely extending means connected to said body wall and engagable with a supporting surface for said rodent trap for maintaining said rodent trap in fixed position on said supporting surface.

7. A rodent trap as recited in claim 6 wherein said bottom end wall is provided with an aperture through which one end of said rubber band extends to provide an external loop of said rubber band and wherein said rubber band is connected to said wall by an elongated anchor lug passed through said loop.

8. A rodent trap as recited in claim 7 wherein said door member is provided with an opening through which a loop of said rubber band extends and further includes an anchor lug extending through said loop for retaining said loop externally of said door member.

9. A rodent trap as recited in claim 8 wherein said door member includes a slot through which one end of said latch member extends and said latch member includes keeper pins extending transversely through said latch member on opposite sides of said door member so as to retain said latch member in said slot.

10. A rodent trap as recited in claim 4 wherein said latch member has an open-ended bait receiving cavity on its end opposite its connection to said door member.

11. A disposable rodent trap comprising a container defining an internal chamber, an end wall having an entry opening therein of sufficient size to permit a rodent to pass therethrough so as to enter said internal chamber, a door member provided externally of said end wall and movable from an open position toward said end wall into a closed position covering and blocking said entry opening, biasing means for urging said door member toward its closed position, latch means having a portion inside said chamber and extending between said door member and a catch surface on, and forming part of, said end wall for normally holding said door member in its open position but being movable by rodent contact inside said chamber out of contact with said catch surface to permit said biasing means to move

6

said door member to its closed position to entrap the rodent in said internal chamber and wherein said container is a disposable beverage can having a cylindrical body wall, a bottom end wall and a dispensing end wall with said entry opening being provided in said dispensing end wall which comprises a wall from which beverage would normally be dispensed during usage of said beverage container for its original purpose and wherein said biasing means comprises an elastic band having one end secured to said bottom end wall, said second end wall includes a small opening spaced from said entry opening and the opposite end of said elastic band extends through said small opening and is secured to said door member by retainer pin means.

12. The invention of claim 11 wherein said latch member comprises an elongated metal tube connected at one end to said door member and having a transverse latch surface medially of its length for engaging said catch surface and further including a lock latch surface extending transversely of said tubular member at a location near the door member for engaging an inner edge surface of said entry opening for latching said door member in said closed position.

13. A rodent trap as recited in claim 12 additionally including a tubular sheath extending between said bottom end wall and said opening in said dispensing end wall for enclosing said elastic band portion inside said internal chamber for preventing any rodent in said chamber from chewing on said rubber band.

14. A disposable rodent trap as recited in claim 13 wherein said door member comprises a can end from a similar can which has one end engaged with said dispensing end wall, said dispensing end wall including a peripheral flange surface which retains said door member in position.

15. A rodent trap as recited in claim 14 wherein said latch member includes attachment means on its end opposite its end connected to said door member for retaining rodent attracting means thereon.

* * * * *

45

50

55

60

65

APPENDIX B

Sample Design
Patents

(12) **United States Design Patent** (10) Patent No.: **US D463,046 S**
Kumar (45) Date of Patent: ** Sep. 17, 2002

(54) **GLASS PUMPKIN CAULDRON VOTIVE HOLDER**

(75) Inventor: **Sanjeev Kumar**, Munster, IN (US)

(73) Assignee: **Hosley International Trading Corporation**, Lynwood, IL (US)

(**) Term: **14 Years**

(21) Appl. No.: **29/149,517**

(22) Filed: **Oct. 11, 2001**

(51) LOC (7) Cl. **26-01**
(52) U.S. Cl. **D26/11; D26/16**
(58) Field of Search D26/9, 10, 11,
D26/16; 431/125, 291; D11/125; D7/612,
628

(56) **References Cited**

U.S. PATENT DOCUMENTS

D128,373 S   * 7/1941 Heisey D26/9
D337,614 S   * 7/1993 Turner D26/9
D412,369 S   * 7/1999 Kumar D26/16
D422,720 S   * 4/2000 Hardy D26/11

* cited by examiner

Primary Examiner—Robin V. Taylor
(74) *Attorney, Agent, or Firm*—Olson & Hierl, Ltd.

(57) **CLAIM**

The ornamental design for a glass pumpkin cauldron votive holder, as shown and described.

DESCRIPTION

FIG. 1 is a perspective view of a glass pumpkin cauldron votive holder of the present invention;

FIG. 2 is a right side elevational view of the glass pumpkin cauldron votive holder;

FIG. 3 is an opposite side elevational view of the glass pumpkin cauldron votive holder;

FIG. 4 is a top plan view of the glass pumpkin cauldron votive holder;

FIG. 5 is a bottom plan view of the glass pumpkin cauldron votive holder;

FIG. 6 is a front elevational view of the glass pumpkin cauldron votive holder; and,

FIG. 7 is a rear elevational view of the glass pumpkin cauldron votive holder.

1 Claim, 2 Drawing Sheets

FIG. 1

FIG. 2

FIG. 3

FIG. 4

FIG. 5

FIG. 6

FIG. 7

(12) **United States Design Patent** (10) Patent No.: **US D463,007 S**

Lord (45) **Date of Patent:** ** **Sep. 17, 2002**

(54) **FAUCET**

(75) Inventor: **Judd A. Lord**, Carmel, IN (US)

(73) Assignee: **Masco Corporation of Indiana,** Indianapolis, IN (US)

(**) Term: **14 Years**

(21) Appl. No.: **29/136,756**

(22) Filed: **Feb. 7, 2001**

(51) LOC (7) Cl. **23-01**
(52) U.S. Cl. **D23/241**; D23/238; D23/242
(58) Field of Search D23/238–257; 4/675–678; 137/801

(56) **References Cited**

U.S. PATENT DOCUMENTS

D287,395 S	*	12/1986	Piesco	D23/255
D318,099 S	*	7/1991	Reid et al.	D23/255
D375,345 S	*	11/1996	Warshawsky	D23/241
D377,516 S	*	1/1997	Doughty et al.	D23/241
D407,466 S	*	3/1999	Hundley et al.	D23/252
D433,106 S		10/2000	Spangler	
D433,735 S		11/2000	Lord	
D434,118 S		11/2000	Lord	
D436,397 S		1/2001	Lord	
D438,292 S	*	2/2001	Lord	D23/249
D439,954 S		4/2001	Spangler	
D439,955 S		4/2001	Spangler	
D448,456 S	*	9/2001	Lord	D23/249

OTHER PUBLICATIONS

U.S. patent application Ser. No. 29/136,750 filed Feb. 7, 2001.

U.S. patent application Ser. No. 29/136,845 filed Feb. 7, 2001.

U.S. patent application Ser. No. 29/136,836 filed Feb. 7, 2001.

U.S. patent application Ser. No. 29/136,760 filed Feb. 7, 2001.

U.S. patent application Ser. No. 29/136,804 filed Feb. 7, 2001.

U.S. patent application Ser. No. 29/136,839 filed Feb. 7, 2001.

U.S. patent application Ser. No. 29/136,833 filed Feb. 7, 2001.

U.S. patent application Ser. No. 29/136,752 filed Feb. 7, 2001.

U.S. patent application Ser. No. 29/136,765 filed Feb. 7, 2001.

U.S. patent application Ser. No. 29/136,769 filed Feb. 7, 2001.

U.S. patent application Ser. No. 29/136,805 filed Feb. 7, 2001.

U.S. patent application Ser. No. 29/136,782 filed Feb. 7, 2001.

U.S. patent application Ser. No. 29/136,761 filed Feb. 7, 2001.

U.S. patent application Ser. No. 29/136,766 filed Feb. 7, 2001.

(List continued on next page.)

Primary Examiner—Louis S. Zarfas
Assistant Examiner—Gregory Andoll
(74) *Attorney, Agent, or Firm*—Myron B. Kapustij; Lloyd D. Doigan

(57) **CLAIM**

The ornamental design for a faucet, as shown and described.

DESCRIPTION

FIG. **1** is a front perspective view of the faucet showing my new design;
FIG. **2** is a rear perspective view thereof;
FIG. **3** is a front elevational view thereof;
FIG. **4** is a left side elevational view thereof, the right side being a mirror image;
FIG. **5** is a rear elevational view thereof;
FIG. **6** is a top plan view thereof; and,
FIG. **7** is a bottom plan view thereof.
The broken line showing of the apertures in FIG. **7** are for purposes of illustration only and form no part of the claimed design.

1 Claim, 7 Drawing Sheets

OTHER PUBLICATIONS

U.S. patent application Ser. No. 29/136,763 filed Feb. 7, 2001.

U.S. patent application Ser. No. 29/136,773 filed Feb. 7, 2001.

* cited by examiner

Figure - 1

237

Figure - 2

238

Figure - 3

239

Figure - 4

240

Figure - 5

Figure - 6

242

Figure - 7

US00D460410S

(12) **United States Design Patent** (10) Patent No.: **US D460,410 S**

Thrasher et al. (45) Date of Patent: ✳✳ **Jul. 16, 2002**

(54) **SIDEWALLS OF A TIRE**

(75) Inventors: **Danny Austin Thrasher**, Anderson; **Sylvain Leynaert**, Greer; **Joseph George Hoover**, Simpsonville, all of SC (US)

(73) Assignee: **Michelin Recherche et Technique S.A.** (CH)

(✳✳) Term: **14 Years**

(21) Appl. No.: **29/152,417**

(22) Filed: **Dec. 18, 2001**

(51) **LOC (7) Cl.** **12-15**
(52) **U.S. Cl.** **D12/605**
(58) **Field of Search** D12/531, 579, D12/588, 594, 595, 600, 601, 605, 900, 901; 152/209.1, 209.12, 209.16, 209.17, 209.25, 523, 524

(56) **References Cited**

U.S. PATENT DOCUMENTS

D59,717 S	✳	11/1921	Coats	D12/605
D120,687 S	✳	5/1940	Moonan	D12/605
2,745,459 A	✳	5/1956	Pennock	152/153
D260,872 S	✳	9/1981	Wright et al.	D12/596
4,915,150 A	✳	4/1990	Takusagawa et al.	152/209.16
D313,777 S	✳	1/1991	Yamashita	D12/596
D319,994 S		9/1991	Manestar	D12/147
5,849,118 A	✳	12/1998	Matsumoto	152/209.11
D442,128 S	✳	5/2001	Allison	D12/605
D444,742 S		7/2001	Dunlap	D12/147
D447,449 S	✳	9/2001	Guspodin	D12/605

OTHER PUBLICATIONS

Tread Design Guide, 2000, p. 79, BFGoodrich Radial Mud–Terrain T/A.
Tread Design Guide, 2000, p. 85, Dayton Daytona Stag XT.
Tread Design Guide, 2000, p. 103, Mickey Thompson Baja Claw Radial.

Tread Design Guide, 2000, p. 103, Mickey Thompson Baja Claw.
Tread Design Guide, 2000, p. 103, Mickey Thompson Baja King.
Tread Design Guide, 2000, p. 103, Monarch Highliner Premium Hwy. Traction ND.
Tread Design Guide, 2000, p. 106, National Durango M/T.

✳ cited by examiner

Primary Examiner—Robert M. Spear
(74) Attorney, Agent, or Firm—Martin Farrell; Robert R. Reed; Alan A. Csontos

(57) **CLAIM**

The ornamental design for sidewalls of a tire, as shown and described.

DESCRIPTION

FIG. 1 is a perspective view of sidewalls of a tire showing our new design, it being undestood that the surface pattern repeats circumferentially throughout the side portion of the tire, the opposite side perspective view being identical thereto;

FIG. 2 is an enlarged fragmentary front elevation view of a tire showing portions of the surface pattern of the tire sidewalls of FIG. 1; and,

FIG. 3 is an enlarged fragmentary side elevation view of one tire sidewall thereof, the surface pattern being repeated throughout the sidewall area, the opposite side elevation view being identical thereto.

The broken line disclosure of the tire tread and inner bead is for illustrative purposes only and forms no part of the claimed design.

1 Claim, 3 Drawing Sheets

Fig. 1

Fig. 2

Fig. 3

Index

Laches, 177, 191–92
Legal estoppel, 49
Licenses, 47–50, 132
Literal infringement, 21, 142–44
Litigation, 67–68, 171–94. *See also*
    Remedies for infringement
    Attorneys' fees, 138, 188
    Bifurcation, 178
    Burdens of proof, 175–76
    Damages, 177, 181–85, 192
    Declaratory judgment, 171, 174–74
    Equitable estoppel, 177, 192–93
    Injunctions, 177, 178–80
    Jurisdiction, 172–73
    Laches, 177, 191–92
    Markman hearing, 178
    Notice and marking, 189–90
    Preliminary injunctions, 178–80
    Presumption of validity, 58, 68–69,
       175
    Role of judge and jury, 176–78
    Statute of limitations, 189
    Summary judgment, 180–81
    Venue, 173–74
Living organisms, 25–26, 78
Lost profits measure of damages,
    182–83

Marking of patented goods, 189–90
Markman hearing, 178
Markush claims, 61
Means-plus-function claims, 56, 63–64,
    152, 163–67
Mental steps doctrine, 202–03
Methods of doing business, 28–29, 136,
    209–10
    Prior use defense, 136
Misuse, 131–34

Natural rights theory of patent law, 2
Near–simultaneous invention, 114–16
New matter, 35, 38, 81
Nexus, 114
Notice and marking, 189–90
Novelty, 14, 67, 90, 104

Obviousness, 10, 14, 67, 103–04,
    107–16, 176–77, 197
    Analogous arts, 110
    Combination of references, 109–11
    Commercial success, 113–15
    Near-simultaneous invention, 114–
       16
    Nexus, 114
    Obviousness-type double patenting,
       124–26
    Ordinary skill in the art, 107–08
    Secondary considerations, 113–16
    Teaching away, 111–12
On-sale bar, 118–21
Ordinary skill in the art, 107–08

Patent and Trademark Office (PTO),
    1–2, 14, 17, 31, 68–69, 71–73, 136,
    166–67, 210
Patentable subject matter, 23–29, 201–10
    Abstract ideas, 24, 204
    Artistic and literary creations, 27
    Computer programs, 10–11, 28–29,
       201–10
    Living organisms, 25–26
    Mental steps doctrine, 202–03
    Methods of doing business, 28–29,
       209–10
    Principles of nature, 24–25, 202
    Printed matter, 27–28
    Useful arts, 27–29
Pioneer patents, 156–57
Plant patents, 26, 198–200
Preambles, 20, 59–60
Preferred embodiments, 19, 55
Preliminary injunctions, 178–80
Presumption of validity, 58, 68–69, 175
Principles of nature, 24–25, 202
Printed matter, 27–28
Printed publications, 90–93, 117
Prior art, 17, 31, 90–96, 155–57, 166
    Printed publications, 90–93
    Prior inventions, 91, 94–96
    Prior knowledge, 90–91
    Prior patent applications, 93–94
    Prior patents, 91
    Prior use, 91

About the Author

Alan L. Durham is a law professor at the University of Alabama, teaching courses in patent law and other forms of intellectual property. Professor Durham formerly practiced law in California's Silicon Valley with the Palo Alto offices of Brown & Bain and Morrison & Foerster, with a particular emphasis on complex, high-technology patent litigation. He is the author of several articles in the fields of patent and copyright law.